The Torture of Children During Armed Conflicts

Sonja C. Grover

The Torture of Children During Armed Conflicts

The ICC's Failure to Prosecute and the Negation of Children's Human Dignity

Springer

Sonja C. Grover
Faculty of Education
Lakehead University
Thunder Bay, ON
Canada

ISBN 978-3-642-40688-1 ISBN 978-3-642-40689-8 (eBook)
DOI 10.1007/978-3-642-40689-8
Springer Heidelberg New York Dordrecht London

Library of Congress Control Number: 2013948859

Printed on acid-free paper

Springer is part of Springer Science+Business Media (www.springer.com)

This book is dedicated with much love to the memory of my brother Albert Gazan

Preface

It has been remarked by legal scholar Sanford Levinson (2005) that:

> Those of us who discuss "torture," "cruel, inhuman, or degrading activities," and "highly coercive interrogations" *must* climb down into the muck and confront the "facts on the ground," rather than merely doing what we do best, which is to proffer (and take refuge in) place-holding abstraction.

In this book we will do both. That is: (i) we will study the facts on the ground with regard to mass atrocities rising to the level of torture committed against children in particular (here understood as persons under age 18) during selected contemporary armed conflicts (given that the cases to date brought before the ICC have involved armed conflict). We will "climb down into the muck and confront the facts"; very abominable facts at that but yet facts that must be looked at; and (ii) we will consider how these facts relate to the elements of the crime of torture as defined under the Rome Statute (the elements of the ICC crime of torture as a war crime, a crime against humanity and/or as a crime occurring in the context of genocide) and address when the individual perpetrator conduct in question is prosecutable as torture under the Rome Statute. There is no intent here to redefine or reinterpret the elements of the crime of torture under the Rome Statute (either more restrictively or more liberally). Rather the objective is in part to highlight and substantiate through ICC case law the indubitable fact that the ICC to date has not been prepared to prosecute torture as a separable ICC crime (even were systematic and/or widespread) in cases where the victims were children in particular. This has been the pattern notwithstanding the fact that some of the ICC cases in question had as their focus child victims of *other* Rome Statute delineated international crimes (i.e., the cases involved the Rome Statue defined crime of recruitment and use of child soldiers and/or Rome Statute defined sexual violence crimes perpetrated against children). At times the ICC has rejected cumulative charges even where, on the view here, torture charges in addition to others such as rape as a war crime were warranted. This is the current state of ICC case law where children in particular are the targeted victims of torture as part of a common plan during armed conflict. This despite the fact that, on the view here, the elements of the crime of torture as set out in one or more of the relevant articles of the Rome Statute have been met in various of the cases brought before the ICC where children were in particular the targeted victims. Of course the analyses here regarding the criminal liability under the Rome Statute of any individual discussed in what follows who has not yet been found guilty by the ICC of the international crime of torture—if they would be so at all—is a matter of the current author's interpretation and opinion on the facts and the law and nothing more. This point is not repeated in the text but should be 'read into' that text or, to put it differently, simply kept in mind.

The ultimate goal in writing this book is then in part to raise awareness that *in practice* there has been a reluctance of the ICC to consider and prosecute the crime of torture (as defined in the Rome Statute) where the victims are children in particular. This has been the case even where the Prosecutor is pursuing other ICC charges for crimes perpetrated against child victims specifically as, for instance, in the Lubanga and Kony cases. The hope is that bringing this issue to light will in small part contribute to: (i) an increased likelihood that the current ICC OTP and future ICC Prosecutors will acknowledge, where it has occurred, the torture of children as particularized targets in the cases brought by the OTP before the ICC on information, for instance, initially provided by direct or indirect victims, NGOs or UN personnel on the frontlines, etc., or in cases developed by the Prosecutor from situations referred by the State or UN Security Council and that (ii) the ICC Prosecutor will be more likely to pursue prosecution for the crime of torture which involved targeting of children in particular and thus hold responsible for that grave violation of a fundamental *jus cogens* norm those individuals who engaged in or who contributed in some other substantial way to the torture of children as part of a common plan during armed conflict. This might involve: (i) bringing separate torture charges (in addition to other charges) where children are the prime target for certain *forms of torture* (i.e., through rape and sexual enslavement of children as the high priority targeted victims, the physical and psychological torture of children through child soldiering etc.) and (ii) considering the torture, in whatever form, of children in particular as an aggravating factor during sentencing.

Generally in ICC cases, the torture of children often coincides with the torture of one or both parents and other family members and especially of the women of the household or other community members. This book, however, is limited in scope with a special focus on: (i) ICC cases where the OTP pursued prosecution of various Rome Statute crimes perpetrated specifically against child victims but failed to address the Rome Statute delineated crime of torture perpetrated against those same child victims and (ii) those ICC cases where torture of adults is prosecuted but child victims of torture are overlooked or their victimization is minimized in some way.

An examination is also made of several torture cases adjudicated by the Inter-American Court of Human Rights (IACtHR), the Special Court of Sierra Leone (SCSL) and the International Criminal Tribunal for the Former Yugoslavia (ICTY) involving child victims. This with a view to lessons to be learned regarding legal issues in analyzing child torture as an international crime and fundamental human rights matter (i.e., one lesson being the need to analyze the case with reference not simply to a particular court or tribunal's enabling statute but also in the broader international human rights and humanitarian law and international customary law (ICL) context). There are lessons to be learned from all these cases: First and foremost there is a lesson about the urgent need of the international community through its international judicial system to prioritize acknowledgment of and judicial redress for the despicable practice of perpetrators during armed conflict of targeting children in particular for torture. In the international human rights court context redress would be pursued from the State that was complicit in the torture of children and/or which failed to protect the child victims of torture. That redress might include a finding that torture was committed by agents of the State; and financial reparations and other forms of remedy such as institutional changes regarding the policy and practice of national security or armed forces that mandates humane treatment of all detainees consistent with ICL, etc. Through the International Criminal Court or an international criminal tribunal; the surviving victims, if any, and their immediate relatives, as well as the international community, seek an international criminal law remedy to be imposed on the individual perpetrators found to be guilty of the international crime of torture. There is both a pressing need and obligation to pursue criminal accountability of individual perpetrators through international criminal forums (including the ICC where necessary) for the violation of the *jus cogens* prohibition against torture also where children are the particularized victim targets. Note that litigation against the State in an international human rights court is *not* a bar to ICC prosecution of the individual perpetrators most responsible for torture. Criminal accountability is vital for maintaining respect for the international rule of law. This is especially the case where the use of torture of children in particular and of others is widespread and systematic and part of an intentional strategy and common plan during armed conflict.

There is an international legal responsibility under international customary law, humanitarian treaty law and international criminal law to hold the individual perpetrators of torture, including those who committed the particularized torture of children; criminally accountable. This may be accomplished via prosecution by the ICC or another international criminal tribunal where a domestic judicial forum is not a realistic or practical option. Universal jurisdiction is also applicable allowing any State that is able to detain the perpetrators to prosecute for torture. In addition, States must be held civilly to account where there was (i) State complicity in the torture of children and/or (ii) a reckless disregard of the plight of the children who were at risk of torture as a common plan during armed conflict and who suffered this fate; or (iii) in situations where the torture of children in particular as a crime against humanity and/or war crime occurred due to the State's inability to protect. The torture of children as particularized high priority targets during armed conflict and as part of a common plan carried out with impunity symbolizes in a most profound way utter chaos. This then undermines international peace and security as the populace in the jurisdictions affected loses what little confidence in the possibility of the rule of law and in international criminal justice these civilians initially may have clung to fervently in understandable desperation.

The book is organized as follows:

Chapter 1 considers the legal concept of torture under the Rome Statute and ambiguities regarding what constitutes torture under international criminal law.

Chapter 2 considers selected ICC cases involving facts revealing the systematic torture of children in particular as part of a common plan during armed conflict but where torture was not charged.

Chapter 3 considers, in contrast, selected ICC cases where torture was charged as a crime under the Rome Statute but the special targeting of children for torture as part of the common plan was not addressed.

Chapter 4 considers some landmark Inter-American Court of Human Rights cases regarding the targeting of children in particular for torture during internal conflict and the instructive lessons regarding the Court's legal analysis (i.e., the value of considering the broader international human rights and humanitarian legal context, recognizing various incarnations of or vehicles for torture etc.).

Chapter 5 examines 'enforced disappearance' as in itself constituting psychological torture for the direct victims and their family members as well as the relation of 'enforced disappearance' to physical and psychological torture and murder.

Chapter 6 discusses the fact that: (i) no charges to date have been brought for 'enforced disappearance' of children or adults in any cases brought before the ICC and that (ii) the relation between 'enforced disappearance' and torture has not been addressed by the ICC. This despite it being the case that 'enforced disappearance' is part of the *modus operandi* of groups such as the LRA and FPLC as they frequently abduct children for child soldiering and/or sexual enslavement. Most often the families of these child victims have no idea where their children are as they move with the forces or even whether the disappeared children are still alive.

Chapter 7 examines extra-judicial executions and wilful killings of civilians as a strategy of war and a form of physical (depending on how the killing occurred) and/or psychological torture.

Chapter 8 concerns the international legal responsibility to provide justice to child victims of torture where: (i) that suffering consequent to torture was inflicted through conduct that incorporates the elements of torture as a war crime and/or crime against humanity or act of genocide and where (ii) torture was for instance used as a component of a common plan during armed conflict. The latter chapter includes also an examination of the issue of UN peacekeepers, while on a UN operational mission, acting as perpetrators of torture against children and the possibility for ICC prosecution even where these are comparatively isolated incidents. Those prosecutions of UN peacekeeper perpetrators would be advanced given the gravity of the crime and the significant adverse impact on the local populace and the international community of the international crime of the torture of children especially when carried out by UN peacekeepers.

Chapter 9 includes a concluding comment regarding the need to dispel faulty stereotypes of who are the typical victims of torture as part of a common plan during armed conflict. That stereotype is one of a male adult who, for instance, perhaps has some vital information sought to be extracted through interrogation by torture and/or who is part of an opposition group being repressed through torture and other international crimes. The ingrained overly restrictive conceptual prototype of the typical torture victim during armed conflict does not include the image of an infant or child victim targeted in particular; the latter a child who may or may not be politically active. Also discussed in Chap. 9 is the ongoing crisis in Syria marked in part by the horrific targeting in particular of children for torture in various forms by the Bashar al-Assad regime as a component of a common plan. To date the regime's physical and psychological torture of targeted civilians including children in particular (for example the torture of those persons including children held in detention centers for that purpose and then not infrequently murdered) has been carried out with complete impunity insofar as criminal liability is concerned as with the other atrocities attributable to the Bashar al-Assad regime.

This book is in the final analysis an attempt to bring increased attention to: (i) the targeting of children in particular for torture as a part of a common plan during armed conflict as well as to (ii) the absence *in practice* of criminal liability before the ICC to date for the international crime of torture where children were amongst the victims *targeted in particular* in cases that were already before that Court involving other charges. The book further is a call for criminal accountability before the ICC (where the case is admissible and the court has jurisdiction), regardless of the official status of the individual perpetrators, where the accused are those most responsible for committing the grave international crime of torture during armed conflict against children in particular.

Thunder Bay, June 2013 Sonja C. Grover

Acknowledgments

My sincere thanks are extended to Dr. Brigitte Reschke, Executive Editor of Law for Springer for her support of this book project and to the anonymous reviewers of the work. As always, I thank my husband Roshan Grover and daughter Angeline for their love and support which make all things possible. With love and respect I acknowledge, in memory of my parents David and Gina Gazan, that it is they who first taught me about fundamental human rights by living its principles and who challenged me intellectually. Finally, I extend recognition and appreciation to the Springer production team for their excellent work.

Contents

Chapter 1
Contentious Issues Regarding What Constitutes Torture

1.1 The Torture of Children by Any Other Name is Still Torture

> Human solidarity manifests itself not only in a spatial dimension—that is, in the space shared by all the peoples of the world,—but also in a *temporal* dimension—that is, among the generations who succeed each other *in time*... The search for the truth constitutes the starting-point for the liberation as well as the protection of the human person; without truth (however unbearable it might come to be) one cannot be freed from the torment of uncertainty, and it is not possible either to exercise ... protected rights...The prevalence of the right to truth is essential to the struggle against impunity, and is ineluctably linked to the very *realization* of justice, and to the guarantee of non-repetition of ...[human rights] violations....[O]ne of the great truths of the human condition [is] that the fate of one is ineluctably linked to the fate of the others. One cannot live in peace in face of the disgrace of a beloved person. And peace should not be a privilege [only] of the dead.[1]

It is known from the empirical evidence that children in armed conflict situations in many State jurisdictions are not spared from torture and that generally the same extremely cruel torture methods are used on children as on adults. Hence no mercy is shown to children in this regard by a vast array of perpetrators of international crime worldwide. However accurate estimates of the numbers of children who have been tortured worldwide are not available. Further, the stark reality of children as the particularized victims of torture as part of a common plan during armed conflict has not for the most part yet entered the general public consciousness:

> Torture of children is a significant worldwide problem, but there are not official or reliable independent statistics to measure the magnitude of the problem.[2]
>
> **Children have not only been targeted as part of the civilian population, but have also been deliberately targeted specifically *because* they are children**. For example, in the former Yugoslavia, elite snipers intentionally shot children in public places to intimidate

[1] Inter-American Court of Human Rights Case of Bámaca Velásquez versus Guatemala, Judgment of 25, November 2000, (Separate Opinion of Judge A.A. Cançado, para 23, 29, 32, 40).

[2] Quiroga (2009), p. 70.

S. C. Grover, *The Torture of Children During Armed Conflicts*,
DOI: 10.1007/978-3-642-40689-8_1,

> the civilian population. In Sierra Leone, rebels amputated the arms and legs of civilians, including many children, as part of a deliberate strategy to spread terror. Many recent conflicts have also involved the pretence of claims of 'ethnicity' in which the enemy is defined through identification with a different group, focusing on children as the 'other' group's hope for the future. **Targeting children**—for extermination, torture, rape and use as sex slaves—**is increasingly being used by parties to a conflict as an effective means of subduing the civilian population as a whole** (emphasis added).[3]

The focus of this book is on making more visible (i) the issue of the torture of children as an international crime under the Rome Statute; (ii) the specific targeting of children for torture by various State and non-State entities and forces and (iii) the lack of accountability before the ICC for the torture of child victims as specific targets in cases brought before the ICC involving international crimes such as child soldiering, gender-based crimes and attacks against civilian populations. In sum the ICC jurisprudence[4] insofar as the *torture* of children as particularized targets as part of a common plan during armed conflict is concerned does not at all reflect the fact that:

> the torturer has become, like the pirate and the slave trader before him, *hostis humani generis*, an enemy of all mankind.[5]

The lack of attention specifically given by the ICC to children as the particularized victims of torture (as reflected in the failure to charge torture in respect of mental and physical sufferings imposed on children during armed conflict that amount to intentional torture) is all the more inexcusable considering that:

> **Clearly, the jus cogens nature of the prohibition against torture articulates the notion that the prohibition has now become one of the most fundamental standards of the international community**. Furthermore, this prohibition is designed to produce a deterrent effect, in that it signals to all members of the international community and the individuals over whom they wield authority that the prohibition of torture is an absolute value from which nobody must deviate (emphasis added).[6]

To date international crimes *specifically targeting* children (save for child soldiering) have been subsumed by international courts under charges concerning the civilian population as a whole. This pattern of neglecting the torture of children as specifically targeted high priority victims (i.e. such that perpetrators are

---

[3] Bedont and Sandvik-Nylund (2002), p. 30.

[4] There is both (i) a failure of the ICC OTP to prosecute for torture when children are systematically targeted in particular for torture during armed conflict and (ii) a failure of the OTP and the ICC Chambers to legally characterize the facts (i.e. extreme sexual violence, child soldiering with a perpetrator group committing mass atrocities, widespread mutilations of children, enforced disappearance of children etc. all used as part of an intentional common plan during armed conflict) as supporting torture charges in addition to other charges based on the same facts (cumulative charging).

[5] Filartiga v. Pena-Irala, 630 F. 2d 876 (2d Cir. 1980).

[6] The Prosecutor v Antonio Furundzija Trial Judgment ICTY (10 December, 1998), p. 59 para 154.

not charged with the targeting of children for torture as a separable crime in the international court system including the ICC) is longstanding:

> **crimes committed against children have not received due attention in previous and current international justice ... mechanisms, most often being mentioned only as part of atrocities committed against the civilian population in general** (emphasis added).[7]

This sidestepping essentially of the issue of the torture of children as particularized targets is entirely inconsistent with the fact that:

> This revulsion [in the international community regarding the use of torture], as well as the importance States attach to the eradication of torture, has led to the cluster of treaty and customary rules on torture acquiring a particularly high status in the international normative system, a status similar to that of principles such as those prohibiting genocide, slavery, racial discrimination, aggression, the acquisition of territory by force and the forcible suppression of the right of peoples to self-determination.[8]

The failure to prosecute before the ICC the widespread and systematic torture of children as particularized targets in armed conflict situations (the focus of this inquiry) belies the UN Security Council's repeated pronouncements on the importance of protecting children during armed conflict. Note that the UN Security Council can refer situations to the ICC such that if these situations meet Rome Statute jurisdictional and gravity criteria and other conditions (such as those relating to admissibility in regards to the complementarity principle); the situation will be developed into cases for ICC prosecution. The UN Security Council Resolution 1314 for instance, by implication, refers to the fact that children are vulnerable to becoming high priority targets for international crimes during armed conflict as it refers to the "deliberate targeting of... children":

> **...the deliberate targeting of** civilian populations or other protected persons, ***including children***, and the committing of **systematic, flagrant and widespread violations of international humanitarian and human rights law, including that relating to *children*, in situations of armed conflict may constitute a threat to international peace and security, and in this regard [the Security Council] *reaffirms* its readiness to consider such situations and, where necessary to adopt appropriate steps** (emphasis added).[9]

In regards to children as particularized targets, it is noteworthy that in fact:

> It is ... possible for the Security Council to find *that a situation characterized by crimes committed against children* is a threat to international peace and security, and, acting under Chapter VII of the UN Charter, refer that situation to the ICC. The Security Council has the power to refer situations to the ICC regardless of where the crimes have occurred and the nationalities of the alleged perpetrators, thereby overriding jurisdictional thresholds that apply to any other case brought to the ICC. *Thus, the ICC has the potential*

---

[7] Bedont and Sandvik-Nylund (2002), p. 12.

[8] The Prosecutor v Antonio Furundzija Trial Judgment ICTY (10 December, 1998), p. 56 para 147.

[9] Security Council Resolution 1314 (11 August, 2000) at para 9.

> *to strengthen the role of the Security Council in enforcing the protection of children affected by armed conflict* (emphasis added).[10]

To date this has not occurred though in Syria,[11] for instance, the children of the opposition have become particularized targets of torture in various guises under the Bashar Al-Assad regime which has been engaged (at the time of writing) for the last 2 years in large part in an unfettered attack on the Sunni civilian population.

We will explore in the conclusion to this inquiry some possible explanations for the failure of the ICC to adequately address the torture of children as prioritized targets of perpetrator groups committing mass atrocities in an armed conflict situation. There has been to date a complete failure of the ICC to hold perpetrators accountable through *separate charges,* grounded on the facts, for the grave crime of torture committed against children as particularized targets during armed conflict. Note that the fact that torture is a grave crime under the Rome Statute and that the prohibition on torture has a high priority (among the highest in international humanitarian, human rights and criminal law as well as international customary law) has done little if anything to lead to ICC prosecution of the systemic and widespread torture of children as particularized targets in cases to date that have been brought before the ICC.[12] As the contemporary conflict situation in Syria under the Al-Assad regime attests, the lack of accountability in the international courts (i.e. ICC) for the specific targeting of children for torture contributes to the persistence of this practice as a tool for the suppression of the civilian populace more generally.[13]

In what follows in the sections concerning ICC case law we will consider and apply the concept of torture *as defined in the Rome Statute* to: (i) cases in which children have in fact been specifically targeted for torture but the torture of children has neither been acknowledged as such in the case nor the crime of torture against children prosecuted by the ICC Office of the Prosecutor (OTP) and to (ii) cases in which torture was charged by the ICC OTP but no reference was made to the particularized targeting of children nor to its legal implications under the Rome Statute. We must begin then with a consideration of what ostensibly constitutes torture under the Rome Statute.

---

[10] Bedont and Sandvik-Nylund (2002), pp. 47–48.

[11] Syria is not a party to the Rome Statute thus the situation in Syria would have to be referred to the ICC by the UN Security Council. The referrals to the ICC to date by the UN Security Council have not focused on the plight of children as a key rationale for the referral.

[12] Note that the OHCHR has recognized in some instances “the vulnerability of the victim (age, gender, status, etc) should be taken into account to determine whether this case amounts to torture…” (Office of the High Commissioner for Human Rights 2011, p. 2).

[13] Note that in regards to the Torture Convention also “The majority of judgments and decisions about torture have been made in relation to adults.” Man (2000), p. 14.

1.1.1 Torture as an International Crime: Remaining Ambiguities in the Legal Concept

Despite having the elements of the various Rome Statute crimes, including torture as a war crime and torture as a crime against humanity, stipulated under the Rome Statute Elements of the Crimes,[14] as we shall see, the legal definition of torture remains elusive. This is in part due to the fact that other Rome Statute crimes not *labeled* 'torture' in the Rome Statute may be properly deemed by the ICC in a particular case before the Court to amount to torture depending on the specific fact pattern in the case[15]:

> *Many acts, conducts or events may be viewed as torture in certain circumstances, while they will not be viewed as torture in some other situations…* In fact, there is no single definition [of torture] existing under international law… It should be recalled that usually in legal dispositions, torture is linked with cruel, inhuman and degrading treatment or punishment or ill-treatment. Torture is not an act in itself, or specific type of acts, but it is the legal qualification of an event or behaviour, based on the comprehensive assessment of this event or behaviour. *Therefore, the difference between these different qualifications, torture, cruel, inhuman and degrading treatment or punishment or ill-treatment depends on the specific circumstances of each case and is not always obvious* (emphasis added).[16]

The term 'torture' is specifically mentioned in the Rome Statute under Crimes against Humanity and the elements of that crime are as follows:

1.1.1.1 Rome Statute Elements of the Crime: Article 7 (1)(f) Crime Against Humanity of Torture

Elements of the Crime of Torture as a Crime Against Humanity

1. The perpetrator inflicted ***severe physical or mental pain or suffering*** upon one or more persons.
2. Such person or persons were in the custody or under the control of the perpetrator.
3. Such pain or suffering did not arise only from, and was not inherent in or incidental to, lawful sanctions.
4. The conduct was committed as part of a widespread or systematic attack directed against a civilian population.
5. The perpetrator knew that the conduct was part of or intended the conduct to be part of a widespread or systematic attack directed against a civilian population (emphasis added).[17]

---

[14] Rome Statute Elements of the Crimes (2002).

[15] Thus the same set of facts could be classified both, for instance, as inhuman treatment and as torture depending on the specific context of the conduct as the Rome Statute elements for both crimes may have been met.

[16] Office of the High Commissioner for Human Rights (2011), p. 2. It is here contended that sometimes *depending on the circumstances*; inhuman, cruel or degrading treatment may also amount to torture.

[17] Rome Statute Elements of the Crimes (2002).

What is especially noteworthy about the ICC crime of torture as a crime against humanity under Article 7 is that: (a) no specific purpose in perpetrating the torture must be proved (as the ICC notes in footnote 14 to Article 7 (1)(f) of the Elements of the Crime); (b) the victims need not necessarily be under *State* custody or control but only in the custody or under the control of the perpetrator; (c) the torture consists of "*severe* physical or mental pain or suffering;" (d) the torture can exist whether there is one or more than one victim; (e) the pain or suffering is not to be a correlate to or inherent in or incidental to "lawful sanctions" (the latter element clearly reflecting State interests in the drafting of the Rome Statute definition of torture as an ICC crime against humanity); (f) the severe pain or suffering inflicted must be committed by a perpetrator as part of a systematic attack on civilians or intended to be a part of such an attack and (g) the crime of torture as a crime against humanity can occur in peace time or in the context of armed conflict (the same is true for torture as an act that formed part of a pattern directed to perpetrating genocide). Clearly some or all of the other crimes against humanity designated in the Rome Statute could also potentially meet the criteria for torture as a crime against humanity depending on the specific factual circumstance. For instance, the crime against humanity of extermination (Article 7(1)(b) could cause and is likely to cause severe mental and likely also physical suffering depending on the vehicle used to effect that extermination and whether the victims had any forehand knowledge that they were to be exterminated. The crime against humanity of rape may cause severe mental suffering not only as a direct consequence of the degradation and humiliation arising from such victimization but also due to the rejection of the rape victim by his or her community (i.e. it often occurs in some jurisdictions that it is the victim who is blamed for his or her own misfortune in being a rape victim and not the perpetrator or that blame is assigned to both victim and perpetrator). Rape may also cause severe physical pain and suffering rising to the level of torture as when permanent damage is done to the reproductive organs for instance as a consequence of gang rape and/or the victim contracts HIV. The foregoing are only two of many further possible examples of other Rome Statute crimes against humanity (aside from Article 7 (1)(f) which explicitly refers to the crime against humanity of torture) where in fact these additional crimes also can be conceptualized as torture[18] under the Rome Statute criteria depending on the specific fact pattern involved.

Despite the seemingly clear cut listing of the Rome Statute elements of the crime of torture; there are in fact remaining legal ambiguities. This is the case notwithstanding the lack of ambiguity of what is perceived as constituting torture for those on the receiving end of such perpetrator conduct. For instance; the section

[18] Thus the perpetrator might be charged by the ICC OTP, for instance, with 'rape' and 'torture' both as crimes against humanity based on the same fact pattern as each crime charged captures another dimension of the perpetrator's intent and the impact of the perpetrator's conduct on the victim.

titled "General Introduction" to the Rome Statute Elements of Crimes document includes the following item:

> 4. With respect to mental elements associated with elements involving value judgement, *such as* those using the terms inhumane or severe, it is not necessary that the perpetrator personally completed a particular value judgement, unless otherwise indicated (emphasis added).[19]

The above item suggests that what constitutes 'severe' or 'inhumane' perpetrator treatment of the victim is a value judgment (though there is not necessarily always a requirement that the perpetrator him or herself will have completed such a value assessment). Dewulf points out further that the notion of psychological torture is also particularly vague with no clear definition in international law.[20] For instance; threats of death to the victims or their family members, and a certain level of intimidation have been found in some instances by the ICTY to constitute psychological torture and in others cases threats to take life, for instance, have been relegated to the category of 'cruel and inhuman treatment' as distinct from 'torture' by the same ICTY court.[21]

We will return later to this question of legal ambiguity regarding what constitutes 'serious', 'severe' or 'inhumane' or 'degrading' perpetrator conduct and consider in detail the implications for acknowledging and prosecuting the torture of children before the International Criminal Court. Given the imprecision of the terms 'serious', 'severe' or 'inhumane'; it is even more likely that various other crimes against humanity can rise to the level of torture as conceptualized under the Rome Statute depending on the specific facts of the case.

What follows are only selected potential examples of perpetrator conduct that might be classified as inflicting torture, physical and/or psychological, depending on the Chamber's assessment of the facts:

1.1.1.2 Rome Statute Elements of the Crime: Article 6(b) Genocide by Causing Serious Bodily or Mental Harm

Torture is also an ICC crime considered as one possible vehicle for perpetrating genocide via inflicting "*serious* bodily or mental harm to one or more persons" in an attempt to destroy in whole or in part a particular national, ethnical (interpreted as ethnic), racial or religious group. Thus, the Rome Statute Elements of the Crimes document specifically mentions at footnote 3 to Article 6(b) 'Genocide by causing **serious** bodily or mental harm' that: "This conduct may include, but is not necessarily restricted to, ***acts of torture***, rape, sexual violence or inhuman or degrading treatment (emphasis added)." It is not required as an element that

[19] Rome Statute Elements of the Crimes (2002).

[20] Dewulf (2011), p. 180.

[21] Dewulf (2011), p. 180.

the victim be in the custody or control of the perpetrator in order to violate Rome Statute Article 6(b) the elements being as follows:

> **Article 6(b)**
>
> **Genocide by causing serious bodily or mental harm**
>
> 1. The perpetrator caused serious bodily or mental harm to one or more persons.
> 2. Such person or persons belonged to a particular national, ethnical, racial or religious group.
> 3. The perpetrator intended to destroy, in whole or in part, that national, ethnical, racial or religious group, as such.
> 4. The conduct took place in the context of a manifest pattern of similar conduct directed against that group or was conduct that could itself effect such destruction.[22]

'Torture' is in respect of Article 6(b) of the Rome Statute Elements of the Crimes then held by the ICC to be one possible manifestation of the perpetrator inflicting *serious* mental and/or physical harm. The wording "serious harm" is thus also used in the Rome Statute to describe the harms encompassed by torture. Thus reference to 'torture' in the Rome Statute is *not* restricted to the statutory terminology of "severe" harm as used, for instance, in Article 7 (1)(f) to delineate what constitutes torture as a 'crime against humanity' (where the nature of the physical pain or suffering involved is described as 'severe'). Hence, under the Rome Statute arguably (and this is the position taken here); it is *not* necessary to distinguish conceptually between the terms 'serious' and 'severe' in referring to the level of suffering and pain inflicted when assessing whether the perpetrator conduct meets the requisite element as to intensity of harms inflicted for the perpetrator conduct to be considered as torture.[23] Also note that 'torture' is in the Rome Statute described both as a 'grave' breach of international law (Article 8(2)(a)(ii) and 'serious' breach (Article 8(2)(c)(i)). 'Torture' under the Rome Statute and as per all other international instruments that address torture then requires as an element some level of significant physical or mental pain or suffering and/or injury. At the same time, however, on the view here, one cannot legitimately attempt to define away 'torture' through the use of descriptors such as 'serious' or 'great' suffering or pain and/or injury, for instance, as opposed to 'severe' suffering or pain and/or injury.

---

[22] Rome Statute Elements of the Crimes (2002).

[23] Dewulf (2011), pp. 92–93 argues also that the Rome Statute uses the term 'serious' to mean the same as the term 'severe' insofar as both can refer to the pain and suffering of torture under the Statute. Dewulf notes as support for this proposition that the Rome Statute Elements of the Crimes (2002) at Article 8(2)(a)(iii) defines "willfully inflicting great suffering" as "The perpetrator caused *great* physical or mental pain or suffering to, or *serious* injury to body or health of, one or more persons (emphasis added)." Dewulf points out however that the ICTY has held that the level of suffering in torture is greater than that required to meet the elements of the war crime of 'willfully inflicting great suffering' and greater than that involved for instance in the war crime of 'cruel treatment'. The latter ICTY perspective is however not unassailable.

1.2 'Child Abuse' vs. 'Child Torture' as Legal Concepts Under International Law

Let us digress for a moment to consider that there are definite distinctions to be made between 'child abuse' as a *conceptual legal category* versus the 'torture' of children:

> … ***while child abuse may cause severe pain or suffering that is not part of the definition***. Physical or mental violence may be considered child abuse regardless of the degree of pain or injury caused. Indeed, treatment that offends a child's dignity may be considered child abuse, regardless of whether it causes pain or suffering (emphasis added).[24]

Furthermore; 'child abuse' implies that the maltreatment was inflicted by parents or someone with caretaker duties acting in *loco parentis*[25] while this is not a necessary or implied feature in respect of the legal concept of 'torture' of a child. 'Child abuse' and 'torture' then do *not* overlap on all legal characteristics (i.e. in respect of the elements of the crime/features of the legal concept) even if the level of suffering and/or pain and/or injury is equivalent for both 'child abuse' and 'torture' *in certain instances*.[26] In addition, the absolute prohibition on torture is part of international customary law unlike the situation for 'child abuse' where: (i) there is a greater impact of cultural relativism in the interpretation of what constitutes the treatment at issue in various States (that is, what maltreatment amounts to/rises to the level of 'child abuse') and for that reason in part (ii) there exists no universal *jus cogens* prohibition on 'child abuse'.[27] Notions of 'child abuse' to some extent then (and unfortunately on the view here) have been often impacted by cultural relativist presumptions while this is less so in regard to the definition of 'torture' (especially given now the Rome Statute listing of the elements of the

---

[24] O'Donnell and Liwski (2010), pp. 3–4. The current author would point out that insults to personal dignity can cause significant mental suffering depending on the nature of the affront to one's human dignity involved.

[25] O'Donnell and Liwski (2010).

[26] For instance, abduction by a *non-custodial* parent of their child to another State (where the *lawful custodial* parent is acting in the best interests of the child) is generally conceived as a form of 'child abuse' that may produce for the child and custodial parent who has lost the child *mental suffering* rising to the level of the severe suffering of torture. Nevertheless, the two legal categories ('child abuse' and 'torture') should not be conflated. There are important distinctions between the two legal concepts that arguably are worth maintaining such that a proper analysis of the facts in each case is required to determine whether the *elements of the crime of torture* of a child are actually met (i.e. abduction of the child by the non-custodial parent may or may not have been intended to cause severe mental suffering also to the child and not just to the lawful custodial parent who has lost the child; and the former element would have to be present for the conduct of the perpetrator parent to be properly considered legally as *torture of a child* as the direct victim).

[27] This is not at all to say that an absolute universal ban on child abuse with *jus cogens* status would not also be of utmost value. Note that Protocols I and II to the 1949 Geneva Conventions (which arguably have attained the status of international customary law) do incorporate prohibitions on child maltreatment during armed conflict that, depending on the facts in the specific situation, might be considered as child abuse or even as torture.

crime of torture as a war crime or crime against humanity and the listing of the elements of various other crimes in the Rome Statute that could rise to the level of torture):

> The prohibition of torture has in fact been put forward as one of the core rights that needs to transcend the feud between universalists and [cultural] relativists. It has been argued that it is one of those rules that has to be given universal acceptance in an unequivocal manner ... It would, moreover, appear somewhat contradictory to allow for cultural, traditional, social or religious factors to play a significant role *vis-à-vis* the interpretation of what constitutes torturous practices, when at the same time, it is generally accepted that States... are actually ... obligated to change such damaging circumstances. Various ... international instruments thus require that cultural, social, traditional, and other practices that are harmful to women and children[28] be modified or eliminated.[29]

'Torture' further is addressed and defined as an offence under international criminal law such as the Rome Statute (as well as a human rights violation under the Torture Convention[30] and a violation of the laws of war per, for instance, Article 3 Common to the 1949 Geneva Conventions[31]). In contrast, 'child abuse' has not been addressed specifically or explicitly as such under international criminal law via the enabling statute of the ICC or any ad hoc international criminal tribunals such as the ICTY. This may be in part due to the fact that there is no *jus cogens* prohibition of child abuse and not even a semblance of an agreed upon international legal definition of the concept.[32] One might consider that the systematic and widespread 'child abuse' by perpetrators who have custody and control over the child victims and occurring during armed conflict falls, for instance, under the category of 'cruel treatment' as the latter is outlined in the Rome Statute (and where that

---

[28] See Convention on the Rights of the Child (1990) Article 24(3): "States Parties shall take all effective and appropriate measures with a view to abolishing traditional practices prejudicial to the health of children." Note that there is no universal consensus regarding whether these harmful traditional practices in any particular instance constitute: (i) 'torture' under international human rights and/or international criminal law or rather (ii) 'child abuse' that may or may not have torturous elements (i.e. severe suffering) but is conduct that does *not* meet the international human rights and/or international criminal law legal definition of torture in all respects.

[29] Dewulf (2011), pp. 132–133.

[30] Convention against Torture and Other Cruel, Inhuman or Degrading Treatment or Punishment (the "Torture Convention") (entered into force 26 June 1987)

[31] See for example Gandhi (2001).

[32] On the view here sex trafficking of children and the use of children as so-called 'child soldiers' by forces perpetrating mass atrocities are both forms of the psychological and physical 'torture' of children. They both involve pain and suffering of the children as an expected and intended objective of the perpetrator (a required element of the legal concept of torture as an international crime) and serve the purpose of establishing the perpetrators as an organized crime entity that has coercive and intimidating power. These issues have been addressed through various international human rights protocols and conventions (i.e. Convention on the Rights of the Child (1990); Protocol to Prevent, Suppress and Punish Trafficking in Persons, Especially Women and Children, Supplementing the United Nations Convention Against Transnational Organized Crime (Entry into force 25 December 2003); Optional Protocol to the Convention on the Rights of the Child on the involvement of children in armed conflict (12 February, 2002)) but generally not dealt with as *instances of torture* as an international crime.

maltreatment of children meets all the other elements of the crime of 'cruel treatment'). Thus it may be that child abuse (child maltreatment) is an embedded concept on some fact scenarios in notions of cruel treatment, inhumane treatment, and/or outrages on personal dignity for instance as defined under the Rome Statute. Note that the enabling statute of the Special Court of Sierra Leone under Article 5 covers the "abuse of girls" of 13 or 14 and "the abduction of girls for immoral purposes" in relation to the State's Prevention of Cruelty to Children Act, 1926 while the rest of the statute deals with crimes against humanity, violations of Common Article 3 of the 1949 Geneva Conventions and other serious violations of international humanitarian law.[33] Thus the latter statute dealt with abuse of girls in relation to Sierra Leone domestic law but the provision was incorporated in the Court's enabling statute along with provisions concerning international criminal law offences that predate the statute in international customary law.

To the extent that the 'torture' of children *as an international crime* (committed by perpetrator agents of a State or non-State group for instance as part of a common plan during armed conflict) is referred to as 'child abuse' or 'child maltreatment' as opposed to 'torture'; there is in fact a concomitant, if implicit, downgrading in the public perception/consciousness of the international crime of 'torture' as an international crime in respect of child victims.[34] Sadly the term "abuse" (implicitly read as 'child abuse'; an offence to date prosecuted under State jurisdiction) was in fact with respect, on the view here, inappropriately used in the outcome document of the 2002 United Nations General Assembly Special Session on Children. This 'abuse' terminology was used in the context of discussing international crimes and child victims. Such 'verbal slippage', if you will, sends a mixed message as to the nature of the offences at issue and the potential role of the ICC in prosecution of the individual perpetrators. The aforementioned passage in the UN Special Session on Children outcome document referred to read as follows:

> *Put an end to impunity, prosecute those responsible for genocide, crimes against humanity, and war crimes,* and exclude, where feasible, these crimes from amnesty provisions and amnesty legislation, and ensure that whenever post-conflict truth and justice-seeking mechanisms are established, ***serious abuses involving children*** are addressed and that appropriate child-sensitive procedures are provided (emphasis added).[35]

Even such a staunch advocate for basic human rights as Human Rights Watch (HRW) has at times used the watered down moniker "abuse" (meaning 'child abuse'), as opposed to the term 'torture', to describe atrocities intentionally inflicted on children in particular to cause maximum pain and suffering on these

[33] Statute of the Special Court of Sierra Leone (14 August, 2000).

[34] This is not at all to suggest that 'child abuse' is not also a grave violation of the fundamental human rights of children that must be prevented and prosecuted wherever and whenever it occurs. Rather it is only to hold that the elements of the *legal concepts* of 'torture' and 'child abuse' do not entirely overlap though the suffering and/or pain and/or injury involved in 'child abuse' can rise to the level of suffering, pain or injury of torture in certain cases.

[35] United Nations General Assembly Special Session on Children (2002) A world fit for children at para 23.

victims as part of a common plan during armed conflict. This was the case where in the same section of a HRW report on the LRA it is acknowledged that the treatment accorded the children by the LRA amounted to brutality; yet the descriptor categorical term used for the conduct was 'abuse' and not 'torture' (i.e. section IV of the Human Rights Watch 2003 report 'Stolen children: Abduction and recruitment in Northern Uganda' is titled 'Abduction and *abuses* against children by the Lord's Resistance Army').[36] It is difficult to conceive of "abuse" rather than torture[37] as the appropriate categorization of the perpetrator conduct for the following LRA behaviours described in the 2003 Human Rights Watch aforementioned report under section IV:

> Children are forced to witness and to participate in the killings of other children, usually those who attempt to escape and are captured. The practice of using the children to collectively kill fosters guilt and fear among them, and sends a powerful message to the children of their potential fate if they attempt to escape.[38]

> Mark T., also 17 years old, spoke of the killings:
>
> One time when we were marching towards Pajule in Pader district, one 18-year-old male tried to escape but was soon captured. Soldiers laid him on the ground and told us to step on him. All the new recruits participated—we trampled him to death. During my time with the LRA, there were other children who escaped and seven of these were caught. Of them, two were hacked to death with machetes and five were clubbed or trampled. We were either made to participate or watch the killings. The youngest recruit killed was maybe nine or 10 years old.[39]

The point then is that the *erroneous* meta-message communicated (whether intentionally or not) through the use of the term 'abuse' in reference to children as particularized targets of atrocity during armed conflict[40] is that children *rightfully* do not fit the mental prototype for victims of torture as an international crime. The risk of course is that (i) children will be disregarded as the targeted victims in particular, which they so often are, of torture as part of a common plan during armed conflict and that (ii) such a horrific and unlawful military and political strategy will be carried out with continued impunity notwithstanding the international criminal justice system and its principles (i.e. torture charges will not be brought where the victims of even systematic and widespread atrocity are children who were targeted as high priority victims given the perpetrator's purpose in creating demoralization and psychological coercion and torture for the general civilian population being suppressed).

---

36 Human Rights Watch (2003a), p. 5.

37 One wonders whether the softer term 'abuse' would be used in reference to describe such treatment by the LRA of adult victims.

38 Human Rights Watch (2003a), p. 8. The adult LRA perpetrator conduct described on the view here amounts to psychological torture.

39 Human Rights Watch (2003a), p. 10.

40 Note that the term 'abuse' is not typically used to describe the treatment and fundamental human rights violations adults have suffered as victims of atrocity during armed conflict.

1.3 More on the Indeterminacy in the Legal Concept of Torture as an International Crime

Returning then to our discussion of Article 6(b) of the Rome Statute 'Genocide by causing serious bodily or mental harm', recall that the elements of Rome Statute Article 6(b) include a contextual element. There is a requirement that the conduct of, for instance, torture[41] directed to destroying the targeted national, ethnic, racial or religious group in whole or in part through the infliction of physical and/or mental harm must have occurred amidst a pattern of similar conduct directed toward the victim group *or was sufficient itself to cause the destruction of the group* (in whole or in part).[42] Arguably the physical and mental suffering inflicted "by causing serious bodily or mental harm" as a genocidal act could be effected also by inflicting on persons in the targeted group "conditions of life calculated to bring about physical destruction" of the group in whole or in part.(Article 6(c)). The Rome Statute Elements of the Crimes stipulates at Article 6(c) footnote 4 that "The term conditions of life may include, but is not necessarily restricted to, deliberate deprivation of resources indispensable for survival, such as food or medical services, or systematic expulsion from homes." The latter conditions could, of course, produce the severe mental and/or physical suffering most often associated with torture and carried out here for a genocidal purpose.[43]

Mental and physical suffering rising to the level of torture for the targeted group as a whole as victim and the individual and family directly targeted could also arise as the result of (i) the forcible transfer of children of the group to the perpetrator group (Article 6(e): genocide by forcibly transferring children to another group) or (ii) by taking measures to prevent births in the group such as forced sterilization of all women and girls (Article 6(d): Genocide by imposing measures intended to prevent births). In addition, genocide by killing (Article 6(a)) could rise to the level of torture, for instance, caused by knowing one's fate is death at the hands of a *genocidaire* and being helpless to avert it or to protect one's loved ones from the same fate.

None of the latter aforementioned Rome Statute articles pertaining to genocide (Articles 6(a); 6(c); 6(d) and 6(e)) reference the *legal characterization* 'torture'. This is the case though it would seem apparent that each perpetrator conduct captured by these

---

[41] Recall that the Rome Statute Elements of the Crimes (2002) in a footnote to Article 6(b) stipulates that 'torture' may be one vehicle for perpetrating 'genocide by causing serious bodily or mental harm'.

[42] Note that genocide does not require as a necessary element under the Rome Statute that the attack on the targeted group be widespread or systematic.

[43] Inflicting on persons in the targeted group "conditions of life calculated to bring about the physical destruction" of the group in whole or in part could, depending on the circumstances, be both an act of 'genocide' and 'torture as a war crime'. The latter since, for instance, (i) there is a discriminatory element involved (the Rome Statute requires a certain purpose connected with 'torture as a war crime' and specifically lists discrimination as a possible purpose) and (ii) the severe pain and suffering inflicted due to the intolerable conditions not fit for survival are part of a common plan in the context of an armed conflict.

articles could properly be so legally categorized in addition to the genocide classification given the intentional infliction of severe mental and/or physical suffering as part of a planned attack on the targeted group (generally a systematic and widespread attack).

The elements of the ICC crime of torture are also specifically delineated in the Rome Statute with reference to torture as a particular war crime taking place either in an international armed conflict situation or one that is not international. The latter criteria are problematic as often contemporary armed conflicts are internal but have important international players as well. This is the case for instance with the conflict in Syria involving the Bashar Al Assad regime's efforts to quell all internal opposition. The Syrian rebel groups are being backed in a very measured way by the U.S and certain of its allies and the Al Assad brutal regime is being backed by China and Russia. The latter appear not overly concerned, if at all, with the gross and widespread fundamental human rights violations being perpetrated by the Assad regime in this conflict as part of a common plan.[44] The elements of the ICC crime of 'torture as a war crime' are described at Article 8(2)(a)(ii)-1 and Article 8(2)(c)(i)-4 of the Rome Statute Elements of the Crimes as follows (note that there is no requirement that the victim(s) be in the custody or control of the perpetrator (State or non-State) in respect of the 'war crime of torture' under the Rome Statute[45]):

Rome Statute: Article 8(2)(a)(ii)-1: War crime of torture (or inhuman treatment, including biological experiments) (International Context) (Grave breach of the Geneva Conventions of 12 August 1949)
Elements

1. The perpetrator inflicted ***severe physical or mental pain or suffering*** upon one or more persons.
2. The perpetrator ***inflicted the pain or suffering for such purposes as: obtaining information or a confession, punishment, intimidation or coercion or for any reason based on discrimination of any kind.***
3. Such person or persons were protected under one or more of the Geneva Conventions of 1949.
4. The perpetrator was aware of the factual circumstances that established that protected status.
5. The conduct took place in the context of and was associated with an ***international armed conflict.***
6. The perpetrator was aware of factual circumstances that established the existence of an armed conflict (emphasis added).[46]

[44] This is not to suggest that atrocities may not have been committed on an isolated basis by the rebels in Syria but there does not appear to be any evidence to date that the rebels are using atrocity as part of a common plan.

[45] Schabas (2010), p. 215.

[46] Rome Statute Elements of the Crimes (2002).

Rome Statute Article 8(2)(c)(i)-4: War crime of torture (Non-International Context) (Serious Violations of Article 3 Common to the Four Geneva Conventions of 12 August 1949)
Elements

1. The perpetrator ***inflicted severe physical or mental pain or suffering*** upon one or more persons.
2. The perpetrator ***inflicted the pain or suffering for such purposes as: obtaining information or a confession, punishment, intimidation or coercion or for any reason based on discrimination of any kind.***
3. Such person or persons were either *hors de combat*, or were civilians, medical personnel or religious personnel taking no active part in the hostilities.
4. The perpetrator was aware of the factual circumstances that established this status.
5. The conduct took place in the context of and was associated with an ***armed conflict not of an international character.***
6. The perpetrator was aware of factual circumstances that established the existence of an armed conflict (emphasis added).[47]

The terminology referencing inflicting "severe physical or mental pain or suffering" which is used at Rome Statute Article 7(1)(f) in delineating the elements of the 'crime against humanity of torture' occurs then also in Rome Statute Article 8 in the description of the elements relating to the 'war crime of torture'. Note that the Rome Statute 'war crime of torture' incorporates as an element (unlike the case for the Rome Statute crime against humanity of torture) that the harms inflicted on the victim(s) were intended to achieve a specific purpose aside from the infliction of pain or suffering *per se;* for instance; obtaining information or a confession, to carry out a punishment, to create intimidation or coercion or for any reason that has a discriminatory basis. The question arises; however, whether in fact it is possible to maintain that the Rome Statute 'crime against humanity of torture' has no purpose given that no list of objectives is stipulated in the Elements of the Crimes document or whether the latter is pure legal fiction. This given the fact that 'torture as a crime against humanity' arguably has a communicative function namely to further intimidate the populace by demonstrating the dreadful measures which the perpetrator is prepared to utilize to suppress any opposition or otherwise achieve perpetrator objectives.

Other war crimes set out in the Rome Statute may rise to the level of torture as well depending on the fact pattern (the following are but selected examples). For instance, Article 8(2)(b)(x)-2; 'the war crime of medical or scientific experiments' in an international armed conflict may constitute torture (see also Article 8(2)(e)(xi)(2); the war crime of medical or scientific experiments in a non- international armed conflict):

Rome Statute Article 8(2)(b)(x)-2: the War Crime of Medical or Scientific Experiments (Other serious violations of the laws and customs applicable in international armed conflict)

---

[47] Rome Statute Elements of the Crimes (2002).

Elements

The perpetrator subjected one or more persons to a medical or scientific experiment.
The experiment caused death or seriously endangered the physical or mental health or integrity of such person or persons.
The conduct was neither justified by the medical, dental or hospital treatment of such person or persons concerned nor carried out in such person's or persons' interest.
Such person or persons were in the power of an adverse party.
The conduct took place in the context of and was associated with an international armed conflict.
The perpetrator was aware of factual circumstances that established the existence of an armed conflict.[48]

Schabas explains that "mutilation is also a serious violation of Common Article 3 [to the 1949 Geneva Conventions] punishable under Article 8(2)(c)(i) of the Rome Statute [mutilation as a war crime in a non-international armed conflict]"[49] That 'mutilation' and 'torture' are both listed as war crimes under Rome Statute Article 8(2)(c)(i) as Articles 8(2)(c)(i)-2 and 8(2)(c)(i)-4 respectively suggests that they are considered by the drafters of the Rome Statute as of comparative gravity. It is here contended that the 'war crime of mutilation' in itself, as with the war crime of medical or scientific experiments, can rise to the level of torture. Recall that the Rome Statute article dealing with '*torture* as a war crime' requires a specific purpose such as "obtaining information or a confession, punishment, intimidation or coercion or for any reason based on discrimination of any kind." Such a specific Rome Statute purpose requirement or element is not present in regards to 'mutilation as a war crime' or 'scientific or medical experiments as a war crime'. Nevertheless, where *children are specifically targeted* as during WWII in respect of certain of the diabolical 'experiments' conducted by Josef Rudolph Mengele on *children in particular*; age discrimination exists in the selection of the victims and the purpose element of *torture* is thus present in that respect along with the infliction of severe mental and physical suffering and pain. Megele's atrocities of course predated the development and entry into force of the Rome Statute and the example is used here as illustrative of scientific or medical 'experiments' targeting children in particular that could have been charged both as torture and the war crime of medical or scientific experiments had the Rome Statute been entered into force and Germany a State party for example:

> ..an estimated 9,432 boys and girls under fourteen [were used] by … Joseph Mengele in his eugenics experiments on twins and for research on various diseases… When it suited him, Dr. Mengele hugged the children and fed them candy … but a child he seemed to dote on one day could be killed with total indifference the next so he could examine [the child's] organs. The conditions under which the children were used was terrible, as a former prisoner assigned to take care of them described: "The anthropological examinations

[48] Rome Statute Elements of the Crimes (2002).

[49] Schabas (2010), p. 238.

> took place as follows: the children were stripped naked and measurements were made for hours (two to five hours)...This was a difficult ordeal for the children.. Terrified, worn-out hungry and shivering they had to get up at six in the morning and walk the one and one-half kilometre road from the [concentration camp] block to the ... 'hospital'...the room in which the tests were conducted was unheated ... After they returned ... the children had fevers, coughs ....even pneumonias... [50]

There may be discrimination in the selection of victims based on ethnicity or some other factor or status as well of course (as there normally is in instances of widespread mutilation or the carrying out of medical and scientific experiments as for instance with the Nazis) such that the purpose requirement for torture is in that way met. In any case; mutilations and scientific or biological experiments of no benefit to the victims, but rather such as to do significant harm to the victims or even cause death; inherently serve the purpose of intimidation of the targeted group of which the victims are members and of the larger populace as well ensuring to some significant degree the suppression of civilian opposition to the perpetrator group. Thus the purpose element of 'torture as a war crime' relating to intimidation and coercion and to (age) discrimination is present also with mutilation of children in particular as in the Kony case to be here discussed later when addressing LRA atrocities.

The war crime of conducting medical and/or scientific experiments on a person or persons held captive by the adversary and causing death or endangering the mental and/or physical integrity and well being of the victim for reasons having nothing to do with the interests of the victim would meet the criteria of inflicting such severe mental and/or physical pain or suffering on the victim that such conduct might be considered as rising to the level of torture. Note in that regard that Rome Statute Article 8(2)(a)(ii) concerning war crimes sets out "Torture or inhuman treatment, *including biological experiments*" as falling into this Rome Statute category of international crime. Thus biological experiments on humans (i.e. scientific or medical experiments) conducted only in the interests of the perpetrator and causing the victims significant harms and other inhuman treatment (each also listed as separable crimes under the Rome Statute) are *also* specifically considered under Rome Statute Article 8(2)(a)(ii) as potentially rising to the level of torture (as a war crime). Note that though these other international crimes (biological experiments on humans not in the interest of the victims, various other inhuman treatment) do not have a specific purpose explicitly listed in the Rome Statute Elements of the Crimes document; they all clearly serve the purpose of intimidation and coercion of the general oppressed civilian population and thus meet the purpose requirement of torture as a war crime. Thus, for instance, 'inhuman treatment' as a war crime in the context of an international armed conflict (Rome Statute Article 8(2)(a)(ii)-2 and 'cruel treatment' as a war crime in the context of a non-international armed conflict (Rome Statute 8(2)(c)(i)-3) may rise to the level also of torture as a war crime given the purpose served i.e. intimidation and coercion of the populace and given the severity of the suffering and harms inflicted on the direct and indirect victims via the aforementioned crimes.

---

[50] Nicholas (2005), p. 29.

Other categories of war crimes under the Rome Statute may also meet the criteria for torture as a war crime depending on the particular fact scenario. These other instances might include, but are not limited to, for instance, the 'war crime of wilfully causing great suffering (Rome Statute Article 8(2)(a)(iii)):

Rome Statute Article 8(2)(a)(iii): War crime of wilfully causing great suffering (Grave breaches of the Geneva Conventions of 12 August 1949)

Elements

1. The perpetrator caused great physical or mental pain or suffering to, or serious injury to body or health of, one or more persons.
2. Such person or persons were protected under one or more of the Geneva Conventions of 1949.
3. The perpetrator was aware of the factual circumstances that established that protected status.
4. The conduct took place in the context of and was associated with an international armed conflict.
5. The perpetrator was aware of factual circumstances that established the existence of an armed conflict.[51]

The war crime of 'wilfully causing great suffering' may also amount to torture depending on the specific facts where the suffering of the victims is, for instance, very apparent to the general populace or even inflicted in public such that it serves to intimidate the general population. The infliction of the suffering may have been for coercive purposes to obtain information from the direct victims or their family members and hence in that respect also may meet the purpose requirement/element for the Rome Statute war crime of torture.

We have seen then that there is inconsistency in the Rome Statute terminology used to refer to the level of pain or suffering required to meet the threshold for torture; must it be 'severe' or 'simply serious' or 'great' or are the terms interchangeable on certain fact patterns as argued here. Further, who but the victim (given his or her age, health, baseline mental status, disability etc.) can in fact realistically assess such a matter in situ at least insofar as whether the subjective threshold for mental and/or physical suffering and/or pain rises to the level of torture:

> ... both objective and subjective elements that relate to both the treatment and the victim are to be assessed. Objective aspects [of torture]leave room for some sort of objective evaluation and must, therefore, form the basis of any assessment.... Yet... objective elements are not (always) decisive on their own. How many slaps in the face are needed before this conduct goes from cruelty to torture? How long must a person be denied sleep before such (inhuman) treatment becomes torturous? All this is not only dependent on objective evaluation. It also demands considering and assessing subjective elements, which makes the assessment far more complex. How do you determine how much an individual suffers?[52]

In any case, the tolerance for pain or suffering, mental or physical, varies from individual to individual and hence general pronouncements on that matter and a

[51] Rome Statute Elements of the Crimes (2002).

[52] Dewulf (2011), pp. 147–148.

pretence to some definitive objective criteria in that regard seems fallacious. It must also be understood based on current medical knowledge that generally speaking "the threshold of pain for children is lower than it is for adults."[53] It would seem also that the threshold for mental suffering may also be lower for children especially those who are dependent on others psychologically, economically and in other ways. Children dependent on their primary caretakers who may have lost those caretakers in the conflict (i.e. the caretakers may have been murdered or the children may simply have been separated from the caretakers due to any number of factors etc.) may then be especially vulnerable to psychological and physical torture such that the threshold for torture may be lower in their case compared to other children who for a variety of reasons are more resilient psychologically and perhaps even physically. It appears that for many children, if not most, the long-term consequences of torture can be even more severe than for adults according to certain medical specialists working with torture survivors "because torture interrupts the process of normal psychological, emotional and social development."[54] Certain researchers have reported, for instance, that children who managed to escape the LRA or were otherwise freed after being captured by Ugandan forces suffered long-term consequences from their time in LRA captivity and what is here viewed as torturous treatment as child soldiers and/or sex slaves:

> The children reported many difficulties spanning the physical, psychological, social, behavioural and economic domains. All were in extremely poor physical condition when they returned and they continued to suffer serious medical problems stemming from their brutal treatment in the bush 2 or 3 years earlier.[55]
>
> Girls particularly suffered from medical conditions and frequent physical pain stemming from their violent sexual abuse, including HIV/AIDS and sexually transmitted infections.[56]
>
> All the children reported symptoms of psychological trauma on their return. These included nightmares, suicidal thinking, extreme fear and anxiety which pervaded their daily lives as they tried to adjust back into their families and communities.[57]

On the matter of the level of pain and suffering required as an element of the crime of torture the ICTY chamber comment is instructive:

> Torture is constituted by an act or an omission giving rise to "severe pain or suffering, whether physical or mental", but ***there are no more specific requirements which allow an exhaustive classification and enumeration of acts which may constitute torture. Existing case-law has not determined the absolute degree of pain required for an act to amount to torture*** (emphasis added).[58]

---

[53] Quiroga (2009), p. 67.

[54] Bauer and Quiroga (2008).

[55] Chrobok and Akutu (2008), p. 27.

[56] Chrobok and Akutu (2008), p. 27.

[57] Chrobok and Akutu (2008), p. 27.

[58] The Prosecutor v Dragoljub Kunaric, Radomir Kovac and Zoran Vukovic ICTY Appeal Chamber Judgment (12 June, 2002), p. 46 para 149.

The aforementioned ICTY perspective is in fact consistent with the view discussed earlier that:

> Torture is not an act in itself, or specific type of acts, but it is the legal qualification of an event or behaviour, based on the comprehensive assessment of this event or behaviour.[59]

Another source of legal ambiguity in the Rome Statute (as with other instruments that include torture as an international crime) concerns the hypothesized theoretical socially constructed legal distinction (if any) between torture versus so-called 'inhuman' and/or 'degrading treatment' and/or punishment and/or attacks or severe or serious harms inflicted in respect of the victim's human dignity. Dewulf makes the point that often a range of acts that are not statutorily distinguished from one another or from torture in terms of distinct definitions are listed in the same line.[60] For instance, Rome Statute Article 8(2)(a)(ii) includes in the same line torture and other acts that appear to be largely if not wholly akin to torture and reads as follows: "Torture or inhuman treatment, including biological experiments."[61] It would appear that the Rome Statute considers torture as but one form of cruel, inhuman and degrading treatment or punishment rather than distinguishing between torture *versus* inhuman and/or degrading and/or cruel treatment as entirely separable categories. The latter is evidenced for instance by Rome Statute Article 55(1)(b) which states that the rights of persons during an investigation include that they not be subjected to torture which by implication of the particular wording in Rome Statute Article 55(1)(b) refers to *a form of* cruel, inhuman or degrading treatment or punishment:

Rome Statute Article 55(1)(b)
Rights of persons during an investigation

In respect of an investigation under this Statute, a person:

> (b) Shall not be subjected to any form of coercion, duress or threat, *to torture or to **any other form** of cruel, inhuman or degrading treatment or punishment* (emphasis added).[62]

This approach is reminiscent of the European Court of Human Rights holding in Ireland v U.K. where the Court referred to torture as a "special stigmata to deliberate inhuman treatment causing very serious and cruel suffering."[63] Note also that the UN 1975 Declaration on Torture at Article 1(2) stated that "torture constitutes an aggravated and deliberate form of cruel, inhuman and degrading

---

[59] Office of the High Commissioner for Human Rights (2011), p. 2.

[60] Dewulf (2011), p. 64.

[61] Rome Statute (2002). All of these acts can serve the purpose of intimidating the general populace.

[62] Rome Statute (2002).

[63] Ireland v. United Kingdom, Judgment of 18 January, 1978, Series A, No. 25; (1978) 2 EHRR 25, para 159.

treatment or punishment."[64] Hence, 'torture' under the Rome Statute, and consistent with previous international humanitarian law interpretations by various international judicial and human rights bodies, is not a legal characterization that is necessarily mutually exclusive to that of 'cruel, inhuman and degrading treatment or punishment' though it may *on some analysis* have certain additional or distinctive features.

At the same time; the Rome Statute does not clarify at what point various "other" inhuman acts rise to the level of 'torture' (assuming then that torture is distinguishable in terms of the level of severity of suffering or pain inflicted) or whether these other inhuman acts are in fact tantamount to torture simply referred to by another name.[65] Note that under the Rome Statute elements of the crime[66] of torture as a war crime (Article 8(2)(a)(ii)-1) and of inhuman treatment as a war crime (Article 8(2)(a)(ii)-2); *both* include the element of inflicting "*severe* physical or mental pain or suffering" suggesting that inhuman treatment is torture under the Rome Statute if the level of suffering or pain is the prime focus. Rather the difference between the war crime of torture and the war crime of inhuman treatment under the Rome Statute appears to be only in terms of *purported* difference in some aspects of context. That is torture as a war crime under the Rome Statute involves the perpetrator having some specific purpose in inflicting the suffering whereas no reference is made in the Rome Statute elements of the crime to purpose in respect of the elements of the crime of inhuman treatment as a war crime. That is purpose need not be proved as an element of the crime of inhuman treatment under the Rome Statute though generally the torturer in armed conflict has a purpose such as intimidation, shaming of the group of whom the victim is a member, coercion etc.[67] However, inhuman treatment can and often does have a purpose as well and one coinciding with the purposes most often perceived as associated with torture.

---

[64] Declaration on the Protection of All Persons from Being Subjected to Torture and Other Cruel, Inhuman or Degrading Treatment or Punishment (1975) This wording regarding torture as an aggravated form of cruel, inhuman and/or degrading treatment or punishment does not appear in the definition of torture in the Torture Convention (1987) but arguably is implied given the international criminal tribunal and ICC jurisprudence.

[65] Recall that 'inhuman' or 'cruel treatment' for instance can, depending on the circumstances, be inflicted to serve the same purposes as is the case with 'torture as a war crime'; purposes "*such as* obtaining information or a confession, punishment, intimidation or coercion or for any reason based on discrimination of any kind." Note also that the Rome Statute list of possible purposes of torture as a war crime is not an exhaustive list but intended only as examples hence the words "such as" in describing the possible purposes at Article 8 (2)(a)(ii)-1 and Article 8(2)(c)(i)-4.

[66] Rome Statute Elements of the Crimes (2002).

[67] Rome Statute Elements of the Crimes (2002).

Note that the UN Convention on Torture draws no objective distinction between torture and inhuman treatment.[68] Consider also that:

> (…) Certain acts which were qualified in the past as inhuman or degrading treatment, not as torture, could be qualified in the future in a different way, that is, as torture, since to the growing demands of protection of human rights and fundamental freedoms ought to correspond a greater firmness to face the infringements to the basic values of democratic societies (…)[69]

The Rome Statute also uses the term 'inhumane' for instance at Article 7(1)(k) describing the crime against humanity of "Other inhumane acts of *a similar character* intentionally causing great suffering, or serious injury to body or to mental or physical health (emphasis added)."[70] Such 'other inhumane acts' when perpetrated against civilians in a systematic and/or widespread manner conceivably could *also* be considered to constitute 'torture as a crime against humanity' (such that the same fact pattern could form the basis for both ICC charges; namely (i) 'torture as a crime against humanity' and (ii) the crime against humanity of 'other inhumane acts of a similar character intentionally causing great suffering, or serious injury to body or to mental or physical health'. The latter being the case insofar as these other inhumane acts also involve the requisite level of mental and/or physical suffering, pain and/or injury to mind or body to meet the Rome Statute element of torture in that regard. Again there is no purpose element in regards to the Rome Statute crime of "Other inhumane acts of a similar character intentionally causing great suffering, or serious injury to body or to mental or physical health" that must be proved. Notwithstanding the fact, however, that the Rome Statute Elements of the Crimes legal document does *not* require a purpose element to prove 'other inhumane acts' or 'inhuman treatment'; such perpetrator conduct accomplishes the purpose of terrorizing a civilian population (even when the conduct does not involve widespread acts such as mass war crimes involving inhuman treatment but where the conduct may have been confined to isolated incidents). Such perpetrator conduct destroys the psychological and often also the physical integrity of the victims. Further, where there is considered to be a (i) purpose element (based on discrimination, directed to intimidation etc.) or (ii) a specific intent element to destroy a group in whole or in part based on nationality, race, ethnicity or religion[71]; 'inhumane acts' may properly be considered by the ICC, on the view here, also to amount to 'torture as a war crime' or torture in the pursuit of genocide respectively.

---

[68] Office of the High Commissioner for Human Rights (2011), p. 6.

[69] Cantoral Benavides versus Peru IACtHR judgment 18 August 2000 at para 99.

[70] Note that the term 'inhumane' is arguably interchangeable with various other terms used in the Rome Statute such as 'cruel', 'inhuman', 'severe', and 'great' to reflect the extent of suffering and/or pain and/or or injury inflicted by the perpetrator.

[71] The current author has argued elsewhere that the list of targeted protected groups mentioned in the genocide provision of the Rome Statute cannot properly be considered to be an exhaustive list and that several of the terms used in the provision such as 'race' and 'ethnicity' are in fact vague (i.e. see Grover 2013a, b.

Rome Statute Article 7(1)(k) "Other inhumane acts of a similar character intentionally causing great suffering, or serious injury to body or to mental or physical health" appears to have been a provision intended as a "residual category."[72] This in order that anything interpreted (correctly or incorrectly) as not covered by the other Rome Statute articles dealing with international crimes would not be so elusive as to escape categorization under Article 7(1)(k). Thus there is then no exhaustive listing of the type of perpetrator acts to be considered as "other inhumane acts" under Rome Statute Article 7(1)(k)[73]:

> Serious physical and mental injury, falling short of murder, can be prosecuted as 'other inhumane acts'. Criminal behaviour deemed to fall within 'other inhumane acts' has included mutilation and other types of severe bodily harm, beatings and other acts of violence, serious physical and mental injury, inhumane and degrading treatment, forced prostitution, forced disappearance, sniping at civilians, and forced marriage.[74]...Referring to article 7(1)(k) of the Rome Statute, the Supreme Court of Venezuela has considered drug trafficking, terrorism, and child prostitution may constitute crimes against humanity.[75]

> Other inhumane acts were charged in the [ICC] arrest warrants in the *Situation in Uganda* where they are alleged to consist of inflicting serious bodily injury and suffering upon the civilian residents of an internally displaced persons camp.[76] In [the ICC case] *Katanga*, other inhumane acts was charged with respect to indiscriminate gunfire and machete blows on civilians who suffered serious and potentially life-threatening injuries. Pre-Trial Chamber I refused to confirm the charge, however, because it held that these were also attempted murders, and that alleged acts cannot simultaneously be prosecuted as murder and as 'other inhumane acts'.[77]

The current author would argue that it is also legally supportable under the Rome Statute to charge 'other inhumane acts' in reference to the mental suffering caused parents and other family members when their children are targeted for child

---

[72] Schabas (2010), p. 184.

[73] According to the ICTY which has the category of "other inhumane acts" incorporated into its enabling statute, "An exhaustive categorization would merely create opportunities for the evasion of the letter of the prohibition" (Schabas 2010, p. 184) "The Appeal Chamber of the International Criminal Tribunal for the former Yugoslavia has insisted that 'other inhumane acts' as formulated in the Statute of the Tribunal is part of customary international law and cannot be considered to violate the principle of *nullum crimen sine lege*." (Schabas 2010, p. 184) "At the Rome Conference, concern that "'other inhumane acts' was too vague and might violate the *nullum crimen sine lege* principle was expressed." (Schabas 2010, p. 185).

[74] Schabas (2010), p. 185 (These examples of acts deemed "other inhumane acts" coming from ICTY and SCSL cases).

[75] Schabas (2010), p. 185.

[76] Schabas (2010), p. 185.

[77] Schabas (2010), pp. 185–186. The current author would, in contrast to the ICC Pre-Trial Chamber I in *Katanga*, maintain that the perpetrators surely would have ensured murder if that was the only objective. Instead their indiscriminate gunfire and machete blows on civilians left some people dead and other surviving with limbs missing and other grievous injuries as a testament to the ferocity and inhumanity of the perpetrators thus serving well the ongoing purpose of terrorizing civilians. Thus, on the view here, it is possible and legally supportable to charge for both attempted murder and other inhumane acts at once as cumulative charges.

soldiering with a group committing mass atrocities, sexually enslaved by the same group, forced as children to commit atrocities against their own family and community, forcibly transferred to another group etc.

The Rome Statute also includes crimes that are specifically designated as degrading or an affront to human dignity or humiliating such as the war crime of 'outrages upon personal dignity.' (Rome Statute Article 8(2)(b)(xxi)). However, arguably many if not most of the Rome Statute designated crimes involve such an element even if the term degrading or outrage on human dignity or humiliation is not specifically mentioned as an element. One can contemplate situations in which such outrages on human dignity *also* constitute torture give the level of physical and mental suffering they create as when a perpetrator group engages in mass rape of the women and girls (and perhaps also at times of the males) in the victim group. The International Criminal Tribunal for the Former Yugoslavia in fact opined that:

> ... *among the possible purposes of torture one must also include that of humiliating the victim.* This proposition is warranted by the general spirit of international humanitarian law: the primary purpose of this body of law is to safeguard human dignity.[78]

If one of the purposes of torture is humiliation of the victim then, for instance, degrading treatment or punishment and outrages on personal dignity-both of which, as specific Rome Statute crimes, imply severe harms—also arguably constitute torture.

Consider in respect of the current inquiry into (i) the torture during armed conflict of children in particular and (ii) the ICC failure to date to prosecute torture in conflict situations directed against children in particular; the succinct definition of torture advanced by the ICTY:

> [the ICTY identified] the crime of torture on the basis of three elements, these being respectively an intentional act, inflicting suffering, and the existence of a prohibited purpose.[79]

As to the 'purpose' element, the torture of children; especially if on a widespread and/or systematic basis will serve to intimidate and terrorize the general civilian populace as the perpetrator group well understands. Hence though torture as a 'crime against humanity' under the Rome Statute does not require that a purpose be proved (unlike the situation for torture as a war crime under the Rome Statute); a purpose in fact is also embedded (as was mentioned previously) in cases involving torture as a crime against humanity. The Rome Statute elements of the crime

[78] ICTY Furundzija case Sentence of 10 December 1998, para 162.

[79] The Prosecutor v Dragoljub Kunaric, Radomir Kovac and Zoran Vukovic ICTY Appeal Chamber Judgment (12 June 2002), p. 41 para 134. The current author, however, endorses the view discussed previously that (i) torture is a *legal characterization* based on a number of factors rather than any specific act or set of acts and that (ii) context is critical including various characteristics of the victim in determining, for instance, the level of suffering or pain inflicted, perpetrator intent etc.

of 'torture as a war crime' provides examples of the purpose element but the list is *not* exhaustive[80]:

> The perpetrator inflicted the pain or suffering ***for such purposes*** as: obtaining information or a confession, punishment, intimidation or coercion or for any reason based on discrimination of any kind (emphasis added).[81]

There is no requirement under the Rome Statute that the perpetrator of the torture (whether as a crime against humanity, genocidal act or war crime) be a state official or person acting in a delegated official state capacity or person acting as an agent of a *de facto* State authority or some other controlling authority. This is unlike the situation with the Torture Convention[82] that is directed to regulating State behaviour in regards to eliminating torture from the State repertoire.[83] Put somewhat differently:

> The public official requirement is ***not*** a requirement under customary international law in relation to the criminal responsibility of an individual for torture outside of the framework of the Torture Convention.[84]

Further to this point recall that the Rome Statute stipulates that the statute applies in terms, for instance, of what crimes may be alleged against a perpetrator and there is *absence* of immunity regardless of whether or not the perpetrator acted in a purported official capacity as agent of a state authority, or of *de facto* state authority or agent of any other authority:

Rome Statute Article 27

Irrelevance of official capacity

> This Statute shall apply equally to all persons without any distinction based on official capacity.[85]

In any case (i) torture cannot be considered to be lawfully within State jurisdiction given that it is a violation of a *jus cogens* ICL norm and (ii) hence torture cannot in fact be carried out by someone supposedly acting in an official capacity when perpetrating acts of torture and is not an official act.

---

80 This point was made by the ICTY Trial Chamber in The Prosecutor v Dragoljub Kunaric, Radomir Kovac and Zoran Vukovic (as was mentioned in The Prosecutor v Dragoljub Kunaric, Radomir Kovac and Zoran Vukovic ICTY Appeal Chamber Judgment (12 June, 2002), p. 43 para 141.

81 Rome Statute Elements of the Crimes (2002).

82 Convention Against Torture and Other Cruel, Inhuman or Degrading Treatment or Punishment (26 June, 1987): Article 1: For the purposes of this Convention, torture means any act by which severe pain or suffering, whether physical or mental, is intentionally inflicted on a person for such purposes as obtaining from him or a third person information or a confession, punishing him for an act he or a third person has committed or is suspected of having committed, or intimidating or coercing him or a third person, or for any reason based on discrimination of any kind, *when such pain or suffering is inflicted by or at the instigation of or with the consent or acquiescence of a public official or other person acting in an official capacity.* It does not include pain or suffering arising only from, inherent in or incidental to lawful sanctions... (emphasis added)

83 See the discussion on this point in The Prosecutor v Dragoljub Kunaric, Radomir Kovac and Zoran Vukovic ICTY Appeal Chamber Judgment (12 June, 2002), p. 45 para 146.

84 The Prosecutor v Dragoljub Kunaric, Radomir Kovac and Zoran Vukovic ICTY Appeal Chamber Judgment (12 June, 2002), p. 46 para 148.

85 Rome Statute (2002).

1.4 Children as the Particularized Targets for Torture During Armed Conflict

It is argued here that the particularized targeting of children of the opposition for the infliction of severe or serious physical and/or mental harms by a perpetrator in the context of armed conflict meets the criteria for torture as a war crime and, depending on the specifics of the context, may also meet the criteria for torture as a crime against humanity and/or a genocidal act.[86] As a war crime; the torture of children is discriminatory based on age and is intended to intimidate the civilian opposition and coerce that opposition into submission. Recall further that children (no age specified) are a special protected group under the Additional Protocols to the 1949 Geneva Conventions[87] in the context of both international and non-international armed conflicts and, in addition, child civilians are protected under Geneva Convention IV.[88] Arguably the status of children as a protected group during armed conflict was part of customary law long before it became formalized in international humanitarian treaty law. Yet often also in contemporary armed conflicts the most heinous cruelties are reserved for children by parties to the conflict that disregard fundamental human rights and international law as we will discuss later when we consider various ICC cases involving the torture of children during armed conflict.[89]

Since 'torture as a war crime' is most often conceptualized as having a specific purpose; namely "obtaining information or a confession, punishment, intimidation or coercion or for any reason based on discrimination of any kind." as per for instance Rome Statute Article 8 (2)(a)(ii)-1 and Article 8 (2)(c)(i)-4; the notion of children as victims of the war crime of torture is generally not

[86] The current author has argued elsewhere that armed perpetrator groups or forces; State or non-State, which appropriate children (persons under age 18) as so-called child soldiers to participate in committing mass atrocities and/or genocide are in so doing committing the international crime of 'genocidal forcible transfer of children' (Grover 2012, 2013a) and that these children retain their status as civilians. On the analysis here; the genocidal forcible transfer of children as child soldiers by such armed perpetrator groups or forces rises to the level of torture of the children in causing them severe mental suffering and most often also extreme physical suffering while also causing severe mental suffering for the children's families.

[87] Additional Protocol I (Article 77) and Additional Protocols II (Article 4(3)) to the 1949 Geneva Conventions (1977). Note that children who participated in the conflict yet have certain special protections as well under the additional protocols i.e. under Additional Protocol I the death penalty is not to be imposed on persons under 18 for an offence related to the conflict while under Additional Protocol II children under 15 who participated directly in the armed conflict and are captured by the adversary are still protected under Article 77 of Additional Protocol II.

[88] Geneva Convention IV (1949).

[89] The point has been made previously by Goldhagen (2009) p. 451 that women and children are commonly the particularized targets for extreme cruelty in genocidal contexts and that this fact has received little attention in the scholarly literature.

acknowledged nor part of the general public consciousness. This is the case in part since: (i) children are most often not considered in the general perception to function as key players in the conflict in the sense that they would, for instance, be entrusted with valuable military information which could be extracted via torture; (ii) there has been a reluctance to acknowledge that certain brutal regimes such as the Al Assad regime have taken to: (a) punishing children using torture and murder (whether extra judicial or sanctioned via kangaroo courts) for the acts of their parents or other adults in the targeted group (that group defined politically, ethnically or in some other terms) and (b) using the torture of their children simultaneously as a vehicle for intimidation and coercion of the adults in the opposition and since (iii) the war crime of torture motivated by discrimination (a purpose listed in the Rome Statute in relation to this category of war crime) is not generally associated with the notion of victims targeted in particular based on age discrimination. That is; it is generally not acknowledged that children and even infants are being targeted *in particular* during armed conflict by perpetrator groups at least in large part precisely due to these victims' young age and the dreadful impact that the torture of children has on the identifiable group of which the children are members (i.e. that group defined politically or according to any other characteristic).

Children as victims of international crimes are, as Goldhagen notes, largely "invisible". This 'invisibility' is especially apparent in regards also to children as the victims of the international crime of torture as a war crime; crime against humanity or an act of genocide. This is in part due to the fact that children are not generally perceived as political or social actors.[91] Children therefore are largely falsely perceived by the world community, in practice, to be the *unlikely* focus of torture as a strategy for suppression of, for instance, a rebellious civilian group; or the general populace; or a rival rebel group within an opposition at war within itself as well as with the State. The treatment of the children of the opposition by the Al-Assad regime in the contemporary Syrian internal conflict is a case in point of the world's relative neglect of the reality that children are being *specifically targeted* for torture and other inhuman treatment during armed conflict as part of a common plan (here by the Al Assad regime and its proxies such as the pro-government Shabiha).[92] Respectfully; certain human rights gatekeepers such as particular UN officials have, on the view here, reacted to the Al-Assad regime's torture of children with proclamations of naïve myopic incredulousness. Consider the following comments by UN Special Representative, Radhika Coomaraswamy as fairly representative in this regard:

> **Torture marks**
> The UN special representative, Radhika Coomaraswamy, told the BBC her team had returned from Syria with "horrific" reports.
> ***She said she had never seen a similar situation where children were not spared—and even targeted—in a conflict.***

---

[91] That characterization may or may not be accurate depending on the context (i.e. see Grover (2004) for a discussion about children as political actors in defending human rights).

[92] Grover (2013b).

> Many former soldiers spoke about shooting into civilian areas, seeing children, young children being killed and maimed, she said.
> We also had testimonies and saw children who had been tortured, and who carried the torture marks with them. We also heard of children being used—this was recounted to us by some children—of being put on tanks and being used as human shields so that the tanks would not be fired upon.
> However, she also criticised the opposition Free Syrian Army for endangering children.
> For the first time we heard of children being recruited by the Free Syrian Army mainly in medical and service orientated jobs but still on the front line, she said.
> ***Ms Coomaraswamy said the suffering inflicted on children in Syria was unusual even for combat situations.***
> ***We are really quite shocked. Killing and maiming of children in cross-fire is something we come across in many conflicts but this torture of children in detention, children as young as 10, is something quite extraordinary, which we don't really see in other places.***
> She said that in recent massacres children under the age of 10 had been summarily killed (emphasis added).[93]

This expression of disbelief is common amongst high profile human rights spokespersons and gatekeepers despite the pattern by the Al-Assad regime and its proxies of targeting children for torture as particularized victims from the start of the conflict and such conduct being a consistent ongoing pattern of conduct for the regime in the Syrian conflict.[94] Note further that the torture of children as particularized victims is in fact a recurrent theme in many if not most contemporary armed conflicts (recall the conflicts in Sierra Leone, Liberia, Rwanda, Democratic Republic of Congo as just a few where children were specially targeted as victims for heinous acts rising to the level of torture). That children continue to be the victims of torture in ever increasing numbers in armed conflict situations[95] globally will become apparent in our consideration of ICC case law concerning contexts where torture was employed by the State or non-State perpetrator group or force.

---

[93] The UN's Special Representative for Children and Armed Conflict (Radhika Coomaraswamy) 12 June, 2012.

[94] Thirty-two children were amongst the at least 90 victims in the Houla massacre in May 2012 (BBC News 26 May, 2012) and at the time of writing this footnote in April 2013 The Syrian Network for Human Rights reports that amongst the at a minimum 2,300 people who have died as the result of torture in Syrian prisons since the outbreak of the recent conflict between opposition groups and the Al-Assad regime and its proxies; there are at least 80 children who have died of such torture. The Syrian Network for Human Rights reports that the latter killings were effected through various heinous torturous acts such as rape, electrocution, hanging and crucifixion. (Child Rights Information Network 16 April, 2013).

[95] This is not at all to suggest that children in significant numbers are not also the victims of torture in various forms in peacetime; see for instance Quiroga (2009).

1.5 The UN Designated Six Grave Crimes Against Children

It has been noted in the 1 February, 2013 report of the UN Special Rapporteur on torture and other cruel, inhuman or degrading treatment or punishment by Juan E. Méndez that:

> Both the European Court of Human Rights (ECHR) and the Inter-American Court of Human Rights have stated that *the definition of torture is subject to ongoing reassessment in light of present-day conditions and the changing values of democratic societies* (emphasis added).[96]

Consistent with the above point; there has been a shift in democratic countries in terms of better recognizing children as separable autonomous human beings with inherent agency and human dignity. This is reflected in part by recognition that children are not the property of the State nor of their parents or any other and that accordingly they are entitled to respect for their fundamental human rights including the right to be free from the infliction of torture, The Convention on the Rights of the Child speaks to this issue of the *jus cogens* prohibition against the torture of children at Article 37 as follows (where the term 'child' is understood, as per Article I of the Convention on the Rights of the Child, to refer to persons under 18 unless a lower age of majority is specified in the applicable law):

> **Convention on the Rights of the Child (Article 37)**
> States Parties shall ensure that:
> (a) No child shall be subjected to torture or other cruel, inhuman or degrading treatment or punishment...[97]

It will be here argued in a later section with reference to specific ICC case law that the UN designated six grave crimes involving the specific targeting of children constitute acts of torture causing severe mental and/or physical pain or suffering. In particular contexts, it is here contended, the acts of torture involving the UN designated six grave crimes against children constitute international crimes incorporating the elements of the Rome Statute crime of torture as a war crime, crime against humanity and/or act of genocide depending on the circumstances. Those UN designated six grave crimes against children include (i) killing and maiming,[98]. (ii) recruitment or use of child soldiers,[99] (iii) rape and other forms of sex-

---

[96] Report of the Special Rapporteur (Juan E. Méndez) (1 February 2013). on torture and other cruel, inhuman or degrading treatment or punishment

[97] Convention on the Rights of the Child (1990).

[98] With regard to killing and maiming "Another worrisome trend is the rise in suicide attacks, and the use of children to carry them out, that lead to the death or serious injuries of children." (Office of the Special Representative of the Secretary-General for Children and Armed Conflict: The Six Grave Violations website (Accessed 22 June 2013)

[99] "The distinction between "voluntary" enlistment and forced recruitment is without meaning because even if children join on a "voluntary" basis, it is a desperate attempt to survive. Ultimately it is the decision of adult commanders to recruit children and they have to be held accountable for their acts." (Office of the Special Representative of the Secretary-General for Children and Armed Conflict: The Six Grave Violations website (Accessed 22 June 2013).

ual violence,[100] (iv) abduction,[101] (v) attacks on schools[102] or hospitals and (vi) denial of access to humanitarian aid.[103]

UN Security Council Resolution 2068 concerns these six international crimes targeting children in particular and in part reads as follows:

> **UN Security Council Resolution** 2068 **(2012)**
> *Noting also* relevant provisions of the Rome Statute of the International Criminal Court
> ...
> 2. *Strongly condemns* all violations of applicable international law involving the recruitment and use of children by parties to armed conflict as well as their re-recruitment, killing and maiming, rape and other sexual violence, abductions, attacks on schools and/or hospitals as well as denial of humanitarian access by parties to armed conflict and *demands* that all relevant parties immediately put an end to such practices and take special measures to protect children;
> 3. ***Expresses deep concern*** **that certain perpetrators persist in committing violations and abuses against children in situations of armed conflict in open disregard of its resolutions on the matter, and in this regard:**
> (a) *Calls upon* Member States concerned to bring to justice those responsible for such violations through national justice systems, ***and where applicable, international justice mechanisms***... (bolded portions reflect emphasis added).[104]

> **UN Security Council Resolution** 1882 **(2009)**
> Under Security Council resolution 1882 (2009), the Council designated sexual violence committed against children as a critical priority and called on parties to armed conflict to prepare and implement action plans to address the violation. Sexual violence is also a trig-

[100] "In some instances sexual violence has been used as a tactic of war designed to humiliate a population or to force displacement." Note that both boys and girls not uncommonly fall victim to sexual violence during armed conflict. "Another aspect that tends to be underestimated is the trauma boys face as witnesses or perpetrators of sexual violence. They may be forced to commit rapes either directly by their commander or indirectly through peer pressure." Mothers of babies born of rape may be forced to stay with the perpetrator group due to stigmatization by their home communities and dependence. Further "These girls and their children are particularly vulnerable to all forms of exploitation including prostitution and trafficking and need special protection." (Office of the Special Representative of the Secretary-General for Children and Armed Conflict: The Six Grave Violations website (Accessed 22 June 2013).

[101] "In times of conflict, children are abducted from their homes, schools and refugee camps. Child abduction often leads to other violations against children such as forced labour, sexual slavery and recruitment. Many children also get trafficked across borders." (Office of the Special Representative of the Secretary-General for Children and Armed Conflict: The Six Grave Violations website (Accessed 22 June 2013).

[102] "Also of great concern is the use of schools for military purposes, as recruitment grounds... Under international humanitarian law, both schools and hospitals are protected civilian objects, and therefore benefit from the humanitarian principles of distinction and proportionality" (Office of the Special Representative of the Secretary-General for Children and Armed Conflict: The Six Grave Violations website (Accessed 22 June 2013).

[103] "It is estimated that in today's conflicts around the globe, 80 millions of children are denied humanitarian assistance. Access can be denied or hampered by parties to conflict for security or political reasons." (Office of the Special Representative of the Secretary-General for Children and Armed Conflict: The Six Grave Violations website (Accessed 22 June 2013).

[104] United Nations Security Council Resolution 2068 (19 September 2012).

> ger for the Secretary-General's list of shame of parties to conflict committing grave violations against children in armed conflict.[105]

Though UN Security Council resolutions are considered 'soft law' (non-binding); the resolutions concerning children potentially could have important legal effects that could significantly benefit children. UN Security Resolutions such as 2068 could, for instance, impact "the development of international law: specifically vis-à-vis the interpretation of treaties and formation of customary international law."[106]

What will be argued here through ICC case law, however, is that the children suffering torture as an international crime during armed conflict as the victims of one or more of the UN designated six grave crimes against children are *not* receiving the full measure of international justice. That is (i) they are not being recognized as particularized torture victims and (ii) in some instances there has been no prosecution for particular systematic widespread crimes amounting to torture and acknowledged by the ICC OTP to have occurred during armed conflict in various cases and involving children as the targeted victims (i.e. gender-based crimes against children were not prosecuted as separable crimes in the Lubanga case let alone as the international crime not only of rape and other sexual violence but also torture as a crime against humanity and/or a war crime).

1.5.1 The Six Grave Crimes Against Children and the Syrian Conflict

Let us consider then the situation in Syria as a current example (though by no means the only example) of the abject forsaking of responsibility *in practice* of the international community in holding to account those who perpetrate torture on children as particularized targets during armed conflict (i.e. As previously mentioned; there has been no referral by the UN Security Council of the Syrian situation to the ICC). In Syria; children as *targeted victims for torture* cannot simply be considered so-called 'collateral damage'; a victim subgroup of the larger civilian population under attack though they are certainly suffering greatly as a result also of the general attacks on the civilian opposition[107]. In a 2013 report Save the Children states:

> From the very beginning of the crisis in Syria, children have been its forgotten victims – facing death, trauma and suffering, and deprived of basic humanitarian aid. Save the Children estimates that nearly 2 million children are in need of assistance in Syria.[108]

---

[105] (Office of the Special Representative of the Secretary-General for Children and Armed Conflict: The Six Grave Violations website (Accessed 22 June 2013).

[106] Field (2013), p. 133.

[107] Nor can the intentional attacks on the general civilian Sunni population in Syria under Al-Assad be considered as "collateral damage".

[108] Martlew (2013), p. 4.

> Two years into the conflict in Syria children are paying the heaviest price….of the 4 million affected people inside Syria, almost 2 million are children, and of the 2 million displaced, 800,000 are children.[109]

The children of the Syrian opposition are in a constant state of terror as are their families. The children are being intentionally and not coincidentally targeted by Al-Assad's henchmen for attack in particular as they are children and many of the children further are losing loved ones[110]:

> Families are struggling to find a safe place to stay, as nearly 3 million buildings have been damaged or destroyed. The lines of fighting move almost daily, so families often do not know if the place they've settled in today will be safe tomorrow. Most displaced families share overcrowded apartments and houses, but an estimated 80,000 internally displaced people are sleeping out in caves, parks or barns (emphasis added).[111]
>
> A new study by a research team from Bahcesehir University in Turkey, found some chilling evidence of what children are experiencing. ***Two-thirds of those interviewed had been in a terrifying situation where they felt they were in great danger***; ***one child in three had been hit, kicked, or shot at…*** (emphasis added).[112]

Further, the children of the opposition in Syria have been targeted for torture thus sending a symbolic message to the opposition not only that the price to be paid for resistance to the Al Assad regime is far too high (namely the destruction of future generations physically and/or psychologically) but also that the regime is capable of unfathomable depravity:

> **Children are being detained and tortured.** Some adults who have been detained reported that children were also present in detention cells. Detained children have given accounts of torture and witnessing the death of other children whilst in detention (emphasis added).[113]
>
> In Syria children have been exposed to grave human rights violations including killing and maiming, sexual violence, **torture**, arbitrary detention, recruitment and use by armed forces and groups, exposure to explosive remnants of war (emphasis added).[114]

Consider then the UN six designated grave crimes perpetrated against children as targeted victims of Al Assad's regime during the current Syrian conflict (with the examples listed under the headings in no way intended to be exhaustive):

> **1. Killing or maiming**
>
> Thousands of children [in Syria] have been killed in their homes and schools, some have died trying to reach hospitals or while hiding in shelters. In addition, cluster munitions have resulted in hundreds of children who have lost hands, arms or legs.[115]

---

[109] UNICEF Crisis Report March 2011–2013, p. 4.

[110] In a recent study of the children interviewed by a research team at Bahcesehir University in Turkey; three of four of the children had lost persons close to them (Martlew 2013, p. 4).

[111] Martlew (2013), p. 4.

[112] Martlew (2013), p. 10.

[113] Child Protection Working Group UNICEF (2013).

[114] UNICEF Crisis Report March 2011 2013, p. 4.

[115] Office of the Special Representative of the Secretary-General for Children and Armed Conflict (18 April, 2013).

> The use of explosive weapons in populated areas [in Syria] has killed and maimed children as well as adults.[116]

> Children [in Syria] face the risk of death or serious injury either from playing with unexploded shells or simply through being forced to live and move around in a landscape scattered with unexploded remnants.[117]

A significant portion of the child deaths are also the result of up close and personal torture inflicted by Al-Assad forces and proxy forces.[118]

> **2. Recruitment or use of child soldiers**
>
> [In Syria] [c]hildren as young as ten are, [on occassion], recruited and used by armed opposition groups for military purposes, including as porters, messengers and combatants. Children are allegedly also being used as human shields by Government forces.[119]

> **3. Rape and other forms of sexual violence**
>
> Rape has been reported as one form of torture leading to death inflicted on children by the Syrian regime.[120]
>
> There is some evidence that [in Syria] girls and boys [of the opposition] as young as 12 are being subjected to sexual violence, including physical torture of their genitals, and rape. The prevalence of such abuses is hard to establish, as survivors often do not report the attacks for fear of dishonouring their family or bringing about reprisals. But fear of sexual violence is repeatedly cited to Save the Children as one of the main reasons for families fleeing their homes.[121]

Note that large numbers of rape victims in armed conflict zones or post-conflict areas are children. For instance, Save the Children reports that 70 percent of the rape victims in conflict affected zones such as Liberia and Sierra Leone are children and refers to this phenomenon erroneously as one of the "*hidden* horrors of war."[122] In fact, this specific category of horror directed toward children is blatantly obvious given its scale within and across many armed conflicts. Nonetheless such widespread targeting of children in particular for grave sexual violation/atrocity constituting Rome Statute international crimes including torture to date has not consistently been prosecuted in cases before the International Criminal Court. Further such sexual violence targeting children in particular has not been prosecuted at the ICC as also a form of torture (both psychological and physical)

---

116 Martlew (2013), p. 10.

117 Martlew (2013), p. 11.

118 Child Rights Information Network 16 April, 2013).

119 Office of the Special Representative of the Secretary-General for Children and Armed Conflict (18 April, 2013).

120 Child Rights Information Network 16 April, 2013).

121 Martlew (2013), p. 11.

122 Save the Children Chief Executive Justin Forsyth cited in Reuters. Most rape victims in conflict zones are children - report, 13 April, 2013 ww.trust.org/alertnet/news/most-rape-victims-in-conflict-zones-are-children-report/?utm_source = MailingList&utm_medium = email&utm_campaign = Weekl Accessed 19 April, 2013.

though, on the view here, cumulative charges for torture and sexual violence against children in particular were warranted in cases such as *Kony* and *Lubanga* discussed here in a later section.

1.5.1.1 Abduction

Children in Syria have been reported by the UN, based on first hand accounts from children, to have been abducted by the Al-Assad regime forces and their proxies and used as human shields.[123]

1.5.1.2 Attacks Against Schools or Hospitals

> It is clear that education is part of the front line of the war on children [in Syria under the regime of Al Assad].[124]
>
> "Schools and hospitals in Syria are systematically attacked and used by parties to the conflict, risking children's lives and jeopardizing their access to education and medical assistance," the Special Representative informed the Security Council. An estimated 2500 educational facilities have been damaged or destroyed while approximately 2000 schools are being used as shelters for Internally Displaced Persons. Around 60 per cent of Syria's health facilities are either damaged or cannot be safely accessed, and approximately 40 per cent of hospitals are inoperative.[125]
>
> One in every five schools in Syria is destroyed, damaged or converted into shelters for displaced families-disrupting schooling for hundreds of thousands of children.[126]
>
> Many hospitals and health workers are being deliberately attacked, so people are reluctant to take the risk of going to hospital…[127]

1.5.1.3 Denial of Humanitarian Access

There has been no guarantee put into effective practice of safe passage for humanitarian workers or fleeing civilians. Nor has the Syrian State provided protection for humanitarian workers attempting to intervene in Syria to provide the necessities of life to a suffering Syrian civilian population and those injured *hors de*

---

123 The UN's Special Representative for Children and Armed Conflict (Radhika Coomaraswamy) 12 June, 2012.

124 Martlew (2013), p. 12.

125 Office of the Special Representative of the Secretary-General for Children and Armed Conflict 18 April, 2013.

126 UNICEF Crisis Report March 2011 2013, p. 4.

127 Martlew (2013), p. 4.

combat. Instead, humanitarian aid has been limited within Syria compared to the magnitude of the need and due to the volatile security situation and government constraints imposed on humanitarian intervention efforts. There is furthermore an ongoing high risk that such humanitarian aid as is being provided will be withdrawn due to the intolerable risks to humanitarian aid workers given the fluidity and intensity of the armed conflict situation within Syria. However to date the UN has maintained the presence of key UN humanitarian agencies within the country:

> The crisis in Syria had increased the risk of humanitarian workers in the country due to the increased risk of indiscriminate shooting by fighting forces, said Sabir Mughal, the UN's chief security adviser in Syria.[128]
>
> ... U.N. agencies are working to provide food, shelter, medical aid and other humanitarian support to the millions in need in the war-ravaged nation. *Many experts have called Syria a humanitarian catastrophe.* The conflict has left much of the nation's infrastructure destroyed, including hospitals, schools, roads and water supply facilities.[129]
>
> [There are] problems of limited access and [the] Office for the Coordination of Humanitarian Affairs' (OCHA) efforts [are] to deliver aid in spite of the constraints on their activities imposed by the government of Syria (emphasis added).[130]
>
> Despite the efforts of the United Nations (UN) and non-governmental organisations (NGOs), millions of people in desperate need in Syria are not receiving enough humanitarian assistance. Some areas have had very little aid or none at all. Insecurity is one of the biggest constraints: 15 aid workers in Syria have lost their lives in the past 2 years. Access is another huge obstacle, as control of access routes shifts continually with the fighting.[131]
>
> Restricted humanitarian access inside Syria means that the international humanitarian response is not able to reach all girls and boys with urgent protection needs. It also means that data on child protection needs and existing child protection structures and capacities is limited and information is difficult to verify.[132]

Restricted access to humanitarian aid and other factors furthermore have led to significant numbers of children in Syria suffering from malnutrition.[133]

1.5.2 The UN Designated Six Grave Crimes Against Children as Torture

Let us turn now to consider how these UN designated six grave crimes against children meet the definition of psychological and/or physical torture. Keep in mind, however, Dewulf's very useful and realistically grounded point that the

[128] BBC (3 December 2012).

[129] Los Angeles Times World News (25 March, 2013).

[130] Under-Secretary-General for Humanitarian Affairs and Emergency Relief Coordinator, Valerie Amos briefing (26 February, 2013).

[131] Martlew (2013), p. 5.

[132] Child Protection Working Group UNICEF (2013).

[133] Martlew (2013), p. 15.

distinction between mental and physical suffering and agony is largely artificial[134] (the distinction is in fact to some extent a 'legal fiction'). Dewulf makes the distinction, however, for ease of reference, based on the means employed to inflict the torture.[135] With respect; the current author would suggest, however, that even reference to 'methods of torture' cannot easily support a distinction between physical and psychological torture. This is the case since physical methods constitute, for all intents and purposes, also psychological methods if they induce through their use (or even anticipated use) simultaneous significant psychological suffering. For simplicity sake only; in that the Rome Statute refers to physical and psychological pain and suffering; reference will nevertheless be made here to physical and psychological torture.

The question we will address is in what way the UN designated six grave crimes against children constitute torture under the Rome Statute specifically. In considering the UN designated six grave crimes targeting children in particular (though not exclusively) as torture under the Rome Statute; we are extending our understanding of crimes under the Rome Statute that may be considered to have been directed against children as prized victims for perpetrator identified symbolic communicative purposes (i.e. to terrorize the general civilian populace). In this respect, for instance, it is noteworthy that not uncommonly torture as a separable category of crime under the Rome Statute is not readily considered as a crime to which children are particularly susceptible and one for which they are particularly targeted. Thus, for example, a 2002 UNICEF Innocenti report on children and international justice does not: (i) list torture as a *separable* Rome Statute crime that can be child-specific in the sense that *children are targeted in particular for torture* by the perpetrator group nor (ii) consider that the crimes listed below in themselves *also constitute torture* as a separable crime under the Rome Statute:

The definitions for genocide, crimes against humanity and war crimes also include a number of crimes specific to children or to which children are particularly vulnerable, such as:

Genocide

- Forcible transfer of children from one group to another;
- Measures intended to prevent birth.

Crimes against humanity

- Crimes of sexual violence, such as rape, sexual slavery, enforced prostitution and enforced sterilization.

War crimes

- Intentional attacks on schools;
- Crimes of sexual violence, such as rape, sexual slavery, enforced prostitution and enforced sterilization;

---

134 Dewulf (2011), p. 188.

135 Dewulf (2011), p. 189.

- Using starvation as a method of warfare;
- Use of children under age 15 as child soldiers (emphasis added).[136]

Consider in this regard a crucial point made by the European Court of Human Rights in regards to the European Convention on Human Rights that applies, on the current author's view, also to any international law instrument (such as the Rome Statute) that serves to criminalize those behaviours that constitute serious or grave violations of fundamental human rights:

> the Convention is a "living instrument which must be interpreted in the light of present-day conditions", **the Court considers that certain acts which were classified in the past as"inhuman and degrading treatment" as opposed to "torture" could be classified differently in future.** It takes the view that the increasingly high standard being required in the area of the protection of human rights and fundamental liberties correspondingly and inevitably requires greater firmness in assessing breaches of the fundamental values of democratic societies (emphasis added).[137]

The current author would argue similarly that the Rome Statute is also a "living instrument which must be interpreted in the light of present-day conditions." This may then require, for instance, a new perspective on what facts support a charge relating to the international crime of the torture of children as particularized targets during armed conflict (whether the torture of children in a specific armed conflict is systematic and/or widespread or more sporadic). New understandings, for instance, about (i) children's development; (ii) the unique medical/physical and psychological short and long-term implications of the UN designated six grave crimes perpetrated against children, and (iii) about children as autonomous human beings with dignity; require new perspectives on the nature of the international crimes committed against children including on what constitutes the torture of children (i.e. as opposed to the 'cruel', 'degrading', 'inhumane' or 'inhuman' treatment or punishment of children where the latter international crimes are, on the view here, erroneously alleged to be *in all instances* of lesser severity in terms of level of suffering/pain or injury inflicted compared to torture). Such is a necessary correlate to a greater recognition by the international community of children's basic human rights and their right to the highest standards of protection feasible in an armed conflict situation. In many instances then, depending on the specific fact pattern, in regards to children as particularized targets, as will be discussed, acts that are legally characterized as 'degrading' or 'inhuman' or 'cruel' or 'inhumane'

[136] Bedont and Sandvik-Nylund (2002), p. 14. Note that the report does state that children can become victim to any of the crimes listed in the Rome Statute.

[137] Office of the High Commissioner for Human Rights (2011) p. 8.

ought to instead be classed as torture; or *additionally* also as 'torture'.[138] That is; children must no longer be denied access to international criminal justice through preconceived notions that exclude them as possible victims of torture consequent to: (i) a legally insupportable refusal to characterize the perpetrator conduct as torture where children are the high priority targets; (ii) a foregone erroneous presumption that the intentional torture of children during armed conflict is generally an isolated occurrence and (iii) a failure to recognize the many forms in which the torture of children during armed conflict presents (i.e. sexual violence, abduction, use as a so-called child soldier, sexual enslavement, physical and psychological torture through well established methods such as electroshock; threats of death or through other more novel means etc.)

Torture carried out as a common plan by a State or non-State group is one of the quintessential international crimes in that it attempts to undercut in the most heinous fashion even the idea of the rule of law as a civilizing force for a humane society and international community dedicated to peace and security for all.[139] Recall in this regard that, in part, the objective in this book is not only to encourage the ICC Office of the Prosecutor in drawing up indictments to include prosecution of perpetrators who target children for all manner of atrocity (a call to action that UNICEF has urged for some time)[140] but also to have the ICC OTP address in the charges *as a separate crime* under the Rome Statute the torture of children as particularized targets where the evidence is present.

Before considering the question of the UN designated six most grave crimes against children as torture, however, we must digress for a moment and consider the matter of intent of the perpetrator to inflict torture on children through the commission of the six grave crimes targeting children. Our focus will be on direct

[138] As discussed previously; there is no consensus in the scholarly community that the level of pain and/or suffering and/or injury or harm, psychological or physical, associated with inhuman, degrading or cruel treatment or punishment is distinguishable from that of torture *in every circumstance*. However, the legal characterization of perpetrator conduct as 'torture' (as opposed to cruel or inhuman or degrading or inhumane treatment or punishment) appears arguably to have for the general international community, to some degree at least, more psychological impact given the common inference regarding a greater level of suffering supposedly associated with torture. This latter inference also commonly induces a greater sense of revulsion in regards to the perpetrators. Note that the current author is, with respect, not in agreement with the view expressed by ICC Pre-Trial Chamber I in *Katanga* that a charge of "other inhumane acts" under the Rome Statute precludes the possibility of any and all charges in addition relating to Article 7(1)(a) to 7(1)(j) including torture (see Schabas (2010), p. 184 referring to the Katanga Pre-Trial Chamber I view on the scope of "other inhumane acts" under Rome Statute Article 7(1)(k)). Torture, as has been here discussed, is not properly defined by any specific act or acts but is rather a legal characterization (see Office of the High Commissioner for Human Rights (2011) p. 2) and hence an act can, on the view here, be legally characterized under the Rome Statute as 'torture' and also fall under the category of 'other inhumane acts'.

[139] For a thought provoking discussion on whether international criminal law is a 'living discipline' see Villaneuva Sanz Pardo (1999).

[140] Bedont and Sandvik-Nylund (2002), p. 26: "The International Criminal Court is urged to focus specifically on crimes committed against children when drawing up indictments…".

intent (*dolus directus*) to inflict torture on children and also intent resulting from acts or omissions undertaken with the full knowledge that the foreseeable consequences would be the torture of children (*dolus indirectus*). We will not concern ourselves here, given the unlikelihood of such a scenario, with torture as the result of negligence or recklessness where the act or omission was intentional but the consequence of torture of children was not the perpetrator objective nor necessarily foreseeable. The contention here is that in the ICC cases to be discussed the targeting during armed conflict of children in particular for the agony of psychological and physical torture was (i) the direct purpose and intent of the perpetrator and/or (ii) deemed, from the perpetrator's perspective, an acceptable and expected outcome of the perpetrator conduct undertaken even if not the prime or even secondary objective. On the analysis here; each of the UN designated six grave crimes targeting children: (1) killing or maiming, (2) recruitment or use of child soldiers, (3) rape and other forms of sexual violence, (4) abduction, (5) attacks against schools or hospitals and (6) denial of humanitarian access; involve physical and psychological suffering rising to the level of torture. All of these acts directly produce terror in children. Killing and maiming, recruitment as a child soldier, rape and other sexual violence, abduction (generally for the purpose of sexual slavery as an appropriated accessory to the perpetrator group and/or for child soldiering) and attacks on schools and hospitals involve actual physical harms to children which are not infrequently grievous and/or life threatening. If particular children are not the direct victims suffering physical *injury* such as that caused by machetes or machine gunfire for instance; they will yet have witnessed these atrocities being perpetrated on other children within their families, schools or communities and this too produces terror and correlated physical symptoms and harms for these children as well. Denial of humanitarian access often over time results in both extreme physical and psychological suffering for children in particular and can and does threaten their very survival in many circumstances. All of the UN designated six grave crimes against children engender desperate feelings of helplessness and terror in the children as well as in their families rising to the level of psychological torture.[141]

[141] The current author has discussed elsewhere (Grover 2012) that children appropriated by perpetrator groups committing mass atrocities and/or genocide are the victims of genocidal forcible transfer and should be considered entirely as non- culpable victims even if they commit atrocities as part of the perpetrator group. The children may be appropriated by such a perpetrator group through abduction, psychological coercion or the children "volunteering" as a strategy for survival in the midst of desperate life circumstances and the perpetrator atrocities committed on anyone who resists. Such children generally take on the perpetrator identity as they have no alterative if they wish to survive. However, beneath any bravado that may be the coping strategy of choice for some of these children lies psychological and most often also physical suffering and injury. This resulting from the children having been appropriated by a perpetrator group committing grave international crimes and all that such appropriation entails (see for instance Bauer and Quiroga (2008); Quiroga (2009); Man (2000)).

The disruption of normal developmental process can add to the suffering of child torture victims:

> A child's world is created by interlocking reference points, such as parents, family, school, friends and the community which not only provide reference points, but also an understanding of how the universe "works". The disappearance of one of these elements, for example the traumatic disruption of a sense of right and wrong through the infliction of torture, or the death of a parent, may fundamentally threaten a sense of identity and security [for a child].[142]

The physical and psychological torture of children through any one of the above mentioned UN designated six grave crimes against children helps then to break down the children's identity.[143] The latter is a prime objective (purpose) of the perpetrator; namely to subjugate and appropriate the child victim to the perpetrator group. This process is facilitated by a breakdown in the child's original identity as an innocent and a contributing valued member of his or her community and family. Whether the child victim is permitted to survive or not, the child torture victim has been forever marked as perpetrator property and at the mercy of the perpetrator group. Furthermore, when children are appropriated as child soldiers (to serve as fighters and/or in other roles such as spies, couriers, etc.) and/or as sex slaves; these children in fact through those forms of torture become the conscripted basis of renewal in the lifeblood of the perpetrator group.[144] Therefore they are not at any time free to leave the perpetrator group on their own volition and must either escape, be rescued or be very occasionally released in small numbers as part of a small token public relations gesture by the perpetrator group to appease the international community represented for instance by NGOs.[145]

This specific aspect of the purpose of torture (to break down the victim's original personality and identity and morph these into the perpetrator group identity and style of being and conduct until no remnant is left of the former self) is often

---

[142] Man (2000), p. 35.

[143] Man (2000), p. 35.

[144] The reference here is to perpetrator armed groups or forces committing mass atrocities and/or genocide.

[145] The UN has urged that the release of child soldiers be part of any negotiated peace settlement in those conflict situations where child soldiering and sexual enslavement of children has been an endemic part of the conflict: **UN Security Council Resolution** 1882 **(4 August, 2009)** "The Security Council ...: 13. Stresses that effective disarmament, demobilization and reintegration programmes for children, building on best practices identified by UNICEF and other relevant child protection actors, are crucial for the well-being of all children who, in contravention of applicable international law, have been recruited or used by armed forces and groups, and are a critical factor for durable peace and security, and urges national Governments and donors to ensure that these community-based programmes receive timely, sustained and adequate resources and funding15. Calls upon Member States, United Nations entities, including the Peacebuilding Commission and other parties concerned to ensure that the protection, rights, well-being and empowerment of children affected by armed conflict are integrated into all peace processes and that post-conflict recovery and reconstruction planning, programmes and strategies prioritize issues concerning children affected by armed conflict..."

at the forefront in the torture during armed conflict of children in particular[146] (though such a perpetrator purpose can also be operative for some adult torture victims). For instance, the breaking down of the child's identity and personality in whole or in part can be accomplished through (i) their child soldiering for groups perpetrating mass atrocities where the child is forced to commit and witness atrocities and through (ii) sexual violence against the appropriated children including sexual enslavement of these children (especially girls) many of whom also act as child soldiers.[147] These child victims then come to be identified by the community at large with the perpetrator group and eventually to also perceive themselves as 'of the perpetrator group'.

The torture (in whatever particular form) of children in particular during armed conflict as part of a common plan serves also the purpose of terrorizing the civilian population. It sends a symbolic message to the general populace that: (i) future generations will not be left physically or psychologically intact should any opposition group pose any challenge to the perpetrator group and that (ii) there is, furthermore, no hope in relying on future generations to free the people from the perpetrator group's oppression as the children will be moulded by the perpetrator group through brutal means to identify with and have allegiance to only the perpetrator group. All children of the opposition, as a consequence of the selection from their child population of children targeted for torture, are traumatized as indirect victims (they know they may at any time be next). The indirect child torture victims come to know thus that despite their status as children they are yet not safe (this notwithstanding the fact that their status as children entitles them to special protection under international law).

Note that the Inter-American Convention to Prevent and Punish Torture[148] captures a critical feature of the purpose of torture that is so key to the torture during armed conflict of children in particular; namely the purpose of breaking down the children's original identities and personalities. This purpose of the perpetrator groups committing one or more of the six grave crimes against children during armed conflict will be evident also in the ICC cases and other cases involving

146 This since the appropriated children are a virtual unlimited source of renewal for many perpetrator groups such as the LRA given the large numbers of available children to be victimized in certain regions and their malleability when appropriated at a young age.

147 See Briggs (2005); Cook (2007); Dallaire (2010) and Singer (2005) for a discussion of child soldiers used as expendable instruments of war. For a historical perspective on child soldiers of various nationalities in WWI and II see for instance Kucherenko (2011) and Van Emden (2005). On the use of a child soldier (Omar Khadr) by a terrorist group and bias in the perception of a Western child soldier as a child soldier see Williamson (Ed.) (2012). For a view (of child soldiers) heavily influenced by cultural relativist perspectives see Drumbl (2012a) and Honwana (2006) and for an opposing view focused on all child soldiers appropriated by groups perpetrating mass atrocities as wholly victims whose universal human right to security of the person, right to family etc have been grossly violated see Grover (2013a and b, 2012).

148 The Inter-American Convention to Prevent and Punish Torture (28 February, 1987).

child torture victims to be here discussed. The Inter-American Convention to Prevent and Punish Torture at Article 2 defines torture thus:

> Article 2
> For the purposes of this Convention, torture shall be understood to be any act intentionally performed whereby physical or mental pain or suffering is inflicted on a person for purposes of criminal investigation, as a means of intimidation, as personal punishment, as a preventive measure, as a penalty, ***or for any other purpose***. **Torture shall also be understood to be the use of *methods upon a person intended to obliterate the personality of the victim* or to diminish his physical or mental capacities, even if they do not cause physical pain or mental anguish.**
> The concept of torture shall not include physical or mental pain or suffering that is inherent in or solely the consequence of lawful measures, provided that they do not include the performance of the acts or use of the methods referred to in this article (emphasis added).[149]

It is to be emphasized that there is no suggestion here that these UN designated six grave crimes against children in any way represent, in the current author's view, an exhaustive list of the acts of torture that have been or could be perpetrated against children as particularized direct victims targeted for torture. In addition, note that children may also be the indirect victims of torture consequent to the six grave crimes targeting selected children or through the witnessing of the torture of adults:

> They [children] may become secondary victims if forced to witness the torture of a family or community member; often this is done deliberately to put pressure on the primary victim to make a confession. Finally, children are also indirect victims when a family or community member has been tortured and whose life changes for the worse as a result.[150]

It is striking that the torture during armed conflict of children in particular has not been highlighted in the cases brought before the ICC already where torture of children in fact has been a prominent feature of the case. This especially since the use of torture against children is abhorrent and even more ghastly when it is used systematically and on a mass scale as it has been in several ICC cases where torture was *not* charged. This is all the more puzzling since:

> [C]learly, the jus cogens nature of the prohibition against torture articulates the notion that the prohibition has now become one of the most fundamental standards of the international community. Furthermore, this prohibition ... signals to all members of the international

---

[149] The Inter-American Convention to Prevent and Punish Torture (28 February, 1987). Note that the Inter-American Convention to Prevent and Punish Torture includes a stipulation that the torture be perpetrated (a)"... by a public servant or employee who acting in that capacity orders, instigates or induces the use of torture, or who directly commits it or who, being able to prevent it, fails to do so or by (b) "A person who at the instigation of a public servant or employee mentioned in subparagraph (a) orders, instigates or induces the use of torture, directly commits it or is an accomplice thereto." The Rome Statute does *not* require as an element of torture that there be any connection to a public servant or employee or any person allegedly acting in an official capacity or on behalf of someone holding a public office.

[150] Bauer and Quiroga (2008).

> community and the individuals over whom they wield authority that the prohibition of torture is an absolute value from which nobody must deviate.[151]

The failure of the ICC OTP, in addition to other charges, to prosecute the systematic mass torture of children during armed conflict in cases that involve this phenomenon and have been brought before the ICC serves *in practice* to undermine the *jus cogens* status of the absolute ban on torture *when the targeted victims are children in particular.*

Let us turn then first to a consideration of ICC cases that considered children as particularized victim targets of certain Rome Statute defined international crimes (such as recruitment and use of children for active participation in armed hostilities) but where torture of those same children was improperly overlooked as a further basis for prosecution by the ICC Office of the Prosecutor. The ICC cases we will consider all involve the context of armed conflict. Note that it appears from the empirical evidence that:

> During political violence and war the high risk children [high risk to become victims of torture] are the children detained during political violence, child soldiers, children internally displaced in refugee camps, detained children during the war against terrorism and children tortured by peacekeeping forces.[152]

In what follows we will consider various of these child groups that are high risk in an armed conflict situation for victimization by torture in various forms.

References

Bauer B, Quiroga J (2008) The war on terror's youngest victims. http//www.irct.org/media-and-resources/irct-news/show-news.aspx?PID=13767&NewsID=1597. Accessed 21 April 2013

Bedont B and Sandvik-Nylund M (2002) International Criminal Justice and Children (No Peace Without Justice; UNICEF Innocenti Research Centre).http://www.unicef.org/emerg/files/ICJC.pdf

Briggs J (2005) Innocents lost: When child soldiers go to war. Basic Books, New York

Cook K (2007) The kidnapped girls of Uganda. Penquin Canada, Toronto

Dallaire R (2010) They fight like soldiers, they die like children. Random House Canada, Toronto

Dewulf S (2011) The signature of evil: (Re) defining torture in international law Intersentia, Antwerp

Drumbl M A (2012a). Reimagining child soldiers in international law and policy. Oxford University Press, Oxford

Gandhi M (2001) Common Article 3 of Geneva Conventions 1949 in the era of international tribunals. ISIL Year Book of International Humanitarian and Refugee Law. http://www.worldlii.org/int/journals/ISILYBIHRL/2001/11.html Accessed 18 June 2013

Goldhagen DJ (2009) Worse than war: Genocide, eliminationism, and the ongoing assault on humanity. Public Affairs/Perseus Book Group, New York

Grover SC (2004) The child as human rights defender: implications for peace education. Intl J Learn 11:1–6

Grover SC (2012) Child soldier victims of genocidal forcible transfer: Exonerating child soldiers charged with grave conflict-related international crimes. Springer, Berlin

[151] ICTY Furundzija case Sentence of 10 December, 1998, para. 154.

[152] Quiroga (2009), p. 66.

Grover SC (2013a) Humanity's children: ICC jurisprudence and the failure to address the genocidal forcible transfer of children. Springer, Berlin
Grover SC (2013b) Child soldiers as victims of 'genocidal forcible transfer': Darfur and Syria as case examples. The International Journal of Human Rights 17 (3): 411-427
Honwana A (2006) Child soldiers in Africa. University of Pennsylvania Press, Philadelphia
Kucherenko O (2011) Little soldiers: how soviet children went to war 1941–1945. Oxford University Press, Oxford
Man N (2000) Children , torture and power: The torture of children by States and opposition groups (A Save the Children report).http://www.savethechildren.org.uk/sites/default/files/docs/Children-Torture-Power.pdf, Accessed 23 April, 2013
Martlew N (2013) Childhood under fire: The impact of two years of conflict in Syria (report on behalf of Save the Children).http://www.savethechildren.org/atf/cf/%7B9def2ebe-10ae-432c-9bd0-df91d2eba74a%7D/CHILDHOOD%20UNDER%20FIRE%20EMBARGOED%20UNTIL%2013TH%20MARCH.PDF, Accessed 2 May, 2013
Nicholas LH (2005) Cruel world: the children of Europe in the Nazi webAlferd A Knopf, New York
O'Donnell D, Liwski N (2010) Child victims of torture and cruel, inhuman or degrading treatment. Innocenti Centre Working Paper No. 2010–2011. UNICEF Innocenti Research Centre, Florence
Quiroga J (2009) Torture in children. Torture Journal on Rehabilitation of Torture Victims and Prevention of Torture 19(2): 65–87
Schabas WA (2010) Oxford commentaries on international law: the international criminal court: a commentary on the rome statute. Oxford University Press, Oxford
Singer PW (2005) Children at war. Pantheon Books, New York
Van Emden R (2005). Boy soldiers of the great war: their own stories for the first time. Headline Book Publishing, London
Villaneuva Sanz Pardo P (1999) Is international criminal law a living discipline? Int J Hum Rights 3(4):92–100
Williamson J (Ed.) (2012). Omar Khadr : Oh Canada. McGill-Queeen's University Press, Montreal

Materials

Chrobok V, Akutu, AS (2008) Returning home: children's perspectives on re-integration a case study of children abducted by the Lord's Resistance Army in Teso, Eastern Uganda (Coalition to Stop the Use of Child Soldiers report). http://reliefweb.int/sites/reliefweb.int/files/resources/9E8CAC8792A99D4CC12574250041975D-Full_Report.pdf
Convention against Torture and Other Cruel, Inhuman or Degrading Treatment or Punishment (the "Torture Convention") (CAT) (entry into force 26 June 1987). http://www.hrweb.org/legal/cat.html Accessed 18 June 2013
Convention on the Rights of the Child (1990) (entry into force 2 September 1990). http://www.ohchr.org/EN/ProfessionalInterest/Pages/CRC.aspxAccessed 19 April 2013
Declaration on the Protection of All Persons from Being Subjected to Torture and Other Cruel, Inhuman or Degrading Treatment or Punishment (1975) G. A. res. 3452 (XXX), annex, 30 U.N. GAOR Supp. (No. 34) at 91, U.N. Doc. A/10034 (1975). http://www1.umn.edu/humanrts/instree/h1dpast.htm. Accessed 2 May 2013
Inter-American Convention to Prevent and Punish Torture (entry into force 28 February, 1987) http://www.oas.org/juridico/english/treaties/a-51.html. Accessed 2 May 2013
International Criminal Tribunal for the former Yugoslavia (ICTY) Furundzija case Sentence of 10 December 1998. http://www.icty.org/x/cases/furundzija/tjug/en/fur-tj981210e.pdf
Los Angeles Times World News (25 March, 2013) U.N. withdrawing staff from Syria, citing danger. http://www.latimes.com/news/world/worldnow/la-fg-wn-un-syria-20130325,0,6661725.story. Accessed 19 April 2013

Office of the High Commissioner for Human Rights (2011) Interpretation of torture in light of the practice and jurisprudence of international bodies. http://www.ohchr.org/Documents/Issues/Torture/UNVFVT/Interpretation_torture_2011_EN.pdf Accessed 1 May 2013
Office of the Special Representative of the Secretary-General for Children and Armed Conflict: The Six Grave Violations (n.d.). http://childrenandarmedconflict.un.org/effects-of-conflict/the-most-grave-violations/killing-and-maiming/ Accessed 22 June 2013
Optional Protocol to the Convention on the Rights of the Child on the involvement of children in armed conflict (entry into force 12 February, 2002). http://www.refworld.org/docid/47fdfb180.html Accessed 17 June, 2013
Office of the Special Representative of the Secretary-General for Children and Armed Conflict 18 April, 2013 Security Council must assure an end to the violence against children in Syria. http://childrenandarmedconflict.un.org/press-releases/sc-must-ensure-an-end-to-the-violence-against-children-in-syria/ Accessed 19 April, 2013
Protocol to Prevent, Suppress and Punish Trafficking in Persons, Especially Women and Children, Supplementing the United Nations Convention Against Transnational Organized Crime (Entry into force 25 December 2003). http://www.uncjin.org/Documents/Conventions/dcatoc/final_documents_2/convention_%20traff_eng.pdf Accessed 17 June 2013
Report of the Special Rapporteur (Juan E. Méndez) (1 February, 2013) to the UN General Assembly on torture and other cruel, inhuman or degrading treatment or punishment. http://www.ohchr.org/Documents/HRBodies/HRCouncil/RegularSession/Session22/A.HRC.22.53_English.pdf Accessed 19 April 2013
Security Council Resolution 1314 11 August, 20000. http://www.securitycouncilreport.org/atf/cf/%7B65BFCF9B-6D27-4E9C-8CD3-CF6E4FF96FF9%7D/CAC%20SRES%201314.pdf Accessed 2 May 2013
Statute of the Special Court of Sierra Leone (14 August, 2000). http://www.sc-sl.org/LinkClick.aspx?fileticket=uClnd1MJeEw%3D& Accessed 18 June 2013
Under-Secretary-General for Humanitarian Affairs and Emergency Relief Coordinator, Valerie Amos briefing to the UN security council Syria briefing on the humanitarian situation 26 February, 2013. http://www.whatsinblue.org/2013/02/syria-briefing-by-un-humanitarian-chief.php Accessed 19 April 2013
UNICEF Crisis Report March 2011-March 2013: Syria's children: A lost generation?. http://www.unicef.org/infobycountry/files/Syria_2yr_Report.pdf Accessed 5 May 2013
United Nations General Assembly Special Session on Children (2002). A world fit for children' United Nations A/S-27/19/Rev.1
United Nations Security Council Resolution 2068 (19 September, 2012). http://www.securitycouncilreport.org/atf/cf/%7B65BFCF9B-6D27-4E9C-8CD3-CF6E4FF96FF9%7D/s_res_2068.pdf Accessed 14 June 2013
UN Security Council Resolution 1882 (4 August, 2009). http://www.securitycouncilreport.org/atf/cf/%7B65BFCF9B-6D27-4E9C-8CD3-CF6E4FF96FF9%7D/CAC%20SRES%201882.pdf Accessed 23 June 2013

Cases

Filartiga v. Pena-Irala, 630 F. 2d 876 (2d Cir. 1980)
Inter-American Court of Human Rights (IACtHR) Cantoral Benavides versus Peru Judgment 18 August, 2000
Ireland v. United Kingdom, Judgment of 18 January 1978, Series A, No. 25; (1978) 2 EHRR 25
The Prosecutor v Dragoljub Kunarac, Radomir Kovac and Zoran Vukovic ICTY Appeal Chamber Judgment (12 June 2002)

Chapter 2
Selected ICC Cases Involving the Systematic Torture of Children Where Torture was Not Charged

... [E]very case tells a story. And every story marks a life. And every life has meaning. Aceves WJ (2007) p. xv.

2.1 The Prosecutor v Joseph Kony, Vincent Otti, Okot Odhiambo, and Dominic Ongwen

The situation in northern and western Uganda involving the Lord's Resistance Army (LRA) insurgency that had started in 1987 was referred to the ICC 16 December, 2003 by the government of Uganda. The referral was due to the fact that the Ugandan government had been unable to secure the arrest of Joseph Kony and the other leaders of the LRA. This as the LRA was operating from bases in Southern Sudan to launch their attacks on the Ugandan civilian population as well as on the Ugandan armed forces (the Ugandan People's Defence Force or UPDF) and on local defence units (LDUs).

> The LRA, a rebel force fighting the government of Uganda, has abducted more than sixty thousand Ugandan children and youth over the duration of the northern Uganda armed conflict that has spanned more than twenty years.[1]
> Among the war-affected population of northern Uganda, one in six female adolescents has been abducted by the LRA.[2]

The charges against Joseph Kony (Commander-in-Chief of the Lord's Resistance Army (LRA) include 33 counts on the basis of his individual criminal responsibility (articles 25(3)(a) and 25(3)(b) of the Statute). At the time of writing; Kony is still at

---

[1] Carlson and Mazurana (2010) p. 236

[2] Carlson K and Mazurana D (2010) p. 236

S. C. Grover, *The Torture of Children During Armed Conflicts*,
DOI: 10.1007/978-3-642-40689-8_2, © Springer-Verlag Berlin Heidelberg 2014

large. The ICC charges against Kony cover the crimes he committed from 1 July, 2002 to 2004[3] and the charges are comprised of the following:

- Twelve counts of crimes against humanity (murder-article 7(1)(a);enslavement-article 7(1)(c); sexual enslavement-article 7(1)(g); rape-article 7(1)(g); inhumane acts of inflicting serious bodily injury and suffering-article 7(1)(k)); and,
- Twenty-one counts of war crimes (violence to life and person; in particular murder-article 8(2)(c)(i); violence to life and person; in particular cruel treatment of civilians-article 8(2)(c)(i); intentionally directing an attack against a civilian population-article 8(2)(e)(i); pillaging-article 8(2)(e)(v); inducing rape-article 8(2)(e)(vi); forced enlistment of children-8(2)(e)(vii)).[4]

The Kony warrant of arrest[5] issued by the ICC Pre-Trial Chamber II described the allegations as follows:

> the LRA has been directing attacks against both the UPDF and LDUs and against civilian populations; ... in pursuing its goals, the LRA has engaged in a cycle of violence and established a pattern of "brutalization of civilians" by acts including murder, abduction, sexual enslavement, mutilation, as well as mass burnings of houses and looting of camp settlements; ... **abducted civilians, including children, are said to have been forcibly "recruited" as fighters, porters and sex slaves to serve the LRA and to contribute to attacks against the Ugandan army and civilian communities** (emphasis added).[6]

The Pre-Trial Chamber held that these LRA perpetrator activities were independently corroborated by several sources including the United Nations, foreign governmental agencies, non-governmental organisations and world media as well as being reported by the government of Uganda. The Pre-Trial Chamber further held that Joseph Kony in concert with Vincent Otti and other senior LRA commanders was responsible for "devising and implementing LRA strategy, including standing orders to attack and brutalise civilian populations."[7] It was found also by the Pre-Trial Chamber that (i) Joseph Kony in or about the middle of 2002 ordered LRA forces to begin attacks against civilians in particular regions and also to abduct civilians for appropriation by the LRA as LRA fighters and that (ii) in 2003

---

[3] The Rome Statute entered into force 1 July, 2002 at which time Uganda accepted the jurisdiction of the ICC.

[4] Pre-Trial Chamber II: Warrant of Arrest for Joseph Kony issued on 8 July 2005 as amended on 27 September 2005 ICC-02/04-01/05. It should be noted that the Ugandan government army to some degree was also guilty of abducting children and using them for direct participation in the conflict.

[5] It should be noted that the Ugandan government army (UPDF-the Ugandan People's Defence Force) was also guilty of abducting children and using them for direct participation in the conflict though none of its leaders were ever charged by the ICC for war crimes involving the recruitment and use of children (aged 15 or under) or for the sexual violence perpetrated by UPDF forces (Chrobok and Akutu (2008), p. 6).

[6] Pre-Trial Chamber II: Warrant of Arrest for Joseph Kony issued on 8 July 2005 as amended on 27 September 2005 ICC-02/04-01/05, para 5.

[7] Pre-Trial Chamber II: Warrant of Arrest for Joseph Kony issued on 8 July 2005 as amended on 27 September 2005 ICC-02/04-01/05, para 9.

Kony issued standing orders to kill civilians including persons living in camps for internally displaced persons and that with respect to certain regions[8] ordered that all the civilians there be killed and to loot. These orders were implemented in a most brutal fashion. Much direct evidence was available as to the allegations against Kony in the form of "intercepted radio communications, accounts from former members of the LRA and accounts from other victims or witnesses."[9]

The admissibility decision was issued 10 March, 2009[10] with Pre-Trial Chamber II ruling the case admissible against Joseph Kony, Vincent Otti, Okot Odhiambo, and Dominic Ongwen (the cases were joined).

2.2 LRA Atrocities Perpetrated Against Children as Constituting Torture

The following two excerpts from the Kony Warrant for arrest are the only points at which child victims are specifically mentioned:

> NOTING that the Prosecutor alleges that, on REDACTED 2004, an armed group attacked the REDACTED IDP Camp, REDACTED, in the REDACTED District, REDACTED and started shooting at and hacking civilians; that the attack resulted in REDACTED houses being burnt REDACTED; that sources, including Ugandan authorities and local hospital records, indicated that the attack resulted in the death of REDACTED civilians **including children** and women, and the wounding of REDACTED civilians..(emphasis added).[11]

> NOTING that, according to the Prosecutor, REDACTED, UPDF soldiers found the bodies of REDACTED men, women **and children** who had been bludgeoned to death, as well as some survivors who were transported to the local hospital; REDACTED; that, according to Ugandan authorities, the attack resulted in the death of REDACTED civilians, the wounding of REDACTED residents of the camp and the killing of REDACTED. (emphasis added).[12]

As mentioned; Kony was charged by the ICC as the prime leader of the LRA for his role as architect and implementer of the strategy of committing mass atrocities against civilians with those international crimes for which Kony was charged taking place from 1 July, 2002 to 2004 in Uganda. Despite the LRA targeting children in

[8] The 27 September 2005 decision re the warrant for arrest contained redactions regarding the specific locations that Kony targeted.

[9] Pre-Trial Chamber II: Warrant of Arrest for Joseph Kony issued on 8 July 2005 as amended on 27 September 2005 ICC-02/04-01/05, para 12.

[10] Situation on Uganda in the Case of the Prosecutor v Joseph Kony, Vincent Otti, Okot Odhiambo, Dominic Ongwen: Pre-Trial Chamber II :Decision on the admissibility of the case under article 19(1) of the Statute 10 March, 2009 ICC-02/04-01/05.

[11] Pre-Trial Chamber II: Warrant of Arrest for Joseph Kony issued on 8 July 2005 as amended on 27 September 2005 ICC-02/04-01/05, para 21.

[12] Pre-Trial Chamber II: Warrant of Arrest for Joseph Kony issued on 8 July 2005 as amended on 27 September 2005 ICC-02/04-01/05, para 24.

particular for torture; Kony was not charged with torture.[13] Instead; he and his high positioned cohorts were charged with offences against the civilian populace more generally. Let us consider then some of the available evidence from NGO's of the LRA's targeting in particular of children for torture during the time frame covered by the ICC charges against Kony and his high-ranking associates:

> UNICEF estimated that about 10,000 children were abducted between May 2002 and May 2003 alone. During 2003 and 2004 some 20,000 rural children, known as "night commuters", sought refuge from abduction by travelling to towns each night.[14]

Abductions of such large numbers of children for appropriation by the LRA are properly legally characterized, on the view here, as crimes against humanity against a special protected group of civilians[15] in terms of but not necessarily limited to 'enslavement' (Rome Statute Article 7(1)(c)); the 'forcible transfer' of the children away from the area in which they were lawfully residing (Rome Statute Article 7(1)(d)) and 'enforced disappearance' (Rome Statute Article 7(1)(i)). In addition, with respect to 'torture' as a crime against humanity; these LRA abductions of masses of children constitute *psychological* torture inflicted on the direct child victims (Rome Statute Article 7(1)(f)) and, depending on the physical force used and pain and suffering and any significant injury caused in the process of the abduction in particular instances, may also involve physical torture.[16] This psychological torture is consequent in part from the children's forced traumatic separation from family and community and, in addition for somewhat older children, the dread of what likely lies in store for them as LRA sex slaves and/or child soldiers based on their knowledge of what the LRA has done to previous abductees. The 20,000 child 'night commuters' were terrorized and hence subjected to severe psychological suffering by the threat of abduction and appropriation by the LRA forces and were thus, at a minimum, the indirect victims of psychological torture as a crime against humanity under Rome Statute Article 7(1)(f). The LRA gender-based crimes causing severe mental and physical suffering to the direct victims also amount to torture (both physical and psychological). It has been noted, for instance, by the ICTY that "rape is one of the worst sufferings that a human being can inflict on another"[17] and that it rises to the level of torture in the context of armed conflict when used, for instance, intentionally as part of a common plan:

---

[13] There is no suggestion here that the LRA did not also torture adults, however, the focus in this inquiry is on the particularized targeting of children for torture as an LRA strategy and the inadequacies of the ICC prosecutorial response in this regard.

[14] Chrobok and Akutu (2008), p. 5.

[15] Children are a special protected group under Protocols I and II Additional to the 1949 Geneva Conventions which arguably are a codification of international customary law (Protocol I and II Additional to the 1949 Geneva Conventions (1977).

[16] This is not to suggest that physical injury is a necessary element of the crime of torture under the Rome Statute either as a war crime or crime against humanity or act carried out with genocidal intent.

[17] The Prosecutor v Dragoljub Kunaric, Radomir Kovac and Zoran Vukovic ICTY Trial Chamber Judgment (22 February, 2001) at para 655.

The ICTY Finding of Rape as Torture When Used as a Strategy of War

(Prosecutor v Dragoljub Kunaric, Radomir Kovac and Zoran Vukovic)

> By raping D.B. himself and bringing her and FWS-75 to Ulica Osmana \ikica no 16, the latter at least twice, to be raped by other men, the accused Dragoljub Kunarac thus ***committed the crimes of torture and rape*** as a principal perpetrator, and he aided and abetted the other soldiers in their role as principal perpetrators by bringing the two women to Ulica Osmana \ikica no 16 (emphasis added).[18]
>
> As far as the ***girls were raped and tortured by other men,*** Dragoljub Kunarac was aiding and abetting the latter by taking the girls to them in the knowledge that they would rape them and by encouraging them to do so. The Trial Chamber therefore finds the accused Dragoljub Kunarac GUILTY of *torture under Counts 1 and 3 and GUILTY of rape under Counts 2 and 4* (emphasis added).[19]

Similarly; the gender-based LRA grave sexual violence international crimes, including 'rape', are properly also legally characterized as 'torture'. As in the ICTY case *Kunaric,*[20] the LRA sexual violence was perpetrated as an intentional part of a widespread systematic attack and terrorizing of a civilian population; this time in Uganda.[21] Yet Kony and his high-ranking cohorts were not charged with 'torture' based on the long-term enslavement of girls by LRA 'military units' for the purpose, among others, of rape and child soldiering and as part of a common plan to oppress the general civilian population.

It is further noteworthy that special attention was given by the ICTY Trial Chamber to the fact that some of the victims of the Serb sexual violence were *children or very young* and this was considered an *aggravating factor* for sentencing purposes as was the fact that some of the victims were subjected to sexual violence for an extended period over months:

> **The youthful age of certain of the victims of the offences committed by Dragoljub Kunarac is considered as an aggravating factor**. At the time of the commission of the offences against them, FWS-87 was about 15 and a half years old, A.S. and D.B were about 19 years old, FWS-50 was about 16 years old, FWS-191 was about 17 years old and FWS-186 was about 16 and a half years old (emphasis added).
>
> He committed these offences over an extended period of time in relation to certain of his victims, for example, two months in relation to the enslavement of FWS-191 and FWS-186. This fact is also considered in aggravation.[22]

---

[18] The Prosecutor v Dragoljub Kunaric, Radomir Kovac and Zoran Vukovic ICTY Trial Chamber Judgment (22 February, 2001) at para 656.

[19] The Prosecutor v Dragoljub Kunaric, Radomir Kovac and Zoran Vukovic ICTY Trial Chamber Judgment (22 February, 2001) at paras 686–687.

[20] The Prosecutor v Dragoljub Kunaric, Radomir Kovac and Zoran Vukovic ICTY Trial Chamber Judgment (22 February, 2001).

[21] Note also that half of the girls and young women forced to become LRA "wives" have given birth to children fathered by the wives' LRA captors (Carlson and Mazurana (2010), p. 237).

[22] The Prosecutor v Dragoljub Kunaric, Radomir Kovac and Zoran Vukovic ICTY Trial Chamber Judgment (22 February, 2001) at paras 864–865.

Thus unlike the situation in the ICC Kony case; the ICTY in *Kunarac* properly took account of the fact that some of the victims of the Serb sexual violence (i.e. rape as torture) were children or very young adults and considered that this was an aggravating factor for sentencing as was the extended period of this form of torture in regards to certain of the older child victims. The consideration of the young age of the victims as an aggravating factor in sentencing is, it is here argued, a proper approach given that: (i) children are a special protected group under international law with certain privileges under ICL and international humanitarian and human rights treaty law that exceed those of the civilian population generally; (ii) the mental and physical suffering for children and young persons may even be greater than for many adults according to medical experts on torture since (a) children have a lower threshold for pain and (b) given the fact that the children and young adults risked through being subjected to extreme sexual violence (such as gang rapes) losing reproductive capacity having never had a child and interference with their normal and healthy sexual and interpersonal relationships.

Consider then how the elements of the Rome Statute crime of torture as a crime against humanity[23] are met in respect of the LRA abductions and threat of abductions of children[24]:

Rome Statute Crime of Torture as a Crime Against Humanity[25]
Elements of the Crime Met Based on Facts Relating to LRA Atrocities

1. **Rome Statute Element**: "The perpetrator inflicted severe physical or mental pain or suffering upon one or more persons"... **LRA**: The children abducted by the LRA were psychologically traumatized and suffered severe anguish as child soldiers and/or sex slaves;
2. **Rome Statute Element**: "Such person or persons were in the custody or under the control of the perpetrator"...**LRA:** The children abducted were in the custody of the LRA as so-called child soldiers and/or sex slaves or playing some other role in support of the LRA while the child 'night commuters' were under the control of the LRA perpetrators in that they were not free to live in their

[23] The current author has argued elsewhere (see Grover 2012 and Grover 2013a) that: (i) children are a 'protected group' *as such* under the Rome Statute genocide provisions and that (ii) appropriation of children by a State or non-state armed force perpetrating mass atrocities and/or genocide constitutes the 'genocidal forcible transfer of children'. However; for the purposes of the present inquiry: (i) the ICC cases considered here will be analyzed only in terms of the broad categories of Rome Statute international crime *actually charged* in the case (genocide, crimes against humanity and/or war crimes) and (ii) the question will be addressed as to why torture was not included as a specific instance of the broader category of crime charged (i.e. under Rome Statute Articles 6, 7 or 8) given that the Rome Statute elements of the crime of 'torture' (of children) were in fact present.

[24] "The LRA is a rebel group originating from Uganda that is now scattered across the DRC [Democratic Republic of Congo], CAR [Central African Region] and South Sudan after being driven out by the [Ugandan] army" Moss (2013).

[25] Rome Statute Elements of the Crimes (2002).

communities without fear of abduction particularly at night and were forced to escape their communities at night in search of safety;

3. **Rome Statute Element**: "Such pain or suffering did not arise only from, and was not inherent in or incidental to, lawful sanctions"... **LRA**: The LRA was and is an unlawful criminal organization perpetrating mass atrocities;
4. **Rome Statute Element** "The conduct was committed as part of a widespread or systematic attack directed against a civilian population"... **LRA**: The child abductions were part of LRA generalized attacks on civilians with children particularly targeted for abduction and other forms of coercive recruitment into the LRA as part of a common plan;
5. **Rome Statute Element**: "The perpetrator knew that the conduct was part of or intended the conduct to be part of a widespread or systematic attack directed against a civilian population"... **LRA**: The LRA leadership (Kony and other high ranking leaders of the LRA) gave specific orders to the LRA rank and file to implement systematic and widespread abductions of children for the purpose of child soldiering and/or sexual enslavement and the latter LRA conduct was part of the various atrocities inflicted en mass against the civilian population in Uganda.[26] (As children are a special protected group under i.e. Additional Protocol II to the 1949 Geneva Conventions[27] (which is customary law); Kony and his cohort of high ranking commanders knew or should have known also that recruitment or use of children (under 15s) by any means for active participation directly or indirectly in combat and/or for the purpose of sexual enslavement is a violation of international humanitarian law).

In addition, the abduction and appropriation of the children by the LRA constitute war crimes including but not limited to the war crime of recruitment and use of children (where the children were 15 or younger) as per Rome Statute article 8(2)(e)(vii); forced enlistment of children. It is here argued that the abduction and forced recruitment of the children by the LRA *also* constitutes the war crime of "violence to life and person, in particular... **torture**."[28] The latter offence is set out in the Rome Statute as one of the "serious violations of Article 3 common to the four Geneva Conventions of 12 August 1949." (Article 8 (2)(c)(i) relating to a non-international armed conflict).[29] The abduction itself involves violence by its very nature and creates in the child abductees severe mental suffering while the actual induction into the LRA and the forced activities thereafter also involves severe violence inflicted against the children mentally and physically creating significant trauma:

> Once in the LRA children were forced to participate in combat, to carry out raids, to loot and burn houses and to kill and mutilate other child soldiers and civilians. They were

[26] Rome Statute Elements of the Crimes (2002).

[27] Additional Protocol II to the 1949 Geneva Conventions (1977).

[28] Rome Statute (2002), Article 8 (2)(c)(i).

[29] Rome Statute (2002).

> trampled to death, beaten or mutilated, either as punishment or if they were physically unable to keep up with their unit. Girls were raped and many have borne children while in the LRA.... large numbers of those abducted, and their children, remain unaccounted for. Many have undoubtedly died in battle, been killed by their abductors or died from physical injury or illness.[30]

Girls sexually enslaved and repeatedly raped by the LRA as abducted children incur mental and physical suffering as a result. In addition, psychological suffering is associated with the sexual violation of these girl victims as (i) in many cases girl LRA abductees have contracted HIV as a result of forced sexual activity with infected LRA commanders and rank and file fighters while (ii) a proportion of the child victims suffered mentally not knowing their HIV status after repeated rapes:

> I was raped twice in the bush by our commander and his bodyguard, in Pader, and I felt so bad because I was still young then and not ready for sex; worse, I am not sure to date if they were free from HIV/AIDS.[31]

Consider now how the elements of the Rome Statute crime of torture as a war crime specifically targeting children are met in respect of the LRA abductions and threat of abductions of children during the period 2002–2004:

Rome Statute Crime of Torture as a War Crime[32] Article 8 (2)(c)(i)-4 (Non-International Armed Conflict)

Elements of the Crime Met Based on Facts Relating to LRA Atrocities

1. **Rome Statute Element**: "The perpetrator inflicted severe physical or mental pain or suffering upon one or more persons"... **LRA**: Children were exposed to extreme mental and physical suffering arising from atrocities inflicted upon them by the LRA such as rape and mutilations; being forced to engage in atrocities as child soldiers as well as from witnessing atrocities carried out by other LRA.[33]
2. **Rome Statute Element**: "The perpetrator inflicted the pain or suffering for such purposes as: obtaining information or a confession, punishment, intimidation or coercion or for any reason based on discrimination of any kind."...

   LRA: Children in particular were targeted by the LRA for abduction[34] as a means of (i) 'recruiting' LRA child soldiers and (ii) for sexual victimization through rape; other sexual violence and sexual enslavement. The children were also targeted for mutilation and generally for the most extreme cruelty via a host of barbaric means. This then constitutes age discrimination in victim targeting in that children were the LRA's high priority targets for victimization though children were not by any means the exclusive targets. The targeting of

---

[30] Chrobok and Akutu (2008), p. 5.

[31] Chrobok and Akutu (2008), p. 11.

[32] Rome Statute Elements of the Crimes (2002).

[33] Severe psychological suffering, particularly if prolonged, often has adverse physical consequences.

[34] Given the highly coercive environment for children and their families created by the LRA atrocities; it is dubious at best to consider that children alleged to have volunteered for LRA child soldiering were in fact making an informed voluntary decision.

children in particular for these various forms of atrocity was and is used by the LRA as a key intimidation and coercion tactic to suppress the general civilian population and to discourage children (including youth) from taking up any opposition cause against the LRA. Such inhuman treatment and punishment of the children appropriated by the LRA is further intended to ensure absolute submission in all respects from these children to LRA commands. In fact, the LRA has forced children to kill their own family members or other community members[35] to make it clear to the children that there is no point in trying to escape the LRA as even if successful there is no family or community to welcome any LRA child escapee home.[36]

3. **Rome Statute Element**: "Such person or persons were either *hors de combat*, or were civilians, medical personnel or religious personnel taking no active part in the hostilities."... **LRA**: The children targeted for atrocities during LRA village massacres were civilians not involved in combat.[37]LRA 'child soldiers'[38] were also forced to commit atrocities against other LRA child soldiers, for instance, if the child soldier victim had tried to escape the LRA. On the analysis here; the appropriated LRA so-called 'child soldiers' were and remained *civilians* forcibly transferred by direct and indirect coercive means to a criminal organization.
4. **Rome Statute Element**: "The perpetrator was aware of the factual circumstances that established this status."... **LRA**: The LRA targeted child civilians in particular for abduction, murder and brutalization of various forms and this was part of a systematic and widespread attack on the civilian population by the LRA. Thus the LRA was well aware that their high priority targets (children) were in fact civilians.
5. **Rome Statute Element**: "The conduct took place in the context of and was associated with an armed conflict not of an international character."... **LRA**: The conflict between the LRA and the Ugandan government was characterized

[35] Note that just the threat that *others* would kill family members has been regarded as constituting psychological torture according to the Special rapporteur on torture (see The Prosecutor v Kvocka et al. ICTY Trial Chamber Judgement at para 144); while in *Kony* the ICC OTP did not charge torture in relation to children being forced by the LRA to kill family members themselves.

[36] Young (2007), p. 20.

[37] Just as a point of interest; note that it would not be unlawful under international law for child civilians to be part of a rebellion (a popular uprising) against an authoritarian perpetrator group such as the LRA which was and still is engaged in committing mass atrocities against civilians.

[38] The current author maintains that so-called 'child soldiers' appropriated by State or non-Sate forces perpetrating mass atrocities as part of a common plan are in fact the victims of a criminal organization which has transferred the children away from their families and communities and to the perpetrator group through various direct and indirect coercive means. These children are then civilians forcibly transferred to the LRA and they properly retain their status as 'protected civilians' under international humanitarian law and ICL (in fact, given the circumstances, these LRA so-called 'child soldiers' remain 'civilians' entitled to *special protection* as children under international humanitarian and ICL regardless their participation or lack of participation in the fighting such that any military attack on such a child is justified only if he or she poses an imminent deadly threat) (i.e. see Grover (2013a) and Grover (2008)).

by the ICC in the Prosecutor v Joseph Kony, Vincent Otti, Okot Odhiambo, Dominic Ongwen as an internal conflict (though from 1994 to early 2005 the LRA received support from the Sudanese government).[39]

6. **Rome Statute Element**: "The perpetrator was aware of factual circumstances that established the existence of an armed conflict."[40] …**LRA**: The LRA, which claims to seek a government based on the biblical Ten Commandments, carried out widespread human rights abuses against the northern Ugandan population, including killings, mutilation, rape and sexual enslavement, the burning and destruction of property and looting. Thus the LRA was well aware of factual circumstances that established the existence of an armed conflict. Between 50,000 and 70,000 people, including thousands of children, were abducted and used in hostilities [at the direction of Kony and other LRA high commanders].[41]

It is in fact striking that Kony and his cohorts charged by the ICC were *not* charged with torture as a war crime and a crime against humanity. That prosecutorial strategy; with respect, it is here argued, was not legally supportable given the ferocity and purposefulness of the extreme atrocities inflicted by the LRA upon children in particular with the purpose in large part of (a) inflicting maximum suffering on the child victims of torture and their communities and (b) as a strategy of intimidation of survivors and of the general populace. Consider the following firsthand account, for instance, of the type of extreme suffering that the LRA was routinely prepared to and did inflict on the children abducted:

> When I was abducted in 2003, we had no food for three days, we lived only on water. Then the rebels made us move and when we reached Asamuk the rebels decided that we should prepare some food. They told us to decide among ourselves who should be eaten. At first, we thought it was a joke until they decided themselves on a certain girl whom they slaughtered and cut into pieces. Then they told us to cook the pieces. When it was ready, the rebels forced us to eat the cooked girl. After that we were told to kill an old man who was helpless. After a week, the rebels brought us to Amaseniko camp [Amuria] where we had been abducted and told us to burn houses. I was told to kill my grandfather. When I tried to refuse, the rebels beat me hard until I accepted to kill him using heavy stones. Then we went ahead to kill two more people we came across" (Girl 13).[42]

Instead of being charged *additionally* with *torture* as a crime against humanity (Article 7(1)(f); and '… cruel treatment *and torture*' as war crimes (Article 8(2)(c)(i)-3 and 8(2)(c)(i)- 4 respectively); Kony's charges included amongst others "other inhumane acts of inflicting serious bodily injury and suffering' as a crime against humanity (Article 7(1)(k)) and cruel treatment of civilians as a war crime Article 8(2)(c)(i). This despite the fact that there was precedent under the ICTY legal

---

[39] Chrobok and Akutu (2008), p. 5.

[40] Rome Statute Elements of the Crimes (2002).

[41] Chrobok and Akutu (2008), p. 5.

[42] Chrobok and Akutu (2008), p. 5.

regime, for example, for considering rape[43] and mutilation[44] as torture; and the fact that rape and mutilation[45] of children in particular were and are consistent in the pattern of grave international crimes perpetrated by the LRA.[46] Further, being forced during an armed conflict to murder members of one's own family and community for the purpose in part of coercion and intimidation of LRA child soldier abductees certainly would seem to qualify as (i) a form of psychological torture as a war crime[47] and b) given the systematic and widespread use of this strategy by the LRA as part of a broader attack on civilians; also torture as a crime against humanity.

The indictment of Kony in respect of Rome Statute Article 8(2)(c)(i) (violence to life and person), on the view here, with respect, misguidedly did not *additionally* legally characterize as *torture*[48] such LRA atrocities as: child abduction; forced soldiering of children; child sexual enslavement and sexual violence against child victims in particular; mutilation[49] and murder, the aforementioned carried out for the purpose of intimidation of the civilian population and the targeting in particular of children. All of these grave international crimes carried out on a systematic and widespread basis were and are emblematic of the LRA 'military' tactic to inflict as severe psychological and physical pain; suffering and harm as possible on children in particular to accomplish LRA objectives. The LRA atrocities against children in particular make manifest the LRA's complete disregard for the human dignity of children as legal persons and as human beings with inherent universal basic rights under international law.

It is here contended then that the aforementioned LRA systematic and widespread atrocities perpetrated against children in particular constitute the physical and psychological torture of the child victims (as a war crime and/or crime against humanity) given: (i) the child victims' lower threshold for pain and suffering and higher

---

[43] The Prosecutor v Anto Furundzija (ICTY CASE NO.: IT-95-17/1-PT) Amended Indictment (2 June, 1998).

[44] According to the ICTY Trial Chamber in *The Prosecutor* v *Delalic* (ICTY) 16 November, 1998 at para 511; causing severe physical injury (presumably mutilation would be included as an instance of the latter) can be legally characterized as 'torture' (as a war crime) where there is present also a prohibited purpose that is covered as an element of torture. In regards to the LRA; that prohibited purpose element per the Rome Statute would include, for instance, intimidation, coercion and age discrimination in selecting infants and children as high priority targets for mutilation.

[45] Kony faced rape as a war crime charge amongst others but not mutilation as a war crime charged under Article 8(2)(c)(i) despite the facts on the ground especially in terms of the harms inflicted on children that would have supported mutilation and rape as torture charges under 8(2)(c)(i) and also a separable independent charge of mutilation as a war crime. Note that on the analysis here amputation is a form of mutilation.

[46] According to the ICTY Trial Chamber in *The Prosecutor* v *Delalic* (ICTY) 16 November, 1998 at para 442; torture is a specific form of inhuman treatment and inhuman treatment is a broader category of offence than is torture.

[47] See The Prosecutor v Kvocka et al. ICTY Trial Chamber Judgement at para 144.

[48] 'Torture' refers here to torture as a war crime and/or crime against humanity depending on the circumstances of each offence.

[49] Dewulf (2011), p. 183 notes that even mock mutilations such as mock amputations have been classed as mental torture.

level of vulnerability in general compared to adults increasing the likelihood that the level of suffering and pain or injury was severe enough to reach the torture threshold; (ii) the LRA purpose of intimidating the general populace through such victimizing of children in particular; and the LRA using such examples of inhuman treatment and punishment of child victims to attempt to coerce child abductees to be submissive to each and every LRA demand and (iii) given age discrimination in the selection of infants and children in particular as high priority victims for LRA extreme cruelty.[50] Instead, the violation of Rome Statute Article 8(2)(c)(i) listed in the Kony ICC warrant for arrest reveals that the charge of 'cruel treatment of civilians' as a war crime was based on the following facts that were *not* classed additionally as torture:

> **Count Seven**
> **(Cruel Treatment at REDACTED IDP Camp Constituting War Crimes)**
> On REDACTED 2003, ordering the commission of war crimes which in fact occurred, namely, the cruel treatment of civilian residents of REDACTED IDP Camp, by abducting them, tying or otherwise restraining them, and forcing them, under ***threat of death***, to carry plundered property, in REDACTED District, Uganda (articles 8(2)(c)(i) and 25(3)(b) of the Statute) (emphasis added).
>
> **Count Twenty-Four**
> **(Cruel Treatment at REDACTED IDP Camp Constituting War Crimes)**
> On REDACTED 2004, ordering the commission of war crimes which in fact occurred, namely, the cruel treatment of civilian residents of REDACTED IDP Camp, by abducting REDACTED residents, forcing them to march under armed guard and ***threat of death***, and then beating them, REDACTED District, Uganda (articles 8(2)(c)(i) and 25(3)(b) of the Statute) (emphasis added).
>
> **Count Thirty-One**
> **(Cruel Treatment at REDACTED IDP Camp Constituting War Crimes)**
> On REDACTED 2004, ordering the commission of war crimes which in fact occurred, namely, the cruel treatment of civilian residents of REDACTED IDP Camp, by ***abducting*** REDACTED residents, forcing them REDACTED District, Uganda (articles 8(2)(c)(i) and 25(3)(b) of the Statute).[51]

As Dewulf notes; the use of *threat of death* by a perpetrator (as mentioned in the facts underlying count seven and 24 of the Kony indictment) has been considered at times as psychological torture in other judicial forums such as the ICTY.[52] Hence in that respect also there was a basis to consider *torture* as one of the factors (as opposed to cruel treatment exclusively) constituting the violation of Article 8(2)(c)(i) listed in the Kony warrant for arrest.[53]

---

[50] This is not to say that certain of these acts (such as mutilation for instance) where directed against adults cannot also amount to torture but the focus of this inquiry is on the child victims of torture.

[51] Pre-Trial Chamber II: Warrant of Arrest for Joseph Kony issued on 8 July 2005 as amended on 27 September 2005 ICC-02/04-01/05.

[52] Dewulf (2011), p. 180.

[53] "The LRA uses brutal tactics to demand obedience from abducted children. Children are forced to beat or trample to death other abducted children who attempt to escape, and are ***repeatedly told they will be killed if they try to run away***…"(Human Rights Watch (2003a), p. 2).

Classifying the LRA's mutilation and hacking of civilians, including children in particular, as 'other inhumane acts' exclusively (as per Rome Statute Article 7(1)(k)); and not also as 'torture' serves to downgrade in the public perception of the international community the meaning of "inflicting 'serious' bodily injury and suffering."[54] As was discussed previously; *torture* is at points described in the Rome Statute as involving acts causing *serious* suffering or pain (psychological and/or physical) such that the term 'severe' is in fact in respect of torture under the Rome Statute somewhat interchangeable with the term 'serious' (i.e. footnote 3 to the Rome Statute genocide provision at Article 6(b) indicates that genocidal acts that cause *serious* bodily or mental harm may include *torture* (directed to one of the protected groups listed). Yet the charges in the Kony ICC indictment sidestep entirely the obvious torture of children in particular inflicted by the LRA in large part through causing 'serious' bodily injury along with severe psychological suffering:

> **Count Twenty-Two**
> (Inhumane Acts at REDACTED IDP Camp Constituting Crimes Against Humanity)
> On REDACTED 2004, ordering the commission of crimes against humanity which in fact occurred, namely, the inhumane acts of inflicting serious bodily injury and suffering upon REDACTED civilian residents of REDACTED IDP Camp, REDACTED District, Uganda (articles 7(1)(k) and 25(3)(b) of the Statute).
>
> **Count Twenty-Nine**
> (Inhumane Acts at REDACTED IDP Camp Constituting Crimes Against Humanity)
> On REDACTED 2004, ordering the commission of crimes against humanity which in fact occurred, namely, the inhumane acts of inflicting serious bodily injury and suffering upon REDACTED civilian residents of REDACTED IDP Camp, REDACTED District, Uganda (articles 7(1)(k) and 25(3)(b) of the Statute).

In fact even *mock* mutilation and *simulated* amputation have been regarded in other contexts as constituting torture:

> In considering individual complaints brought against Uruguay and Bolivia, the Human Rights Committee found that... simulated... amputations amounted to torture.[55]

In the Kony case; actual amputations and mutilations of children in particular were not legally characterized *additionally* as 'torture'. This though there is precedent for such a categorization from the ICTY jurisprudence for instance in the Kvocka case:

> 144. The UN Special Rapporteur on Torture, human rights bodies, and legal scholars have listed several acts that are considered severe enough per se to constitute torture and those that are likely to constitute torture depending on the circumstances. Beating, sexual violence, prolonged denial of sleep, food, hygiene, and medical assistance, as well as threats

---

[54] Rome Statute Article 7(1)(k) reads as follows: "Other inhumane acts of a similar character intentionally causing great suffering, or ***serious*** *injury to body or to mental or physical health* (emphasis added)." Footnote 3 to Article 6(b) of the Rome Statute reveals that with respect to serious bodily or mental harm: "This conduct may include, but is not necessarily restricted to, acts of ***torture***, rape, sexual violence or inhuman or degrading treatment." (Rome Statute 2002, emphasis added).

[55] The Prosecutor v. Miroslav Kvočka, Dragoljub Prcać, Milojica Kos, Mlađo Radić and Zoran Žigićv ICTY Trial Judgement (2 November 2001) IT-98-30/1-T, p. 43, para 146.

> to torture, rape, or kill relatives were among the acts most commonly mentioned as those likely to constitute torture. **Mutilation of body parts would be an example of acts *per se* constituting torture (bolded emphasis added).**[56]

It is here contended then that additional charges of torture as a war crime and a crime against humanity, based in part on LRA acts of mutilation/amputation of children in particular, was entirely legally supportable in *Kony*.

There have been ongoing mass atrocities perpetrated by the LRA involving international crimes that postdate the time frame of the 2005 ICC Kony arrest warrant.[57] The LRA specifically targets children for extreme cruelty amounting to torture such as but not limited to abduction and forced soldiering and causing the children to witness atrocities perpetrated against their family members and other members of their community; a *continuing pattern from the earlier crimes* attributed to Kony:

> Between December 14 and 17, 2009, the Lord's Resistance Army (LRA), a Ugandan rebel group, carried out a horrific attack in the Makombo area of Haut Uele district in northeastern Democratic Republic of Congo, near the border with Sudan. In a well-planned operation, the LRA killed more than 321 civilians and abducted more than 250 others, *including at least 80 children*. The vast majority of those killed were adult men who were first tied up before LRA combatants hacked them to death with machetes or crushed their skulls with axes or heavy wooden sticks (emphasis added).[58]

> ***The LRA's brutality against children has been particularly grotesque*: it continues to replenish its ranks through the abduction of children, forcible training and use of children in combat operations, and compelling compliance through threats, violence, and mind control** (emphasis added).[59]

> In late December 2008 and into January 2009, the Lord's Resistance Army (LRA) brutally killed more than 865 civilians and *abducted at least 160 children* in northern Democratic Republic of Congo (DRC). *LRA combatants hacked their victims to death with machetes or axes or crushed their skulls with clubs and heavy sticks. In some of the places where they attacked, few were left alive* (emphasis added).[60]

> Even by LRA standards, the Christmas massacres in Congo were especially brutal. LRA combatants struck quickly and quietly, surrounding their victims as they ate their Christmas meal in Batande village, or as they gathered for a Christmas day concert in Faradje. In Mabando village, the LRA sought to maximize the death toll by luring their victims to a central place, playing the radio and forcing their victims to sing songs and to call for others to come join the party. In most of the attacks they tied up their victims, stripped them of their clothes, *raped the women and girls, and then killed their victims by crushing their skulls. In two cases the attackers tried to kill three-year-old toddlers by twisting off their heads.* The few villagers who survived often did so because their assailants thought they were dead (emphasis added).[61]

This evidence supports the contention that additional charges for LRA atrocities (including those post the time frame covered in the original Kony ICC indictment),

---

56 The Prosecutor v Kvocka et al. ICTY Trial Chamber Judgement at para 144.

57 Human Rights Watch (2010).

58 Human Rights Watch (2010), p. 3.

59 Human Rights Watch (2010), p. 13.

60 Human Rights Watch (2009), p. 4.

61 Human Rights Watch (2009), p. 5.

including the torture in particular of child and other civilians, ought to be added to the Kony et al. ICC charges in an amended indictment.[62] No less is required if the ICC is to honor its commitment to justice for the mass victims of grievous international crimes especially where the perpetrator group such as the LRA targets children for extreme cruelty and torture. The struggle continues against the LRA as of April 2013[63] and the LRA leadership facing ICC charges including Kony remain at large at the time of writing.

The LRA under Kony's command has been actively involved in committing the UN designated six grave crimes perpetrated against children which crimes, on the view here, constitute torture; namely a) *killing and maiming* of children, b) *mass rape and other sexual violence* perpetrated against children abducted to serve as LRA child soldiers and/or sex slaves and against other child civilians, c) *abduction* of children primarily to serve as LRA child soldiers and/or LRA sex slaves, d) *recruitment and use of child soldiers* (persons under 15), e) *attacks on schools* for the purpose of abducting children and f) *denial of humanitarian access* for children brutalized by the LRA in the villages or in LRA camps or as child soldiers.[64] Extreme cruelty of the LRA towards their child victims is the quintessential signature in fact of the LRA.[65]

2.3 The Backlash Against the Kony 2012 YouTube Video: Inconvenient Truths Regarding Barriers to Justice for Child Torture Victims under International Criminal Law

The torture, as part of a common plan during armed conflict, of children in particular is symptomatic of: (i) the State's failure to provide security to the vulnerable within its jurisdiction and (ii) in some instances, of the State's complicity in this most grave violation of the *jus cogens* prohibition against torture. The systematic and/or widespread torture in an armed conflict of children in particular is furthermore symbolic of a debased and depraved authoritarian perpetrator regime; be it a State or *de facto* State entity; or instead a rebel authority or rebel group still struggling for power. The reality of tortured children belies any façade of legitimacy that the perpetrator group responsible for the torture may present. It is the case, nevertheless, that there are *in practice* significant inexcusable barriers to child victims of torture (that torture

[62] Note that Kony is still commander-in-chief of the LRA at the time of writing.

[63] Deputy spokesperson for the Secretary-General Ban Ki-Moon (2 April, 2013).

[64] The current author contends that (i) all persons *under 18* recruited or used to participate indirectly or directly in armed conflict are so-called 'child soldiers' (to use the colloquial non-legal term) and (ii) where these children are appropriated by groups or forces perpetrating international crimes; they are the victims of the genocidal forcible transfer of children who in law retain their civilian status (i.e. Grover (2013a).

[65] See for example Human Rights Watch (2003b).

perpetrated during armed conflict as part of a common plan) obtaining justice through the international criminal law system such as the ICC. In part this is not surprising given a segment of the international community of States (which segment varying depending on the situation) adopting strategies such as prioritizing attempts to uphold the legitimacy[66] of the State regime by minimizing the scale or denying even the occurrence of the atrocities against children within the jurisdiction at issue and declaring that State sovereignty[67] precludes an international response to the atrocities (such as prosecutions of the perpetrators most responsible) even where the State is unable and/or unwilling to ensure the justice interests of child torture victims. (The situation in Syria being a case in point in this regard with the Syrian regime carrying on with its brutal repression of civilians, including the torture of children of the opposition, and Russia and China blocking attempts to organize among UN Security Council members, in an effort to stop further bloodshed, any substantive response to the oppression by the Syrian regime and blocking referral of the Syrian situation to the ICC). Other strategies include: (i) engaging in 'politically correct' *irrelevant* cultural relativist rhetoric[68] in regards to the State(s) where the atrocity of child torture (and other atrocity) is occurring on a systemic and widespread basis during armed conflict and/or (ii) adopting erroneous rationales for the denial of access to international criminal justice for child torture victims such as this blocked access being but an unfortunate by- product of the need to keep good inter-State relations[69] in the interest of peace and security. This 'reframing' of the issue of the violation of the *jus cogens* prohibition against torture -notwithstanding children being the particularized victims in many of these situations- undermines international public pressure to ensure child torture victims' access to justice under international criminal law. On the view here; interestingly and sadly this misguided 'reframing' regarding atrocities perpetrated against children during armed conflict is occurring also in some quarters of the scholarly community. This is reflected, for instance, in the vituperous negative reaction among some legal scholars and social scientists to the *Kony 2012* youtube video [hereafter referred to as *Kony 2012*].[70] Let us consider then a series of articles written on the topic of *Kony 2012* and published

---

[66] A state or other entity in authority or power or a rebel group accused of torture as a common plan during armed conflict loses, to some extent at least, esteem and perceived legitimacy in the perception of the international community with this effect likely magnified when the victims include children.

[67] The perpetrating of international crimes is not a lawful function within the jurisdiction of any State or *de facto* State or other entity in power or having authority by any means.

[68] That is to say that cultural relativist rationales for torture in whatever form are without merit and that determinations can be made under international human rights and criminal law as to whether: (i) the level of suffering, pain and, if present, injury rise to the level of torture and (ii) whether the infliction of this suffering and mental and/or physical harm was carried out for one of the prohibited purposes that would render the crime a war crime under international criminal law as per i.e. the Rome Statute in addition to or instead of a crime against humanity.

[69] This author would maintain as many other scholars have that any lasting peace and security requires as a precondition justice and respect for basic human rights.

[70] The video discussing LRA atrocities and Kony's role as commander-in-chief of the LRA.

in the *International Journal of Human Rights Practice* as well as a report published by the Outreach Council of the African Studies Association regarding critical analysis of *Kony 2012* as a media message and in regard to its impact. It seems, on the current author's respectful view, that the aforementioned analyses of *Kony 2012* inappropriately largely shifts the focus away from the plight and reality of LRA child torture victims and their lack of any forthcoming remedy via the international criminal justice system (i.e. the ICC) and onto other matters:

> **"React and Respond:**
> **The Phenomenon of *Kony 2012* (Guidelines for Teaching about Issues Raised by *Kony 2012*)"**[71]
> **Introduction**
> The unprecedented attention generated by the ***Kony 2012*** video, which has been viewed by well over 100 million people worldwide since its release on March 5, provides a unique "*teaching moment*" *about* a number of crucial issues, including *representations of Africa,* resolving international conflicts, *evaluating charities and social justice organizations* [such as 'Invisible Children'], *and campaigns spread by social media* [such as the campaign to arrest Kony; the leader of the LRA] (emphasis added).[72]

Note that in the "introduction" setting the stage for the "Guidelines for teaching about issues raised by *Kony 2012*" section of the report 'React and Respond' (produced for the 'Outreach Council of the African Studies Association')[73] and quoted above; the reality of child torture victims of the LRA is not part of the focus but is rather background information. Instead, issues regarding, for instance (i) the credibility of the social justice agency 'Invisible Children' (which produced the *Kony 2012* you tube) are raised as are (ii) issues related to the purported image rehabilitation deemed necessary for Africa as a whole pursuant to the alleged damaging impact on that image in the international public perception due to *Kony 2012* and its depiction of LRA atrocities against children.[74] "As educators, we encourage our students to "complicate" their analysis of important, complex issues. *This is certainly true when trying to understand the issues related to the atrocities committed by the*

---

[71] Brown et al. (13 April, 2012).

[72] Brown et al. (13 April, 2012), p. 4.

[73] Brown et al. (13 April, 2012).

[74] A brief history of the brutality by both the LRA and the Ugandan government is given in the 'React and Respond' report (authored by Brown et al. (13 April, 2012)) in a section prior to the 'teaching guidelines' section (as background). The focus of the report is, however, on critical 'media literacy.' Consider then the issue of an audience, for whatever reason, reacting defensively to extremely disturbing realities presented in any particular media format (such as the disturbing reality of mass child torture in various forms carried out by the LRA and depicted in *Kony 2012*). That defensive response can include somehow 'reframing' the horrific reality depicted in the media message such as to undermine its impact (the latter constituting an aspect of *media illiteracy* if you will). The issue of such 'defensive deflection', at some level, of a horrendous reality depicted in a media social justice campaign such as *Kony 2012* is a topic that is not discussed in the 'React and Respond' report. On the contrary, arguably, one might consider that the following admonition in the report refers to a mechanism for just such 'defensive deflection' away from horrific realities:.

LRA and the failure of central African governments to arrest Kony." (Brown et al. (13 April 2012)). The current author would argue that while the history and evolution of the armed conflict in Northern Uganda may be complex, the reality of child torture by the LRA as part of a common plan during that conflict and the violation of a *jus cogens* norm such violence represents is not. Hence a paralysis in prosecutorial efforts (domestic and/or international) in respect of bringing to justice those LRA most responsible for atrocities in Northern Uganda, CAR, DRC and South Sudan cannot properly be excused based on alleged complexity of the situation. There is no question that the authors of the above cited report of course abhor torture and the targeting of children for torture (as was prevalent with the LRA in Uganda) and that discussion of a broad range of issues is legitimate in relation to *Kony 2012*. Notwithstanding the latter, however, the aforementioned report inadvertently, in this author's respectful view, through indirect means, serves to "soften the blow", if you will, of the harsh truth that such targeting of children in particular for torture was part of a common plan of the LRA and did not represent an isolated random set of instances. This unfortunate 'pasteurizing' to some degree of the LRA horrors, it is here contended, is further the inadvertent result of specific wording in the report such as in the following paragraph:

> **Providing historical context**: The *Kony 2012* video vividly depicts the atrocities of Joseph Kony and the Lord's Resistance Army (LRA) committed over the past two decades. *While these atrocities certainly took place and should be condemned, the video does not provide, nor does it suggest that it would be appropriate to explore, the historical context that gave rise to the LRA* (emphasis added).[75]

The specific wording of the quote immediately above would seem to imply subtly and tacitly, however unintentionally, that previous Ugandan army atrocities make the LRA atrocities less shocking insofar as these LRA atrocities were, when placed in historical context, more of a 'foreseeable' or even 'understandable' outcome in some way. While of course historical context is useful in understanding the origins of an armed conflict; no such context can in fact provide 'insight' *qua* an 'explanation' *from any perspective* for the torture of children or any group civilian or non-civilian. (Note further that the child victims depicted in *Kony 2012* represent symbolically the thousands more child victims of the LRA in Uganda and neighbouring States).[76] The torture of children (and any other persons) is a violation of a *jus cogens* norm and is 'manifestly unlawful'. Thus one need not explore the historical context in a particular situation to decipher the meanings or import of torture for humanity generally; especially in respect of the torture of children; a group of persons entitled to special protection under ICL and international humanitarian and human rights law. Indeed a focus on historical context relating to a specific situation *in an attempt to 'explain' systematic and widespread torture during*

[75] Brown et al. (13 April, 2012), p. 5.

[76] Since being pushed out of Uganda, the LRA has operated in the Central African Region, South Sudan and the Democratic Republic of Congo but is now thought to number only about 200 (Associated Press (9 March, 2012)).

armed conflict, including child torture, occurring in that context (such as that carried out by the LRA in Uganda) in some ways, however inadvertently, implicitly detracts from the very notion of *erga omnes* in regards to the prohibition against torture. The 'torture truths' (for lack of a better term) depicted in *Kony 2012* thus, the current author would maintain, 'speak for themselves' with or without any further historical context as they relate to the matter of a universal most fundamental human right; namely the right to be protected against torture.

The authors of 'React and Respond' are rightfully concerned with negative stereotypical images of Africa, if any, that may unintentionally stem from or be reinforced by *Kony 2012* and properly encourage critical analysis of the video and any issues it raises. However, surely proposed solutions that do not deal effectively *as an urgent matter* with LRA violence will do nothing to dispel the presumed negative stereotypes about Africa which can arise to which the authors of 'React and Respond' allude.[77] The 'React and Respond' report suggests that "negotiated solutions" are in order not military ones and certainly a negotiated settlement with the LRA would be the preferred solution. Yet it seems clear that the children who are suffering LRA violence as the perpetrator group's high priority targets will not find relief based on a negotiated settlement with the LRA. Consider in this regard that since 2000 Uganda has granted amnesty under the Amnesty Act to 26,000 members of armed groups; mostly low ranking LRA members.[78] Yet the LRA (admittedly weakened) continues to attack civilians mostly in neighbouring States (since the LRA was ousted from Uganda in 2006). A peace settlement also seems impossible since the ICC does not recognize amnesty for those responsible for grave international crimes such as the LRA and there are ICC warrants out for the arrest of key LRA leaders. Further, the Ugandan government (Uganda being a party to the Rome Statute and accepting the jurisdiction of the ICC) has excluded (in theory at least) top LRA leaders from its 2000 Amnesty Act.[79] Thus Kony has rejected a peace settlement given that his ICC warrant does and will stand and he is not to be granted amnesty by Uganda. In addition; it is not at all clear that the direct and indirect surviving victims of the LRA support amnesty for all of the

[77] Certainly the torture of children in armed conflict is not in any way simply an African phenomenon but rather has occurred in many other parts of the globe as in the Serb-Bosnian conflict, the Afghan conflict, the Syrian conflict and others where torture of children has been made manifest in various forms from forcing children to live in conditions not conducive to survival to child soldiering to the infliction of other physical and psychological agonies.

[78] IRIN (30 May, 2013). The amnesty granted to these LRA adult perpetrators means that their surviving child direct victims (i.e. child 'returnees' who escaped the LRA or were rescued or otherwise returned to their communities) and indirect victims must endure the psychological torture of living alongside their tormenters; reliving their trauma and fearing a repetition of atrocities perhaps instigated by the same people.

[79] "Key sections of Uganda's Amnesty Act were allowed to lapse in May 2012, meaning that members of armed groups, notably the Lord's Resistance Army (LRA), no longer automatically escaped prosecution if they willingly abandoned their armed struggle. Earlier this month [in May, 2013], these sections of the act were reinstated and will remain in force for two years. *Only top LRA commanders are ineligible for amnesty*." (emphasis added) (IRIN (30 May, 2013).

LRA or even some (this notwithstanding the more positive views on the issue of amnesty for LRA members endorsed by some scholars, many Western, and by segments of the Ugandan population often not those directly affected by the LRA violence).[80] The residents note that those calling for amnesty have never faced the direct results of rebel atrocities. "Those who lived in towns can of course forgive but not those who were affected directly," says Francis Okello a resident of Lira, where Kony started his operations after taking over from Alice Lakwena, the woman believed to be Kony's cousin.

Further what of the right of the child victims of the LRA and their families and communities to international criminal justice; at a modicum through the prosecution of Kony and other key LRA commanders before the ICC? For some, misguidedly on the analysis here, a 'children's rights' perspective (which is in a fact a 'human rights' perspective) seems insufficient to justify either *Kony 2012* or the social movement it has inspired that has focused international attention on the LRA and Kony as a fugitive from the ICC that must be brought to justice sooner rather than later. Consider in this regard as one example the following comment by a prominent Ugandan re *Kony 2012*:

> Ogenga Latigo, a politician from northern Uganda who previously led the opposition in Uganda's Parliament, said Invisible Children's perspective was too narrow to be allowed to define the popular understanding of an insurgency that displaced millions and in which thousands were killed or abducted. "Theirs is a narrow perspective," he said of Invisible Children's work. "They just want the war to end so that children can go back home. That's all."[81]

The current author argues that both peace and the rule of law demand that at least those most responsible for grave international crimes such as the torture (in whatever form) of children as particularized victim targets during armed conflict as part of a common plan (as for instance perpetrated by the LRA) be prosecuted. To do otherwise is both to devalue children as human beings and to normalize to an extent the widespread violation of the torture prohibition.

"Child Soldiers and Clicktivism: Justice, Myths, and Prevention"[82]
Respectfully, on the view here, Drumbl (author of *Child Soldiers and Clicktivism: Justice, Myths, and Prevention*) trivilaizes the *Kony 2012* video and its vital message (urging activism and more earnest and effective measures to capture Kony and bring him to justice before the ICC) in part due to his concern that *Kony 2012*

[80] Baryio (26 February, 2013): Residents of northern Uganda oppose any type of amnesty for the LRA, saying they have witnessed Kony's atrocities. They say the LRA stole their children for soldiers, raped their women, killed families and looted properties.

[81] Associated Press (9 March, 2012).

[82] Drumbl (2012a).

allegedly presents the issue of child soldiers as "Africanized."[83] In fact; *Kony 2012* simply addresses the LRA phenomenon (hence the *a propos* name *Kony 2012*) and the LRA victims' right to international criminal justice. It seems unfair and, more importantly, inaccurate to suggest that the video presents an 'Africanized' image of child soldiering by virtue of the fact that the video was focused on the LRA and was not a general documentary on child soldiering. As the head of 'Invisible Children' Jason Russell says in the video; the purpose of the video is to stop the LRA and to stop Kony.[84] The charge that *Kony 2012* 'Africanizes' the phenomenon of child soldiering seems rather to be, on the view here, a product of 'political correctness' run amok. *Kony 2012* was in fact missing 'politically correct' rhetoric designed to assuage those who erroneously regard every frank discussion of fundamental human rights abuses in a particular locale as an attack on culture and lack of respect for the general populace in that specific jurisdiction.[85]

Since atrocities against children (i.e. various forms of torture carried out by the LRA against children in particular) are of concern to the international community: (i) there can be no constraints on who is properly permitted to speak on such matters and (ii) in some instances internationally coordinated solutions are the only option though of course the State involved would ideally be the key player in any such international effort.[86] In fact; timidity in discussing the horrendous atrocities committed against children in particular in any certain jurisdiction; be it Uganda or any other State: (i) does little to foster vigorous attempts to hold those most responsible for these atrocities to account in a national or an international criminal forum (i.e. the ICC where there is jurisdiction and the case is admissible) and (ii) may inadvertently reinforce an outcome in which the nature and extent of the atrocities perpetrated against children in the jurisdiction in question are mitigated *in the international public perception and consciousness*. This then inevitably

---

[83] Others such as Fisher (2012) have even gone so far as to blatantly accuse the Kony video makers of promoting "soft bigotry"; a claim that the current author finds unjustified based on the *Kony 2012* and the *Kony 2012 II: Beyond Famous* video content regardless the certain limitations that all docu videos and this one in particular have in providing all relevant historical context. Further, Jason Russell's personal religious beliefs are irrelevant but yet misguidedly mentioned at times (i.e. see Hickman (2012)) as allegedly pertinent in assessing the video. The *Kony 2012* and *Kony 2012 Part II* videos, at least as to communicating the realities on the ground regarding LRA torture of children in various unspeakable ways, have important information that should not lead to 'shooting the messenger' due to the unpalatable facts of Kony's severely cruel victimization of children.

[84] As Drumbl (2012b) points out; only 40 per cent of the world's child soldiers are in Africa. One wonders if the complaint would have been made had the video addressed child soldiering in some non-African context that the video was 'Europeanizing', the phenomenon of child soldiering.

[85] This is not to say that the *Kony 2012* film could not have been improved upon (i.e. *Kony 2012 Part II* for instance includes more African voices on the issue of the LRA and that was an improvement) but the same could be said for any docu- style brief video from at least some perspective.

[86] It was, it should be recalled, the President of Uganda, Yoweri Museveni, who in December 2003 referred the situation involving LRA atrocities in that State to the ICC.

does a great injustice to the child victims and their right to: (i) have the truth about the nature and extent of their suffering fully acknowledged and (ii) to have proper acknowledgement of the State's and the international community's failure to protect them as children during armed conflict (an obligation under international humanitarian and human rights law that is in fact also part of customary law). The objective and realization of holding to account the perpetrators of mass atrocities is important for an appreciation of what constitutes the full measure of justice and access to justice also for child victims; and for the upholding of the very ideal of the rule of law. Child victims of torture in its many guises as part of a common plan during armed conflict, such as the child victims of the LRA, have a right to access the ICC for a remedy as persons with juridical personality[87]:

> ...children are subjects of rights and not only object[s] of protection. In fact, the subjects of law are the children, and not infancy or childhood.... *The limitations of legal capacity [do] nothing [to] subtract from legal personality. The titulaire of rights is the human being, of flesh and bone and soul, and not the existential condition in which he finds himself temporari*ly...(emphasis added).[88]
>
> It is certain that the juridical personality and capacity keep a close relationship, but at the conceptual level they are distinguished from each other. It may occur that an individual may have juridical personality without enjoying, as a result of his existential condition, full capacity to act. Thus, in the present context, one understands by personality the aptitude to be titulaire of rights and duties, and by capacity the aptitude to exercise them by himself (capacity of exercise). *Capacity is, thus, closely linked to personality; nevertheless, if by any situation or circumstance an individual does not enjoy full juridical capacity, this does not mean that thereby he is no longer subject of right[s]. It is the case of the children* (emphasis added).[89]
>
> *In fact, as the Law ineluctably recognizes juridical personality to every human being* (whether he is a child, an elderly person, a person with disability, a stateless person, or any other), irrespectively of his existential condition or of his juridical capacity to exercise his rights for himself (capacity of exercise),—*we may, thus, visualize* ***a true right to the Law...that is, the right to a legal order*** *(at domestic as well as international levels)* ***which effectively protects the rights inherent to the human person*** [which rights include also the right of child victims of the international crime of torture in whatever form to a judicial remedy].[90]

Child victims of grave international crimes then must not be relegated to a 'remedy' in terms of transitional justice measures (such as Truth and Reconciliation

[87] That remedy including prosecution of perpetrators and potentially also reparations paid through the ICC victims fund.

[88] Juridical status and human rights of the child, Advisory Opinion OC-17/02, August 28, 2002, Inter-Am. Ct. H.R. (Ser. A) No. 17 (2002). Concurring Opinion of Judge A.A. Cancado Trindade at point 6–7.

[89] Juridical status and human rights of the child, Advisory Opinion OC-17/02, August 28, 2002, Inter-Am. Ct. H.R. (Ser. A) No. 17 (2002). Concurring Opinion of Judge A.A. Cancado Trindade at point 8.

[90] Juridical status and human rights of the child, Advisory Opinion OC-17/02, August 28, 2002, Inter-Am. Ct. H.R. (Ser. A) No. 17 (2002) Concurring Opinion of Judge A.A. Cancado Trindade at point 71.

Commission forums) as the routine and *only* option in their case. Transitional justice mechanisms such as Truth and Reconciliation forums are arguably a kind of mass group therapy process intended in large part to diffuse lingering tensions in the general populace. Such mechanisms do not always operate to serve effectively the 'best interests' of child victims or indeed their right to justice.[91]

On another issue, the current author is in accord with Drumbl's comment (in his analysis of *Kony 2012* and its depiction of LRA child soldiers) that many factors may facilitate child soldiering (i.e. child displacement and separation from family during armed conflict, children being orphaned during armed conflict, child hunger, the small arms trade etc.). The current author would argue however that child soldiering as it occurs in the midst of mass atrocity would not occur on the scale it does *but for* the intention of those who, as a common plan and strategy of war, choose to perpetuate it and exploit children's already oppressive circumstances to that end. Hence statements such as the following by Drumbl, in this author's view, unjustifiably downplay the aforementioned fact:

> It is, moreover, convenient to blame a handful of *crazed commanders* for child soldiering.[92] But the ease of blame fails to uproot the many factors that conspire to facilitate child soldiering. These factors include the small arms trade, state political alliances, poverty, and illegal export of pilfered natural resources (emphasis added).[93]

The holding to account of those most responsible for the targeted torture of children as part of war strategy and as a crime against humanity (i.e. Kony as commander-in-chief of the LRA) is a reaffirmation of the rule of law and highlights for the international community an example of what constitutes crossing the line into behaviour to be condemned as uncivilized and abhorrent to the conscience of the international community. That holding to account then is more than just a tiny step toward justice though it tragically is far from sufficient to stop the full extent of the suffering.[94] *Kony 2012* and the follow-up video *Kony 2012 Part II: Beyond Famous*[95] contribute

---

[91] For a discussion of Truth and Reconciliation mechanisms see, for instance, Grover (2012) at 263–287 and Parmar et al. (2010).

[92] If as Drumbl suggests Kony is but a 'crazed commander'; the question arises whether Dumbl also maintains that Kony could avail himself of a mental status defence before the ICC under Rome Statute Article 31(a) ("mental disease or defect") and/or Article 31 (b) (intoxication).

[93] Drumbl (2012b), p. 484.

[94] Contrast this view with that of Drumbl(2012b) who states: "However laudable, the fact remains that criminally prosecuting and convicting commanders who illicitly recruit children into armed forces or groups represents only a tiny step towards justice." (p. 483) The latter step toward justice, it is here contended, is not "tiny" in terms of its symbolic value as a reaffirmation of the international community's 'responsibility to protect' and of inherent universal fundamental human rights.

[95] *Kony 2012 Part II: Beyond Famous* includes more African voices than did *Kony 2012* and "revises the sites of Kony's war more clearly away from northern Uganda and into South Sudan, the Central African Republic and the Democratic Republic of the Congo" (Hickman (2012), p. 477).

to the movement to hold Kony to account and for any international pressure in that regard we can, it is here contended, be properly grateful:

> *Kony 2012* dispenses with the sad-eyed African poster-child and puts up 'Wanted' posters for Joseph Kony instead. Prosecution replaces pity.[96]

> He [Jason Russell co-founder of Invisible Children and chief creative officer] too is assembling an army [i.e. social activists] not only to bring a torturer and mass murderer of children before the courts [ICC], but also to 'change the world'[by using social media to foster international social justice].[97]

International pressure for criminal prosecution is undoubtedly often a necessary element if perpetrators of mass atrocities are to be captured and held to account[98] for their grave international crimes (including the targeting of children in particular for torture and other atrocities) regardless where they are propagating this extreme violence. Such perpetrators create severe international human rights and humanitarian crises for civilians. The child victims, whether on the African continent or elsewhere, are not at all then interested in 'cultural relativist' purported explanations of why they have suffered so mercilessly nor are they placated by 'politically correct' niceties in addressing the alleged complexities of the circumstances surrounding their physical and psychological torture. These child victims deserve better-that is: (i) urgent humanitarian intervention; (ii) practical effective interventions post conflict to help them rebuild their lives as best they can (iii) their entitlement to a judicial remedy respected and realized in terms of prosecution of those most responsible as well as (iv) reparation.[99]

2.4 The Prosecutor v Thomas Lubanga Dyilo

Lubanga was convicted of being co-perpetrator (Rome Statute Article 25(3)(a)) with respect to enlisting and conscripting children younger than age 15 into his armed force (the FPLC)[100] and using them to participate actively in the internal conflict in Ituri region in violation of Rome Statute Article 8(2)(e)(vii) from early September 2002 to 2 June, 2003.[101] (The legal characterization of the facts relating to the nature of the

---

96 Waldorf (2012), p. 470.

97 Hickman (2012), p. 475.

98 This judicial accountability might be through the ICC or another competent and fair international criminal justice body that is relevant where the State is unable and/or unwilling to fairly investigate and prosecute or such prosecutions may be in some instances carried out by a competent and fair domestic prosecutorial system.

99 Reparation for instance through the ICC Victim Fund and the State if the State was complicit in some way in allowing the torture of these child victims en masse during armed conflict or simply failed to protect.

100 Forces Patriotiques Pour la Liberation du Congo (FPLC) was a rebel militia of which Lubanga was Commander-in Chief and which was comprised of persons of Hema ethnicity. The FPLC was the military wing of the political entity headed by Lubanga and known as the UPC-Union des Patriots Congolais.

101 The Situation in the Democratic Republic of the Congo; The Prosecutor v Thomas Lubanga Dyilo Summary of the "Judgment Pursuant to Article 74 of the Statute" 14 March, 2012.

armed conflict in the DRC in the relevant time period was ultimately changed by the Trial Chamber in *Lubanga* such that the conflict in Ituri was classed as *non-international*. This as the Trial Chamber held that outside involvement was not extensive enough to consider the conflict international. The Pre-Trial Chamber had originally classed the conflict as international due to the involvement of Uganda in the DRC).[102]

It is striking that in the Prosecution closing statements 25 August, 2011 in the Lubanga case; counsel for the ICC Office of the Prosecutor; Ms. Bensouda (now Chief Prosecutor of the ICC) held that the children who had been 'recruited' by the FPLC and used to participate actively in the hostilities had suffered ***torture*** due to that experience. That *torture*, she argued before the ICC, was such that if the child victims survived; the suffering of traumatic aftereffects continued:

> The Prosecution submits that even those children who survived the ***tortures*** suffered during training continue to be ***tortured,*** that those who have no visible scars of the wounds received have internal scars that will remain with them for years to come, that even if you see no blood on the body of a former child soldier, they are internally bleeding (emphasis added).[103]

Notwithstanding counsel for the ICC Prosecution's eloquent oratory in closing, however, the ICC OTP did *not* at any time pursue torture charges against Lubanga either as a war crime or a crime against humanity.[104] Interestingly and sadly the representative for the victims in *Lubanga* did not petition the ICC Pre-Trial Chamber at some point before the trial to amend the charges to include torture (i.e. physical and psychological torture inflicted through sexual violence perpetrated against the LRA child members; psychological torture through forcing child 'recruits' to perpetrate atrocities against their families and communities etc.) Rather the victims' representative made an unsuccessful plea for a legal recharacterisation of the facts at the trial stage[105] in support of the following additional charges:

- sexual slavery as a crime against humanity
- sexual slavery as a war crime in an international armed conflict
- sexual slavery as a war crime in a non-international armed conflict

[102] Kammer (2012).

[103] The Situation in the Democratic Republic of the Congo; The Prosecutor v Thomas Lubanga Dyilo Prosecution Closing Statements 25 August, 2011, p. 10.

[104] Large numbers of children were 'recruited' by Lubanga into the FPLC often through abduction, and subjected to torturous treatment in a myriad of gruesome ways constituting a widespread systematic attack on the civilian population in Ituri : "Mr. Thomas Lubanga's crimes… are not just *crimes committed against the community* in Ituri…" The Situation in the Democratic Republic of the Congo; The Prosecutor v Thomas Lubanga Dyilo Prosecution Closing Statements 25 August, 2011, p. 6.

[105] That plea purportedly, according to the ICC Appeal Chamber, ran afoul of ICC procedural rules given, for instance, the timing of the victims' representative's motion. In any case, according to the ICC Appeal Chamber, the facts re sexual violence in *Lubanga* were not properly part of the factual basis considered at trial since no sexual violence charges had been confirmed by the Pre-trial Chamber nor was an amendment to the charges properly sought by the OTP in this regard before trial. Hence there was allegedly no factual basis regarding sexual violence at trial that could be properly included in the record supporting a legal recharacterisation of the facts that would have led to additional charges relating to FPLC sexual violence.

- inhuman treatment as a war crime
- cruel treatment as a war crime in a non-international armed conflict[106]

Given the change in legal characterization of the DRC conflict as internal; ultimately had the victims' representative's plea been accepted the additional charges would have been 'sexual slavery as a crime against humanity'; 'sexual slavery as a war crime in a non-international armed conflict' and 'cruel treatment as a war crime in a non-international armed conflict'.

Rather than referring to the treatment accorded the children in the FPLC military training camps as *'torture'*, the so-called 'training' was referred to in the closing statement by the Prosecutor as "*cruel treatment*":

> Mr. Thomas Lubanga took these children and subjected them to the more—to the most ***cruel training***. He forced them to stay in camps where boys and girls were beaten when they were sick or when they were tired. They were forced to beat and to abuse fellow child soldiers just to train them to obey orders. ***They lived in constant fear. They were taught to hate and to shoot and to kill unarmed civilians, the elderly, women, and children*** (emphasis added).[107]

In any case, no charges were in fact brought against Lubanga for *torture or cruel treatment of the children* in violation of Rome Statute Article 8(2)(c)(1) "Violence to life and person, in particular... *cruel treatment* and *torture* (emphasis added)."[108]

2.4.1 FPLC Child Soldiering: Torture as a War Crime

Lubanga 'recruited' hundreds of children from across Ituri for the work of FPLC mass atrocity[109]and many of these children were under age 15.[110] The FPLC in fact targeted children in particular to be so-called FPLC 'soldiers' in large part as there was less resistance from children to FPLC torture meted out to them in various ways and stages of FPLC indoctrination:

> Why did the UPC/FPLC want to use children as soldiers? Well, it was because they could exploit their youth and their experience, because children are daring. They don't understand the consequences of their actions. ***They could manipulate them, and they could control them*** (emphasis added).[111]

[106] Heller (August 10, 2009).

[107] The Situation in the Democratic Republic of the Congo; The Prosecutor v Thomas Lubanga Dyilo Prosecution Closing Statements 25 August, 2011, p. 9.

[108] Torture in a non-international armed conflict situation.

[109] The Situation in the Democratic Republic of the Congo; The Prosecutor v Thomas Lubanga Dyilo Prosecution Closing Statements 25 August, 2011, p. 11.

[110] One commander estimated that about 35% of the children at the largest of the 20 training camps in Ituri were under 15 (The Situation in the Democratic Republic of the Congo; The Prosecutor v Thomas Lubanga Dyilo Prosecution Closing Statements 25 August, 2011, p. 11).

[111] The Situation in the Democratic Republic of the Congo; The Prosecutor v Thomas Lubanga Dyilo Prosecution Closing Statements 25 August, 2011, p. 12.

> Most of them, he said, were about 10 or 13 to 22. He said, and I quote, "*We preferred to use young persons as body-guards*." It was a conscious choice (emphasis added).[112] (Witness 0041)
> They explained that children were enlisted because they are fearless, ***because they strictly obey orders*** (emphasis added)[113](Witness 0038 and Witness 0017; two former military officers).

The FPLC was a criminal organization given its policy and pattern of perpetrating systematic and widespread grave international crimes. Given that pattern of mass atrocity; none of the FPLC members had a legal right under international humanitarian law to participate in combat and cannot therefore be considered 'combatants'[114] or 'non-civilians' or 'soldiers' under international humanitarian or military law. The FPLC was thus a criminal organization that inflicted atrocities on its opposition and also used torture in various forms on the FPLC child soldier 'recruits' (i.e. the extreme cruelty of FPLC 'training' included commanding the children to commit atrocities).

Note that the UN Security Council in resolution 1071[115] refers to the recruitment and use of children in combat as an "inhumane and abhorrent practice." Child soldiering and children's active participation in conflict as an appropriated member of a perpetrator group committing mass atrocities has also been variously referred to by State representatives before the U.N. Security Council as "inhuman"; "heinous," "barbaric"; all terms that well conjure up a vision of child soldiering for a perpetrator group as *torture* as, on the view here, is the proper characterization:

> Let me once again voice our horror at one of the most despicable actions of the Liberian warlords: their practice of recruiting, training, and deploying children for combat. *Training and often drugging children, many of them aged seven to fourteen, who often end up killing relatives and terrorizing their neighbourhoods, is an unconscionable crime.* Words alone do not suffice to condemn this **heinous** behaviour. This behaviour must be stopped immediately, by every means the international community has available, including that of writing some provision, the framework of what will soon become the international criminal court, in order to bring to justice the perpetrators of such intolerable acts (emphasis added).[116]

> The representative for Poland expressed his appreciation of the condemnation of "**making children fight and kill**" which he called an "**inhuman practice** (emphasis added)."[117]

---

[112] The Situation in the Democratic Republic of the Congo; The Prosecutor v Thomas Lubanga Dyilo Prosecution Closing Statements 25 August, 2011, p. 12.

[113] The Situation in the Democratic Republic of the Congo; The Prosecutor v Thomas Lubanga Dyilo Prosecution Closing Statements 25 August, 2011, p. 12.

[114] The term 'combatant' is one used in law only in reference to international conflicts and the armed conflict in *Lubanga* was ultimately legally characterized by the ICC Trial Chamber as an internal conflict.

[115] UN Security Council in resolution 1071 (1996).

[116] Italy Statement before the UN Security Council UN Doc. S/PV.3694, 30 August 1996, p. 6. (Commentary of Italy on the Situation in Liberia).

[117] Poland, Statement before the UN Security Council, UN Doc. S/pv.3694, 30 August 1996, p. 14 (Commentary of Poland on the Situation in Liberia) cited in The Prosecutor v Sam Hinga Norman Amicus Curiae Brief of the United Nations Children's Fund (UNICEF) on child recruitment 21 January, 2004 Special Court of Sierra Leone (SCSL), p. 26, para 76.

> The representative for Chile echoed these words, calling it an "**inhuman and barbaric practice** (emphasis added)."[118]

Let us consider then next how FPLC activities meet the elements of the Rome Statute crime of torture as a war crime in the context of a non-international armed conflict:

Rome Statute War crime of Torture (Non-International Context) Article 8 (2) (c) (i)–4

Elements of the Crime[119] **Met Based on Facts Relating to FPLC Activities**

1. **Rome Statute**: "The perpetrator inflicted severe physical or mental pain or suffering upon one or more persons."... **FPLC**: the children 'recruited' by the FPLC suffered severe physical and mental pain and suffering due to: (i) the torture inflicted by FPLC adult members and by other FPLC children (the latter perpetrators acting on command of FPLC ranking adult members) to ensure compliance and to make an example of any child who resisted; (ii) the trauma of their active participation in combat and the forced commission of atrocities against their own families, communities and/or others including other child FPLC compatriots (i.e. who had attempted to escape, who were ill, those who could not keep up with the rigours of the FPLC training etc.) and (iii) separation from parents and family to live in constant fear as an appropriated ostensible 'member' of the FPLC
2. **Rome Statute**: "The perpetrator inflicted the pain or suffering for such purposes as: obtaining information or a confession, punishment, intimidation or coercion or for any reason based on discrimination of any kind."... **FPLC**: the FPLC targeted children in particular for FPLC recruitment hence implementing a recruitment strategy that in large measure was based on age discrimination. Further, the brutalization/torture of the children abducted or otherwise recruited was a means to suppress any opposition from the general population and to obtain absolute submission in all respects from the children to FPLC commands. Hence the pain and suffering inflicted on the child recruits served both the intimidation and coercion objectives of the FPLC in regards to the child recruits and the general populace.
3. **Rome Statute**: "Such person or persons were either *hors de combat*, or were civilians, medical personnel or religious personnel taking no active part in the hostilities."... **FPLC**: The FPLC targeted children, including under 15s, for child soldiering. Additional Protocol II to the 1949 Geneva Conventions (which is recognized as international customary law) makes it clear that children under

[118] Chile, Statement before the UN Security Council, UN Doc. S/pv.3694, 30 August 1996, p. 14 (Commentary of Chile on the Situation in Liberia) cited in The Prosecutor v Sam Hinga Norman Amicus Curiae Brief of the United Nations Children's Fund (UNICEF) on child recruitment 21 January, 2004 Special Court of Sierra Leone (SCSL), p. 27, para 77.

[119] Rome Statute Elements of the Crimes (2002).

15 are to be considered as a special protected group of *civilians* who cannot in law consent to recruitment or participation in combat. Hence the prohibition in Additional Protocol II on recruitment or use of children under 15 for direct or indirect participation in combat is one of the Fundamental Guarantees to *Civilians*. [120] Further of course the FPLC targeted for atrocity children and other civilians in the villages.

4. **Rome Statute**: "The perpetrator was aware of the factual circumstances that established this status."... **FPLC**: The FPLC targeted for abduction (as part of a common plan during the armed conflict) child civilians for child soldiering and sexual enslavement or 'recruited' through other coercive methods such as threats to families which forced the surrender of their children[121] for recruitment into the FPLC. The FPLC made no effort to avoid recruitment of under 15 s but instead recruited children with 'blanket sweeps' such that children as young as 8 or 9 were recruited. As under 15s, according to customary law, are to be considered a special protected group of civilians (compare Additional Protocol II to the 1949 Geneva Conventions)[122]; the FPLC may be considered as having had such knowledge or it may be considered that the FPLC should have had the knowledge of the special protected *civilian status* of the under 15s. Further the FPLC knew or should have known that it was recruiting under 15s in large numbers given its indiscriminate child recruitment strategy that did not consider age, health status or other such relevant factors.
5. **Rome Statute**: The conduct took place in the context of and was associated with an armed conflict not of an international character. **FPLC**: The ICC Trial Chamber in *Lubanga* legally re-characterized the conflict as *internal* as the involvement of Uganda was not sufficient to classify the conflict as international.
6. **Rome Statute**: "The perpetrator was aware of factual circumstances that established the existence of an armed conflict"...**FPLC**: The FPLC rebel militia perpetuated the armed conflict insofar as: (i) there was no thought by the FPLC leadership of disbanding during the time frame covered in *Lubanga* and (ii) the FPLC committed mass atrocities against civilians (relying in large part on so-called child soldiers to do this bidding) thus creating a climate of insecurity and desperation non-conducive to peace.

---

[120] The Prosecutor v Sam Hinga Norman Amicus Curiae Brief of the United Nations Children's Fund (UNICEF) on child recruitment 21 January, 2004, p. 6 (SCSL).

[121] "The UPC/FPLC also forced families to give up their children on pain of military punishments or fines. As Witness 0031 described it, if parents didn't send their children, it was at the risk of their own life... If the villages refused to hand over their children for Thomas Lubanga's army, the villagers would be left unprotected during attacks." (The Situation in the Democratic Republic of the Congo; The Prosecutor v Thomas Lubanga Dyilo Prosecution Closing Statements 25 August, 2011, p. 13).

[122] Additional Protocol II to the 1949 Geneva Conventions (1977) Article 4(3).

2.4.2 Sexual Violence Perpetrated Against the FPLC Child 'Recruits': Torture as a War Crime

Sexual violence charges under the Rome Statute were *not* advanced by the ICC OTP in *Lubanga* nor was extreme sexual violence by the FPLC used to ground a charge of torture as a war crime or a crime against humanity (the FPLC widespread and systematic attacks on the civilian population included sex crimes perpetrated by the FPLC against girls in particular though not exclusively):

> *As the evidence showed, girls were particularly singled out for particular abuse.* They were either raped by fellow soldiers or were handed over to Lubanga's commanders as sexual slaves and forced to be wives to these commanders (emphasis added).[123]
>
> The Prosecution requests the Chamber to make clear that these girls are not the wives, are not the wives, of commanders. They also are the victims of the crimes of recruitment and have to be particularly protected by the demobilisation programmes and by this Court.[124]

On the matter of the ICC Chief Prosecutor in *Lubanga* not bringing forward charges relating to sexual violence; the ICC Trial Chamber had the following comment:

> The Chamber strongly deprecates the attitude of the former Prosecutor in relation to the issue of sexual violence. He advanced extensive submissions as regards to sexual violence in his opening and closing submissions at trial, and in his arguments on sentence he contended that sexual violence is an aggravating factor that should be reflected by the Chamber. However, not only did the former Prosecutor fail to apply to include sexual violence or sexual slavery at any stage during these proceedings, including in the original charges, **but he actively opposed taking this step during trial when he submitted that it would cause unfairness to the accused if he was convicted on this basis.** Notwithstanding this stance on his part throughout these proceedings, he suggested that sexual violence ought to be considered for purposes of sentencing (emphasis added). [125]

The current author contends that in *Lubanga* the ICC Trial Chamber legally re-characterizing the facts to support: (i) adding *separate charges relating to sexual violence* (i.e. rape, sexual enslavement etc.) and (ii) sexual violence also as an instance of the war crime of torture and/or the crime against humanity of torture such that *torture would be an additional potential charge* (based on the same facts) would *not* have unfairly compromised the defendant Lubanga's due process rights.[126] This is the case as it can be properly held that Lubanga and his cohort of high ranking FPLC commanders and UPC political leaders knew or should have known that: (i) the mass systematic sexual violence perpetrated by the FPLC

---

[123] The Situation in the Democratic Republic of the Congo; The Prosecutor v Thomas Lubanga Dyilo Prosecution Closing Statements 25 August, 2011, p. 9.

[124] The Situation in the Democratic Republic of the Congo; The Prosecutor v Thomas Lubanga Dyilo Prosecution Closing Statements 25 August, 2011, p. 10.

[125] Trial Chamber I, Situation in the Democratic Republic of Congo, Prosecutor v. Lubanga, ICC-01/04-01/06-2901, Decision on Sentence pursuant to Article 76 of the Statute (July 10, 2012).

[126] These potential additional charges would then have had to be confirmed by the ICC Pre-Trial Chamber.

against children (girls in particular) was a form of physical and psychological torture; and that (ii) torture is absolutely prohibited under international customary law, including the laws of war, without exception. The charges of torture relating to the sexual violence perpetrated against children by the FPLC would not then have been entirely unforeseen given: (i) the *jus cogens* nature of the prohibition on torture and the obligation in every instance to prosecute torture especially when it is as systematic and widespread as that perpetrated by the FPLC against girls in particular and considering (ii) the amount of time in the ICC Prosecutor's opening statement spent discussing widespread sexual violence perpetrated by the FPLC against children in particular.[127] Hence, on the view here, legally re-characterizing the facts at trial[128] to include those supporting additional separate charges of (i) sexual violence crimes such as rape and sexual enslavement and (ii) torture as a war crime and/or crime against humanity related to the systematic widespread sexual violence perpetrated against children by the FPLC would *not* have deprived the defendant Lubanga of proper notice.

Recall that acts of sexual violence during armed conflict were considered to be torture in the ICTY case *The Prosecutor v Dragoljub Kunaric, Radomir Kovac and Zoran Vukovic*. The current author holds that such should have been the case also in *Lubanga* and *Kony* and the other ICC cases where systematic sexual violence (especially against children in particular) was not so legally characterized. The ICTY Appeal Chamber commentary in *The Prosecutor v Dragoljub Kunaric, Radomir Kovac and Zoran Vukovic* on *sexual violence as torture* is, on the view here, highly instructive as to why sexual violence can in some circumstances be considered as torture:

> Sexual violence necessarily gives rise to severe pain or suffering, whether physical or mental, and in this way justifies its characterisation as an act of torture (emphasis added).[129]
>
> … even if the perpetrator's motivation is entirely sexual, it does not follow that the perpetrator does not have the intent to commit an act of torture or that his conduct does not cause severe pain or suffering, whether physical or mental, since such pain or suffering is a likely and logical consequence of his conduct.[130]

Hence in the ICC cases *Lubanga* and *Kony*, for instance, the sexual violence perpetrated against children in particular by the rebel groups commanded by the

[127] "Thirty of the 129 victims participating in the [Lubanga] trial referred to suffering or witnessing acts of sexual violence, and the prosecution mentioned these acts in their opening and closing statements" (Kammer (2012), p. 12).

[128] This is not at all to suggest that the preferable strategy was not rather for the ICC OTP to (i) ask for an amended indictment at the Pre-Trial stage to address the sexual violence offences as separate charges including torture as a war crime and/or crime against humanity or (ii) to have addressed these issues in the first application for a warrant to the ICC Pre-Trial Chamber for its consideration when deciding on confirmation of charges and issuing of a warrant in the first instance.

[129] The Prosecutor v Dragoljub Kunaric, Radomir Kovac and Zoran Vukovic ICTY Appeal Chamber Judgment (12 June, 2002), p. 46, para 150.

[130] The Prosecutor v Dragoljub Kunaric, Radomir Kovac and Zoran Vukovic ICTY Appeal Chamber Judgment (12 June, 2002), p. 47, para 153.

aforementioned does, on the current analysis, amount to torture. This is the case in that: (i) these acts produced severe mental and physical pain and suffering for the direct child victims and psychological suffering for their family members and (ii) the sexual violence was inflicted intentionally and with a prohibited purpose; namely to terrorize the general population and the children into submission. Furthermore, the sexual violence targeted children in particular though not exclusively. Thus there existed some degree of age discrimination in respect of who was considered a most valued target for sexual victimization as the perpetrator group attempted to appropriate the children through sexual violence. The latter in the hope that the children's original identity would be replaced by allegiance and identification with the oppressive perpetrator armed group (the FPLC and LRA respectively) thus winning longevity; it was anticipated by these rebels, for the perpetrator group. There was of course also an element of ethnic discrimination in *Lubanga* in the targeting also of non-Hema children and adult victims (the Lendu) for sexual violence. Likewise Kony targeted a selected population in particular though not exclusively; namely the Acholi.[131] (The Acholi population is comprised of about 54 major clans and a number of sub-clans all of which have long-standing traditional tied to Acholiland).[132] The Acholi for the most part perceive themselves as a distinct ethnic group (though they may in practice place more emphasis on clan membership and various members of the group may have different interpretations of the basis for Acholi ethnic identity as distinct) and are regarded by other ethnic groups in Uganda as a distinct group.[133] The Acholi speak a particular language Luo and practice certain unique cultural traditions.)[134]

The current author has discussed *sexual violence as torture* separately from *'child soldiering' as torture* and maintains that these can be considered as separate counts of torture even though based on some overlapping facts. (The current author contends that children appropriated as sex slaves by the perpetrator armed group are also properly considered to be child soldiers). Child soldiering as torture then encompasses the recruitment and training process and use of children for active participation directly or indirectly in the conflict by armed groups perpetrating mass atrocities. Sexual violence as torture perpetrated by armed groups committing mass atrocities on their child recruits encompasses the sex acts performed on these children (i.e. rape etc.), forced "marriage', forced pregnancy, and the children's sexual enslavement by the perpetrator group.[135] It is to be emphasized that this author is in accord with the position of Judge Odio Benito in *Lubanga* on the relationship between 'child soldiering' and being sexually enslaved/sexually victimized by these perpetrator armed groups. That is; the current author concurs

[131] Brown et al. (2012).

[132] Okot (11 March, 2013).

[133] Davenport (2011).

[134] Davenport (2011).

[135] The sexual violence against children in particular was, it should be noted, also targeted against children outside the perpetrator group and against adults as well.

that: (i) 'active participation' in the conflict includes being subjected to sexual violence as an appropriated member of the perpetrator group[136] and that (ii) the girls appropriated most often performed as children various traditional soldiering functions (fighting, serving as bodyguards to commanders, being couriers, spying etc.) as well as serving as sex slaves for the rebel commanders and various others in the perpetrator group.

Lubanga, according to the ICC Trial Chamber, could not be held responsible for sexual violence against FPLC child soldiers as part of a *common plan* as the Trial Chamber held there was allegedly not sufficient evidence in that regard. However, respectfully, it is here maintained that the evidence across situations involving perpetrator armed groups using so-called child soldiers and committing mass atrocities, the FPLC being no exception and as discussed by the OTP at trial, shows that sexual violence against child soldiers, especially girls, is endemic for such groups and generally part of the common plan for appropriation of the girl child soldiers in the first instance.

The FPLC under Lubanga's command had been actively involved in committing the UN designated six grave crimes perpetrated against children which crimes, on the view here, constitute torture; namely (a) killing and maiming of children, (b) mass rape and other sexual violence perpetrated against children abducted to serve as FPLC child soldiers and/or sex slaves and against other child civilians, (c) abduction of children primarily to serve as FPLC child soldiers and/or FPLC sex slaves, (d) recruitment and use of child soldiers (persons under 15) for active participation in hostilities, (e) attacks on schools for the purpose of abducting children and (f) denial of humanitarian access for children brutalized by the FPLC in the villages or in FPLC military camps in which child soldiers also were 'trained'. Extreme cruelty of the FPLC towards their child victims is, as with the LRA, a prime signature of the FPLC.

2.5 Situation in the Republic of Cote D'Ivoire in the Case of the Prosecutor v Simone Gbagbo

The atrocities that are at issue in the Simone Gbagbo case arose in the aftermath of the election of Ivorian President Alassane Ouattara in May, 2010. Former President Laurent Gbagbo's refused to accept the electoral results even though those results were certified by the United Nations (UN). Quatarro turned to the rebel forces in the North for support. These same rebels (along with Former President Laurent Gbagbo now in ICC custody and facing four counts of crimes against humanity) had

[136] Judge Odio Benito in Lubanga wrote "The use of young girls and boys bodies by combatants within or outside the group is a war crime and as such encoded in the charges against the accused" [the charges being the recruitment and use for active participation in hostilities of child soldiers] (Cited in Kammer (2012), p. 15).

committed various mass atrocities[137] during the 2002–2003 armed conflict between the rebels and the government of the day. Human Rights Watch reports that none of those from the Ouattara camp responsible for atrocities have been charged while 150 from the Gbagbo side have been charged domestically.[138]

Simone Ggagbo, the Ivory Coast former first lady, faces ICC charges for her criminal responsibly in regards to:

> the crimes against humanity of murder, rape and other forms of sexual violence, persecution and other inhumane acts committed during the post-election crisis from 28 November 2010 onwards by the Ivorian Defence and Security Forces ("FDS"),**which were reinforced by youth militias** and mercenaries loyal to President Gbagbo ("pro-Gbagbo forces"), in Abidjan, including around the Golf Hotel and elsewhere in the country.[139]

> **Charges**
> [The arrest warrant for Simone Gbagbo sets out] her alleged criminal responsibility within the meaning of Article 25(3)(a) of the Statute for the **crimes against humanity** of: (1) **murder** under Article 7(l)(a), (2) **rape and other forms of sexual violence** under Article 7(l)(g), (3) **other inhumane acts** under Article 7(l)(k) and (4) **persecution** under Article 7(l)(h) of the Statute committed in the territory of Côte d'Ivoire during the period between 16 December 2010 and 12 April 2011.[140]

It is here held with respect to children[141] that the use of youth militia by the Gbagbo forces to perpetrate atrocities is itself a form of torture and that it also constitutes the genocidal forcible transfer of children (where child is understood to refer to persons under age 18) to a perpetrator armed group. (Note by the same token that the forces loyal to President Alassane Ouattara (the Forces Républicaines de Côte d'Ivoire, FRCI), the armed forces of Côte d'Ivoire, committed widespread human rights abuses against young men from pro-Gbagbo ethnic groups, including mass arbitrary arrests, illegal detention, extortion, cruel and *inhuman treatment*, and, in some cases, *torture*").[142] As explained here previously; such a perpetrator armed group completely appropriates the identity of the children through committing atrocities against them such as torture and/or having the children themselves participate in atrocities against others[143]:

> Most of the militia killings took place in broad daylight. Victims were typically stopped at illicit checkpoints and ordered to show their identification cards. If the militiamen

---

[137] "At least 3,000 people were killed and 150 women raped during the [2002-2003] crisis, often in targeted acts perpetrated along political, ethnic, and religious lines" Human Rights Watch (2013), p. 1.

[138] Human Rights Watch (2013), p. 1.

[139] Situation in the Republic of Cote D'Ivoire in the case of The Prosecutor v Simone Gbagbo Pre-Trial Chamber II Warrant of Arrest 29 February 2012 at Para 2.

[140] Situation in the Republic of Cote D'Ivoire in the case of The Prosecutor v Simone Gbagbo Pre-Trial Chamber II Warrant of Arrest 29 February 2012.

[141] The term children here refers to persons under age 18.

[142] Human Rights Watch (2013a), p. 3.

[143] The so-called "Young Patriots" youth militia group loyal to Laurent Gbagbo was responsible for burning their victims alive (targeted northern Ivorians who aligned with Alassane Ouattara) a practice colloquially referred to as "Article 125" – named after the cost of a litre of fuel and matches" (Mark (2012)).

> believed from the person's style of dress or surname that he was a Muslim or from an ethnic group that tended to support Ouattara, the militiamen would surround him, accuse him of being a "marcher" or "rebel," and beat the victim to death with iron bars, pieces of wood, and bricks. **Victims and witnesses generally identified the attackers as members of FESCI or the Young Patriots**, as a result of prior personal knowledge of the attacker, because the attacker said he was from the group, or because of where the attack took place—often directly outside a Young Patriot assembly point or a FESCI-run student housing building (emphasis added).[144]

The appropriation of children by the perpetrator armed group continues even after the conflict subsides or ends. This as the children are generally forever perceived by at least a segment of the larger community as part of the perpetrator group having been marked as 'perpetrator property' through various forms of torture (i.e. child soldiering for a murderous group, being victimized themselves through mutilation, rape etc.). Furthermore these perpetrator armed groups will generally not give up some sort of indefinite control over those child "recruits' and often, if the opportunity arises, re-recruit them through various means including abduction.[145] Note that the child soldiers recruited into the so-called pro-Gbagbo *youth militias* to perpetrate atrocities included children at least as young as 14 if not younger as well as 'youth'[146]:

> **General Philippe Mangou–The head of the armed forces under former President Gbagbo.** Mangou oversaw troops who appear to have committed war crimes and likely crimes against humanity On March 21, Mangou appeared with Blé Goudé at military headquarters to address several thousand **Young Patriots**—already implicated in scores of killings and rapes...*Mangou was quoted by numerous outlets as promising—as youth chanted "we want Kalashnikovs"—that* **the army would take "everyone, without regard to qualifications or age.** The only thing that counts is the will and determination of each person.... **Everyone will be enrolled in the army." The Young Patriots would continue to commit atrocities in subsequent weeks** (emphasis added).[147]

Despite children under and over 15 being tortured, at a minimum, psychologically as part of the pro-Gbagbo youth militia (given their having been trained and commanded to commit atrocities) there were no torture charges or child soldiering charges brought by the ICC against Simone Gbagbo or her husband former President Laurent Gbagbo both of whom were indicted by the ICC:

> Laurent Gbagbo–The former president was the commander-in-chief of armed forces that committed war crimes and likely crimes against humanity. ***He appointed as Minister of Youth his longtime ally Charles Blé Goudé, providing a direct link to the Young Patriots, who engaged in widespread killings along ethnic lines***. Despite clear evidence of grave crimes committed by his military and militia supporters, Gbagbo neither denounced nor took steps to prevent or investigate the crimes (emphasis added).[148]

---

[144] Human Rights Watch (2011b).

[145] Grover 2013a.

[146] "Children as young as 14 are being trained, armed and used as scouts according to a recent report by the campaigning group Human Rights Watch". RT News (11 June 2012).

[147] Human Rights Watch (2011b), p. 104.

[148] Human Rights Watch (2011b), p. 103.

2.6 The Situation in the Central African Republic in the Case of the Prosecutor v Jean-Pierre Bemba Gombo

Former ICC Prosecutor Moreno-Ocampo had the following comments in regards to the significance of the Bemba Gombo case[149] to prosecution of gender-based international crimes:

> Mr. Bemba's arrest is a warning to all those who commit, who encourage, or who tolerate sexual crimes. There is a new law called the Rome Statute. Under this new law, they will be prosecuted. **The Bemba case therefore is unique as sexual violence and rape is central to his prosecution.** It is also important as Bemba is not accused of personally raping women but prosecutors argue that he is criminally responsible for the rape, under command responsibility in that he reportedly failed to punish or stop the soldiers from committing these crimes, even though he was purportedly aware that they were being committed. According to Lieberman, 'The trial marks the first major prosecution of rape as a weapon of war and a fulfillment of years of international legal advocacy for female war victims' (emphasis added).[150]

As is revealed in what immediately follows; the former ICC Prosecutor was not completely successful in prosecuting the gender-based crimes in *Bemba Gombo* according to the full scope of the human rights violations they actually entailed. That is, *the ICC did not agree to the legally characterization of the mass rape and other sexual violence during the armed conflict as torture* despite the prosecutor's advancing rape as torture charges pertaining both to rape as a crime against humanity and rape as a war crime. We will consider and challenge here the refusal of ICC Pre-Trial Chamber II in *Bemba Gombo* to accept the Prosecutor's bringing of cumulative charges of rape and also *torture* and *outrages on personal dignity* based on the same facts underpinning the rape and other sexual violence charges. Let us review then some selected relevant excerpts from the Pre-Trial Chamber II *Bemba Gombo* confirmation of charges decision as relates to the issue of cumulative charging.

2.6.1 Bemba Gombo: Selected Excerpts from the Pre-trial Chamber II Confirmation Decision (15 June, 2009)

> …
>
> **V. CRIMES CHARGED BY THE PROSECUTOR**
>
> **A. Crimes Against Humanity**
>
> 71. In the Amended DCQ the Prosecutor charges Mr Jean-Pierre Bemba with **murder** (article 7(l)(a) of the Statute), **rape** (article 7(l)(g) of the Statute) and **torture** (article 7(l)(f) of the Statute) as **crimes against humanity** falling within the jurisdiction of the Court.

---

149 The Chamber considers that the opposing forces were essentially, on the one hand, a segment of the armed forces of the Central African Republic which remained loyal to Mr Ange-Félix Patassé [President of CAR at the time] and allied with the combatants of the Mouvement de Libération du Congo ("MLC") led by Mr Jean-Pierre Bemba commonly referred to as the "Banyamulengue", and, on the other hand, the forces of Mr François Bozizé. (The Prosecutor v Jean-Pierre Bemba Gombo; ICC Pre-Trial Chamber III Warrant of Arrest for Jean-Pierre Bemba Gombo (23 May, 2008).

150 ICC Prosecutor Moreno-Ocampo Comments on the Bemba Gombo case (Cited in Wachala (2012), pp. 543–544).

72. Having reviewed the Disclosed Evidence as a whole, the Chamber finds that there is sufficient evidence to establish substantial grounds to believe that acts of murder and rape constituting crimes against humanity within the meaning of articles 7(l)(a) and 7(l)(g) of the Statute were committed as part of a widespread attack directed against the civilian population carried out in the CAR from on or about 26 October 2002 to 15 March 2003. **However, the Chamber rejects the cumulative charging approach of the Prosecutor and declines to confirm count 3 of torture as a crime against humanity within the meaning of article 7(1)(f) of the Statute. The Chamber bases this finding on the following considerations.**

...

93. In the Amended DCC, the Prosecutor alleges that (...) the MLC troops looted, raped, and killed CAR civilians....Men, women **and children were raped by multiple MLC perpetrators** (...) Civilians that were killed included those who tried to prevent or resist rapes, attacks or lootings.

...

109. In the Amended DCC, the Prosecutor alleges that: Women were raped on the pretext that they were rebel sympathizers. (...) **Many of the women and girls who were raped feared being shot by combatants.** By subjecting the CAR civilian population to cruel, inhuman and humiliating attacks, the MLC troops instilled a general climate of fear in the CAR population, with the hope of effectively destabilizing the opposing army.

...

(bb)The death of the baby of witness 80

152.The Chamber is not satisfied by the evidence presented by the Prosecutor and hence does not rely on the evidence related to the death of witness 80′s baby on 8 November 2002 at PK 12202 for its determination regarding the count of murder. ISS. The Chamber carefully examined the statement of witness 80 who stated that an ***MLC soldier threw her baby on the ground before he raped her***. The witness further states that she had breast-feeding problems as a result of the medical treatment she underwent after the rape. Witness 80 states that she contracted staphylococcus. **The witness believes that the baby probably got infected and subsequently died as a result of her rape.** Witness 80 thus maintained that her baby died of diarrhoea and anaemia because it could not be breast-fed properly.

...

154. **The Chamber firstly notes that there is no indication in the witness statement that the baby died as a direct result of having been thrown to the ground. Secondly, the Chamber does not find any further clear evidence which would establish a causal link between the act of rape committed by the MLC soldiers and the death of the baby.**

(b) Specific elements of the act of rape as a crime against humanity (count I)

159. In the Amended DCC, the Prosecutor alleges that:

[from on or about 26 October 2002 to 15 March 2003], Jean-Pierre Bemba committed, jointly with another, Ange-Félix Pattasé, crimes against humanity through acts of *rape upon civilian men, women and children* in the Central African Republic, in violation of [article] 7(l)(g) (...) of the Rome Statute.

160. **The Chamber finds that there is sufficient evidence to establish substantial grounds to believe that acts of rape constituting crimes against humanity directed against CAR civilians were committed by MLC soldiers as part of the widespread attack against the CAR civilian population from on or about 26 October 2002 to 15 March 2003, with the knowledge of the attack by MLC soldiers...**

...

165. Having reviewed the Disclosed Evidence, and in particular, the statements of direct witnesses 23, 29, 42, 68, 80, 81, 87 and 22, the Chamber finds that they consistently describe the multiple acts of rape they directly suffered from and detail the invasion of their body by the sexual organ of MLC soldiers, resulting in vaginal or anal penetration. The evidence

shows that direct witnesses were raped by several MLC perpetrators in turn, that their clothes were ripped off by force, that they were pushed to the ground, immobilised by MLC soldiers standing on or holding them, raped at gunpoint, in public or in front of or near their family members. The element of force, threat of force or coercion was thus a prevailing factor.

...

(ii) Findings of the Chamber

197. **The Chamber recalls that the Prosecutor framed count 3 of the Amended DCC as torture "through acts of rape or other forms of sexual violence". At the Hearing, the Prosecutor presented evidence showing not only (aa) acts of rape that would allegedly amount to torture, but also (bb) material facts other than acts of rape which he legally characterised as acts of torture. In his closing statement, the Prosecutor highlighted that "[t]he main physical acts underpinning the charges of rape, torture and outrages upon personal dignity is rape in this case"**

198. **The Chamber, in particular, draws the attention to the following events and the evidence related thereto:**
(aa) Alleged acts of torture through acts of rape or other forms of sexual violence

199. **The Prosecutor used a cumulative charging approach by characterising count 3 of the Amended DCC as "[torture] through acts of rape or other forms of sexual violence".** ***He avers that the same criminal conduct can be prosecuted under two different counts, namely the count of torture as well as the count of rape, the acts of rape being the instrument of torture***.

200. The Chamber acknowledges that the cumulative charging approach is followed by national courts, and international tribunals under certain conditions.

201. The Chamber deems it necessary to recall paragraph 25 of the Decision of 10 June 2008 in which the following was clearly stated:
(...) **the Prosecutor appears on occasion to have presented the same facts under different legal characterizations. [The Chamber] wishes to make it clear that the Prosecutor should choose the most appropriate characterization. The Chamber considers that the Prosecutor is risking subjecting the Defence to the burden of responding to multiple charges for the same facts and at the same time delaying the proceedings. It is for the Chamber to characterize the facts put forward by the Prosecutor**. The Chamber will revisit this issue in light of the evidence submitted to it by the Prosecutor during the period prior to the confirmation of charges, having regard to the rights of the Defence and to the need to ensure the fair and expeditious conduct of the proceedings.

202. **By its decision, the Chamber intended to make it clear that the prosecutorial practice of cumulative charging is detrimental to the rights of the Defence since it places an undue burden on the Defence. The Chamber considers that, as a matter of fairness and expeditiousness of the proceedings, only distinct crimes may justify a cumulative charging approach and, ultimately, be confirmed as charges. This is only possible if each statutory provision allegedly breached in relation to one and the same conduct requires at least one additional material element not contained in the other**.

203. In addition, the Chamber further recalls that the ICC legal framework differs from that of the ad hoc tribunals, since under regulation 55 of the Regulations, the Trial Chamber may re-characterise a crime to give it the most appropriate legal characterisation. **Therefore, before the ICC, there is no need for the Prosecutor to adopt a cumulative charging approach and present all possible characterisations in order to ensure that at least one will be retained by the Chamber.**

204. **The Chamber considers that in this particular case, the specific material elements of the act of torture, namely severe pain and suffering and control by the perpetrator over the person, are also the inherent specific material elements of the act of rape.**

However, the act of rape requires the additional specific material element of penetration, which makes it the most appropriate legal characterisation in this particular case.

205. **The Chamber, after having carefully reviewed the factual circumstances submitted by the Prosecutor, concludes that the evidence he presented reflects the same conduct which underlies the count of rape, as identified in the statements of witnesses 22, 23, 29, 68, 80, 81, 87 and Unidentified Victims 1 to 35.** ***The Chamber therefore considers that the act of torture is fully subsumed by the count of rape.***

(bb) Other alleged acts of torture, other than acts of rape

206. Having reviewed the Disclosed Evidence pertaining to other alleged acts of torture, other than acts of rape, the Chamber finds that the Amended DCC fails to specify as to which other facts of torture the Prosecutor relies upon.

207. The Chamber notes that the Prosecutor presented evidence pertaining to other acts of torture, other than acts of rape, but did not specify so in the Amended DCC. To the contrary, without any information in the Amended DCC on the link between the facts underpinning the act of torture and the individual concerned, the Chamber resorted to the Disclosed Evidence in order to properly interpret the Amended DCC. The Prosecutor presented only at the Hearing some material facts parenthetically. However, the Chamber clarifies that the presentation of partially relevant material facts at the Hearing to support the submission that some acts of torture are different from acts of rape does not cure the deficiencies and imprecision of the Amended DCC.

...

209. Applying these principles, the Chamber is of the view that in the Amended DCC, the Prosecutor neither detailed the material facts of torture other than acts of rape nor the method of commission of the alleged acts of torture. As a consequence, Mr Jean-Pierre Bemba was not in a position to properly identify the facts underpinning the act of torture and adequately prepare his defence. **Therefore, the Chamber declines to confirm count 3 of torture as a crime against humanity through other acts of torture, other than acts of rape.**

..

(c) Specific elements of torture as a war crime (count 4)

289. In the Amended DCC, the Prosecutor alleges that:

From on or about 26 October 2002 to 15 March 2003, Jean-Pierre BEMBA committed, jointly with another, Ange-Félix Patassé, **war crimes by inflicting severe physical or mental pain or suffering through acts of rape or other forms of** ***sexual violence, upon civilian men, women and children*** **in the Central African Republic, in violation of [article] 8(2)(c)(i) (...) of the Rome Statute**.

290. The Prosecutor alleges that the facts characterised as acts of torture constituting crimes against humanity occurred also in the context of the armed conflict not of an international character.

291. Lacking precision in the Amended DCC as to the specific purpose required for the commission of torture within the meaning of article 8(2)(c)(i) of the Statute, the **Chamber declines to confirm count 4 of torture as a war crime**.

...

297. Given the identical submission of the Prosecutor in the Amended DCC with regard to the act of torture and the underlying criminal conduct pertaining to acts of rape, **the Chamber refers to the Prosecutor's submission at the Hearing that MLC troops "used torture through acts of sexual violence for the purpose of punishing and intimidating the civilian population for allegedly sympathizing with Bozizé's rebels, as well as for the purpose of discriminating against their victims"**.

...

299. The Chamber observes that indeed the Prosecutor failed to provide the factual basis in the Amended DCC underpinning the charge of torture as a war crime. Even at the Hearing, **the Prosecutor only recalled a selection of factual circumstances pertaining**

to acts of rape in order to substantiate the count of torture as a war crime. However, he did not elaborate on the specific intent of alleged MLC soldiers which would have clearly characterised the alleged acts as acts of torture as a war crime.
300. Therefore, the Chamber considers that the Prosecutor did not discharge properly his duty under article 61(3) of the Statute and regulation 52(b) of the Regulations. The duty to present evidence in relation to each legal requirement of the crime cannot be compensated by the Chamber.

…

302. The Chamber rejects the cumulative charging approach of the Prosecutor and therefore declines to confirm count 5 of outrage upon personal dignity as war crime in violation of article 8(2)(c)(ii) of the Statute.

..

308. The Chamber further notes that, only at the Hearing, the Defence was in a position to properly identify the factual basis pertaining to count 5 when **the Prosecutor clarified that "any act of rape is humiliating, degrading and a violation of a person's dignity. Therefore, any act of rape constitutes an outrage upon personal dignity". Albeit acknowledging the different nature of both crimes, the Prosecutor maintained at the Hearing that the crime of outrage upon personal dignity is fulfilled because MLC soldiers humiliated, degraded and violated the dignity of civilians by (1) gang-raping them, (2) raping them at gunpoint, (3) ripping off their clothes before the rape, (4) raping them in front of their families or in public, and (5) because of the powerlessness of the families witnessing the rapes, (6) the severity of the rapes and (7) the impact of the rapes on the families of rape victims and the CAR population in general.**

310. As identified above in the context of the count of torture as a crime against humanity, the Chamber notes that also in the context of outrages upon personal dignity the Prosecutor presented the same conduct, related mainly to acts of rape, under different legal characterisations, namely articles 8(2)(c)(ii) and 8(2)(e)(vi) of the Statute. ***In the opinion of the Chamber, most of the facts presented by the Prosecutor at the Hearing reflect in essence the constitutive elements of force or coercion in the crime of rape, characterising this conduct, in the first place, as an act of rape. In the opinion of the Chamber, the essence of the violation of the law underlying these facts is fully encompassed in the count of rape.***

…

312. **With reference to the Chamber's previous findings concerning cumulative charging, *it therefore holds that in this particular case the count of outrage upon personal dignity is fully subsumed by the count of rape*, which is the most appropriate legal characterisation of the conduct presented.**

…

490. **The Chamber finds sufficient evidence to establish substantial grounds to believe that Mr Jean Pierre Bemba-who was at all times relevant to the charges, a military-like commander with effective authority and control over the MLC troops-failed to take all necessary and reasonable measures within his power to prevent or repress the commission by the MLC troops of the crimes against humanity of murder and rape and the war crimes of murder, rape and pillaging in the CAR from on or about 26 October 2002 to 15 March 2003.**
FOR THESE REASONS, THE CHAMBER

(a) determines that the Case falls within the jurisdiction of the Court and is admissible pursuant to articles 17(1) and 19(1) of the Statute;
(b) declines to confirm that Jean-Pierre Bemba Gombo is criminally responsible within the meaning of article 25(3)(a) of the Statute for the charges of crimes against humanity and war crimes as described in the Amended Document Containing the Charges;
(c) declines to confirm that Jean-Pierre Bemba Gombo is criminally responsible within the meaning of article 28(b) of the Statute for the charges of crimes against humanity and war crimes as described in the Amended Document Containing the Charges;

(d) **confirms that Jean-Pierre Bemba Gombo is criminally responsible within the meaning of article 28(a) of the Statute for the following charges:**

(i) ***murder constituting a crime against humanity*** (count 7) within the meaning of article 7(l)(a) of the Statute;
(ii) ***rape constituting a crime against humanity*** (count 1) within the meaning of article 7(1) (g) of the Statute;
(iii) ***murder constituting a war crime*** (count 6) within the meaning of article 8(2)(c) (i) of the Statute;
(iv) ***rape constituting a war crime*** **(count 2)** within the meaning of article 8(2)(e) (vi) of the Statute; and
(v) ***pillaging constituting a war crime*** (count 8) within the meaning of article 8(2) (e)(v) of the Statute;

(e) **declines to confirm that Jean-Pierre Bemba Gombo is criminally responsible within the meaning of article 28(a) of the Statute for the following charges:**

(i) ***torture constituting a crime against humanity*** (count 3) within the meaning of article 7(1) (f) of the Statute;
(ii) ***torture constituting a war crime*** (count 4) within the meaning of article 8(2)(c)(i) of the Statute;
(iii) ***outrages upon personal dignity constituting a war crime*** (count 5) within the meaning of article 8(2)(c)(ii) of the Statute...[151]

Let us reconsider then the issue of cumulative charging by the ICC OTP Prosecutor in Bemba Gombo in relation to rape not only as a Rome Statute war crime and crime against humanity but also constituting *torture* as a war crime and crime against humanity and outrages on personal dignity as a war crime.

2.6.2 *Mass Rape as 'Torture' and an 'Outrage on Personal Dignity': The Cumulative Charging Issue*

It is here suggested that the ICC Prosecutor was legally justified in *Bemba Gombo* to advance cumulative charges in relation to ***mass rape*** given the realities of mass rape during armed conflict (as causing enormous and severe suffering as part of a general attack on civilians or a targeted segment of the civilian populace; occurring generally in conjunction with other crimes against humanity and used also as a war strategy to intimidate the general populace). Those cumulative charges on the same facts included also separate charges of *rape as torture* and *rape as an outrage on personal dignity* (both, as discussed, *not* confirmed by the Pre-Trial Chamber in *Bemba Gombo*). Recall that the Rome Statute Elements of the Crimes allows that "A particular conduct may constitute one or more crimes."[152] Respectfully then it is

[151] Situation in the Central African Republic in the Case of the Prosecutor v Jean-Pierre Bemba Gombo Pre-Trial Chamber Confirmation Decision (15 June, 2009) ICC-01/05-01/08.

[152] Rome Statute Elements of the Crimes: General Introduction (2002) (point 9).

here contended that the *crimes of torture and outrage on personal dignity are **not subsumed** under the crime of rape contrary to the presumptions on this point of ICC Pre-Trial Chamber II in Bemba Gombo.* This is the case in that the charge of rape alone is not sufficient to capture the essence of the crime of *systematic mass rape* carried out in part with the *specific intent and for the purpose of torture of and attacks on the personal dignity of not only the direct victims but a larger targeted group of which the direct rape victims are members.* While any rape for any particular individual direct victim likely amounts to psychological and physical torture and an outrage on personal dignity; this may or may not be the specific intent or purpose of the perpetrator in every instance of *isolated cases of rape* occurring in the context of armed conflict (even where these *isolated* instances of rape occur amidst other war crimes and/or crimes against humanity that are unrelated to sexual violence).[153] These isolated instances of rape during armed conflict are, furthermore, not part of a to perpetrate torture and to humiliate and undermine psychologically the larger group of which the direct victims are members. However, *mass rape carried out as part of a common plan*, it is here argued, has as a specific purpose and reflects the intent of the perpetrator group as a whole (as opposed to the perpetrators as individuals who actually committed the rapes) to: (i) torture the civilian group of which the direct rape victims were members be that group defined politically and/or ethnically or in some other fashion (not just the direct victims) and to (ii) commit insults on the personal dignity not just of the direct victims of the mass rapes but on the civilian populace as a whole or that segment of the populace targeted for atrocities (i.e. the alleged opposition groups within the general populace). It is here argued then that the common plan in *Bemba Gombo* involved mass rape and that the *dolus directus in the first degree* or *direct intent* of this component of the common plan was one of psychological torture and attacks on the personal dignity of the targeted civilian group and not just harms to the direct rape victims. It was precisely for that reason that Bemba Gombo, who had effective control over the MLC troops, did *not* take the necessary, sufficient and reasonable action to prevent or repress the mass rapes. That is, the mass rapes were in accord with a prime objective of the common plan; that is to torture and humiliate the targeted segment of the general populace as a means of suppression. In this regard; further recall that the Rome Statute Elements of the Crimes allows that the "existence of intent and knowledge can be inferred from relevant facts and circumstances."[154] Here it is sug-

[153] One might say that the perpetrators involved in isolated instances of rape in an armed conflict situation may rightfully have attributed to them *dolus directus in the second degree.* That is, the perpetrators can be assumed to be aware that a rape may be perceived by the direct victim as an outrage on the victim's personal dignity and as psychological and physical torture. However, the latter (torture and outrage on the victim's personal dignity) may not be the specific intent and purpose of the perpetrators in committing this form of sexual violence *for reasons other than as part of a common plan.*

[154] Rome Statute Elements of the Crimes (2002) General Introduction (point 3).

gested that: (i) the very occurrence of the mass rapes and non-intervention by Bemba Gombo as Commander-in-Chief of the MLC to prevent or stop the rapes, (ii) the MLC military committing gang rapes as a matter of course, (iii) the commission of the rapes in front of other family members, (iv) the gang rapes of children and other such facts allow for the inference that: a) the MLC perpetrators had the knowledge that they were committing *torture* and perpetrating *outrages on the personal dignity of individual victims and the victims' larger group* and b) that this was precisely their intent as part of a common plan under the leadership and guidance of Bemba Gombo among others to suppress any opposition.

The mass rapes committed in CAR while Bemba Gombo was President and Commander-in-Chief of the MLC (Movement for the Liberation of Congo) then amounted to much more than horrific sexual violence that grounded the charges against Gombo of rape as a war crime and rape as a crime against humanity. These mass rapes were not simply allegedly motivated by the sexual urges and proclivities of the individual direct perpetrators. Rather, these mass rapes were, on the analysis here, part of a common plan of which Bemba Gombo was fully aware and in which he was complicit. That common plan then included mass rape as a component designed to achieve the specific objective or purpose of psychological torture and outrages on the personal dignity of not only the direct individual victims of the mass rapes but also the targeted segment of the civilian population perceived as supporters of the opposition.

Recall now *the elements of torture* under the Rome Statute Elements of the Crimes[155] that include an element regarding knowledge that the *conduct constituting torture* was: (i) part of something broader (i.e. a common plan of attacking the general populace or a targeted segment of the civilian population such as a particular opposition group or ethnic group (torture as a crime against humanity) and/or (ii) had a very specific intended purpose such as intimidation of the general populace (torture as a war crime). In both cases- torture as a crime against humanity or torture as a war crime- the individual perpetrator *mens rea* is to: (i) **commit torture *qua* inflicting "severe physical or mental pain or suffering" using mass rape as the vehicle** and to (ii) **participate in implementing the *common plan* which has as a prime objective to inflict psychological torture not only on direct victims but also on the general populace or a targeted segment thereof** (*mass rape* being an ideal vehicle for inflicting psychological torture and humiliation on the direct victims and the larger group to which they belong especially in countries where women are extremely modest and their virginity before marriage and sexual availability only to their husbands is dictated by strict religious and cultural practice).

Consider then the elements of torture under the Rome Statute and the element of knowledge and intent of the individual perpetrators, those who had command

155 Rome Statute Elements of the Crimes (2002).

responsibility over them and those who aided and abetted them where mass rape was the vehicle for torture as part of a common plan:

Elements of the Crime of Torture as a Crime Against Humanity

1. The perpetrator inflicted **severe physical or mental pain or suffering** upon one or more persons.
2. Such person or persons were in the custody or under the control of the perpetrator.
3. Such pain or suffering did not arise only from, and was not inherent in or incidental to, lawful sanctions.
4. The conduct was committed as part of a widespread or systematic attack directed against a civilian population.
5. **The perpetrator knew that the conduct [torture actualized as mass rape] was part of or intended the conduct to be part of a widespread or systematic attack directed against a civilian population [as part of a common plan]** (emphasis added and portion in square brackets added)[156]

Article 8(2)(a)(ii)-1
War crime of torture (International armed conflict)
Elements

1. The perpetrator **inflicted severe physical or mental pain or suffering** upon one or more persons.
2. **The perpetrator inflicted the pain or suffering for such purposes as: obtaining information or a confession, punishment, intimidation or coercion or for any reason based on discrimination of any kind. [i.e. the torture through mass rape was knowingly and intentionally inflicted on women and girls in particular as part of a common plan directed to intimidation of a targeted larger group.]**
3. Such person or persons were protected under one or more of the Geneva Conventions of 1949.
4. The perpetrator was aware of the factual circumstances that established that protected status.
5. The conduct took place in the context of and was associated with an international armed conflict.
6. The perpetrator was aware of factual circumstances that established the existence of an armed conflict (emphasis added and portion in square brackets added).[157]

Elements of the Crime of Torture as a War Crime (non-international armed conflict)
Article 8(2)(c)(i)-4
War crime of torture
Elements

1. The perpetrator **inflicted severe physical or mental pain or suffering** upon one or more persons.
2. The perpetrator inflicted the pain or suffering for such purposes as: obtaining information or a confession, punishment, intimidation or coercion or for any reason based on discrimination of any kind [**i.e. the torture through mass rape was knowingly and intentionally inflicted on women and girls in particular as part of a common plan directed to intimidation of a targeted larger group.]**
3. Such person or persons were either hors de combat, or were civilians, medical personnel or religious personnel taking no active part in the hostilities.

---

156 Rome Statute Elements of the Crimes (2002).

157 Rome Statute Elements of the Crimes (2002).

4. The perpetrator was aware of the factual circumstances that established this status.
5. The conduct took place in the context of and was associated with an armed conflict not of an international character.
6. The perpetrator was aware of factual circumstances that established the existence of an armed conflict (emphasis added and portion in square brackets added).[158]

The suggestion here then is that: (i) Bemba Gombo and his MLC troops "knew that the conduct [*namely torture*] was part of" and "intended the conduct to be part of a widespread or systematic attack directed against a civilian population" and (ii) knew and intended that mass rape be the instrument for that torture as alleged by the ICC Prosecutor. Torture through mass rape in CAR during the relevant time period was then, on the analysis here, itself an objective or purpose of the common plan implemented under Bemba Gombo (as Commander-in-Chief of the MLC) along with other leaders of the group. **The *intent to commit psychological torture by inflicting severe suffering or pain*[159] *using mass rapes as the vehicle* (and targeting not only the direct victims of the rapes but also the larger civilian perceived opposition group to which they belonged) constitutes an element that is *not* part of the elements of the Rome Statute international crime of rape *per se*** (not every perpetrator of a rape *as an isolated incident* intends to inflict psychological torture). Hence the following requirement set out by the Pre-Trial Chamber in *Bemba Gombo* for a separate charge of torture in addition to the charge of rape based on the same conduct (mass rapes) is met:

> only distinct crimes may justify a cumulative charging approach and, ultimately, be confirmed as charges. ***This is only possible if each statutory provision allegedly breached in relation to one and the same conduct requires at least one additional material element not contained in the other*** (emphasis added).[160]

Hence, on the analysis here, even on the above reasoning of the Pre-Trial Chamber in *Bemba Gombo* the additional charges of: (i) torture as a crime against humanity and (ii) torture as a war crime were legally supported. ***Similarly the intent or purpose to perpetrate an 'outrage on personal dignity' qua "humiliation and degradation"*[161] *(of direct victims and the larger group of civilians to which they belong) is not an element of the crime of rape per se.***[162] However, it was *a purpose and intent* associated with the ***mass rapes** in CAR* as part of the common plan intended to humiliate

---

158 Rome Statute Elements of the Crimes (2002).

159 Rome Statute Elements of the Crimes (2002): (i) The crime against humanity of torture: Element one: "The perpetrator inflicted severe physical or mental pain or suffering upon one or more persons" (Article 7(1)(f)) (ii)The war crime of torture: Element one: "The perpetrator inflicted severe physical or mental pain or suffering upon one or more persons." (Article 8 (2)(a)(ii)-1 (international armed conflict) and Article 8(2)(c)(i)-4 (non-international armed conflict)).

160 Situation in the Central African Republic in the Case of the Prosecutor v Jean-Pierre Bemba Gombo Pre-Trial Chamber Confirmation Decision 15 June, 2009 ICC-01/05-01/08 at para 202.

161 Rome Statute Elements of the Crimes Article 8(2)(b)xxi war crime of outrages on personal dignity; Eelement one: "The perpetrator humiliated, degraded or otherwise violated the dignity of one or more persons".

162 This is not at all to dispute that most if not all rape victims would perceive a rape to be an outrage on their personal dignity but only to say this may or may not have been the intent of a perpetrator committing an *isolated instance* of rape during armed conflict.

and demoralize not just the direct victims but also the opposition group through mass rape of its women and girls This then justifies the charge of 'outrages on personal dignity' as a war crime in addition to rape and torture as war crimes and rape and torture as crimes against humanity in *Bemba Gombo.* Recall that the ICC Prosecutor in Bemba Gombo alleged:

> that the crime of outrage upon personal dignity is fulfilled because MLC soldiers humiliated, degraded and violated the dignity of civilians by (1) gang-raping them, (2) raping them at gunpoint, (3) ripping off their clothes before the rape, (4) raping them in front of their families or in public, and (5) because of the powerlessness of the families witnessing the rapes, (6) the severity of the rapes and (7) the impact of the rapes on the families of rape victims and the CAR population in general.[163]

The mass rapes in CAR during the period covered in the Bemba Gombo ICC case were *intentionally* and systematically carried out in front of family members[164] and were of extreme severity in that gang rapes were the common practice of the MLC. The latter facts also speak to these mass rapes being used as a vehicle for *psychological torture* and perpetrating *outrages on the dignity of a targeted segment of the larger civilian population* (that is the opposition group) and reveal that they did not simply constitute violence directed against the direct victims of the rapes themselves. These mass rapes in CAR during the period covered in Bemba Gombo thus cannot be fully understood by reducing the intent and purpose of the individual perpetrators to simply that of committing acts of sexual violence *per se* against individual direct victims. This is the case then since the intent of the individual perpetrators of the mass rapes[165] during armed conflict *as part of a common plan* is of a larger scope than just fulfilling the purpose of humiliating and causing severe pain and suffering to the direct victims of the rapes. The mass rapes in CAR under Bemba Gombo as part of a common plan were a vehicle rather for the psychological torture, demoralization and humiliation of the targeted segment of the populace (the perceived opposition) as a means of suppression and repression.

It is also argued here that the *mass rape of children* as particularized targets[166] and not only of women in CAR is further testament to the fact that *torture* and

---

[163] Situation in the Central African Republic in the Case of the Prosecutor v Jean-Pierre Bemba Gombo Pre-Trial Chamber Confirmation Decision 15 June, 2009 ICC-01/05-01/08 at para 308.

[164] "In *Kvočka* the Trial Chamber found that the "presence of onlookers, particularly family members, also inflicts severe mental harm **amounting to torture** on the person being raped." In 1998, the *Furundzija* Trial Chamber held that being forced to watch acquaintances being victimized in severe sexual attacks was **torture** for the forced observer." (Women's Initiatives for Gender Justice, 2005, p. 20).

[165] Rapes committed as isolated events during armed conflict, unlike the rapes perpetrated by the MLC *as part of a common plan* during the period covered in *Bemba Gombo*, are directed against individual victims and are not intended generally to inflict harms on the lager civilian population or a segment thereof (though the perpetrators may have knowledge that this likely will be an additional consequence).

[166] "Men, women and **children** were raped by multiple MLC perpetrators" (Situation in the Central African Republic in the Case of the Prosecutor v Jean-Pierre Bemba Gombo Pre-Trial Chamber Confirmation Decision 15 June, 2009 ICC-01/05-01/08 at para 93).·

outrage on the personal dignity of the targeted segment of the general populace was the objective of perpetrating the mass rapes in CAR during the period covered in *Gombo*. Nothing could be more devastating for the civilian populace than the torture (in all its various forms including for instance mass rape, enforced disappearance and extra-judicial killings) of its children. Hence, on the view here, the facts pertaining to the gang rapes of children in CAR during the relevant period also justified additional charges of *torture* and *outrages on personal dignity* being brought against Bemba Gombo based on the mass rapes.

In fact it is here contended that the failure of the Pre-Trial Chamber in *Bemba Gombo* to confirm the Prosecutor's well-grounded legal characterization of the facts pertaining to mass rape to allow for not only rape charges but also (i) torture as a crime against humanity and (ii) torture as a war crime as well as (iii) outrages on person dignity as a war crime is *inadvertently discriminatory both in respect of gender and age*. This is the case in that mass rape is not being properly charged by the ICC as 'torture' and as 'outrages on personal dignity' where women and children (especially female children) are the primary (though not exclusive) victims of mass rape as a key component of common plan[167] (that common plan being fashioned and implemented by commanders who have a specific intent and purpose to inflict 'torture' also on the targeted segment of the populace as well as 'outrages on the personal dignity' of the latter larger civilian group in addition to inflicting such severe suffering on the direct victims of the rapes).[168] *This then results in unequal protection for women and children under the Rome Statute against the crimes of torture and outrages on personal dignity where mass rape is used as the vehicle for accomplishing these aforementioned Rome Statute crimes.*

Recognizing that *mass rape as part of the common plan in the context of armed conflict constitutes 'torture'* would be quite helpful in de-stigmatizing the rape victims and in highlighting the gravity of the crime of mass rape.[169] This may in turn encourage victims to come forward and share their stories with a view to international criminal prosecution for mass rape both as rape and torture (as war crimes and crimes against humanity) and as an outrage on personal dignity (a war crime).

[167] The failure to charge 'torture' and 'outrages on personal dignity' may be an erroneous (on the view here) decision of the ICC Prosecutor as in *Lubanga* or may be due to other factors such as the Pre-Trial Chamber (as in *Bemba Gombo*) declining to confirm the latter charges.

[168] Note that in regard to the individual perpetrators during armed conflict of mass rape (as a crime against humanity) "**the last element should *not* be interpreted as requiring proof that the [individual] perpetrator had knowledge of all characteristics of the attack or the precise details of the plan or policy of the State or organization**. In the case of an emerging widespread or systematic attack against a civilian population [as part of a common plan], the intent clause of the last element indicates that this mental element is satisfied if the perpetrator intended to further such an attack." (Rome Statute Elements of the Crimes 2002: Introduction to the Elements of the Crimes against Humanity at point 2).

[169] This is not at all to detract from the gravity of isolated instances of rape during armed conflict.

In respect of this issue note, for example, the findings of Amnesty International on the stigmatization of victims of mass rape perpetrated during armed conflict:

> Amnesty International reported on the situation of women who had been raped in the Bosnian war in the early 1990s, and that "[m]any victims… pointed out that the public perception of rape was preventing them from rebuilding their lives and integrating with the society. **[One complained that] "I do not have any rights. Wherever I go people perceive me–I am sorry to use this word–as a whore. But did I choose this life?** (emphasis added)"[170]

Note as an additional point that Rome Statute Article 7(1)(g) regarding systematic or widespread sexual violence as a crime against humanity states:

> (g) Rape, sexual slavery, enforced prostitution, forced pregnancy, enforced sterilization, or *any other form of sexual violence of comparable gravity* (emphasis added).[171]

It is here suggested, however, that any mass sexual violence *whatever its form* perpetrated against civilians bespeaks a common plan with the objective of inflicting torture on the populace and is therefore to be considered of sufficient gravity as contemplated by the legal concept of crimes against humanity.

One final point; the Pre-Trial Chamber in *Bemba Gombo* in, on the view here, respectfully, an unfounded accusatory fashion alleged that the ICC Prosecutor was trying to 'hedge his bets' re confirmation of at least some charges in the case by using a strategy of cumulative charging with that purpose in mind:

> 203. In addition, the Chamber further recalls that the ICC legal framework differs from that of the ad hoc tribunals, since under regulation 55 of the Regulations, the Trial Chamber may re-characterise a crime to give it the most appropriate legal characterisation. **Therefore, before the ICC, there is no need for the Prosecutor to adopt a cumulative charging approach and present all possible characterisations in order to ensure that at least one will be retained by the Chamber (emphasis added).**[172]

In fact, however, it would appear that the ICC Prosecutor was simply charging numerous Rome Statute crimes in relation to the mass rapes in CAR during the relevant period that reflect the realities of *mass rape as part of a common plan.* That is, the cumulative charges reflected the fact that the MLC common plan under Bemba Gombo and his co-perpetrators called for mass rape as a vehicle for torture and humiliation of both the targeted segment of the general populace and the direct rape victims. Each crime charged by the ICC Prosecutor involved a unique *mens rea* element connected to the specific crime (i.e. (i) knowledge of torture through mass rapes as part of the common plan and intent to commit *torture* as a war crime and crime against humanity using mass sexual violence, (ii) knowledge of outrages on personal dignity through mass rapes as part of a common plan and the intent to commit *outrages on personal dignity* as a war crime using sexual violence and (iii) the knowledge that mass rape was part of the common plan and intent to commit mass *rape* as

---

170 Amnesty International (2009), p. 59.

171 Rome Statute (2002).

172 Situation in the Central African Republic in the Case of the Prosecutor v Jean-Pierre Bemba Gombo Pre-Trial Chamber Confirmation Decision 15 June, 2009 ICC-01/05-01/08 at para 203.

a war crime and crime against humanity). Each of the ICC Prosecutor charges related in fact to the *perpetrator group common plan purpose of intimidation and humiliation of the targeted civilian group and of the direct rape victims*.

The current author also respectfully contests the Bemba Gombo Pre-Trial Chamber's suggestion that confirmation of the cumulative charges relating to the mass rapes in CAR would have placed an undue burden on the defence. Recall the Pre-Trial Chamber's pronouncement on this point:

> 201 (...) the Prosecutor appears on occasion to have presented the same facts under different legal characterizations. [The Chamber] wishes to make it clear that the Prosecutor should choose the most appropriate characterization. The Chamber considers that the Prosecutor is risking subjecting the Defence to the burden of responding to multiple charges for the same facts and at the same time delaying the proceedings. It is for the Chamber to characterize the facts put forward by the Prosecutor....
>
> 202. By its decision, the Chamber intended to make it clear that the prosecutorial practice of cumulative charging is detrimental to the rights of the Defence since it places an undue burden on the Defence. The Chamber considers that, as a matter of fairness and expeditiousness of the proceedings, only distinct crimes may justify a cumulative charging approach and, ultimately, be confirmed as charges. This is only possible if each statutory provision allegedly breached in relation to one and the same conduct requires at least one additional material element not contained in the other.[173]

In fact where cumulative charging under the Rome Statute (i.e. for rape', 'torture' and 'outrages on personal dignity') is justified, as it is on the view here in *Bemba Gombo*, there is no undue burden on the defence. Each of these aforementioned grave international crimes (grounding the ICC Prosecutor's cumulative charges in *Bemba Gombo*) contained an element of *mens rea* to commit the *distinct* separable crime as can be inferred from various facts here already discussed. Respectfully it is here maintained that not permitting the ICC Prosecutor to advance separate charges relating to these distinct crimes was unfair to the victims who are entitled to: (i) the full measure of international criminal justice and to (ii) an acknowledgement of the full scope and nature of their suffering and of the various international crimes and human rights violations to which they were subjected without mercy.

References

Literature

Aceves WJ (2007) The anatomy of torture :A documentary history of Filartiga v Pena Irala Martinus Nijhoff Publishers, Leiden

Carlson K, Mazurana D (2010) Accountability and reconciliation in northern Uganda: accountability for sexual and gender-based crimes by the lord's resistance army. In Parmar S, Roseman MJ, Siegrist S, Sowa T (eds) Children and transitional justice: truth-telling,

[173] Situation in the Central African Republic in the Case of the Prosecutor v Jean-Pierre Bemba Gombo Pre-Trial Chamber Confirmation Decision 15 June, 2009 ICC-01/05-01/08 at para 201–202.

accountability and reconciliation p 232–292 http://www.unicef-irc.org/publications/pdf/tj_chapter7.pdf Accessed 29 April 2013
Davenport DL (2011) Acholi clan, ethnic, and national identities in post-conflict Northern Uganda In: A case study in Koch Goma sub-county, Nwoya District (2011). Independent Study Project (ISP) Collection. Paper 1206. http://digitalcollections.sit.edu/isp_collection/1206 Accessed 2 May 2013
Dewulf S (2011) The signature of evil: (Re) Defining torture in international law Intersentia, Antwerp
Drumbl MA (2012a) Reimagining child soldiers in international law and policy. Oxford University Press, Oxford
Grover SC (2013a) Humanity's children: ICC jurisprudence and the failure to address the genocidal forcible transfer of children. Springer, Berlin
Grover SC (2012) Child soldier victims of genocidal forcible transfer: exonerating child soldiers charged with grave conflict-related international crimes. Springer, Berlin
Grover SC (2008) 'Child Soldiers' as 'Non-Combatants': the inapplicability of the refugee convention exclusion clause. Int J Hum Rights 12(1):53–65
Hickman D (2012) Jason and the Internauts. J Hum Rights Pract 4(3):475–480
Parmar S, Roseman MJ, Siegrist S, Sowa T (2010) Children and transitional justice: truth-telling, accountability and reconciliation, Published by the Human Rights Program at Harvard Law School, Cambridge (Mass)
Wachala K (2012) The tools to combat the war on women's bodies: rape and sexual violence against women in armed conflict. Int J Hum Rights 16(3):533–553
Waldorf L (2012) White noise: hearing the disaster. J Hum Rights Pract 4(3):469–474
Young A (2007) Preventing, demobilizing, rehabilitating and reintegrating child soldiers in African conflicts. J Int Policy Solu 7:19–24

Materials

Amnesty International (2009) Whose justice?' the women of Bosnia and Herzegovina are still waiting" (AI Index EUR/63/006/2009) http://www.amnesty.org/en/library/info/EUR63/006/2009 Accessed 27 May 2013
Associated Press (2012). Ugandans criticize Kony video sensation for oversimplifying a complicated history http://www.thespec.com/news-story/2154458-ugandans-criticize-kony-video-sensation-for-oversimplifying-a-complica/ Accessed 29 June 2013
Baryio A (2013) for the Washington Times: Communities. Kony 2013: Africa designates more troops to fighting Joseph Kony http://communities.washingtontimes.com/neighborhood/africa-relayed/2013/feb/26/kony-2013-africa-designates-more-troops-fighting-j/ Accessed 30 June, 2013
BBC News Syrian Crisis: Houla child massacre confirmed by UN 26 May, 2012 http://www.bbc.co.uk/news/world-middle-east-18221461Accessed 19 April 2013
Brown BB, Metzler J, Root C, and Vinck P (2012) React and respond: The phenomenon of Kony 2012 (on behalf of the Outreach Council of the African Studies Association) http://illinois.edu/1363/kony_react_respond_4_13_12.pdf Accessed 2 May 2013
Chrobok, V, Akutu, AS (2008) Returning home: children's perspectives on re-integration a case study of children abducted by the Lord's resistance army in Teso, Eastern Uganda (coalition to stop the use of child soldiers report) http://reliefweb.int/sites/reliefweb.int/files/resources/9E8CAC8792A99D4CC12574250041975D-Full_Report.pdf
Deputy spokesperson for the Secretary -General Ba Ki-Moon (2013) UN office in central Africa says Ugandan soldiers continue fight against LRA http://www.un.org/sg/spokesperson/highlights/index.asp?HighD=4/5/2013 Accessed 26 April 2013
Fisher M (2012) The soft bigotry of Kony. The Atlantic. 8 March. http://www.theatlantic.com/international/archive/2012/03/the-soft-bigotry-of-kony-2012/254194

Heller KJ (2009) Re-characterizing facts in lubanga opinio juris http://opiniojuris.org/2009/08/10/recharacterizing-facts-in-lubanga/ Accessed 28 April 2013
Human Rights Watch (2013a) Turning rhetoric into reality: accountability for serious international crimes in the Cote d'Ivoire available for download at http://www.hrw.org/reports/2013/04/04/turning-rhetoric-reality Accessed 8 May 2013
Human Rights Watch (2013b) Syria: A stream of bodies in Aleppo's River http://www.hrw.org/news/2013/06/04/syria-stream-bodies-aleppo-s-river Accessed 9 June 2013
Human Rights Watch (2011b) They killed them like it was nothing the need for justice for Côte d'Ivoire's post-election crimes http://www.hrw.org/sites/default/files/reports/cdi1011WebUpload.pdf Accessed 8 May 2013
Human Rights Watch (2010) Trail of Death: LRA atrocities in Northeastern Congo http://www.hrw.org/sites/default/files/reports/drc0310webwcover_0.pdf Accessed 23 April 2013
Human Rights Watch (2003a) Stolen children: Abduction and recruitment in Northern Uganda 15(7A) http://www.hrw.org/reports/2003/uganda0303/uganda0403.pdf Accessed 26 April 2013
Human Rights Watch (2003b) Human Rights abuses by the Lord's resistance army http://www.hrw.org/reports/2003/uganda0703/uganda0703a-04.htm Accessed 7 May 2013
IRIN (2013) Rebel Amnesty reinstated in Uganda http://www.irinnews.org/report/98133/rebel-amnesty-reinstated-in-uganda
Italy Statement before the UN security council UN Doc. S/PV.3694, 30 August 1996
Juridical status and human rights of the child, advisory opinion OC-17/02, August 28, 2002, Inter-Am. Ct. H.R. (Ser. A) No. 17 (2002) http://www1.umn.edu/humanrts/iachr/series_A_OC-17.html Accessed 1 July 2013
Kammer S (2012) Deconstructing Lubanga, the ICC's first case: The trial and conviction of Thomas Lubanga Dyilo (American Non-Governmental Organizations Coalition for the International Criminal Court (AMICC) http://www.amicc.org/docs/Deconstructing_Lubanga.pdf Accessed 26 April 2013
Mark M (2012) Ivory Coast militia leader is willing to face trial, says lawyer: The Guardian online 10 May, 2012) http://www.guardian.co.uk/world/2012/may/10/ivory-coast-militia-leader-trial
Moss K (2013) Lord's Resistance Army funded by elephant poaching, report says (Guardian, UK, 4 June, 2013) http://www.guardian.co.uk/environment/2013/jun/04/lords-resistance-army-funded-elephant-poaching Accessed 25 June 2013
Okot B (11 March, 2013) Uganda: Breaking the links between the land and the people (for the International Institute for Environment and Development) http://www.iied.org/uganda-breaking-links-between-land-people Accessed 2 May 2013
Poland, Statement before the UN Security Council, UN Doc. S/pv.3694, 30 August 1996, p. 14 (Commentary on the Situation in Liberia)
Protocol Additional to the Geneva Conventions of 12 August 1949, and relating to the Protection of Victims of International Armed Conflicts (Protocol I), 8 June 1977. http://www.icrc.org/ihl.nsf/WebART/470-750099 Accessed 18 April 2013
Protocol Additional to the Geneva Conventions of 12 August 1949, and relating to the Protection of Victims of Non-International Armed Conflicts (Protocol II), 8 June 1977. http://www.icrc.org/applic/ihl/ihl.nsf/Treaty.xsp?documentId=AA0C5BCBAB5C4A85C12563CD002D6D09&action=openDocument Accessed 18 April 2013
Rome Statute Elements of the Crimes (2002) http://www.icc-cpi.int/NR/rdonlyres/9CAEE830-38CF-41D6-AB0B-68E5F9082543/0/Element_of_Crimes_English.pdf

Cases

Pre-Trial Chamber II Warrant of Arrest for Joseph Kony issued on 8 July 2005 as amended on 27 September 2005 ICC-02/04-01/05
The Prosecutor v Delalic et al ICTY Trial Judgement 16 November, 1998 (Case No. IT 96-21- T) http://www.ess.uwe.ac.uk/documents/part1.htm Accessed 25 June 25 2013

The Prosecutor v Dragoljub Kunaric, Radomir Kovac and Zoran Vukovic ICTY Trial Chamber Judgment 22 February 2001

The Prosecutor v Anto Furundzija (ICTY CASE NO.: IT-95-17/1-PT) Amended Indictment (2 June, 1998) http://www.icty.org/x/cases/furundzija/ind/en/fur-1ai980602e.pdf 25 Accessed June 2013

The Prosecutor v Sam Hinga Norman Amicus Curiae Brief of the United Nations Children's Fund (UNICEF) on child recruitment 21 January, 2004 Special Court of Sierra Leone (SCSL) SCSL-2003-08

The Prosecutor v Thomas Lubanga Dyilo Prosecutor Closing Statement (25 August, 2011) http://212.159.242.181/iccdocs/doc/doc1210316.pdf Accessed 26 May 2013

The Prosecutor v Miroslav Kvočka, Dragoljub Prcać, Milojica Kos, Mlađo Radić and Zoran Žigićv ICTY Trial Judgement (2 November, 2001) IT-98-30/1-T

Chapter 3
Selected ICC Cases in which Torture Charges Were Brought but the Special Targeting of Children for Torture Not Addressed

3.1 Situation in the Democratic Republic of Congo in the Case of the Prosecutor v Sylvester Mudacamura

The case against Sylvester Mudacamura was developed after the Government of the DRC on 3 March, 2004 referred the situation in the DRC to the ICC. The ICC issued a warrant for the arrest of Sylvester Mudacamura 13 July, 2012. It is alleged that Mudacamura, as Supreme Commander of the Forces Démocratiques pour la Libération du Rwanda (FDLR), was responsible as *indirect co-perpetrator* for nine counts of war crimes committed from 20 January 2009 to the end of September 2010, in the context of the conflict in the Kivus, in the Democratic Republic of Congo (DRC).[1] The ICC Pre-Trial Chamber did *no*t find that Mudacamura could be charged as a direct co-perpetrator in that the Pre-Trial Chamber held that there were *not* reasonable grounds to believe that his orders had a direct effect in regards to fostering the commission of the crimes nor that he was head of a well organized armed force with control over the major functions in regards to administering the force or with disciplining nor that he was involved with the cover ups of criminal acts at the Mianga and Busurungi attacks in May 2009.[2]

- The conflict opposed the Forces Démocratiques pour la Libération du Rwanda (FDLR), an organized armed group sometimes in coalition with other groups, to the Forces Armées de la République Démocratique du Congo (FARDC), in coalition with the Rwanda Defence Forces (RDF) during operation Umoja Wetu and with the United Nations Organization Mission in the DRC (MONUC) during operations Kimia II and Amani Leo;

---

[1] ICC information sheet Situation in the Democratic Republic of Congo in the Case of the Prosecutor v Sylvester Mudacamura ICC-01/04-01/12.

[2] ICC information sheet Situation in the Democratic Republic of Congo in the Case of the Prosecutor v Sylvester Mudacamura ICC-01/04-01/12

DOI: 10.1007/978-3-642-40689-8_3,

- From February to December 2009, the FDLR allegedly conducted attacks in the Kivus, including in: Busurungi and surrounding villages, Kipopo, Malembe, Manje, Mianga, and Mutakato.[3]

Charges

> In accordance with the warrant of arrest, Sylvestre Mudacumura has allegedly engaged his criminal responsibility as an indirect co-perpetrator under Article 25(3)(b) of the Rome Statute for nine counts of war crimes, allegedly committed in the Kivu Provinces of the DRC, between 20 January 2009 and the end of September 2010:
>
> (i) Murder;
> (ii) Mutilation;
> (iii) Cruel treatment;
> (iv) **Torture;**
> (v) Outrage upon personal dignity;
> (vi) Attack against the civilian population;
> (vii) Pillaging;
> (viii) Rape;
> (ix) Destruction of property.[4]

The torture charge was issued with the following specific alleged facts as the basis:

> **Torture constituting a war crime (Article 8(2)(c)(i) of the Rome Statute) The Prosecutor alleges in Count 9 that:**
>
> MUDACUMURA is criminally responsible for the **war crime of torture inflicted through severe assaults, aggravated rape, mutilation and/or inhumane treatment involving the infliction of severe physical or mental pain or suffering upon the victims for the purpose of intimidation, punishment or in discrimination based on their perceived allegiance to the FARDC forces**; at or near various locations in the Kivu Provinces, DRC, including Busurungi and surrounding villages, Walikale territory. North Kivu, on or about the 9–10 May 2009; [REDACTED] (emphasis added).
>
> **On the basis of the overall material presented, the Chamber finds reasonable grounds to believe that torture was committed, within the meaning of Article 8(2)(c) (i) of the Statute, whereby FDLR soldiers inflicted severe physical or mental pain or suffering upon one or more civilians for the purpose of punishment in:** (i) Busurungi and surrounding villages on or about 9–10 May 2009, where civilians were beaten, raped, mutilated and subjected to inhumane acts by the FDLR to punish them for their perceived support of FARDC forces, [REDACTED] and [REDACTED] (emphasis added).[5]

---

[3] ICC information sheet Situation in the Democratic Republic of Congo in the Case of the Prosecutor v Sylvester Mudacamura ICC-01/04-01/12

[4] ICC information sheet Situation in the Democratic Republic of Congo in the Case of the Prosecutor v Sylvester Mudacamura ICC-01/04-01/12

[5] Situation in the Democratic Republic of Congo in the Case of the Prosecutor v Sylvester Mudacamura Pre-Trial Chamber II Decision the Prosecutor's Application under Article 58, p. 18.

3.2 Commentary on the Prosecutor v Sylvester Mudacamura

It is striking that Sylvester Mudacamura was charged with torture that occurred in the context of general attacks on a civilian population perceived to be affiliated with the opposition. Sylvester Mudacamura was charged with *torture* on the same type of facts (i.e. severe assaults, aggravated rape, mutilation and/or inhumane treatment) that occurred in *Kony* and *Lubanga* who did *not* face torture charges brought by the ICC Prosecutor. Unlike Kony and Lubanga; *the torture of children in particular* in various forms (mutilation, rape, sexual enslavement and/or child soldiering) is not automatically synonymous with the name Sylvester Mudacamura though the question remains whether this characterization may also have fit the facts.[6] In the cases of Kony and Lubanga; the torture of children in various forms was used as an intimidation and coercive technique in regards the general populace or a segment thereof. Hence the conduct of the LRA and the FPLC meets the element also of the war crime of torture relating to the infliction of the severe suffering; pain and often severe injury having a specific perpetrator purpose.

Sylvester Mudacamura's acting as an indirect co-perpetrator of mutilation; rape and inhumane treatment of civilians, along with other grave crimes, netted him the ICC charge of *torture* as a war crime in a non-international armed conflict. In contrast, in the Kony case, similar facts resulted in respect of Rome Statute Article 8(2)(c)(i) only in the charge of *cruel treatment* as opposed to also 'torture'. Yet in *Kony* it is the case that children were very much the high priority particularized targets for extreme LRA atrocities. As discussed previously, the threshold for pain and suffering for children is lower than for most healthy fairly young adults such that a legal characterization of 'torture' is often legally supportable in considering the children's pain and suffering and the context in which it occurred. These extreme LRA atrocities caused the children severe mental and physical suffering and often death or if certain of the child victims survived; the damage inflicted resulted in horrendous permanent physical and mental harms. Hence, not charging torture (in addition to *cruel treatment* and the remaining existing charges) in *Kony*, for instance, sends a powerful message to the international community; namely that the suffering of children, no matter how extreme, does *not*, for some reason, fall into the rarified legal category of 'torture' as a war crime and/or crime against humanity (i.e. as per the Rome Statute). That message is in fact highly adverse to children's best interests and undermines child torture victims' access to the full measure of international criminal justice. In *Lubanga*; a violation of Article 8(2)(c)(i) was not even charged (i.e. violence to life and person, in particular murder … mutilation, cruel treatment and torture) despite the rapes and other sexual violence

[6] This question was not formally addressed in the case and hence no definitive conclusions can be based on the judgment in the case in regard to whether children were victimized as prized targets by the FDLR.

amongst other atrocities perpetrated in particular against children by the FPLC and the severe suffering children were forced to endure both during training and as fighters or support persons for the FPLC.

3.3 Situation in Darfur and the Prosecutor v Ahmad Muhammad Harun ("Ahmad Harun") and Ali Muhammad Ali Abd-Al-Rahman ("Ali Kushayb")

The situation in Darfur relevant to the indictment of Harun relates to the armed conflict that occurred from August 2002 until at least 27 April, 2007 (the date of the warrant for Harun). The parties to the conflict were as follows: the Government of the Sudan including fighters from the Sudan People's Armed Forces ("the Sudanese Armed Forces") and the Popular Defence Force (the "PDF") along with the pro-government Militia/Janjaweed against organised rebel groups including the Sudanese Liberation Movement/Army (SLM/A) and the Justice and Equality Movement (JEM) in Darfur, Sudan.[7] Harun was from April 2003 until about September 2005, Minister of State for the Interior of the Government of Sudan. As such he was in charge of the security portfolio and hence coordinating various bodies (i.e. the police, Sudanese armed forces, the national security and intelligence service, and the militia/Janjaweed) in the fight against the rebels. From this role derives Harun's criminal culpability in the Rome Statute crimes charged against him:

> Due to his position at the Darfur Security desk and through his overall coordination and personal participation in key activities of the Security Committees, namely the recruiting, arming and funding of the Militia/Janjaweed in Darfur, Ahmad Harun intentionally contributed to the commission of the ...crimes, knowing that his contribution would further the **common plan** carried out by the Sudanese Armed Forces and the Militia/Janjaweed, which consisted of attacking the civilian populations in Darfur (emphasis added).[8]

It is alleged in the warrant that as the head of the government's security operations against the rebels; Harun knew of the crimes being committed against civilians and the methods being used to suppress the population (which methods constituted grave international crimes under the Rome Statute). The ICC Pre-Trial Chamber also found that Harun's public speeches indicated he knew of the Janjaweed/militia attacks on civilians and the brutality they were inflicting and that he personally encouraged the commission of these crimes.[9]

---

[7] The Prosecutor v. Ahmad Muhammad Harun ("Ahmad Harun") and Ali Muhammad Ali Abd-Al-Rahman ("Ali Kushayb") 2007.

[8] The Prosecutor v. Ahmad Muhammad Harun ("Ahmad Harun") and Ali Muhammad Ali Abd-Al-Rahman ("Ali Kushayb") 2007, p. 5.

[9] The Prosecutor v. Ahmad Muhammad Harun ("Ahmad Harun") and Ali Muhammad Ali Abd-Al-Rahman ("Ali Kushayb") 2007, p. 5.

Charges

Mr Harun is allegedly criminally responsible for 42 counts on the basis of his individual criminal responsibility under Articles 25(3)(b) and 25(3)(d) of the Rome Statute, including:
Twenty counts of crimes against humanity: murder (Article 7(1)(a)); persecution (Article 7(1)(h)); forcible transfer of population (Article 7(1)(d)); rape (Article 7(1)(g)); inhumane acts (Article 7(1)(k)); imprisonment or severe deprivation of liberty (Article 7(1)(e)); and ***torture*** (Article 7(1)(f)); and
Twenty-two counts of war crimes: murder (Article 8(2)(c)(i)); attacks against the civilian population (Article 8(2)(e)(i)); destruction of property (Article 8(2)(e)(xii)); rape (Article 8(2)(e)(vi)); pillaging (Article 8(2)(e)(v)); and outrage upon personal dignity (Article 8(2)(c)(ii)).

In regards to the torture charges in *Harun,* he was charged with *torture* committed as part of the attacks on Fur, Zaghawa and Masalit by the Sudanese Armed Forces and the Militia/Janjaweed:

Count 21
(Persecution in Mukjar town and surrounding areas constituting a crime against humanity)
Between August 2003 and March 2004, Ahmad Harun, as part of a group of persons acting with a common purpose, contributed to the persecution of the primarily Fur population of Mukjar town and surrounding areas by acts of murder, attack of the civilian population, imprisonment or severe deprivation of liberty, ***torture***, pillaging and destruction of property (Articles 7(1)(h) and 25(3) (d) of the Statute);

Count 35
(Torture in Mukjar town and surrounding areas constituting a crime against humanity)
Beginning in or about August 2003, Ahmad Harun, as part of a group of persons acting with a common purpose, contributed to the **torture** of at least 60 civilians from the primarily Fur population of Mukjar town and surrounding areas (Article 7(l)(f) and 25(3)(d) of the Statute)[10]

In *Harun,* there was no recognition of the fact that children were and are a high priority target for torture by the Al Bashir forces and its allied armed groups. Rather children as victims of torture were considered as but part of the victim group subject to attack as civilians of a particular ethnicity (Fur)[11] by the Al Bashir forces and to torture in the process of that attack. Not surprisingly then child specific acts of torture such as child soldiering, abduction and sexual

[10] The Prosecutor v. Ahmad Muhammad Harun ("Ahmad Harun") and Ali Muhammad Ali Abd-Al-Rahman ("Ali Kushayb") 2007, p. 12.

[11] Thus the discriminatory aspect, based on age, in the Al Bashir forces selecting children as high priority targets for torture was not considered despite the fact that this aspect would be relevant as an aggravating factor in sentencing should there be a conviction.

enslavement of children, and attacks on schools were also not addressed in *Harun* though they were mentioned in the Inquiry into Darfur:

> According to the JEM, extensive rape has been committed by the Government and the Janjaweed...*the Government and the Janjaweed have repeatedly abducted women and **children***.[12]
>
> In many cases a ground attack began with soldiers appearing in Land Cruisers and other vehicles, followed by a large group of Janjaweed on horses and camels, all with weapons such as AK47 s, G3 s and rocket-propelled grenades. Many of the attacks involved the *killing of civilians, including women and* ***children***, the burning of houses, *schools* and other civilian structures, as well as the destruction of wells, hospitals and shops (emphasis added).[13]
>
> As an example of a case of mass killing of civilians documented by the Commission, the attack on Surra, a village with a population of over 1700, east of Zalingi, South Darfur, in January 2004, is revealing. Witnesses interviewed in separate groups gave a very credible, detailed and consistent account of the attack in which more than *250 persons were killed, including women and* ***a large number of children... They forced women to take off their maxi (large piece of clothing covering the entire body) and if they found that they were holding their young sons under them, they would kill the boys*** (emphasis added).[14]
>
> **The Commission also notes that Janjaweed have, on a number of occasions, *specifically targeted and killed children* including in Kailek and Surra referred to above. The Commission received *many reports of random and/or targeted killing of children, sometimes in horrific circumstances such as by burning or mutilation*** (emphasis added).[15]
>
> The Commission interviewed several eyewitnesses who confirmed that following the joint attacks by Government soldiers and Janjaweed in the area, up to 30,000 people were confined in Kailek, South Darfur, for about 50 days. ***Women and children were separated from the men, confined in an area around the Mosque, and later taken away by their captors to be raped. They were subjected to gang rapes which lasted for protracted periods of time. Girls as young as 10 years old were raped*** (emphasis added).[16]
>
> ***Inhumane acts such as throwing people, including children, into fire were committed by the Janjaweed during several attacks***. Five such incidents were reported from Urbatete, Tarabeba, Tanako, Mangarsa and Kanjew villages in West Darfur. In most of these incidents victims were burnt to death. **Extreme mental torture was inflicted on many mothers who saw their children burn alive after they were snatched from their arms by the Janjaweed and thrown into the fire. *Houses were set on fire with the inhabitants still inside. Most of the victims in such incidents were children***. Inhumane forms of

[12] Report of the International Commission of Inquiry on Darfur to the United Nations Secretary-General 25 January, 2005, p. 60, para 221.

[13] Report of the International Commission of Inquiry on Darfur to the United Nations Secretary-General 25 January, 2005, p. 63, para 242.

[14] Report of the International Commission of Inquiry on Darfur to the United Nations Secretary-General 25 January, 2005, p. 74, para 272.

[15] Report of the International Commission of Inquiry on Darfur to the United Nations Secretary-General 25, January, 2005 p. 76, para 278.

[16] Report of the International Commission of Inquiry on Darfur to the United Nations Secretary-General 25 January, 2005, p. 90, para 343.

> killings used by the Janjaweed include **crucifixion of victims** during the attack on the village of Hashab in North Darfur in January 2004. ... (emphasis added).[17]

> The persons under attack, predominantly from African tribes, were commonly subjected to beatings and whipping by the Janjaweed. These included ***women and young girls. In many incidents victims were subjected to severe beatings as a form of torture.*** The Commission has seen several victims who still bear scars of these beatings, and some who suffered permanent physical damage as a result (emphasis added).[18]

Clearly the Janjaweed as an agent for the Government of Al Bashir targeted children *in particular* for mutilation, rape, and other forms of the most heinous *torture* such as being burned alive. However there was no special consideration of these facts by the ICC OTP in charging torture. This was the case notwithstanding the fact that hundreds of children *in particular* were the specific high priority targeted victims of this torture. Instead *Harun* faced only one count of torture in relation to but 60 civilian victims and torture was mentioned as one of the acts relating to the charge of 'persecution as a crime against humanity'. *In regards to the latter charge of* ***persecution through torture****; the persecution referred to in Harun was in relation to targeted* ***ethnic groups*** *but* ***not also based on discrimination relating to the young age of certain of the specially targeted victims (i.e. children and infants)***. In fact the Rome Statute legal characterization of 'persecution as a crime against humanity' permits that the persecution be based on any ground of targeting "an identifiable group or collectivity" that is "universally recognized as impermissible under international law":

Rome Statute Article 7(1)(h):

> **Persecution against any identifiable group or collectivity on** political, racial, national, ethnic, cultural, religious, gender as defined in paragraph 3, or **other grounds that are universally recognized as impermissible under international law**, in connection with any act referred to in this paragraph or any crime within the jurisdiction of the Court...[19]

The *persecution in particular of children* (the term 'children' here including also youth and infants; persons under age 18)[20] through torture is clearly prohibited under international law (i.e. under international customary law and under the

---

[17] Report of the International Commission of Inquiry on Darfur to the United Nations Secretary-General 25 January, 2005, pp. 96–97, para 365.

[18] Report of the International Commission of Inquiry on Darfur to the United Nations Secretary-General 25 January, 2005, p. 97, para 366.

[19] Rome Statute (2002).

[20] The International Committee of the Red Cross makes clear in its commentaries on the Additional Protocols I and II that it is children under 18 who are entitled to special respect and protection under Additional Protocols I and II to the 1949 Geneva Conventions in provisions therein stipulating special protections for children where the age of the child is not specified (International Committee of the Red Cross (ICRC) Commentary on Protocols I and II Additional to the 1949 Geneva Conventions (1987).

Additional Protocols I and II to the 1949 Geneva Conventions[21] (which arguably are now part of international customary law) as well as under international human rights law such as the Convention on the Rights of the Child (1990)).[22] *Age discrimination in prioritizing the targeting of child victims for torture* in many of the Darfurian instances can thus be regarded as a ground for a charge of persecution through torture under the Rome Statute (Article 7(1)(h). This author contends further that *torture as part of a common plan* should be charged also as an act of genocide; specifically the 'genocidal forcible transfer of children', when it is perpetrated against children *in particular as a protected group* as is and was the case in Darfur as outlined in *Harun*.[23] The current author has argued elsewhere (see Grover (2013a), pp. 1–49 and (2013b)) that: (i) the notion of 'protected group' in respect of the genocide provisions of the Rome Statute and other treaty law is properly interpreted to include any identifiable group or collectivity targeted *as such* for genocide and that (ii) the examples of 'protected groups' listed at Article 6 of the Rome Statute are not an exhaustive list, nor intended to be, of potential protected groups targeted for genocide *as such* (as a group or collectivity)

References

Literature

Grover SC (2013a) Humanity's children: ICC jurisprudence and the failure to address the genocidal forcible transfer of children. Springer, Berlin

Grover SC (2013b) Child soldiers as victims of 'genocidal forcible transfer': Darfur and Syria as case examples. The International Journal of Human Rights 17(3):411–427

Cases

ICC information sheet Situation in the Democratic Republic of Congo in the Case of the Prosecutor v Sylvester Mudacamura ICC-01/04-01/12

The Situation in the Democratic Republic of Congo (2008) The Prosecutor v Germain Katanga and Mathieu Ngudjolo Chui Pre-Trial Chamber I Decision on the Confirmation of Charges 30 September, 2008 ICC-01/04-01/07

---

[21] Additional Protocols I and II to the 1949 Geneva Conventions (1977).

[22] Convention on the Rights of the Child (1990). Sudan is not a party to the CRC.

[23] Note that *torture* as a means of "the perpetrator caus[ing] serious bodily or mental harm to one or more persons" with the objective of *genocide* is mentioned at footnote 3 to Rome Statute Article 6(b). Genocide was a factor in Darfur and part of the *common plan* of the Al Bashir forces leading to targeting peoples also based on ethnicity as revealed by the facts in *Harun* regarding persecution of the Fur ethnic group.

The Prosecutor v. Ahmad Muhammad Harun ("Ahmad Harun") and Ali Muhammad Ali Abd-Al-Rahman ("Ali Kushayb") Pre-Trial Chamber I Warrant of Arrest for Ahmad Harun 27 April, 2007 ICC-02/05-01/07

Materials

Rome Statute Elements of the Crimes (2002) http://www.icc-cpi.int/NR/rdonlyres/9CAEE830-38CF-41D6-AB0B-68E5F9082543/0/Element_of_Crimes_English.pdf
Convention on the Rights of the Child (1990) (entry into force 2 September 1990) http://www.unicef.org/crc/Accessed 19 April, 2013
International Committee of the Red Cross (ICRC) (2013) Commentary on Protocol 1 additional to the 1949 Geneva conventions http://www.icrc.org/ihl/INTRO/470(1987). Accessed 20 May, 2013
Additional Protocol to the Geneva Conventions of 12 August 1949, and relating to the Protection of Victims of International Armed Conflicts (Protocol I), 8 June 1977. http://www.icrc.org/ihl.nsf/WebART/470-750099 Accessed 18 April, 2013

Chapter 4
Lessons From the Inter-American Court of Human Rights: Addressing Child Torture

Monica Feria Tinta, a human rights lawyer who has represented victims before the Inter-American Court of Human Rights (IACtHR) in several landmark cases, has noted in referencing The Gomez Paquiyaur case that the family members of torture victims have the right to know what happened to their loved ones where this is not the case and ***to have those facts acknowledged "for what they were***".[1] As Tinta points out; the prime rationale for bringing the cases involving child torture victims before the Inter-American Court of Human Rights:

> ...was the need to have the facts acknowledged for what they were, if one was to prevent this type of recurrent behavior from happening again: ''***no, this is not casual, incidental ill-treatment; this is torture*** (emphasis added)".[2]

In the Gomez Paquiyaur case the facts supported the conclusion that the child victims at issue were tortured and then murdered by agents of the Fujimori administration of Peru in 1991 and the Inter-American Court of Human Rights (IACtHR) found as such. The IACtHR has in such cases: (i) shone the light of international justice on *the torture of children in particular as part of a common plan* of certain authoritarian regimes; (ii) acknowledged the conduct perpetrated against the child victims in particular clearly as *torture* and (iii) as the Inter-American Court of Human Rights is mandated to address State obligations to uphold certain human rights guarantees; held the States involved accountable. In contrast the ICC, on the case analysis here, has generally *not* acknowledged the torture of children as particularized targets during armed conflict and has not held the individuals most responsible (as is *its* mandate) to account for that torture. We will consider next the Gomez Paquiyaur Brothers case concerning children targeted for the grave crimes of 'enforced disappearance' and 'torture' as part of a common plan and based on the perceived political affiliation of the children's parents and certain other relatives. This case is here considered in order to highlight that properly such enforced disappearance and torture of *children as particularized targets* ought be

---

[1] Tinta (2009), p. 120.

[2] Tinta (2009), p. 120.

S. C. Grover, *The Torture of Children During Armed Conflicts*,
DOI: 10.1007/978-3-642-40689-8_4, © Springer-Verlag Berlin Heidelberg 2014

treated as grave international crimes that *must* be acknowledged wherever part of the fact pattern. In fact it is here contended that the torture of children as high priority targets (torture committed via the enforced disappearance of the children and other acts such as physical torture) as part of a common plan ought not only to be charged by the ICC OTP as separate counts of the crime of torture[3] but to be considered also as an aggravating factor in sentencing in cases brought before the ICC.

The torture of children as particularized targets as a component of a common plan may, as mentioned previously, constitute a strategy for genocide, crimes against humanity and/or war crimes. Further; "[I]n situations of massive human rights violations, the systematic use of torture has as its aim the intimidation of entire populations" or of large identifiable segments of the civilian population and not just the infliction of suffering and pain on the direct individual victims.[4]

> **Modern torture is designed for political control of entire populations at once**-it is not any more primarily to get information, to punish, or to convert. Therefore, for torture to be effective, large numbers of victims are chosen, some even deliberately at random. People see that no one is safe… (emphasis added).[5]

What must also be recognized, however, is that, as the empirical evidence across armed conflict situations demonstrates, children become highly likely particularized targets of torture in a context where torture is being used as part of a common plan during armed conflict to intimidate an entire population or an identifiable segment of the population that is oppositional to the ruling authority or to a rival rebel group. This is the case since the children of a targeted group are inevitably highly valued by that victim group as the hope for the future and for cultural continuity. The torture of the targeted victim group's children inflicts a deep psychological wound that the perpetrator group hopes and feels confident will be an effective intimidation tactic.

We turn now then to the Gómez-Paquiyauri Brothers v. Peru case which has as its focus the torture of children as particularized targets acknowledged as central to the Peruvian perpetrator group common plan. Note that torture in this case and other similar cases before the IACtHR was held by the Court not only to involve: (i) the inflicting of severe pain and suffering on the individual child victims but to (ii) have functioned also as an attempt by the agents of the State to obliterate the personality of the child victims; the purpose being one of: (a) intimidation of a population and, as the current author understands it, (b) appropriation of the children's identity (even in death) to the perpetrator group.

---

[3] This as opposed, for instance, to the systematic and widespread torture of children in particular being subsumed under other charges such as attacks on civilians or the torturous conduct being misclassified as inhuman treatment or inhumane acts *not* rising to the level of torture.

[4] Tinta (2009), p. 128.

[5] Gray (1998) at p. 152.

4.1 Case of the Gómez-Paquiyauri Brothers v. Peru

The American Convention of Human Rights[6] violations attributed to the State of Peru in the Gómez-Paquiyauri brothers case (violations involving the torture and other fundamental human rights violations perpetrated against the brothers Emilio Moisés and Rafael Samuel Gómez Paquiyauri; respectively 14 and 17 years old) filed February 5, 2002 by the Inter-American Commission of Human Rights before the Inter-American Court of Human Rights were as follows:

> Articles 4 (Right to Life), 5 (Right to Humane Treatment), 7 (Right to Personal Liberty) and 19 (Rights of the Child) **for the alleged detention, *torture*, and extra-legal execution of the brothers Emilio Moisés and Rafael Samuel Gómez Paquiyauri,** as well as Articles 8 (Right to Fair Trial) and 25 (Right to Judicial Protection) of the American Convention...all the above in combination with the obligation set forth in Article 1(1) (Obligation to Respect Rights) of that same Convention. **Likewise, the Commission asked the Court to find that the State breached Articles 1, 6 and 8 of the Inter-American Convention to Prevent and Punish Torture (hereinafter "the Inter-American Convention against Torture)"** to the detriment of the Gómez Paquiyauri brothers. Finally, the Commission asked the Court to order the State to make a number of pecuniary and non-pecuniary reparations, as well as to pay the costs generated by processing of the case under domestic venue and before the Inter-American System (emphasis added).[7]

The Gomez-Paquiyauri children had been the victims of enforced disappearance and were tortured by agents of the authoritarian Peruvian State of the time because "they had been perceived by the State as children from a family [allegedly] with a history of "terrorist" connections and as such, "deserving" [in the view of the State] of the treatment to which they were subjected."[8]

Various sources of evidence regarding the torture of the Gómez Paquiyauri brothers were proffered including but not limited to:

> **Documentary Evidence**
> **Expert opinion of Bent Sorensen, a surgeon and an expert in treatment and prevention of torture**
>
> The expert headed the delegation of the United Nations Committee Against Torture (CAT) that visited Peru between August and September 1998 and he was responsible for drafting the report that was unanimously adopted by the members of the CAT. Said report found that torture, as defined in Article 1 of the United Nations Convention against Torture and other Cruel, Inhuman or Degrading Treatment or Punishment (hereinafter "the UN Convention against Torture"), was practiced systematically in the country, both by the Dirección Nacional Contra el Terrorismo, (hereinafter "DINCOTE"), and by the División de Investigación Criminal, DIVINCRI...
>
> Regarding to Rafael Samuel and Emilio Moisés Gómez Paquiyauri, he pointed out that the blows they received, as described in the significant photographs and documents, caused grave suffering and pain; the act was intentional, as the beating began when they were

---

[6] American Convention of Human Rights (entry into force 1978).

[7] Gómez-Paquiyauri Brothers v. Peru Judgement 8 July, 2004 at para 2.

[8] Tinta (2008), p. 154.

arrested; the purpose of the acts seemed to be that of investigating, but it may also have been to intimidate or coerce… **The expert witness stated his conclusion that "[t]here is no doubt that the two boys were tortured before they were murdered** (emphasis added)."

Regarding to Lucy Rosa Gómez Paquiyauri, sister of the alleged victims, the expert witness stated that **the mental suffering of a 15 year old girl, when she learned that her two brothers were tortured to death, is "obvious"**.The mental and physical torture caused during the interrogation and deprivations of liberty of Lucy Rosa, was inflicted intentionally by police and prison officers, with the aim of intimidating and "coercing" her. **As a conclusion, the expert witness stated that Lucy suffered physical and mental torture** (emphasis added).

Regarding to the rest of the surviving family, the expert witness stated that the significant documents describe in detail that the DINCOTE visited the home of the Gómez Paquiyauri family and interrogated the family many times over several years, and this caused them mental suffering. Said actions were intentionally carried out by the DINCOTE with the aim of intimidating or coercing. **The above led the expert witness to conclude that the whole family was mentally tortured** (emphasis added).[9]

[Selected] Testimony and Expert Opinion:

(a) **Testimony of Lucy Rosa Gómez Paquiyauri, sister of the alleged Victims**

The man took them [family members] to the hospital, where he told them that Rafael and Emilio were dead. They went to the room where the bodies were and saw that they were wet, full of dirt, soiled. Her brother Rafael "smelled of urine" and "had an expression of horrible pain." Their eyes were empty, there was encephalic mass on their hair, she could see that her brother Rafael's chest was full of holes, and that they were both filthy and full of dirt. At that time, she "fe[lt] that [her] life was falling apart." **Both bodies had a sign that said "NN [Unidentified], light build, olive-skinned, approximate age" 24 years on Emilio's card and 27 years on Rafael's, "arrived as a corpse** (emphasis added)".[10]

Note that the State had tried to conceal that the torture victims were minors by intentionally misidentifying the children; obvious minors (in fact aged 14 and 17); as adults at the hospital. The State was well aware of the gravity of the fundamental human rights violation of torture as a breach of a *jus cogens* norm and the exacerbating aspect that the victims were children.

(b) **Testimony of Marcelina Paquiyauri Illanes de Gómez, mother of the alleged victims**

Rafael and Emilio were dead, with their faces disfigured. Emilio's mouth was half open, his teeth full of dirt, his clothes full of dirt, wet, full of urine. She said that Rafael was the same, "his eyes empty," his thumb shot off, as if it had been cut but with a bullet wound and some skin still holding a piece of the "phalanx" and the palms of the hands also had holes, as if they had been burned.[11]

Rafael's body was identified as: "approximately 27, NN [unidentified], arrived as a corpse," and Emilio's as: "approximately 24 years old, unidentified, arrived as a corpse."

[9] Gómez-Paquiyauri Brothers v. Peru Judgement 8 July, 2004 at para 44.

[10] Gómez-Paquiyauri Brothers v. Peru Judgement 8 July, 2004 at para 49.

[11] Gómez-Paquiyauri Brothers v. Peru Judgement 8 July, 2004 at para 49.

Due to her desperation she [the mother of the child torture victims] began to scream and to ask why they gave them that age if they were children (emphasis added).[12]

(c) **Testimony of Ricardo Samuel Gómez Quispe, father of the alleged victims**

His sons, aged 14 and 17, were cruelly tortured and murdered. Rafael's body had a mark that said "NN [unidentified], 27 years old", and it was full of dirt, blood on his clothes, a broken finger on one of his hands, a piece of flesh dangling, and holes in both hands. Emilio's body said "24 years old." There were other corpses at that place in like conditions...The following day, he heard the names of his sons on a television report about a confrontation with the police, in which "three [alleged] terrorists" died (emphasis added).[13]

Note the State's attempt at dissemblance by claiming the children, who had no political affiliations themselves; and had not been involved in any political or opposition act against the regime that day or any other day, were "terrorists". These child torture victims were labelled by the media thus as anonymous 'terrorists'. It is in fact the case that States that perpetrate the torture of children in particular rarely if ever claim official recognition of the same. This though the public is generally well aware of State directed torture as a fact where it occurs. Clearly the State is cognizant of the abhorrent nature of torture and of the torture of children in particular. While non-State groups and forces frequently are also guilty of torture as the ICC cases here previously discussed attest, there is often a particular problem of acknowledgement of torture where the State is complicit. Further, the only recourse, though often in practice tragically non-feasible for various reasons in particular cases, may be to the international human rights courts or the ICC for instance with protection for witnesses and family members provided also through such an international court:

The involvement of an actor or actors of the state in torture is central to the problem... **The involvement of such actors [agents of the State] means that Governments do not 'officially' commit or ever publicly condone torture on adults let alone on children—no one admits to being a torturer. The very essence of [State] torture is secretive and hidden** (emphasis added).[14]

Indeed, often it is those who commit the violation that are charged with investigating the very crimes that they have committed. Even if the case reaches the courts, corruption, disorganisation and collusion with the perpetrators means that convictions are rare. Finally, in the climate of fear that pervades societies in which people's rights are systematically violated, survival is the first and most significant deterrent to any action.[15]

(d) **Testimony of Miguel Ángel Gómez Paquiyauri, brother of the alleged victims**

When the facts took place, on June 21, 1999, he was 8 years old... The event left its mark on the child and harmed him "a lot"; he had nightmares, he dreamt of them, and his

---

[12] Gómez-Paquiyauri Brothers v. Peru Judgement 8 July, 2004 at para 49.

[13] Gómez-Paquiyauri Brothers v. Peru Judgement 8 July, 2004 at para 49.

[14] Man (2000), p. 8. (In practice, however, in at least some instances, the State or non-State group perpetrating the torture of children in particular may wish to acknowledge torture in using tortured children as symbols of its power and control and as a means to intimidate the general populace as a whole or a more limited identifiable opposition).

[15] Man (2000), p. 8.

> nerves were in very bad shape. After he saw the bodies and the photographs, he felt deep grief, "I have no words to describe, it was something that truly hurt me deeply to see them like that." He felt that he was left practically alone, because Emilio and Rafael were the ones who defended him if something happened to him. If he needed something, Rafael, who was working, bought it for him, they were "like my parents [...] they cared for me as if they were my parents, and overnight I was left alone, with no one." **Regarding the memory of the event, the witness stated that he preferred "to bury it but it cannot be done, it is something that cannot be erased and is always going to be there if justice is not found** (emphasis added)."[16]
>
> **Expert opinion of Inge Genefke, a neurologist and an expert in treatment and prevention of torture.**
> The concept of a "**secondary victim**" refers to the closest members of the family who, after the torture episode, suffer and in fact have secondary consequences. **In this case, the family has suffered. The way they were shown the bodies, with no prior preparation, was a traumatic shock. Even today they are under the effects of that suffering. In this sense, the next of kin of the alleged victims may be called "secondary victims."** The authorities persecuted the family instead of helping them (emphasis added).[17]

What is evident from the testimony is that the effects of torture in terms of mental suffering is something that impacts the entire surviving family and is inter-generational as well. That trauma is compounded significantly when justice is not rendered in holding to account the individual perpetrators and the State whether the State was actively complicit in the torture through its agents as part of an intentional common plan or instead simply at fault due to the failure to protect arising from negligence or lack of will and/or lack of resources.

Note that Article 5 of the American Convention on Human Rights states:

> 1. Every person has the right to have his physical, mental, and moral integrity respected.
> 2. **No one shall be subjected to torture or to cruel, inhuman, or degrading punishment** or treatment. All persons deprived of their liberty shall be treated with respect for the inherent dignity of the human person.[...][18]

The failure of the State to acknowledge the torture of children as particularized victims where the facts in the case evidence the same would amount, on the view here, also to a violation of the following but not limited thereto: (i) *the Right to juridical personality* under the American Convention of Human Rights which states that: "Every person has a right to recognition as a person before the law" (Article 3)[19] and (ii) *the Right to Judicial Protection* under the American Convention of Human Rights which states that: "Everyone has the right to simple and prompt recourse, or any other effective recourse, to a competent court

---

[16] Gómez-Paquiyauri Brothers v. Peru Judgement 8 July, 2004 at para 49.

[17] Gómez-Paquiyauri Brothers v. Peru Judgement 8 July, 2004 at para 49.

[18] Gómez-Paquiyauri Brothers v. Peru Judgement 8 July, 2004 at para 104.

[19] This is to say that the failure of the State to acknowledge and prosecute the specific targeting of children for torture is in effect to dehumanize children before the law and hence to deny their juridical personality.

or tribunal for protection against acts that violate his fundamental human rights recognized by the constitution or laws of the State concerned, or by this Convention, even though such violations may have been committed by persons acting in the course of their official duties." (Article 25).[20]

Articles 1, 6 and 9 of the Inter-American Convention Against Torture[21] were also held by the petitioners violated in the Gómez-Paquiyauri Brothers case[22]:

> In the instant case of the Gómez Paquiyauri Brothers, the testimony of the next of kin of the two victims before this Court, and throughout the instant Judgment, concur in that when their bodies were found at the morgue, with a sign that read "unidentified", they were both wet, dirty, with their clothes full of dirt and blood, with an expression of "horrible pain," and their faces mangled; the eye sockets of both brothers were empty, and there was encephalic mass on their hair; one of them (Rafael) was missing a thumb, which had been shot off, and the palms had holes in them, as if they had been burned; the other deceased brother's mouth (Emilio's) was half-open, his teeth full of dirt. One of the surviving brothers (MiguelÁngel Gómez Paquiyauri) stated before the Inter-American Court that "he had no words to describe" what he saw. **The father of the two youths (Ricardo Samuel Gómez Paquiyauri) added that "his children, 14 and 17 years old, were cruelly tortured and murdered** (emphasis added)."[23]

> In the instant Judgment in the case of the Gómez Paquiyauri Brothers, the Court has, in short, found that **one of the proven facts is that "At the morgue the bodies of Rafael Samuel and Emilio Moisés Gómez Paquiyauri were full of blood and dirt, wet, dirty; there was encephalic mass on their hair, and one of Emilio's fingers was missing. In both of them, the eyes were missing" (para. 67(j))** (emphasis added).[24]

The IACtHR made reference in *Gómez-Paquiyauri Brothers* to the finding of the European Court of Human Rights in *Ireland v. the United Kingdom* that a legal characterization of *torture depends on all the circumstances of the case including age of the victims*:

> ... **analysis of the gravity of the acts that may constitute cruel, inhumane or degrading treatment or *torture*, is relative and depends on all the circumstances of the case, such as** duration of the treatment, its physical and mental effects and, in some cases, the sex, **age,** and health of the victim, among others (emphasis added).[25]

---

[20] This is to say that the failure of the State to acknowledge and prosecute the particularized torture of children as part of a common plan in a context of armed conflict is to deny the surviving child torture victims, if any, and the immediate family members a judicial remedy and to, hence, deny symbolically as well the deceased child torture victims', if any, the right to protection.

[21] Inter-American Convention Against Torture (entry into force 28 February, 1987).

[22] Gómez-Paquiyauri Brothers v. Peru Judgement 8 July, 2004 at para 105.

[23] Separate Opinion of Judge Antônio Augusto Cançado Trindade IACtHR Gómez-Paquiyauri Brothers v. Peru Judgement 8 July, 2004 at para 3.

[24] Separate Opinion of Judge Antônio Augusto Cançado Trindade IACtHR Gómez-Paquiyauri Brothers v. Peru Judgement 8 July, 2004 at para 9.

[25] Gómez-Paquiyauri Brothers v. Peru Judgement 8 July, 2004 at para 113 (referencing European Court of Human Rights Case: Ireland v. the United Kingdom, Judgment of 18 January 1978, Series A No. 25, para. 162).

The Inter-American Court of Human Rights in *Gómez-Paquiyauri Brothers* gave special consideration to the fact that the victims of the torture in the case were children (minors):

> ... **the Court deems that as a whole the facts that have been pointed out, taking especially into account that the alleged victims were minors, constitute evident signs of torture,**[26] in light of the definition in Article 2 of the Inter-American Convention against Torture, in violation of Article 5 of the American Convention, in combination with Article 1(1) of this same Convention, and of the obligations set forth in Articles 1, 6 and 9 of the Inter-American Convention against Torture, to the detriment of Rafael Samuel and Emilio Moisés Gómez Paquiyauri (emphasis added).[27]
>
> Also, as the Court analyzed the matter in the chapter on abridgment of Article 5 of the Convention and the provisions of the Inter-American Convention against Torture ... **the fact that the alleged victims were children requires applying the highest standard in determining the seriousness of actions that violate their right to humane treatment** (emphasis added).[28]

The Inter-American Court of Human Rights (IACtHR) also considered and found that the immediate surviving family members were indirect victims of the State torture of Rafael Samuel and Emilio Moisés Gómez Paquiyauri:

> All this generated suffering and powerlessness of their immediate next of kin vis-à-vis the State authorities, for which reason, in this case, **the next of kin can be considered the victims of cruel, inhumane and degrading treatment**, in violation of Article 5 of the American Convention (emphasis added).[29]

The IACtHR also found that there had been absolute impunity for those responsible for the torture of the children; Rafael Samuel and Emilio Moisés Gómez Paquiyauri.[30] There was, among other IACtHR holdings in the case, a finding that Article 19 of the American Convention on Human Rights was violated which article reads as follows:

> **Article 19. Rights of the Child**
> Every minor child has the right to the measures of protection required by his condition as a minor on the part of his family, society, and the state.[31]

On the issue of the torture victims in the case being children; the Inter-American Court held as follows:

> ***Rafael Samuel and Emilio Moisés Gómez Paquiyauri were children, respectively 14 and 17 years old, when they were unlawfully and arbitrarily detained, tortured, and***

---

[26] Recall that the threshold for pain and suffering is generally lower for children than for healthy adults and hence children's suffering and pain may be more readily legally characterized as torture depending on all the circumstances.

[27] Gómez-Paquiyauri Brothers v. Peru Judgement 8 July, 2004 at para 117.

[28] Gómez-Paquiyauri Brothers v. Peru Judgement 8 July, 2004 at para 170.

[29] Gómez-Paquiyauri Brothers v. Peru Judgement 8 July, 2004 at paras 118.

[30] Gómez-Paquiyauri Brothers v. Peru Judgement 8 July, 2004 at para 147-148.

[31] Gómez-Paquiyauri Brothers v. Peru Judgement 8 July, 2004 at para 160.

> ***extra-legally executed by agents of the Peruvian National Police. The Court deems that cases in which the victims of human rights are children are especially grave***, as their rights are reflected not only in the American Convention, but also in numerous international instruments, broadly accepted by the international community -notably in the United Nations' Convention on the Rights of the Child that "establish the duty of the State to adopt special protection and assistance measures in favor of children under their jurisdiction" (emphasis added).[32]
>
> Regarding the matter of protecting the rights of the child and adopting measures to attain said protection, **the principle of the best interests of the child prevails, based "on the very dignity of the human being, on the characteristics of children themselves, and on the need to foster their development, making full use of their potential"** (emphasis added).[33]
>
> **Compulsory Law (Jus Cogens) and the Establishment of the Aggravated International Responsibility of the State**
>
> It is highly significant that, in establishing the international responsibility of the State in the instant case of the Gómez Paquiyauri brothers, the Inter-American Court, when it found that Articles 5 and 4 of the American Convention were breached, explicitly recognized that an international juridical system of absolute prohibition of all forms of torture and extra-legal executions has been constituted in our day, and it is now part of the sphere of international jus cogens (paras. 111–112 and 128, respectively). **Therefore, there is an aggravated international responsibility (for the wrongful acts committed and the persons murdered, two children), with direct consequences regarding reparations** (emphasis added).[34]

It is here contended that the *rights of the child in particular* underlie several of the Rome Statute provisions[35] and can be properly held to apply also to those Rome Statute provisions concerning *torture*. For instance; the rights of the child in relation to ICC prosecution of torture are respected when (i) the legal characterization of torture in cases with child victims takes into account that the threshold for pain and suffering (psychological and physical) is lower for children than for healthy adults not of advanced age and that (ii) the torture of children should be considered an aggravating factor in sentencing given the special protection entitlements of children under international law (which protections exceed those of adult civilians).

---

[32] Gómez-Paquiyauri Brothers v. Peru Judgement 8 July, 2004 at para 162.

[33] Gómez-Paquiyauri Brothers v. Peru Judgement 8 July, 2004 at para 163.

[34] Separate Opinion of Judge Antônio Augusto Cançado Trindade IACtHR Gómez-Paquiyauri Brothers v. Peru Judgement 8 July, 2004 at para 37.

[35] For example; the following Rome Statute articles explicitly refer to children: Article 6 (e) Forcibly transferring children of the group to another group. Article 8 (2)(b) (xxvi) Conscripting or enlisting children under the age of fifteen years into the national armed forces or using them to participate actively in hostilities. Article 8 (2)(e)(vii) Conscripting or enlisting children under the age of fifteen years into armed forces or groups or using them to participate actively in hostilities.

Further; in that the Rome Statute is part of a broader corpus of international law that in part emphasizes the fundamental rights of the child; the Rome Statute must also be interpreted with that context in mind in cases involving direct child victims (the latter victims being a segment of or the totality of the victim group at issue). Recall in this regard Article 21 of the Rome Statute which states:

Rome Statute Article 21
Applicable law

1. The Court shall apply:
(a) In the first place, this Statute, Elements of Crimes and its Rules of Procedure and Evidence;
(b) **In the second place, where appropriate, applicable treaties and the principles and rules of international law, including the established principles of the international law of armed conflict;**
(c) Failing that, general principles of law derived by the Court from national laws of legal systems of the world including, as appropriate, the national laws of States that would normally exercise jurisdiction over the crime, provided that those principles are not inconsistent with this Statute and with international law and internationally recognized norms and standards.
2. The Court may apply principles and rules of law as interpreted in its previous decisions.
3. ***The application and interpretation of law pursuant to this article must be consistent with internationally recognized human rights, and be without any adverse distinction founded on grounds such as*** gender as defined in article 7, paragraph 3, age, race, colour, language, religion or belief, political or other opinion, national, ethnic or social origin, wealth, birth or other status (emphasis added).[36]

Schabas has commented, and the current author concurs, that while the Rome Statute Elements of the Crimes are key to interpretation of the Statute; they are not the only guide and "In practice, all of the sources listed in article 21 [of the Rome Statute] will be helpful to the Court in its effort to interpret the Statute."[37] It must be recalled that the Elements of the Crimes according to Article 9 of the Rome Statute ***assist*** the Court in interpretation.[38] However, there may still be lacuna in the Statute that may be properly filled in respect of interpretation by considering also other international law

Rome Statute Article 21 thus mandates, in part, that interpretation and application of the provisions of the Rome Statute (such as those that concern torture) be: (i) "consistent with internationally recognized human rights", (ii) "be without any adverse distinction founded on gender…***age***, race, colour, language, religion or

[36] Rome Statute (2002).
[37] Schabas (2010), p. 385.
[38] Rome Statute (2002).

belief, political or other opinion,[39] national, ethnic or social origin, wealth, birth or other status" or any other potential grounds of adverse distinction and (iii) where relevant be consistent with the international law of armed conflict. Hence, the failure to even charge torture and apply the Rome Statute to the facts of torture where children are the particularized targets of torture as part of a common plan during armed conflict (as has occurred, on the view here, with certain ICC cases such as in *Kony* and *Lubanga)* is *not* consistent with the requirements of Rome Statute Article 21. Those aforementioned requirements of Rome Statute Article 21 are that the Statute not be interpreted or applied with any adverse distinction in regards to age (i.e. including young age). The same can be said in regards to the failure to consider as an *aggravating factor* the fact of there being child victims of torture (i.e. amongst the general group of direct victims of torture in a particular ICC case).

The contention here further is that Rome Statute Article 21 requires that where children in particular are targeted for torture; interpretation and application of the Rome Statute to the facts of the case must be consistent with relevant treaty law and international human rights principles (such as the relevant provisions of the Convention on the Rights of the Child). This is the case in practice in that consideration of this broader context of children's fundamental human rights in international law facilitates the ICC Chamber addressing in its case analysis: (i) the *special protected status of children* under international humanitarian and human rights law and ICL (that special protected status of children arguably reflecting a *jus cogens* norm that children are not to be intentionally targeted for harms during armed conflict as part of a common plan) and (ii) the implications for the findings of the ICC Chamber of the fact that children were particularized targets for torture as part of a common plan. Given such a children's human rights international law perspective in combination with the international criminal law perspective of the Rome Statute; the ICC would, it is here contended, be more likely then to find: (i) perpetrator treatment of the child victims that involved inflicting severe pain, suffering (and perhaps also injury) *amounted to torture*; (ii) the perpetrators most responsible knew or should have known that they were implementing a common plan that included perpetrating *torture* on children; the latter being a *manifestly unlawful* act and one that is in contravention of international law (including the Rome Statute) and iii) the fact that the direct victims of torture included children (or were completely comprised of children) is an aggravating factor in sentencing potentially justifying a more severe sentence than would otherwise have been

[39] Note that children are often prioritized by the perpetrator group as victim targets for torture as part of a common plan during armed conflict because of their parents' political affiliation. Yet this aspect of torture as part of a common plan and its implications for the case analysis (i.e. determining that the torture of the children served the purpose of suppressing a political opposition and hence may have been a war crime) has not to date been dealt with by the ICC in cases it has considered where children were the victims of torture.

imposed. Consider then, as examples, two selected provisions of the Convention on the Rights of the Child (CRC) relevant in regard to interpretation and application of the Rome Statute in respect of torture as a war crime or as a crime against humanity where some, most, or all of the direct torture victims in the ICC case at bar are children:

Convention on the Rights of the Child
Article 37
States Parties shall ensure that:

(a) ***No child* shall be subjected to *torture* or other cruel, inhuman or degrading treatment or punishment** (emphasis added).[40]

Convention on the Rights of the Child
Article 2

1. States Parties shall respect and ensure the rights set forth in the present Convention to each child within their jurisdiction without discrimination of any kind, irrespective of the child's or his or her parent's or legal guardian's race, colour, sex, language, religion, political or other opinion, national, ethnic or social origin, property, disability, birth or other status.
2. **States Parties shall take all appropriate measures to ensure that the child is protected against all forms of discrimination or punishment on the basis of the status, activities, expressed opinions, or beliefs of the child's parents, legal guardians, or family members** (emphasis added).[41]

The above CRC provisions highlight the fact that: (i) the torture of children as particularized targets is a grave human rights violation under international law including the CRC and that (ii) children often are targeted for torture as a form of 'punishment' [of others through their-the children's- suffering) due to the status or political or other affiliations of the parents, legal guardians or family members of the targeted children.

Note that the Convention on the Rights of the Child (CRC) stipulates at Article one that 'child' refers to persons under age 18 "unless under the [domestic] law applicable to the child, majority is attained earlier."[42] Hence technically the CRC provides rights and protections-for instance protection against torture- only to persons considered as minor children domestically under the applicable national law.[43] However, at the same time, the *jus cogens* prohibition in international law against torture is part of international customary law and applies as well to persons who are under 18 but yet may be considered under national law in certain domains to have attained the age of majority (as that *jus cogens* prohibition pertains also to victimizing persons 18 and over through torture). Hence the CRC is contradictory

[40] Convention on the Rights of the Child (1990).

[41] Convention on the Rights of the Child (1990).

[42] Convention on the Rights of the Child (1990).

[43] Many States, however, do consider 18 to be the age of majority in many if not most respects such as in regard to eligibility to vote in local, regional or national governmental elections.

in some ways since, for instance, it includes an ***age limited*** *provision against torture* (at Article 37 of the CRC read in conjunction with Article 1 of the CRC) which prohibition under ICL, international humanitarian, *other* human rights law and international criminal law is applicable regardless the age of the victim. The latter then implying also a State obligation to protect, among others, all persons under age 18 against torture.

Article one of the CRC then defers to the domestic law in defining who is a 'child' and thus does not extend the protections and rights *of the CRC* (i.e. the right of the child to be protected against torture) to persons under age 18 who are not defined as 'children' domestically under the applicable national law. Article one of the CRC, insofar as it does not stipulate that all human beings under age 18 are defined as 'children' under the Convention (the CRC), is thus highly problematic. The CRC—though it is a specialized international legal instrument entirely focused on the rights and freedoms of the child—potentially offers no protection against torture to some persons under 18; namely those *not* defined as 'children' domestically under the applicable law. In this respect then the CRC offers *less* protection to 'children' regarding one of the bedrock rights of international law-the right to be protected against torture—than do other international legal instruments such as the Convention Against Torture (CAT) that involve no age limitations regarding who can be considered a *child* torture victim under that Convention.[44]

The situation arises, however, that due to the specific terms of the CAT (the element that a State official or someone acting in an official capacity inflicted the torture); that often children, particularly young children, are *erroneously* not conceptualized in the international public consciousness as amongst the likely potential torture victims that the CAT is intended to protect.[45] Further obscuring

[44] Convention against Torture and Other Cruel, Inhuman or Degrading Treatment or Punishment (the "Torture Convention") (entry into force 26 June, 1987).

[45] The UN Committee Against Torture has, on occasion, however, addressed the violation of the CAT rights of children in some of its responses to State reports on alleged compliance with the CAT (entry into force 26 June, 1987) and in consideration, for instance, of certain individual complaints (an example of the latter is mention of the psychological suffering of the young daughter of Armenian parents who were tortured by the National Security Service in Azerbaijan after being deported to Azerbaijan from Sweden having been being refused asylum in Sweden (see Committee Against Torture, Communication No. 374/2009 Decision of 25 November, 2011). In that case, however, the teen daughter was ultimately granted a residential permit by Sweden and hence the complaint filed on behalf of the daughter in the original communication was discontinued by the Committee. The complaints of the parents against Sweden were found by the Committee to be meritorious based on the fact that the family had been deported from Sweden despite the considerable risk that they would be tortured in Azerbaijan).

the reality of children as high priority targets for torture by perpetrator groups is the fact that violations of the CAT most often involve persons who have been tortured for: (i) political reasons that relate to the victims' *direct* political involvement; and/or (ii) the purpose of extracting a confession or information; and/or (iii) the purpose of intimidation or coercion of others also directly involved in the opposition; and/or (iv) some discriminatory reason such as furthering ethnic cleansing (in the latter case the focus is generally more so on a targeted ethnic civilian group *per se* rather than on the particularized targeting of children within that group for torture). Children most often are *not* conceived of as *political activists*[46] and hence are generally mistakenly not considered by the international community as actually being *likely high priority targets for torture* by a perpetrator group in violation of the CAT. The occurrence and scope of the problem of children as particularized high priority targets for torture as a tactic of intimidation and coercion in respect of the larger group to which the children's parents or other kin belong (i.e. a political opposition) is something which the international community has in fact been very slow to fully acknowledge and address if it has done so at all.

Consider now that: (i) the recruitment and use of persons *under age 18* for 'soldiering'[47] in the midst of mass atrocities can be viewed as a form of the *torture of children* (i.e. by having child soldiers live in constant fear, endure brutalization by commanders, be forced to witness and commit atrocities etc.) and, as such, (ii) lead to a charge under the Rome Statute of the war crime or crime against humanity of torture. The latter approach, it is here contended, is consistent with the International Committee of the Red Cross (ICRC) position in its commentaries that the "special respect and care" that children are entitled to under Additional Protocols I and II to the 1949 Geneva Conventions during armed conflict is *not* to be considered restricted to only under 15s. This was the ICRC position though the Committee acknowledged that it was unable, despite its vigorous efforts, to extend in Additional Protocols 1 and II to the 1949 Geneva Conventions the prohibition on recruitment and use of children for

[46] The current author considers that children (persons under age 18) appropriated as child soldiers by a group such as the LRA which group is perpetrating mass atrocities are the victims of 'genocidal forcible transfer' regardless the mode of 'recruitment' or any professed allegiance of the child victims to the perpetrator group. These children, on the view here, retain their civilian status and can by no means be considered as political activists. This is not at all to negate the fact that children have been and continue to be social rights/political activists in other contexts (i.e. children were major contributors to the anti-apartheid movement in South Africa).

[47] Recall that the current author holds that perpetrator groups, whether State or non-State, committing mass atrocities are *not* functioning as 'soldiers' as that term is understood under international law and military law and hence any child member of such a group (essentially a criminal organization) is not in any sense under international law a (child) 'soldier'.

participation in hostilities to cover all persons under age 18 and not just under 15s as certain States resisted.[48]

On the above analysis then the charge under the Rome Statute of *torture* (i.e. through using children for 'soldiering' with a perpetrator group committing mass atrocities and/or genocide) where the children were *under 15* would be an *additional charge* to that relating to the Rome Statute offence of recruitment and use of children under age 15 for active participation in the armed hostilities. However; for children 15 and over but under 18 subjected to torture through soldiering with a perpetrator group committing mass atrocities and/or genocide; the charge of torture would stand alone in respect of the aforementioned facts (since the Rome Statute offence of recruitment and use of children for active participation in hostilities applies only to under 15s). In respect of a Rome Statute charge of torture of 'children' (persons under age 18) through 'soldiering' (that is child soldiering with a perpetrator group committing mass atrocities and/or genocide) the fact that these persons were children at the relevant time could then also be considered an aggravating factor for sentencing purposes (regardless whether all the children were under 15 or some or all were 15 and over but under 18). Note that persons under age 18 are considered 'children' under the Rome Statute as is evidenced by the fact that under the Rome Statute **general principles of law** the ICC has no jurisdiction over persons aged under 18.[49]

As we have seen; the ICC *in practice* to date in its case judgments has not given special consideration to the targeting for ***torture of children in particular*** and, in this way, has inadvertently undermined the notion of children's right to special protection during armed conflict (as per, for instance, international customary and humanitarian treaty law). This though the special protection entitlement

---

[48] Article 77 of Protocol I Additional to the 1949 Geneva Conventions (1977) states at paragraph one: "Children shall be the object of special respect … The Parties to the conflict shall provide them with the care and aid they require, whether because of their age or for any other reason." Note that no age is specified for the term "child." The ICRC commentary in regards to paragraph one and four of Article 77 of Protocol I in part states: "The word "children" is not clarified in any way, and this omission is intentional. The Rapporteur said: "**It should also be noted that the Committee [the ICRC] decided not to place specific age limits in paragraphs 1 and 4 and that there is no precise definition of the term children**" (emphasis added). (International Committee of the Red Cross Commentary on Protocol I additional to the 1949 Geneva Conventions (1987)) Article 4 of Protocol II Additional to the 1949 Geneva Conventions (1977) reads in part:" Children shall be provided with the care and aid they require…" The ICRC commentary on Article 4 reads in part: "**The Conference intentionally did not give a precise definition of the term "child"**… ***It is important not to exclude the possibility that aid is required by children over the age of fifteen… The fact of having been recruited does not in itself automatically deprive a child of the aid required by his age***. As regards judicial proceedings, it must be recalled that the death penalty for an offence related to the conflict cannot be pronounced on a person under the age of 18 years, in accordance with the provisions of Article 6 '(Penal prosecutions),' paragraph 4, of the Protocol (emphasis added)." (ICRC comentaries available at:http://www.icrc.org/applic/ihl/ihl.nsf/vwTreatiesByTopics.xsp)

[49] For a discussion on this issue see, for instance, Grover (2012), pp. 76–79. Note that the Rome Statute exclusion of persons under age 18 from criminal responsibility is not just a jurisdictional matter but rather a principle of general law under the Statute.

of children during armed conflict has, in certain ICC cases, been raised by the ICC OTP, victims' representatives and expert witnesses including UN officials. Charges relating to ***torture*** (*perpetrated against children in particular*) have not been laid by the ICC Prosecutor as separate charges apart from charges relating to the child-specific Rome Statute offence of perpetrating child soldiering (see for instance the *Lubanga* and *Kony* cases). The fact that the threshold for suffering and pain is lower for children than healthy adults has not then been considered by the ICC in making determinations about children as potential victims of torture in various forms (through child soldiering, sexual enslavement, rape and other sexual victimization etc.) in any particular ICC case.

In other instances the torture of children in particular has not been addressed directly in any substantive way but rather subsumed under charges such as cruel treatment, and/or inhumane and degrading treatment and/or torture of civilian victims in general. The torture of children as particularized targets has hence not either been considered by the ICC as an aggravating factor in sentencing for any charge such as attacks on civilians or persecution of a targeted civilian group and other grave crimes perpetrated against civilians. Rape and other forms of sexual violence committed against children as perpetrator targeted high priority victims has also not been charged by the ICC Prosecutor as torture. Further the recruitment and use of children in armed conflict by perpetrators of mass atrocities and/or genocide has not also been charged as torture (nor has this been the case either with various other crimes under the Rome Statute such as enforced disappearance of children as prioritized targets which it is here contended constitute torture). **It is here argued that in fact there is, at present, an ongoing adverse distinction based on age in the ICC interpretation and application of the Rome Statute crime of torture** which is reflected in the :(i) reluctance to charge torture of children as particularized targets even where the evidence supports such a charge; (ii) the failure to consider torture of children as an aggravating factor in sentencing notwithstanding, for instance, children's right to special protection during armed conflict under international customary and treaty law and (iii) the failure to recognize *also* as torture various systematic and widespread grave crimes committed by a perpetrator group against children as high priority particularized targets (i.e. enforced disappearance of children, rape and other sexual violence against children, recruitment of children into a perpetrator group to participate in mass atrocities etc.).

By not charging *torture* (in addition to other applicable charges) where children are particularized targets of torture in various forms (i.e. child soldiering, sexual enslavement, forced disappearance etc.), the ICC is not in fact fully considering customary law as arguably encoded in Protocol I and II Additional to the 1949 Geneva Conventions which requires recognition of the special protections to which children have a right. That right certainly includes the right to be protected from torture. Not classifying, for instance, child soldiering and sexual enslavement of children as *torture* (as well as charging under Rome Statute provisions dealing with sexual violence and child soldiering) undermines children's special protection rights especially for older children under age 18 but 15 or over[50] where perpetrators will typically make claims that the children consented to becoming a child soldier or providing sexual "services".[51] The latter when in fact the oppressive overall circumstances of armed conflict and the threats that such perpetrator groups perpetrating mass atrocities and/or genocide pose make untenable the notion of children of any age giving truly informed voluntary consent. Further, the failure to recognize children as particularized targets of torture, respectfully on the view here, is a reflection of the ICC OTP and ICC Chambers' disregard of relevant other international law treaties such as the Convention on the Rights of the Child (CRC). The CRC for instance stipulates at Articles 2 and 37, as mentioned, the child's right to be protected from harms such as torture directed against the child based on the perceived political affiliation or social activism of the children's parents or legal guardians. In fact in many of the ICC cases involving the torture of children as part of the fact pattern; the children in particular were targeted for various forms of torture as a very deliberate strategy and based on the parent's perceived political alliances.

References

Gray G (1998) Treatment of survivors of political torture: Administrative and clinical issues. J Ambul Care Manag 2(21):39–42. (Cited in Tinta MF (2008) The landmark rulings of the Inter-American Court of Human Rights on the rights of the child. Martinus Nijhoff Publishers, Leiden)

Man N (2000) Children, torture and power: The torture of children by States and opposition groups (A Save the Children report) http://www.savethechildren.org.uk/sites/default/files/docs/Children-Torture-Power.pdf Accessed 23 April 2013

Tinta MF (2008). The landmark rulings of the Inter-American Court of Human Rights on the rights of the child. Martinus Nijhoff Publishers, Leiden

Tinta MF (2009) Legal consequences for torture in children cases: the Gomez Paquiyauri brothers v Peru case. Torture 19(2):118–131

Schabas WA (2010) Oxford commentaries on international law. The international criminal court: a commentary on the Rome Statute. Oxford University Press, Oxford

[50] Children aged 15 and over are not protected by the Rome Statute war crimes provisions prohibiting the recruitment and use for active participation in hostilities of only persons **under 15** for active participation in hostilities.

[51] On the view here (i) children under 15 in international customary law cannot consent to child soldiering with; or sexual victimization by; a perpetrator group committing grave international crimes and (ii) children 15 and over cannot be considered to have consented- even where there is so-called alleged 'voluntary' recruitment for child soldiering and/or for sexual slavery—given the oppressive circumstances of a context of mass atrocities and the potential consequences for themselves and their families in showing resistance to the child soldiering recruitment campaigns of perpetrator groups committing mass atrocities and/or genocide. In any case; no person of any age can be considered in law to have consented to sexual slavery/enslavement.

Materials

American Convention on Human Rights entry into force (1978) http://www.oas.org/dil/treaties_B-32_American_Convention_on_Human_Rights.htm. Accessed 10 May 2013 BBC News Syria crisis: Obama warns Assad over chemical weapons ww.bbc.co.uk/news/world-middle-east-20583966 Accessed 19 April 2013

Convention against Torture and Other Cruel, Inhuman or Degrading Treatment or Punishment (the "Torture Convention") (CAT) (1987) (entry into force 26 June, 1987) http://www.hrweb.org/legal/cat.html Accessed 18 June 2013

Convention on the Rights of the Child (1990) (entry into force 2 September 1990) http://www.ohchr.org/EN/ProfessionalInterest/Pages/CRC.aspx Accessed 19 April 2013

International Committee of the Red Cross (ICRC) (1987) Commentary on Protocol 1 additional to the 1949 Geneva Conventions http://www.icrc.org/ihl/INTRO/470 Accessed 20 May 2013

Cases

United Nations Committee Against Torture (2011) Communication No. 374/2009 Decision of 25 November, 2011 (CAT/C/47/D/374/2009) http://www.bayefsky.com/pdf/sweden_t5_cat_374_2009.pdf Accessed 8 July 2013

European Court of Human Rights Case (1978) Ireland v. the United Kingdom, Judgment of 18 January 1978, Series A No. 25

Inter-American Court of Human Rights (IACtHR) (2013) Gómez-Paquiyauri Brothers v. Peru Judgement 8 July, 2004 http://www.corteidh.or.cr/docs/casos/articulos/seriec_110_ing.pdf Accessed 10 May 2013

Chapter 5
The Enforced Disappearance of Children as Torture

5.1 Introduction

> The last several decades have witnessed a dramatic change in the methods of warfare. Civilians are now increasingly targets of violence, not just simply victims of collateral damage. **Among civilians targeted, children and youth are subject to acts of violence, including enforced disappearances and enforced conscription. Children have been forcibly disappeared and forcibly conscripted in many countries** including Argentina, El Salvador and northern Uganda (emphasis added).[1]

The 'enforced disappearance' of *children as particularized targets* is a common form of *torture* used by both State and non-State political and military organizations during armed conflict (internal conflict or conflict also with international dimensions). 'Enforced disappearance' is set out as a crime against humanity in the Rome Statute when carried out in a systematic or widespread manner. Often that 'enforced disappearance' has resulted from the children's abduction and use as a child soldiers and/or sex slaves and child soldiering charges may have been brought as in *Lubanga* for instance.[2] The 'enforced disappearance' of children, it is here argued, is torture under the Rome Statute and must be considered as such in addition to being classed as 'enforced disappearance' *per se*. This is the case in that torture, as the Inter-American Convention to Prevent and Punish Torture,[3] acknowledges at Article 2 not only inflicts great physical and/or mental pain and/or suffering but also seeks to

---

[1] Harvey-Blankenship et al. (2010), p. 1.

[2] Lubanga's FPLC was the military wing of a political entity the UPC "Enforced disappearance of persons" [as the term is used in the Rome Statute] means "the arrest, detention or abduction of persons by, or with the authorization, support or acquiescence of, a State or a political organization, followed by a refusal to acknowledge that deprivation of freedom or to give information on the fate or whereabouts of those persons, with the intention of removing them from the protection of the law for a prolonged period of time." (Article 7(1)(i) Rome Statute 2002).

[3] Inter-American Convention to Prevent and Punish Torture (28 Feb 1987).

S. C. Grover, *The Torture of Children During Armed Conflicts*,
DOI: 10.1007/978-3-642-40689-8_5, © Springer-Verlag Berlin Heidelberg 2014

obliterate the personality of the victim. Certainly the 'enforced disappearance' of children accomplishes all of these torture objectives as well as serving the purpose of intimidating the general populace or a targeted segment thereof:

> Enforced disappearances result in severe secondary harm to children, such as the loss of identity including nationality, name and family relations.[4]

Not only the child victims but their families suffer incredible mental harms amounting to psychological torture due to the enforced disappearance of the children. Not uncommonly; children forcibly disappeared are subjected to grave physical harms as well as was evidenced for instance in the Kony case with LRA child soldiers. Often it seems there is little hope of recovery of the disappeared children when the family is reliant on the very groups or institutions that were complicit in the 'enforced disappearance' in the first instance.[5] Family reunification upon recovery of the disappeared children may be difficult due to estrangement issues on the part of the children and/or the families and the home communities. Due to custody issues where the child is still a minor upon recovery, reunification may be considerably delayed causing even more psychological suffering for the children and/or their family members as such matters are sorted.[6]

'Enforced disappearance', like other forms of torture, may not be publicly acknowledged by the State or non-State group responsible though there is generally a silent understanding by the populace that the perpetrator group is responsible for the forced disappearance of the child victims. Often the disappeared are never recovered and there is no knowledge of whether the victim is alive or dead:

> **Forced disappearance is characterized, among other matters, by creating a situation of overwhelming uncertainty about whether the victim is alive or dead**; in other words, about whether he continues or has ceased to exist. This situation arises from the fact that the authors of the disappearance, not only cut off all forms of communication between the person who has disappeared and the society to which he belongs, but also eliminate any trace or information, about either the survival or death of the person in question (except for the mere passage of time as a growing sign of the probability that the victim is dead). In other words, the abductors create a state of uncertainty about the existence of the person who has disappeared (emphasis added).[7]

Forced disappearances of children where the children have been abducted to serve as child soldiers and/or sex slaves most often involve also the cutting off completely of the children's ties with their families and communities. Further, these child victims many times are sent to areas far from home to hot conflict zones within the jurisdiction (or in an international conflict; even to hot spots in neighbouring States).

---

[4] Harvey-Blankenship et al. (2010), p. 2.

[5] Harvey-Blankenship et al. (2010), p. 2.

[6] Harvey-Blankenship et al. (2010), p. 2.

[7] IACtHR Case of Bámaca-Velásquez v. Guatemala Judgment of November 25, 2000 Separate Opinion of Judge De Roux Rengifo, p. 1.

It has been argued that enforced disappearance where the families do not know the fate of their loved one(s); and are not given access to the remains where the victim is deceased; violates the right to truth for society as a whole:

> the right to truth applies ultimately also as a sign of respect for the dead and the living. The hiding of the mortal remains of a disappeared person, in a flagrant lack of respect to them, threatens to disrupt the spiritual bond which links the dead to the living, and attempts against the solidarity which ought to guide the paths of the human kind ...[8]

> **the right to truth is essential to the struggle against impunity, and is ineluctably linked to the very realization of justice, and to the guarantee of non-repetition of those violations** (emphasis added).[9]

Further 'enforced disappearance' as a form of psychological torture functions to reinforce that one is not protected by the rule of law such as may be alleged to exist in the particular context in which the enforced disappearance took place :

> **The forced disappearance of a person victimizes likewise his close relatives (at times disrupting the family nucleus itself), not only for the intense suffering and the desperation ensuing therefrom, but also from substract [of] all from the protecting shield of Law** (emphasis added).[10]

> **In its final arguments, the Commission alleged that, as a result of the disappearance of Bámaca Velásquez, the State violated the right to the truth of the next of kin of the victim and of society as a whole.** In this respect, the Commission declared that the right to the truth has a collective nature, which includes the right of society to "have access to essential information for the development of democratic systems", and a particular nature, as the right of the victims' next of kin to know what happened to their loved ones, which permits a form of reparation. The Inter-American Court has established the obligation of the State to investigate the facts while there is uncertainty about the fate of the person who has disappeared, and the need to provide a simple and prompt recourse in the case, with due guarantees. Following this interpretation, the Commission stated that this is a right of society and that it is emerging as a principle of international law under the dynamic interpretation of human rights treaties and, specifically, Articles 1(1), 8, 25 and 13 of the American Convention (emphasis added).[11]

It is argued here that not classifying 'enforced disappearance' as in itself torture, also violates, in its own way, the collective right of society to the truth. That *torture* inflicted using the vehicle of 'enforced disappearance' involves psychological torture in that: (i) the direct victim's ties to family and community are disrupted (ii) often the identity and personality of the victim is obliterated and (iii) in a significant portion of the cases; physical torture of various kinds is also inflicted (child soldiers are subjected to cruel and inhuman treatment rising to the level of torture in being subjected to physical tortures as part of training, for disobedience, to set an example to other child 'recruits' etc.) and this physical torture has

---

[8] IACtHR Case of Bámaca-Velásquez v. Guatemala Judgment of November 25, 2000 at para 31.

[9] IACtHR Case of Bámaca-Velásquez v. Guatemala Judgment of November 25, 2000 at para 32.

[10] IACtHR Case of Bámaca-Velásquez v. Guatemala Judgment of November 25, 2000 at para 40.

[11] IACtHR Case of Bámaca-Velásquez v. Guatemala Judgment of November 25, 2000 at para 197.

psychological torture correlates. In certain cases; the deceased victim of enforced disappearance is never recovered as the perpetrator group wishes to conceal the signs of torture on the body[12] while at other times, as in Syria, child torture victims who had been disappeared for a period are intentionally returned to the family (often in death) to cause further mental suffering and intimidation for these immediate next of kin. Let us consider next then an example where the Inter-American Court of Human Rights addressed specifically the enforced disappearance of a child (in the Molina Theissen case) in order to consider some of the lessons to be learned on the topic of torture through 'enforced disappearance'.

5.2 Additional IACtHR Cases Re the 'Enforced Disappearance' of Children

While the previous IACtHR case here discussed (the case of the Gomez Papquiyauri Brothers) also involved 'enforced disappearance' of children; in that case the children's bodies were recovered and there was clear evidence of the physical torture the children endured aside from the psychological torture that was established based on the facts. In the cases to be discussed next not all of the forcibly disappeared children were recovered. Nonetheless; the enforced disappearance of the children in and of itself can legally be considered as torture for the direct and indirect victims; the indirect victims being the immediate family members.

5.2.1 Excerpts from Molina Theissen v Guatemala

The Court considers that the following facts have been established:

Concerning the internal armed conflict and the forced disappearance of persons.
40(1) When the facts took place, the forced disappearance of persons was a State practice carried out principally by members of the security forces. The purpose of this practice was to dismantle movements or organizations that the State identified as having "insurgency" tendencies and to instill fear into the population;

40(2) The State based itself on the "National Security Doctrine" to characterize a person as "subversive" or as an "internal enemy," and this could be anyone, who genuinely or allegedly supported the fight to change the established order. The victims hailed from all sectors of Guatemalan society: leaders of grass-roots or opposition organizations, workers, peasants, teachers, student leaders, members of religious orders or their lay helpers;

40(3) This practice was implemented by the army, the civil self-defense patrols (hereinafter "the PAC"), the military commissioners, the military footpolice, the national police, the judicial police and the "death squadrons";

[12] IACtHR Case of Bámaca-Velásquez v. Guatemala Judgment of November 25, 2000 at para 145(d).

40(4) The detention, abduction, torture and subsequent assassination of those who were "disappeared" was carried out by heavily armed groups of individuals, who introduced and identified themselves as belonging to one of the State's different investigation or security units. During these operations, they did not provide information on the motives for the alleged detention or the centers to which those detained would be transferred. These groups acted with total impunity and traveled in cars similar to those used by the police forces or identified as belonging to security units, with deteriorated license plates or without the road use permit;

40(5) Violence was inevitably used in the forced disappearance of persons carried out by members of State security units. These acts of violence were directed against the victims, their next of kin, and any witnesses to the events. The threats and intimidation of the victims' next of kin continued for some time after the detention, so as to curb their initiatives to locate the persons detained and to heighten their fear;

40(6) Between 1979 and 1983, the period coinciding with the exacerbation of the internal conflict in Guatemala, boys and girls were subjected to many human rights violations, and were direct victims of forced disappearance, arbitrary execution, torture, abduction, rape, and other acts that violated their fundamental rights. The threats and torture to which they were subjected were used as a way of torturing their families, and were designed to instill exemplary terror in them;

Concerning Marco Antonio Molina Theissen and his next of kin 40(7) **Marco Antonio Molina Theissen was born on November 30, 1966, and was 14 years and 10 months old when the facts took place**. He lived with his family in Guatemala City. He was in third year of high school at the Guatemalan-Israeli College and hoped to complete his high school certificate and continue on to university….

40(9) **The members of the Molina Theissen family and other next of kin**, such as Marco Antonio's brothers-in-law, are members of the administrative, academic, political and social areas of the Universidad de San Carlos and **were identified as political opponents or "subversives" by the security forces;…**

40(9)(iv) **Emma Guadalupe Molina Theissen, the victim's sister**, was a member of "*Juventud Patriótica del Trabajo,*" which was attached to the Guatemalan Labor Party (PGT). Julio César del Valle Cóbar, her companion, was a leader of the FRENTE student party at the Universidad de San Carlos, in Guatemala City, at the end of the 1970s and the beginning of the 1980s. On March 19, 1976, both of them were detained when they were conducting a census of one of the urban settlements established after the earthquake of February 4, 1976… Emma Guadalupe and Julio César were accused of "subversion" and subsequently acquitted; **her case was heard by the minor's court, because *she was just under 15 years of age*. While she was detained by her captors, before being handed over to the competent judicial authorities, she was raped and tortured for several days.** As of this time, it is believed that military intelligence opened a dossier on both of them. On March 22, 1980, Julio César del Valle Cóbar was found tortured and shot in his car. According to reports, the "para-military forces" were responsible for this act. As a result of her companion's assassination, Emma Guadalupe had to go into hiding and flee Guatemala City.

On September 27, 1981, Emma Guadalupe was detained by members of the armed forces, who kept her in illegal and clandestine custody for nine days in the installations of the "Manuel Lisandro Barillas" Military Barracks in Quetzaltenango. During her detention, she was maintained incommunicado, blindfolded and handcuffed to the leg of a bunk bed. She was interrogated constantly and violently, suffering many kinds of torture: repeated rape by members of the army, blows, kicks, electric shocks and psychological torture. She did not receive food or water. On the ninth day of her detention, October 5, 1981, she had lost so much weight that she was able to slip off the handcuffs and escape by the window;

Concerning the disappearance of Marco Antonio Molina Theissen

40(10) On October 6, 1981, two individuals armed with automatic weapons entered the home of the Molina Theissen family, located on 6th Avenue, No. 2-35, Zone 19, Colonia La Florida, in Guatemala City, and a third person remained on watch outside the residence. **The child, Marco Antonio Molina Theissen was in the house, together with his mother**, Emma Theissen Álvarez. One of the individuals shackled Marco Antonio, tied him to the arm of a chair, and gagged him with a piece of masking tape. The other person hit Emma Theissen Álvarez and tried to lock her up in one of the rooms of the house;

40(11) **The individuals searched the Molina Theissen family's home. When they had completed the search, *they took the child, Marco Antonio Molina Theissen, put him in a nylon sack and threw him into the back of a green pick-up with official license plate 17675. Emma Theissen Álvarez was able to get out of the house and she ran after the vehicle, although she was unable to do anything. This was the last time she saw her son*;**

40(12) **The detention and subsequent forced disappearance of Marco Antonio Molina Theissen was carried out by the Guatemalan army, presumably as a reprisal for the escape of his sister, Emma Guadalupe Molina Theissen, from the "Manuel Lisandro Barillas" Military Barracks, and to punish a family they considered to be an "enemy**"…(emphasis added).[13]

The Inter-American Court of Human Rights found in the case that the State

47(3) violated the rights embodied in Articles 4(1) (Right to Life), 5(1) and 5(2) (Right to Humane Treatment), 7 (Right to Personal Liberty), 8 (Right to a Fair Trial), 17 (Rights of the Family), 19 (Rights of the Child) and 25 (Judicial Protection) of the American Convention on Human Rights, and that it failed to comply with the obligations established in Articles 1(1) (Obligation to Respect Rights) and 2 (Domestic Legal Effects) thereof, to the detriment of Marco Antonio Molina Theissen; the State also failed to comply with the obligation established in Articles I and II of the Inter-American Convention on Forced Disappearance of Persons to the detriment of Marco Antonio Molina Theissen [and]… violated the rights embodied in Articles, 5(1) and 5(2) (Right to Humane Treatment); 8 (Right to a Fair Trial); 17 (Rights of the Family), and 25 (Judicial Protection) of the American Convention on Human Rights, and that it failed to comply with the obligations established in Articles 1(1) (Obligation to Respect Rights) and 2 (Domestic Legal Effects) thereof, to the detriment of the next of kin of Marco Antonio Molina Theissen: Emma Theissen Álvarez vda. de Molina (mother), Carlos Augusto Molina Palma (deceased father), Emma Guadalupe, Ana Lucrecia and María Eugenia Molina Theissen (sisters)….

Concerning the measures taken

40(14) The parents of Marco Antonio Molina Theissen took various measures to try and locate their son: they visited military posts, they went to hospitals, and they contacted army officers, senior members of the police and Government, representatives of the Catholic Church, and international human rights organizations. His parents contacted several individuals to negotiate his liberty; in this regard, they were asked to give money and to exchange the father for the son. The family accepted the terms and conditions of the negotiation, but the individuals never fulfilled the agreement;

40(15) The victim's parents filed several writs of habeas corpus on the day of the facts. On July 9, 1997, the victim's next of kin, with the legal advice of the *Grupo de Apoyo Mutuo*, filed another writ of habeas corpus before the Supreme Court of Justice of Guatemala in favor of Marco Antonio Molina Theissen, but received no reply. Subsequently, on August

[13] IACtHR Molina Theissen v Guatemala Judgment of 4 May, 2004.

> 11, 1997, the next of kin of Marco Antonio Molina Theissen again filed a writ of habeas corpus before the Supreme Court of Justice in his favor. The same day, the Second Trial Court of the Municipality of Mixto ordered the Ministry of National Defense and the Ministry of the Interior to inform it whether they had received or knew of any order of detention or investigation against **the child**, or whether they had proceeded to arrest him. On August 13, 1997, the said Ministries informed the court that they had not received any order of detention against the victim and were not aware that any investigation had been initiated into the reported facts. On August 15, 1997, the Second Trial Court of the Municipality of Mixto rejected the writ of habeas corpus that had been filed[14];

The fact pattern manifest in the Molina Theissen case in regards to 'enforced disappearance' of a child is typical of this grave crime regardless of the jurisdiction in which it occurs. Currently at time of writing, for instance, Syria has engaged in the 'enforced disappearance' of children of the opposition; most often if not always also subjecting these children to gruesome physical tortures and often murdering them as well. Yet there has been no referral by the UN Security Council of the Syrian situation to the ICC despite this and other atrocities being committed by the Al Assad regime.

As is typical with cases of enforced disappearance of children as an international crime; Marco Molina Theissen was forcibly disappeared in order to inflict severe psychological suffering upon and intimidate his parents and other family members perceived to be part of the political opposition. In addition, the enforced disappearance of Marco Antonio Molina Theissen was in retaliation for the escape of his sister when as an adult she had been abducted by agents of the State and tortured (the sister herself as a 15 year old had also been abducted and tortured at that time for being a member of "*Juventud Patriótica del Trabajo,*" which was attached to the Guatemalan Labor Party). Thus it mattered not whether a child was (i.e. Emma Guadalupe Molina Theissen) or was not (i.e. Marco Antonio Molina Theissen) politically active. In both cases they were not safe from 'enforced disappearance' in Guatemala at the time based on the regime's targeting of children of the perceived opposition as a common plan of intimidation and coercion of the civilian opposition.

The Inter-American Court of Human Rights in *Molina Theissen* highlighted then this specific targeting of children for 'enforced disappearance' (most often accompanied by other forms of torture and often also murder of the disappeared child). In doing so the Inter-American Court of Human Rights: (i) affirms the child's inherent human dignity and right to respect as an autonomous person separate from the family; (ii) implicitly affirms the right of the child to be protected from any adverse consequences due to the parent's or family's political stance and also (iii) affirms the child's right to freedom of expression. Thus such cases are important in reinforcing children's fundamental human rights including their civil and political rights. Further, the case, in highlighting the specific targeting of children for enforced disappearance, reaffirms the fact that (i) children under international customary and treaty law are entitled to special protections and that (ii) any particular international law instrument must be properly interpreted, when there are child victims of grave international crimes, also with consideration of other relevant international law concerning children; such as but not limited to the Convention on the Rights of the Child.[15]

---

[14] IACtHR Molina Theissen v Guatemala Judgment of 4 May, 2004.

[15] Convention on the Rights of the Child (1990).

5.3 'Enforced Disappearance' of Children as Torture Gone Unacknowledged by the ICC

Enforced disappearance is defined under the Rome Statute as:

> "Enforced disappearance of persons" means the arrest, detention or abduction of persons by, or with the authorization, support or acquiescence of, a State or a political organization, followed by a refusal to acknowledge that deprivation of freedom or to give information on the fate or whereabouts of those persons, **with the intention of removing them from the protection of the law for a prolonged period of time** (emphasis added).[16]

'Enforced disappearance' of *children as particularized targets* and perpetrated by a State group or some other political entity to date has not been properly acknowledged by the ICC (referring here to the particular Rome Statute defined offence of 'enforced disappearance'). This is contrary to the urging of the UN Human Rights Council that particular attention be given to the specific targeting of children for enforced disappearance given their right to special protection and their vulnerability and the gravity of this continuous crime:[17]

> Children's evolving stages of physical and mental maturity, as well as their reliance on adults, places them in a situation of particular vulnerability. **As such, the specific nature of the rights violations and the specific State obligations in cases of child victims of enforced disappearance must be properly understood and underscored** (emphasis added).[18]

> **The Working Group recognizes that children must be afforded special protections and acknowledges the salience of relevant instruments that specifically address violence against children.** These include the Convention on the Rights of the Child (CRC) and its three Optional Protocols on the involvement of children in armed conflict; on the sale of children, child prostitution and child pornography; and on a communications procedure (emphasis added).[19]

> **Armed conflicts increase children's vulnerability, jeopardize their survival and development, and increase their risk of marginalization, abuse, and exploitation and particularly of becoming victims of enforced disappearances.** Treating children as objects susceptible of appropriation harms their dignity and personal integrity, and it is the

---

[16] Rome Statute Article 7(2)(i).

[17] UN Human Rights Council Resolution 7/12 'Enforced or involuntary disappearances" (in part) urges the Working Group on Enforced or Involuntary Disappearances "To pay particular attention to cases of children subjected to enforced disappearance and children of disappeared persons and to cooperate closely with the Governments concerned in searching for and identifying these children" and notes at point 4 that enforced disappearance of children is a continuous crime with long-term effects on children that can continue for the victims even after age of majority (27 March, 2008).

[18] UN Working Group on Enforced or Involuntary Disappearances General Comment (2012).

[19] UN Working Group on Enforced or Involuntary Disappearances General Comment (2012).

> State that should ensure their protection and survival, as well as prioritize measures to promote family reunification (emphasis added).[20]

Furthermore, this grave international crime involving children targeted in particular for 'enforced disappearance'[21] has not been characterized as constituting *also* torture under the Rome Statute (in addition to meeting the elements of the Rome Statute crime of 'enforced disappearance'). Yet, as noted in the General Comment of the UN Human Rights Council Working Group on Enforced or Involuntary Disappearances, children especially suffer grave harms as a result of enforced disappearance:

> Article 1 of the Declaration establishes that an enforced disappearance "inflicts severe suffering" on the victims "and their families". The Working Group recognizes that child victims of enforced disappearance suffer particularly severe harm in these situations (emphasis added).[22]

'Enforced disappearance' is but one form of perpetrator *torturous conduct* often directed against children as high priority targets but not acknowledged as torture[23] by the ICC:

> When a child is forcibly removed from its legitimate family ...then this constitutes a perfidious usurpation of duty. The repressors who took the disappeared children from their homes, or who seized mothers on the point of giving birth, were making decisions about people's lives in the same cold-blooded way that booty is distributed in war. Deprived of their identity and taken away from their parents, the disappeared children constitute, and will continue to constitute, a deep blemish on our society. **In their case, the blows were aimed at the defenceless, the vulnerable and the innocent, and *a new type of torment was conceived.*** – *Nunca Más* (emphasis added)[24]

To date the ICC OTP has not prosecuted the crime of 'enforced disappearance' of children (where children were the high priority targets for this form of severe psychological and physical torture). This though charges of torture in relation also to the charge of enforced disappearance involving child victims were justified on the facts as in several ICC cases where the children were abducted as child soldiers and sex slaves, their whereabouts and status; alive or dead, remaining unknown to their families and communities for a prolonged period or even indefinitely.

---

[20] UN Working Group on Enforced or Involuntary Disappearances General Comment (2012).

[21] In any specific context, such as in the current situation in Syria under the Al Assad regime, it may be that children are targeted in particular for enforced disappearance and torture and that adults are also amongst the victims.

[22] UN Working Group on Enforced or Involuntary Disappearances General Comment (2012).

[23] The torture encompasses both psychological and often also physical torture relating to the mechanism of the forced disappearance and often also additional physical torture inflicted by the perpetrators subsequent to the forced disappearance.

[24] From the report Nunca Más ("Never Again"), based on testimony of witnesses and visits to hundreds of secret detention centres in Argentina. Cited in Harvey-Blankenship et al. (2010), p. 4.

Included as children subjected to enforced disappearance must be recognized also the children born in captivity. Certainly in the situation where female children are abducted to become child soldiers and/or sex slaves; many pregnancies have occurred due to the repeated rapes of these young female victims. In fact the term 'forced mother' has been used in referring to these girl child soldier victims.[25] The resulting offspring of this sexual violence perpetrated in particular (though not exclusively) against female child soldiers sexually enslaved are properly classified under international criminal law also as forcibly disappeared persons. This is the case in that these offspring are cut off from their home communities and the mother's families as are their mothers.

> **Based on its experience, the Working Group recognizes three particular situations in which children become victims of enforced disappearance.** ***The first involves children who are themselves subjected to enforced disappearance*****,** as it is defined in the Declaration. ***A second particular situation occurs when children are born during the captivity of a mother subjected to enforced disappearance***. In this case, children are born in secret detention centres and, most of the time, documents attesting to their true identity are suppressed or altered. **Finally, children are victimized by the fact that their mother, father, legal guardian or other relative is subjected to enforced disappearance. An enforced disappearance creates a network of victims that extends far beyond the individuals that are directly subjected to this human rights violation** (emphasis added).[26]

> In addition to these three situations of enforced disappearance, the Working Group is aware of other situations in which children may become victims of enforced disappearance ***...The forced recruitment of child soldiers***[27] ***also places them in a potential situation of enforced disappearance, especially when they are recruited by armed groups distinct from the regular armed forces of a State but operating with the support, consent or acquiescence of the State*** (emphasis added).[28]

5.4 A Case Example: 'Enforced Disappearance' in Darfur

'UN Watch' urged the UN Working Group on Minorities to acknowledge the crime occurring in Darfur at the behest of the Al Bashir regime of 'enforced disappearance':

> Therefore, UN Watch urges this Working Group, and the Commission generally, to assume their above mentioned responsibilities under Article 9 of the Declaration, and to

---

25 Tonheim (2012), p. 280.

26 UN Working Group on Enforced or Involuntary Disappearances General Comment (2012).

27 As previously discussed, on the view here, even children 15 and over but under 18 appropriated by perpetrator groups committing widespread atrocities and/or genocide cannot be considered to be voluntary recruits.

28 UN Working Group on Enforced or Involuntary Disappearances General Comment (2012).

adopt and reinstate, in the report of the Working Group, the demands that were dropped from the Item 9 draft, which are:

1. To Condemn:

    (a) Indiscriminate attacks against civilians, including killings, **torture**, **enforced disappearances**, destruction of villages, **violence including widespread rape and sexual violence against women and children**, pillaging and forced displacement, conducted on a widespread and systematic basis, as well as arbitrary detentions and illegal incommunicado detentions, as documented by the International Commission of Inquiry,
    (b) The fact that most attacks have been deliberately and indiscriminately directed against civilians, many of them under the direct responsibility or tolerance of the Government of Sudan,
    (c) The climate of impunity concerning violations of human rights and breaches of international humanitarian law committed in Darfur,
    (d) The continuing violations of the N'Djamena Ceasefire Agreements of 8 April 2004 and the Abuja Protocols of 9 November 2004 by all parties,
    (e) Support to Janjaweed militias by the Government of Sudan, and its failure to disarm them...[29]

The fact is then that in the ICC's consideration of cases stemming from the situation in Darfur; crimes against *children in particular* were not fully addressed. This is reflected in the fact that none of the ICC accused from Darfur were charged by the ICC OTP with the (i) enforced disappearance of children or with (ii) such enforced disappearance as a form of torture. This though the regime and its proxy agents, the Janjaweed, were responsible for mass rape and abduction of children and use of children as child soldiers and sex slaves thus placing these child victims in a situation of 'enforced disappearance' (as has been noted by the UN Working Group on Enforced Disappearance is potentially the case in circumstances:**("The forced recruitment of child soldiers also places them in a potential situation of enforced disappearance")**[30]: The UN Working Group on Enforced or Involuntary Disappearances has stated further that:

> Children are the most vulnerable victims. Severe violations of human rights against children include killing, attacks, sexual violence including rape, killing of family members, **abduction of children and recruitment into armed groups**, burning of houses and crops, poisoning of wells, looting of property and animals, humiliation of relatives, and harassment and intimidation. **One of the most odious of these crimes is rape. Thousands of girls—children—have been victimized.**
>
> Rape of civilians is a war crime. Perpetrators bear individual criminal responsibility. Rape is also a crime against humanity, constituting a serious attack on human dignity. These

---

[29] Inlander (2005) Statement on behalf of United Nations Watch to the 11th session of the UN Working Group on Minorities (30 May–3 June, 2005).

[30] UN Working Group on Enforced or Involuntary Disappearances General Comment (2012). These children abducted as child soldiers or and/or sex slaves thus suffered the psychological torture involved in the violent implementation of enforced disappearance plus the brutalities subsequent to the enforced disappearance which in most cases also rises to the level of physical and/or psychological torture (i.e. repeated rapes, being forced to participate and to witness mass atrocities).

> crimes are occurring in Darfur as part of a systematic practice of atrocities committed against the civilian population (emphasis added).[31]

Thus, child soldier recruitment and the sexual enslavement of children by armed groups perpetrating mass atrocities, such as in Darfur, generally also involves enforced disappearance as an additional mode of torture.

It is here suggested that the reason that 'enforced disappearance' of children in particular was not charged against the war criminals and *genocidaires* of the Al Bashir regime and its associated militia and other agents in Darfur is in part because this grave international crime has been traditionally viewed as perpetrated directly against political actors. Since children are not generally considered as themselves political actors they have erroneously not been considered by the ICC as potential direct victims of 'enforced disappearance' as that crime is defined under the Rome Statute.[32] This is tragically ironic as in contemporary times, as in the current Syrian conflict, children are increasingly being targeted for enforced disappearance and torture in various forms in part due to their perceived connection to adults who are alleged to be part of the opposition to the perpetrator group.

5.5 Some History on the Prosecution of 'Enforced Disappearance' Under International Criminal Law

It appears to be the case that there was initially some reluctance to incorporate 'enforced disappearance' during armed conflict as an international crime in the Rome Statute:

> …the delegations negotiating the Rome Statute of the International Criminal Court (ICC) were unaware of any prior precedent for the prosecution of enforced disappearance and were initially reluctant to include the offense as a crime against humanity, on par with murder, rape, and torture.[33]

Certain scholars however contend that enforced disappearance was an international crime prior to the enactment of the Rome Statute and that its origins as a legal concept are embedded in the laws of war:

> By tracing the roots of the prohibition of enforced disappearance by the laws of war as interpreted by the Nuremberg Tribunals, I show that the **criminalization of enforced**

---

[31] UN Working Group on Enforced or Involuntary Disappearances General Comment (2012).

[32] For the same reason (perceiving children not to be political actors generally speaking) Truth Commissions often do not focus on the grave international crime of 'enforced disappearance' of children: "In the 1980s and early 1990s, commissions in Chile, El Salvador and Haiti documented violations against children. However**, since most of the violence targeted the political opposition, the activities of these commissions focused on adults. Their reports mention children and adolescents predominantly in relation to crimes against members of their families,** ***particularly disappearance, torture and killings***. An exception is the Commission in Argentina, which called substantial attention to the issue of kidnapped babies, p. 10.

[33] Finucane (2010), p. 172.

> **disappearance initially served the humanitarian function of protecting "family rights" during armed conflict.** Like other aspects of the laws of war, the prohibition of enforced disappearance protects noncombatants and promotes key international values by constraining the conduct of belligerents. ***Here, the protected object is the family and the international value is familial integrity*** (emphasis added).[34]

Clearly the enforced disappearance of children strikes at the heart of the family and undermines to some extent inter-generational continuity. 'Enforced disappearance' during armed conflict viewed as an attack on family thus makes it all the more clear why children are often prioritized targets for the international crime of enforced disappearance. This is the case since children in some ways symbolize the essence of the existing family as well as representing the vehicle for future generations of that family.

The current author concurs with Finucane that: "Only through the prosecution of enforced disappearance are the specific harms caused by the continuing uncertainty of disappearance acknowledged and condemned."[35] It appears that in fact enforced disappearance was recognized as both a prohibited war crime and a crime against humanity under international customary law according to certain of the judgments of the Nuremberg Tribunals.[36] Historical documents of the Nazi WWII era reveal that:

> By terrorizing the occupied populations of Western Europe through a program of enforced disappearance, Hitler hoped to suppress resistance.[37]

Thus it appears that 'enforced disappearance' during armed conflict has long been recognized as an international crime under international customary law (ICL) violating the right to family. By not prosecuting as 'enforced disappearance' (in addition to whatever other charges might apply): (i) the recruitment and use of child soldiers and (ii) the enslavement of children as sex slaves during armed conflict by State or non-State forces perpetrating mass atrocities and/or genocide, there is no foregrounding of these crimes as, amongst other things, a denial of the children's[38] right to family. Conversely charging 'enforced disappearance' in relation to child soldiering and sexual enslavement perpetrated by a group committing mass atrocities and/or genocide, in addition to the other relevant offences, reinforces the notion that children have as much right to family as parents have to their children. This is the case in that children too have certain inherent autonomous and universal basic human rights including amongst them the right to family.

'Enforced disappearance' as a weapon of war was a prominent feature of the Serb perpetrators' strategy in 1992 in the Bosnia Herzegovina conflict:

> Approximately twenty-seven thousand persons were missing in Bosnia and Herzegovina by the end of the war in 1995. The overwhelming majority of these persons were Muslims who disappeared during the "ethnic cleansing" of eastern Bosnia by Bosnian Serb forces. Despite over a decade of work by organizations such as the ICRC, the International

[34] Finucane (2010), p. 173.

[35] Finucane (2010), p. 173.

[36] Finucane (2010), p. 175.

[37] Finucane (2010), p. 176.

[38] 'Child' or 'children here referring respectively to a person or persons under age 18.

Commission for Missing Persons, and the Missing Persons Institute of Bosnia and Herzegovina, over ten thousand individuals remain unaccounted for in Bosnia and Herzegovina. **The WCC has held that many of the missing persons in the country disappeared under conditions satisfying the definition of *enforced disappearance as a crime against humanity*** (emphasis added).[39]

Since enforced disappearance has existed as a crime under ICL pre WWII; there is no issue with retrospective justice should the ICC charge this offence just as there was no issue for prosecution of this offence for the ICTY. (Note that while the international human rights courts are concerned with State liability for the human rights violations involved in 'enforced disappearance'; the ICC and international criminal tribunals address the individual criminal liability that attaches to the international crime of 'enforced disappearance' as a war crime and/or crime against humanity in any particular context).

5.6 The Connection between the International Crimes of 'Enforced Disappearance', Torture and Murder

Enforced disappearance of children is often correlated with the murder of the disappeared children as evidenced by the experience in various jurisdictions:

Selected Examples:
Argentina

Between 1976 and 1983, up to an estimated thirty thousand Argentines disappeared during the rule of the military junta as part of a systematic purge of perceived political subversives.[40]

Men, women *and children* from all walks of life were systematically abducted, imprisoned in hundreds of detention centres, *tortured and murdered. Estimates suggest that hundreds of pregnant women and young children were among those who disappeared* (emphasis added).[41]

El Slavador
The Salvadoran military engaged in systematic disappearances during the country's armed conflict from 1980 through 1992. At least 2,598 people were disappeared, including children living in areas believed to be rebel strongholds. The abductions resulted from efforts to quell a growing leftist rebellion.[42]

Guarjila, in the northeast sector of Chaletanango, witnessed heavy fighting during the conflict. Shortly after the signing of the peace agreement, Father Jon Cortina, a Jesuit priest in Guarjila, began to hear from parishioners who had suffered abuses at the hands of the military during the war. **Father Cortina was particularly struck by hearing from mothers and other family members about government soldiers snatching their chil-**

39 Finucane (2010), p. 188.

40 Harvey-Blankenship et al. (2010), p. 3.

41 Harvey-Blankenship et al. (2010), p. 3.

42 Harvey-Blankenship et al. (2010), p. 9.

> **dren, sometimes from their very arms. Others recounted seeing their abducted children boarded onto military helicopters and flown away**(emphasis added).[43]

> **Pro-Búsqueda estimates that government troops and their allied security forces were responsible for the disappearances of children in 52 % of their documented cases while the FMLN was responsible for 8 %. The group further estimates that over 65 % of the children who disappeared were under the age of seven** (emphasis added).[44]

Many El Salvadoran children forcibly disappeared by the military during the 1980–1992 conflict have never been recovered alive or dead and a certain segment of these forcibly disappeared children can be presumed to have been murdered. This especially since many if not most of the children were forcibly disappeared by the *Atlacatl Battalion*:

> an elite unit of the Salvadoran army trained as a rapid-response and counter-insurgency unit at the US Army's School of the Americas. *The Battalion was responsible for carrying out some of the worst atrocities of the armed conflict,* including the massacre at El Mozote in December 1981 and the assassination of six Jesuit priests, their housekeeper and her daughter in November 1989 (emphasis added).[45]

Northern Uganda

The Human Rights Centre at the University of California at Berkeley estimates that 54,000–75,000 people had been abducted in Northern Uganda by the LRA between 1986 and 2006, about half of them 18 years old or younger at the time of abduction (an estimated 25,000–38,000 children).[46] However, others estimate that the number is even higher.[47] It is unknown how many of these children have been murdered by the LRA[48] but based on the pattern of LRA activities it is highly probable that a significant number have met that fate:

> The LRA's method of warfare had a profound psychological impact on the population. Not accepted as a liberation movement representing all Acholi, the LRA used extreme violence, especially against civilians, to instill terror in the community. *The violence has ranged from low-intensity attacks to major massacres killing hundreds of people. Civilians have been the main targets.* ***The LRA have mutilated their victims, including cutting off lips, ears and noses, and have abducted children and youth of both sexes, forcing them to serve as soldiers, porters and (the females) sexual slaves***. Many attacks were conducted at night, including raids on villages or IDP camps for food and other supplies. *Young people were often forced to commit atrocities as soon as they were abducted to make it more difficult for them to contemplate returning to their communities* (emphasis added).[49]

Clearly, the rights of children who are forcibly disappeared are violated in terms not limited to the violation of their right to family. The forcibly disappeared children, such as those appropriated by a perpetrator group for child soldiering and/or sexual enslavement,

---

43 Harvey-Blankenship et al. (2010), p. 10.

44 Harvey-Blankenship et al. (2010), p. 11.

45 Harvey-Blankenship et al. (2010), p. 13.

46 Pham et al. (2008), p. 404.

47 Harvey-Blankenship et al. (2010), p. 19.

48 Harvey-Blankenship et al. (2010), p. 20.

49 Harvey-Blankenship et al. (2010), pp. 17–18.

suffer torture psychologically, for instance, by not knowing whether they will survive or by being directly threatened with certain death and then, in some instances, being summarily executed or executed after a prolonged period of unspeakable torture.

5.7 The Continuous Nature of the Crime of 'Enforced Disappearance' of Children

The international crime of 'enforced disappearance' as referred to in the Rome Statute and certain other international law instruments is, on the view here, a 'continuous crime'. The current author would argue that even if and when a forcibly disappeared child is recovered, the crime continues as the child will, in many if not most cases, forever struggle with his or her identity. This is due to the fact that the child is perceived by the broader society to some extent, and often also by the immediate family and even themselves, as forever tainted by the perpetrator group and identified to some degree with that perpetrator group. This is particularly the case where the disappeared children were required as part of the perpetrator group to witness and participate in atrocities and where the children have been subjected to sexual violence (which may also have included, for girls, a *de facto* forced 'marriage' to a member of the perpetrator group and, in some instances, 'forced motherhood'). The acknowledgement, on the analysis here, that 'enforced disappearance' of children is a form of *torture* in which the individual children's personalities and identities are obliterated[50] thus leads to a broader conception of the *continuous* nature of the crime of 'enforced disappearance.' The loss, to a great or even complete extent, of one's original identity and personality are potentially indefinite *continuing elements* of the crime of 'enforced disappearance'. This reinforces the general point that where children are particularized targets of grave international crimes such as 'enforced disappearance'; additional considerations must be addressed (i.e. the ICC considering that 'enforced disappearance' may constitute *torture* especially in respect of child victims given: (i) children's lower threshold for pain and suffering (psychological and physical) (ii) the greater likelihood that the crime of 'enforced disappearance' of children is a *continuous crime* with psychological sequelae amounting to psychological torture lasting for some or an indefinite period (due to trauma and since the children's identities were likely highly fragile (due to age and maturity level) at the time the children were forcibly disappeared such that their identities and personalities may be forever adversely altered to some extent); (iii) the frequency of children forcibly disappeared serving as child soldiers and/or child sex

[50] See for instance the Inter-American Convention to Prevent and Punish Torture: Article 2: "For the purposes of this Convention, torture shall be understood to be any act intentionally performed whereby physical or mental pain or suffering is inflicted on a person for purposes of criminal investigation, as a means of intimidation, as personal punishment, as a preventive measure, as a penalty, or for any other purpose. **Torture shall also be understood to be the use of methods upon a person intended to *obliterate the personality of the victim* or to diminish his physical or mental capacities, even if they do not cause physical pain or mental anguish**" (emphasis added). (The Inter-American Convention to Prevent and Punish Torture (February 28, 1987)).

slaves during armed conflict with groups perpetrating mass atrocities and/or genocide such that these children, if recovered alive, are highly likely to suffer psychological torture for years to come as an after-effect of their traumatisation in the aforementioned manner etc.). Note that the term 'child' as used here refers to persons under age 18. It is here contended that through charges, for instance, of 'enforced disappearance', 'torture' and even potentially the 'genocidal forcible transfer of children' (supported by the evidence in situations where children are abducted and forcibly disappeared as child soldiers and/or sex slaves by perpetrator armed groups committing mass atrocities and/or genocide); children 15 and older but under 18 may potentially also access redress through the ICC (via prosecution of the perpetrators most responsible and potentially also reparations paid from the ICC Victims Fund). This in contrast to ICC cases where, as in *Lubanga*, this would not be the outcome as the charges pertained only to the recruitment and use of children as child soldiers as war crimes perpetrated on children under age 15 (as per the relevant Rome Statute war crimes provisions).

Where children are the victims of forcible disappearance; their personalities and identities have been forever reshaped by the perpetrator group and in the perception of others; this continuing even after the child's death and impacting the next of kin. Hence, respectfully, a broader notion of the continuous nature of the crime of 'enforced disappearance' (of children) is required than that proffered by the 'UN Working Group on Enforced or Involuntary Disappearances' which envisions the crime potentially being completed in all its elements at a certain point in time:

> Enforced disappearances are prototypical continuous acts. The act begins at the time of the abduction and **extends for the whole period of time that the crime is not complete, *that is to say until the State acknowledges the detention or releases information pertaining to the fate or whereabouts of the individual*** (emphasis added).[51]

> **Even though the conduct violates several rights, including the right to recognition as a person before the law, the right to liberty and security of the person *and the right not to be subjected to torture* or other cruel, inhuman or degrading treatment or punishment and also violates or constitutes a grave threat to the right to life**, the **Working Group considers that an enforced disappearance is a unique and consolidated act, and not a combination of acts.**[52] Even if some aspects of the violation may

[51] Working Group on Enforced or Involuntary Disappearances: General Comment on Enforced Disappearance as a Continuous Crime.

[52] This author respectfully argues that the 'UN Working Group on Enforced or Involuntary Disappearances' is in error in suggesting, by implication, that the ***legal characterization*** of the facts cannot refer to a ***number of separate Rome Statute offences*** such as, for instance, 'torture' *and* 'enforced disappearance.' The latter is a legally supportable position, it is here contended, even if the separate charges are based on the same facts as this is permissible under the Rome Statute. At the same time; 'enforced disappearance' can be viewed as "a unique and consolidated act, and not a combination of acts" in practical terms (the occurrence as actualized 'on the ground'). The foregoing analysis offered by the current author does not at all negate the possibility of charging 'enforced disappearance' based on an instrument that was enacted after the enforced disappearance began. This given the continuous nature of the enforced disappearance (i.e. (i) the victims still being missing and the perpetrator group not providing any information as to whether the persons are alive or dead or about their whereabouts and/or based on (ii) recovered surviving victims experiencing ongoing psychological and/or physical suffering (amounting to torture) due to having been the victims of enforced disappearance and the harms inflicted as a result).

> have been completed before the entry into force of the relevant national or international instrument, if other parts of the violation are still continuing, until such time as the victim's fate or whereabouts are established, the matter should be heard, and the act should not be fragmented (emphasis added).[53]

> Thus, when an enforced disappearance began before the entry into force of an instrument or before the specific State accepted the jurisdiction of the competent body, the fact that the disappearance continues after the entry into force or the acceptance of the jurisdiction gives the institution the competence and jurisdiction to consider the act of enforced disappearance as a whole, and not only acts or omissions imputable to the State that followed the entry into force of the relevant legal instrument or the acceptance of the jurisdiction....[54]

> Similarly, in criminal law, the Working Group is of the opinion that one consequence of the continuing character of enforced disappearance is that it is possible to convict someone for enforced disappearance on the basis of a legal instrument that was enacted after the enforced disappearance began, notwithstanding the fundamental principle of non retroactivity. The crime cannot be separated and the conviction should cover the enforced disappearance as a whole (emphasis added).[55]

It is here argued, consistent with the view of the 'UN Working Group on enforced or involuntary disappearances' that the grave international crime of enforced disappearance should be charged such as to cover the conduct of enforced disappearance as a whole given its continuous nature. That is, the forced disappearance should be considered as a whole even if the enforced disappearance occurred before the Rome Statute entered into force or before a particular State became a State party and accepted the jurisdiction of the ICC and then continued after those dates. In other words, the view here is that such an approach does not in fact violate the non-retroactivity principle[56] but rather reflects the reality of enforced disappearance in a significant number of cases.

On the analysis here, as mentioned, a State or non-State armed force committing acts of terror and atrocity and acting as agent of a political entity (i.e. the FPLC) appropriating children for child soldiering commits the continuing crime of 'enforced disappearance'.[57] This has not been the approach of the ICC. For instance, in *Lubanga*, the ICC OTP did not also legally categorize the recruitment and use of child soldiers as constituting, in addition, the Rome Statute offence of

---

[53] Working Group on Enforced or Involuntary Disappearances: General Comment on Enforced Disappearance as a Continuous Crime.

[54] Working Group on Enforced or Involuntary Disappearances: General Comment on Enforced Disappearance as a Continuous Crime.

[55] Working Group on Enforced or Involuntary Disappearances: General Comment on Enforced Disappearance as a Continuous Crime.

[56] See Rome Statute (2002) Article 11 Jurisdiction ratione temporis:

1. The Court has jurisdiction only with respect to crimes committed after the entry into force of this Statute.
2. If a State becomes a Party to this Statute after its entry into force, the Court may exercise its jurisdiction only with respect to crimes committed after the entry into force of this Statute for that State, unless that State has made a declaration under article 12, paragraph 3.

[57] This view as discussed is consistent with that of the UN Working Group on Enforced or Involuntary Disappearances on enforced disappearance as a continuous crime.

'enforced disappearance'. The OTP in *Lubanga* argued further that the continuous nature *of the crime of recruitment and use of child soldiers in hostilities* was *limited in duration* to the time period the child was in FPLC custody or the child is still under age 15 (15 being the age at which children are considered 'underage', to use the Prosecutor's terminology, in respect of recruitment and use of children for active participation in armed conflict):

> The Prosecution submits that the war crime of enlisting and conscripting children under the age of 15 is a crime of a continuous nature committed as long as the child remains in the armed group or is underage.[58]

Legally characterizing (as is here contended is supportable) the facts underlying the Rome Statute war crime of enlisting; conscripting and using children under the age of 15 *also* as 'enforced disappearance' (where the perpetrator group is committing mass atrocities and does not allow the child to have contact with their families once 'recruited') allows for the proper acknowledgement of these facts as constituting also a Rome Statute crime (enforced disappearance) which is: (i) continuous beyond the point of perpetrator custody of the child victims and (ii) continuous even after the child reaches the age of 15 or over (given the continuing damage to the child's perceived identity and any ongoing psychological and physical sequelae of the enforced disappearance due to the severe harms inflicted for the purpose of using the child victims for child soldiering).

The ICC OTP's aforementioned position in *Lubanga* regarding the recruitment and use of child soldiers as a continuous crime fails to acknowledge that: (i) children under age 18 but 15 and over are also the victims of *enforced disappearance* as FPLC child soldiers; (ii) children over and under age 15 could not in fact make a truly voluntary choice to join the FPLC given the FPLC murderous rampage and perpetrating of other mass atrocities; and (iii) children forcibly disappeared as child soldiers and/or sex slaves by the FPLC suffered the continuous harm of having their perceived identity forever changed and tainted by their connection to the FPLC and by FPLC responsibility for grave international crimes perpetrated against often the child's family and home community as well as other communities. Hence, it is here argued that the FPLC appropriation of children as child soldiers and/or sex slaves was a continuous crime also *as enforced disappearance* (a separate charge) that persisted beyond the period the child was in FPLC custody or was no longer "underage" for child soldiering (per the Rome Statute war crime provisions dealing with child soldiering below age 15). This analysis of the facts underlying child soldiering in *Lubanga* (and like cases) in terms of 'enforced disappearance' as a continuous crime applies even if one contends that the ICC Prosecutor was correct in holding that the *war crimes of enlisting; conscripting and using children under 15* persist as a continuous crime only as long as the child "remains in the armed group or is underage."[59]

---

[58] The Situation in the Democratic Republic of Congo The Prosecutor versus Thomas Lubanga Dyilo Office of the Prosecutors Closing Statements (25 August, 2011), p. 10.

[59] This is not to suggest that the current author is in agreement with the former ICC Prosecutor Moreno-Ocampo's holding that there are time limitations on the continuous nature of the crime of recruitment and use in hostilities of children under age 15 as he articulated in *Lubanga*.

5.8 The IACtHR Serrano Cruz Sisters Case: Enforced Disappearance as a Continuous Crime

This issue regarding the continuous nature of enforced disappearance and the temporal jurisdiction of a court was addressed in the context of the Inter-American Court of Human Rights case of the Serrano Cruz Sisters which is informative on this point. That case involved the abduction of Ernestina and Erlinda Cruz Serrano 7 and 3 years old respectively by the El Salvadorian army during a military operation named "Cleaning Operation" in 1982. When the Inter-American Commission filed a complaint to the Inter-American Court of Human Rights in 2003; the two girls 21 years later were still forcibly disappeared. The two sisters were among the 721 cases of disappeared children who were taken during the civil war of that period (1980-1991). The government of El Salvador in response to the Commission's complaint initially denied the Serrano Cruz children had ever existed.[60] Yet, ultimately:

> For families of the disappeared and their advocates, the Serrano Cruz decision constituted a watershed. Previously, the State had refused to even acknowledge that children had been disappeared by the military.[61]

The Serrano Cruz Sisters case was put into context during the IACtHR hearing in part by the testimony of the Director of the *Asociación Pro-Búsqueda* (J.M.R. Cortina Garaícorta) an organization established in August 1994 to help trace the disappeared children of the El Salvador civil war. That testimony in part was as follows:

> **(…) During the armed conflict in El Salvador, there was a *systematic pattern of child disappearance during military operations*.** The case of Erlinda and Ernestina fits perfectly into the general pattern of child disappearance during the conflict. The Armed Forces and the humanitarian institutions that kept the children did nothing to find their families; they were taken to orphanages and to military barracks or they were 'sold in adoption.' It was sufficient for a judge to declare that a child had been materially and morally abandoned for its adoption to be authorized. These adoptions were based on the lie of abandonment and that the children were orphans. 126 children have been found abroad, in 11 countries of America and Europe. All of them have been naturalized as citizens of the country in which they live and almost all of them do not speak their mother tongue (emphasis added).[62]

The Inter-American Court of Human Rights; while it accepted that the Serrano Cruz sisters were forcibly disappeared by agents of the El Salvadorian government; held that it had no jurisdiction to investigate events that occurred 6 months *prior* to the date that El Salvador agreed to accept the jurisdiction and competence

60 Tinta (2008), pp. 172–173.

61 Harvey-Blankenship et al. (2010), p. 1.

62 Dissenting Opinion of Judge Cancado Trinidade in the IACtHR Judgement in Serrano Cruz Sisters Case 9 September, 2005 at para 26.

of the IACtHR (the date of acceptance being 6 June 1995).[63]As Tinta remarks; this decision of the IACtHR "denied that the phenomenon of disappearance is a continuous violation and not an act that could be placed in time at the moment of the kidnapping of the victims only."[64] The Court's decision in this regard was especially tragic in that the girls were still disappeared so many years after 6 June 1995.[65] Let us consider then through selected excerpts the illuminating dissenting opinion of Judge Cancado Trinidade on the issue of the temporal jurisdiction of the Court (IACtHR) and enforced disappearance as a continuous crime for the lessons implicit regarding ICC jurisdiction as well:

5.8.1 *Excerpts from the Dissenting Opinion of Judge Cancado Trinidade: IACtHR Judgement in Serrano Cruz Sisters Case*

I. Towards overcoming excesses of State voluntarism

...

9. As I recalled in my dissenting opinion in the judgment on preliminary objections in this case, the respondent State itself made it plain, by its arguments, that its purpose was very clearly to exclude consideration of each and every human rights violation that had originated in the internal armed conflict which plagued the country and its people for more than a decade (1980-1991) from the jurisdiction of the Inter-American Court. ...

10. The respondent State's objection was thus of a *ratione temporis* and *ratione materiae* nature, forming an *imbroglio* of indeterminate time and broad, general and undefined scope; this objection was accepted by the Court for reasons that I fail to understand, when the Court should have declared them inadmissible and invalid. As I stated in my abovementioned dissenting opinion:

"By proceeding in this way, accepting the terms of this preliminary objection, the majority of the members of the Court accepted State voluntarism, leaving unprotected those who consider themselves the victims of the *continuing human rights violations* of a particular gravity that occurred during the Salvadoran armed conflict, as a result of the documented practice of the *forced disappearance of children and the elimination of their identity and name during this armed conflict*."

11. **By accepting State voluntarism, the Court limited itself unduly and regressively, and unfortunately it did so in an important human rights case that represents**

[63] Tinta (2008), p. 173.

[64] Tinta (2008), p. 173.

[65] Note that the 1993 El Salvadoran Truth Commission addressing the crimes of the civil war "included the disappearance of children in the global situation of disappearances, and described 30 cases of major massacres and some cases of disappearances as examples. (...)"Dissenting Opinion of Judge Cancado Trinidade in the IACtHR Judgement in Serrano Cruz Sisters Case 9 September, 2005 at para 26: Testimony of J.M.R. Cortina Garaícorta. This subsuming of international crimes targeting children in particular amongst other crimes is characteristic also of the ICC approach to date (save for the issue of recruitment and use of children under 15 for active participation in armed conflict as child soldiers by perpetrator groups).

a microcosm of one of the greatest tragedies suffered by the countries of Latin America in recent decades: the tragedy of the children who disappeared in the Salvadoran armed conflict. As I stated in my previous dissenting opinion in this case (judgment on preliminary objections)...

II. A lost opportunity to develop case law
1. **The relevance of the right to identity**

(a) The meaning and scope of the right to **<u>identity</u>**
13. Given the circumstances of this case, I do not see how it is possible to avoid the question of **the *right to identity of the two sisters who are still disappeared***, Ernestina and Erlinda Serrano Cruz. It is an issue on which the Court should have *developed case law*, because, in my opinion, **there is no way in which the right to identity can be disassociated from the legal personality of the individual as a subject of domestic and international law.** Therefore, the Court should have examined jointly the alleged violations in this case to the right to a name (Article 18 of the American Convention) and the rights of the family (Article 17 of the Convention)**. Respect for the right to identity enables the individual to defend his rights and, consequently, also has an impact on his legal and procedural capacity in both domestic and international law.**

14. The right to identity presumes the right to know personal and family information, and to have access to this, to satisfy an existential need and safeguard individual rights. This right also has an important cultural (in addition to social, family, psychological and spiritual) content, and is essential for relationships between each individual and the rest of society, and even for his understanding of the outside world, and his place in it.
15. ***Without a specific identify, one is not a person***. The individual is constituted as a being that includes his supreme purpose within himself, and realizes this throughout his life, under his own responsibility. In this optic, safeguarding his right to an identity becomes essential. The legal personality is expressed as a legal category in the sphere of law, as the unitary expression of the aptitude of a human being to be a holder of rights and obligations at the level of regulated human relations and behavior

16. **The right to identity expands the protection of the human being; it exceeds the category of subjective rights rooted in the sphere of law; it also supports the legal personality as a category in itself in the conceptual sphere of law. The identity expresses what is most personal in each human being, extending to his relationships with his fellow human being and with the outside world.** The concept of the right to identity began to be developed more thoroughly in the 1980 s and 1990 s.

18. However, as I stated in my concurring opinion in the Court's Advisory Opinion No. 17 on the *Juridical Status and Human Rights of the Child* (2002), it cannot be denied that:

... Universal human rights, superior to, and preceding, the State and any form of politico-social organization, and inherent to the human being, affirmed themselves as opposable to the public power itself. ...**The international juridical personality of the human being crystallized itself as a limit to the discretion of State power**. Human rights freed the conception of the subjective right from the chains of legal positivism.

19. **The right to identity reinforces the protection of human rights, protecting each individual against the denigration or violation of his "personal truth**." The right to identity, which encompasses the attributes and characteristics that individualize each human being, seeks to ensure that the individual is faithfully represented in his projection towards his social environment and the outside world. Hence, its relevance which has a direct impact on the legal personality and capacity of the individual in both domestic and international law.

(b) Components of the right to identity
20. Even though the right to identity is not expressly established in the American Convention, its material content is implied, in the circumstances of the specific case, particularly from Articles 18 (Right to a Name) and 17 (Rights of the Family) of the American Convention...

21. **The right to identity, like the right to the truth, is inferred by specific rights embodied in the American Convention; it is more a necessary development of case law that, in turn, leads to the progressive development of the *corpus juris* of international human rights law**

...

73. **Indeed, there is no oblivion there can be no oblivion. The sisters, Ernestina and Erlinda Serrano Cruz, who have remained disappeared since June 2, 1982, are still present in the memory of their loved ones, and their drama is now consigned to the annals of international human rights case law.**[66]

This author concurs with the dissenting opinion of IACtHR Judge Cancado Trinidade in the Serrano Cruz Sisters case that the 'enforced disappearance' of children is a 'continuous crime' that continues after the act which was located at a specific time and place that first rendered the children forcibly 'disappeared.' This in that the children in many cases remain disappeared for some significant period or, as in the Serrano Cruz Sisters case, remain disappeared indefinitely; most often without the family even knowing if the disappeared children are alive or dead. Furthermore; the forced disappearance profoundly impacts the child victims psychologically and in many instances if not most alters the child victims' self-perceived and other perceived identity in the long-term to some considerable extent. This may be due to a variety of factors i.e. in some cases to the perpetrators shaping a new identity for the disappeared children (i.e. the LRA transforming disappeared children into LRA child soldier perpetrators) or as a result of the psychological suffering the child has endured, physical and other tortures inflicted etc. This obliteration or significant modification in the disappeared children's sense of self is also exacerbated by the fact that their true personal identity at the time of disappearance may not have been firmly and fully established for most children; especially in the case of younger children. This too, on the analysis here, contributes to the continuous nature of the crime of 'enforced disappearance' even if the children are eventually recovered by their family alive. This reminds us that 'enforced disappearance' of children in particular is a form of *torture* involving, at a minimum, severe psychological suffering wherein the personalities and true identities of the children are obliterated as part of a process that begins with ripping the children from their families and home communities. Recall that the Inter-American Convention to Prevent and Punish Torture[67] specifically refers to torture

[66] Dissenting Opinion of Judge Cancado Trinidade in the IACtHR Judgement in Serrano Cruz Sisters Case 9 September, 2005 (emphasis added).

[67] Inter-American Convention to Prevent and Punish Torture Article 2 28 February, 1987.

as involving as an objective and process also the obliteration of personality which can be taken to include the attempted elimination of the person's self-perceived and other perceived personal identity.

Judge Cancado Trinidade makes the further point that being denied one's personal identity is a profound violation also in that the right to identity cannot be disassociated from "the legal personality of the individual as a subject of domestic and international law."[68] Recall in this regard also that the American Convention on Human Rights affirms the right to juridical personality "Every person has the right to recognition as a person before the law."[69] As Judge Trinidade puts it: "Respect for the right to identity enables the individual to defend his rights and, consequently, also has an impact on his legal and procedural capacity in both domestic and international law."[70] **Thus not only does 'enforced disappearance' of children in particular constitute a vehicle for *torture*; but it is designed to remove child victims from the protection of the law.** This is accomplished through the mechanism of eliminating, *in practice*, for all intents and purposes, the disappeared child victims' birth right to their true identity. Recall in this regard, for instance, consistent with the aforementioned analysis; that *El Salvador initially declined to accept that the Serrano Cruz sisters even ever existed.*

Judge Cancado Trinidade's dissenting opinion in the Serrano Cruz Sisters case is profound also in that, on the view here, it implicitly recognizes how the Court (in this case the IACtHR) can inadvertently, and contrary to its purpose, *deny the personhood of child victims of grave international crimes* such as 'enforced disappearance' and other such grave crimes. This the Court does, in part, by not recognizing the specific impacts of various grave international crimes on *children in particular*. For instance, respectfully, the IACtHR in *Serrano Cruz Sisters*: (i) failed to grasp the true nature and scope of the crime of 'enforced disappearance' as inflicted on children (i.e. in terms of understanding how and why the crime of enforced disappearance inflicted on children in particular is a continuous one that extends beyond a specific time and place and beyond age of majority); (ii) declined to acknowledge that the crime of 'enforced disappearance' of children continues whether or not the children are recovered alive given the permanent alteration of the children's perceived identities and the ensuing psychological suffering for the direct child victims and their kin and (iii) failed to recognize that there is a continuing violation of the children's right to his or her *untainted identity* whether the disappeared children are alive or deceased and whether or not recovered alive or dead.

The Court may even fail to assume jurisdiction over the case despite well grounded charges regarding the 'enforced disappearance' of children (as in the

---

[68] Dissenting Opinion of Judge Cancado Trinidade in the IACtHR Judgment in Serrano Cruz Sisters Case 9 September, 2005 at para 13.

[69] American Convention on Human Rights entered into force in 1978.

[70] Dissenting Opinion of Judge Cancado Trinidade in the IACtHR Judgement in Serrano Cruz Sisters Case 9 September, 2005 at para 13.

Serrano Cruz sisters case) due to a failure to appreciate the continuous nature of the crime of 'enforced disappearance' as it affects children in particular[71] (that is, the Court may hold that it does not have jurisdiction *ratione temporis* since the enforced disappearance occurred before the Court's enabling statute had entered into force and the State has not agreed to acknowledge the Court's jurisdiction over the matter). In such an instance then the perpetrators of the children's enforced disappearance have in fact been successful in removing the child victims from the protection of the law and in negating for *all practical purposes* the disappeared children's personhood under the law. The same result can occur also when enforced disappearance of children is not charged i.e. in child soldiering cases (as in *Lubanga*) and the charges brought (i.e. recruitment and use of children under 15 for active participation in hostilities) are considered to be time limited as was previously here discussed.

Note that the 'enforced disappearance' of children is also often accompanied, as this author has discussed elsewhere,[72] with the 'genocidal forcible transfer of children' such that the latter additional separate charges are also frequently warranted in cases involving the enforced disappearance of children. For instance, when children are forcibly disappeared to become so-called child soldiers in a State or non-State force perpetrating mass atrocities; their cultural ties are broken in large part or completely and their perceived identity is remade into that of the perpetrator group.[73] This then becomes an effective strategy for destroying, in whole or in part, the perpetrator targeted group of origin of the disappeared child victims.

The current author holds that the Rome Statute implicitly affirms the child's right to identity[74] given: (i) the Rome Statute offence of genocidal forcible transfer of children; (ii) the Rome Statute offence of enforced disappearance and (iii) the Rome Statute offences regarding inhumane; inhuman or degrading or torturous treatment or punishment. The articles regarding the prohibition on the forcible genocidal transfer of children and on enforced disappearance both imply the child's right to family and to his or her true personal identity. Compare in this regard the following statement from the dissenting opinion of Judge Cancado Trinidade in the IACtHR Serrano Cruz case on the right to family as related to the

---

[71] This is not to suggest that enforced disappearance of adults cannot also be a continuing crime (i.e. if the person is disappeared for a period beyond the initial kidnapping or indefinitely).

[72] Grover (2013a, b) and Grover (2012).

[73] As was mentioned, the current author holds that children are in themselves a 'protected group' *as such* under the Rome Statute provision regarding the 'genocidal forcible transfer of children'. Children as a protected group as such is a category that, in addition, most often also overlaps' depending on the situation, with the children's group of origin (or home community) targeted based on other distinctive characteristics i.e. national, ethnic, religious. The political affiliations of the parents of the child victims also most often overlap with other characteristics such as ethnicity as in Syria where the opposition to the Al Assad regime is associated in large part with the Sunni majority.

[74] The right to identity, as has been here discussed, is negated through 'enforced disappearance' (see Dissenting Opinion of Judge Cancado Trinidade in the IACtHR Judgement in Serrano Cruz Sisters Case 9 September, 2005).

right to one's true personal identity. In addition Judge Cancado Trinidade links the right to identity also to juridical personality.

> The right to identity, in *the Serrano Cruz Sisters* case heard under the American Convention, is inferred particularly from the right to a name and the rights of the family (Articles 18 and 17 of the Convention, respectively). But, in other circumstances, in another case, it could equally be inferred from other rights embodied in the Convention (such as the right to juridical personality (Article 3); the right to personal liberty (Article 7); the right to freedom of conscience and religion (Article 12); the right to freedom of thought and expression (Article 13), and the right to nationality (Article 20)).[75]

It is here contended that the same inherent human rights referred to by Judge Cancado Trinidade in the Serrano Cruz Sisters case (for example the right of children to juridical personality, their right to family and to their true identity etc.) are some of the rights that also underlie the designation, for instance, of 'enforced disappearance', 'torture', and the 'genocidal forcible transfer of children' as Rome Statute crimes (this not being an exhaustive list of Rome Statute defined international crimes that have as their objective, in part, to destroy the personalities and identities of the victims; a significant number of whom are children).

At this point recall that the Rome Statute, according to Article 21(3) of that statute, must be interpreted in accord with "internationally recognized human rights" (i.e. the universal inherent rights of the child to juridical personality and to his or her true personal identity):

> **The application and interpretation of law pursuant to this article must be consistent with internationally recognized human rights, and be without any adverse distinction founded on grounds such as** gender ... **age**, race, colour, language, religion or belief, political or other opinion, national, ethnic or social origin, wealth, birth or other status.[76]

The current author holds thus that, pursuant to Article 21(3) of the Rome Statute; the conceptualization of the 'enforced disappearance' of children as a denial of the children's right to their true identity and to juridical personality and as a form of *torture* must be developed through ICC case law.[77] Such "progressive development of the *corpus juris* of international law" (to borrow a phrase from Judge Cancado Trinidade) reflects the fact that the Rome Statute as international criminal law is not to be interpreted according to only a certain historical period (as with the parchment of the dead sea scrolls) but rather is properly regarded as a living instrument to be imbued with current developed universal rights values and sensitivities and a greater respect for children as legal persons with inherent human dignity.

---

[75] Dissenting Opinion of Judge Cancado Trinidade in the IACtHR Judgment in Serrano Cruz Sisters Case 9 September, 2005 at para 22.

[76] Rome Statute (2002).

[77] As here previously discussed, children forcibly disappeared to become child soldiers and/or to be sexually enslaved by perpetrator groups committing systematic widespread atrocities have *not* to date been acknowledged by the ICC also as child victims of the Rome Statute offences of 'enforced disappearance' or 'torture' (through the vehicles of child soldiering and sexual enslavement).

References

Finucane B (2010) Enforced disappearance as a crime under international law: a neglected origin in the laws of war. Yale J Int Law 35:171–197

Grover SC (2013a) Humanity's children: ICC jurisprudence and the failure to address the genocidal forcible transfer of children. Springer, Berlin

Grover SC (2013b) Child soldiers as victims of 'genocidal forcible transfer': Darfur and Syria as case examples. Int J Human Rights 17(3):411–427

Grover SC (2012) Child soldier victims of genocidal forcible transfer: exonerating child soldiers charged with grave conflict-related international crimes. Springer, Berlin

Pham PN, Vinck P, Stover E (2008) The Lord's Resistance Army and forced conscription in Northern Uganda. Human Rights Quart 30:404–411

Materials

Harvey-Blankenship M, Pham PM, Shigekane R (2010) Genetic tracing, disappeared children and justice (Innocenti Working Paper). http://www.unicef-irc.org/publications/pdf/iwp_2010_12.pdf. Accessed 12 May 2013

Inter-American Convention to Prevent and Punish Torture (entry into force 28 February, 1987). http://www.oas.org/juridico/english/treaties/a-51.html. Accessed 2 May 2013

Inter-American Court of Human Rights (IACtHR) Molina Theissen v Guatemala Judgment of 4 May, 2004

Convention on the Rights of the Child (1990) (entry into force 2 September 1990). http://www.ohchr.org/EN/ProfessionalInterest/Pages/CRC.aspx. Accessed 19 April 2013

Inlander MW (2005) Statement on behalf of United Nations Watch to the 11th session of the UN Working Group on Minorities (30 May to 3 June, 2005). http://www.unwatch.org/site/apps/nlnet/content2.aspx?c=bdKKISNqEmG&b=1313923&ct=1747993&printmode=1n. Accessed 13 May 2013

UN Human Rights Council Resolution 7/12 'Enforced or involuntary disappearances'. http://ap.ohchr.org/Documents/E/HRC/resolutions/A_HRC_RES_7_12.pdf. Accessed 12 May 2013

UN Working Group on Enforced or Involuntary Disappearances General Comment on children and enforced disappearances adopted by the Working Group on Enforced or Involuntary Disappearances at its ninety-eighth session (31 October–9 November 2012). http://daccess-dds-ny.un.org/doc/UNDOC/GEN/G13/112/64/PDF/G1311264.pdf. Accessed 12 May 2013

Cases

The Situation in the Democratic Republic of Congo: The Prosecutor v Germain Katanga and Mathieu Ngudjolo Chui Pre-Trial Chamber I Decision on the Confirmation of Charges 30 September, 2008 ICC-01/04-01/07

Chapter 6
The Non-Materialization of ICC Charges of 'Enforced Disappearance'

6.1 On 'Enforced Disappearance' in Darfur: Re-Examining the View of Former ICC Prosecutor Mr. Moreno-Ocampo

Former Prosecutor Moreno-Ocampo at one point contemplated the charge of 'enforced disappearance' against certain Libyan leaders stating that "the behavior is abduction, torture and disappearance. This is a tool to establish fear…"It [the enforced disappearance ICC charges] is being used for the first time because of the circumstances, but it is important that this is established as a crime against humanity,"[1] He further made the comment that "This is different from Bashir in Darfur where it was killings and rape or Milosevic".[2] In fact, however, children were specifically targeted for 'enforced disappearance' and 'torture' in Darfur through the vehicles of child soldiering and/or sexual violence and enslavement and subjected to other atrocities. including murder. subsequent to their forced disappearance (this during the period covered by the ICC charges relating to the situation in Darfur from about March 2003 to at least 14 July, 2008). This pattern of continuing atrocities in Darfur targeting children in particular (amongst others) is addressed in the following excerpts from the UN Child Soldiers Global Report (2008) regarding 'enforced disappearance' of children targeted by various groups and forces in Darfur for child soldiering and sexual violence:

> Throughout 2007 the SAF, the Janjaweed and Darfur armed groups continued to commit serious human rights abuses. Continuing violence and NCP intransigence severely limited access for humanitarian agencies in Darfur. As of July 2007, 2.2 million displaced people lived in camps in Darfur, and an estimated 80 per cent of the camp population were women and children. A UN arms embargo was imposed on Darfur under UN Security Council Resolution 1591 of March 2005. **However, the IDP camps were increasingly violent and militarized.** ***Rape and other sexual violence against women and girls were widespread. Younger girls were specifically targeted for rape, and many victims***

[1] Agence-France Press Al Aarabiya News (8 June, 2011)

[2] Agence-France Press Al Aarabiya News (8 June, 2011)

S. C. Grover, *The Torture of Children During Armed Conflicts*,
DOI: 10.1007/978-3-642-40689-8_6, © Springer-Verlag Berlin Heidelberg 2014

identified the perpetrators as members of the SAF, the central reserve police and the Janjaweed. In August 2006 over 200 women and girls were sexually assaulted over a five-week period in Kalma camp in south Darfur (p. 317).[3]

6.1.1 Child Recruitment and Deployment

6.1.1.1 Sudan Armed Forces (SAF)

The SAF denied recruitment or use of children in their forces, but military officials acknowledged that children from armed groups were transferred into their forces during the unification process. In May 2006, child soldiers were seen in a newly integrated SAF unit. In August 2006 the SAF estimated that there were approximately 19,000 soldiers in these units and it was thought that a significant number of them were under 18. **There were reports of children associated with both the SAF and allied militias in Darfur** (See Footnote 3).

6.1.1.2 Sudan People's Liberation Army (SPLA):

The SPLA acknowledged that it had child soldiers in its ranks and made high-level commitments to end their recruitment and use. However, 47 children were reported in the Kilo 7 barracks in Bentiu (Unity state) in July 2006, and they were not released until July 2007. These children had been enticed by SPLA junior officers who promised education in Southern Sudan. **SPLA forces raided a school in Nasir, Upper Nile, in October 2006 and abducted 32 boys for the purpose of recruitment. All but two were subsequently released. In September 2007 the UN confirmed the presence of children associated with SPLA forces in Southern Sudan. The youngest of the children was nine and the average age 16** (See Footnote 3).

6.1.2 Armed Groups:

6.1.2.1 Militias and armed groups associated with the SPLA

Militias increased recruitment, including child recruitment, before incorporation into either the SAF or SPLA in order to bolster their numbers and strengthen their negotiating power. Commanders from Southern Sudan were confirmed to be actively recruiting children in Khartoum. Some armed groups in the SSDF continued to recruit children after their incorporation into the SPLA in January 2006. The Pibor Defence Forces, a group allied to the SPLA in April 2007, was responsible for the recruitment and use of at least 78 children, the youngest of whom was a boy aged six. The Southern Sudan Disarmament, Demobilization and Reintegration (DDR) Commission was notified of their presence. Following the formal change of alliance from the SAF to the SPLA in April 2007, ***the whereabouts of the children were unknown.*** (See Footnote 3)

---

[3] UN Child Soldiers Global Report (2008).

6.1.3 Armed Groups in Darfur

> **Thousands of children were recruited and used by numerous armed groups in Darfur and actively involved in the armed conflict between May and July 2006. IDPs interviewed in May 2006 following Sudan government-backed Janjaweed militia attacks on villages near Kutum, northern Darfur, said that many armed child soldiers were among those who attacked them and Janjaweed were known to have recruited children from Sudanese refugee camps in Chad in 2006. In May 2006 SLA-Minawi was observed forcibly recruiting boys in Gereida, and in April 2007 armed children believed to be as young as 12 were identified with SLA-Minawi in northern Darfur. Recruitment continued in 2007 by SLA-Minawi, factions of the SLA which had not signed the DPA and the opposition JEM (Peace Wing)** (See Footnote 3).

6.1.4 Chadian-Backed Sudanese Armed Opposition Groups

> **Massive recruitment by Sudanese armed opposition groups took place in March and April 2006 among the refugee and IDP communities in eastern Chad. *Recruitment was at times carried out forcibly, with reports of torture as a coercive means*. In July 2007 the UN reported that the Chadian government had alleged that more than 1,000 children had been recruited by the SLA in refugee camps in the east.** In March 2006 the G-19 faction of the SLA, working in co-operation with Chadian government officials, recruited, some forcibly, 4,700 Sudanese refugees, including hundreds of **children, from the Breidjing and Treguine UN-supervised refugee camps** 50 km west of Adré in eastern Chad. Most of these people subsequently returned to the camps. **In 2006 Sudanese children were recruited from the Djabal and Goz Amir refugee camps in eastern Chad, where teachers were among the recruiters. In January 2007, 39 children were recruited from the Breidjing refugee camp by Sudanese armed opposition groups** (See Footnote 3).

6.1.5 Lord's Resistance Army (LRA):

> The Lord's Resistance Army (LRA), a Ugandan armed opposition group, was present in southern Sudan and attacked and killed civilians. Peace talks between the LRA and the Ugandan government began in July 2006 in Juba and a cessation-of-hostilities agreement was signed in August 2006. **The LRA forcibly recruited children from southern Sudan in the first half of 2007. While the total number of remaining LRA fighters remained unknown, up to 2,000 women and children were believed to remain in LRA camps** (emphasis added).

In sum then, on the analysis here, respectfully, contrary to the above claim of former ICC Prosecutor Moreno-Ocampo; there was in fact ample evidence in the Darfur situation to charge 'enforced disappearance' against the ICC Darfur defendants. This is the case given that the disappeared children were forcibly taken as child soldiers and for the purpose of sexual violation in Darfur and were, for all intents and purposes, the victims of the Rome Statute crime of 'enforced disappearance' (in respect of the families not knowing where their children were and whether or not they were still alive).

Let us consider next then the enforced disappearance ICC charges as they relate to the situation in Libya.

6.2 Situation in the Libyan Arab Jamahiriya: Prosecutor v Muammar Mohammed Abu Minyar Gaddafi, Saif Al-Islam Gaddafi, and Abdullah Al-Senussi

As mentioned previously; the Libyan cases are the first ICC cases in which the charge of 'enforced disappearance' was contemplated by the OTP:

> 35. In sum, the evidence demonstrates that GADDAFI conceived a plan to quell the popular demonstrations of February 2011 by all means, including through the use of extreme and lethal violence. Pursuant to this plan, the Security Forces carried out a widespread and systematic policy of attacks against civilians perceived as dissidents with the purpose of maintaining GADDAFI's power. SAIF AL-ISLAM and ALSENUSSI played key roles in the implementation of the plan. As a result, GADDAFI, SAIF AL-ISLAM and AL-SENUSSI are criminally responsible for the killings, arrests, detentions, ***disappearances*** and acts of ill-treatment against unarmed demonstrators and alleged dissidents committed by the Libyan Security Forces as of 15 February 2010.[4]
>
> 1. **Jurisdiction**
>
> 50. The situation in Libya was referred to the Office of the Prosecutor by the United Nations Security Council, which decided, by Resolution 1970 (2011) and acting under Chapter VII of the Charter of the United Nations, to refer the situation in the Libyan Arab Jamahiriya since 15 February 2011 to the Prosecutor of the International Criminal Court (emphasis added).[5]

Ultimately, the case against Muammar Mohammed Abu Minyar Gaddafi was terminated due to his death and the remaining accused (Abu Minyar Gaddafi, Saif Al-Islam Gaddafi, and Abdullah Al-Senussi) were *not* charged with 'enforced disappearance' but rather with murder and persecution according to the respective warrants. There were then no enforced disappearance charges brought despite the fact that:

> At least 370 Libyans have been reported missing in the eastern part of the country since mid-February 2011, some of them known or suspected to be in Libyan government custody, Human Rights Watch said today.
>
> Human Rights Watch documented 72 cases in the east of people who are missing or were apparently disappeared by government forces. The Libyan Red Crescent Society in Benghazi has recorded 370 missing person cases from Benghazi and Baida.

---

[4] Situation in the Libyan Arab Jamahiriya: Prosecutor's v Muammar Mohammed Abu Minyar Gaddafi, Saif Al-Islam Gaddafi, and Abdullah Al-Senussi16 May, 2011 ICC-01/11.

[5] Situation in the Libyan Arab Jamahiriya: Prosecutor's v Muammar Mohammed Abu Minyar Gaddafi, Saif Al-Islam Gaddafi, and Abdullah Al-Senussi 16 May, 2011 ICC-01/11.

> "At least 370 Libyans from the east-civilians and suspected fighters-have gone missing, some of them last seen in government hands," said Peter Bouckaert, emergencies director at Human Rights Watch, currently working in eastern Libya. "*Given the lack of information and Gaddafi's record with torture and killings, the families of these people fear the worst.*"
>
> The Libyan government has released no information about the number or location of people it has arrested across the country since anti-government protests began on February 15 in eastern Libya and then devolved into heavy fighting between the government and armed opposition groups (emphasis added).[6]

Hence to date the ICC OTP has yet to pursue 'enforced disappearance' charges in any case; though, as discussed, there were ample situations in which such charges were, on the analysis here, justified not only against the Libyan perpetrators but also in regards to various other situations addressed by the ICC.

References

Cases

Agence-France Press Al Aarabiya News (8 June 2011) Qaddafi first to face ICC 'enforced disappearance' charge http://english.alarabiya.net/articles/2011/06/08/152439.html Accessed 15 May 2015

UN Child Soldiers Global Report (2008) http://www.refworld.org Accessed 15 May 2013

Human Rights Watch (2011a) Libya: at least 370 missing from country's east: fate of libyans in government custody unknown. http://www.hrw.org/news/2011/03/30/libya-least-370-missing-countrys-east. Accessed 15 May 2013

[6] Human Rights Watch (2011a).

Chapter 7
'Murder', 'Wilful Killing' or 'Extra-Judicial Killings' of Children as Conflict Strategy and a Form of Torture

7.1 Extra Judicial Killing: Inter-American Commission of Human Rights Report No. 33/04 in Jailton Neri Da Fonseca v Brazil 11 March, 2004

On the issue of whether extra-judicial execution (or killing) constitutes psychological torture[1] consider the findings of the Inter-American Commission of Human Rights in *Jailton Neri Da Fonseca v. Brazil (a case that does not happen to have occurred in the context of armed conflict which is discussed below)*:

> **Excerpts From Jailton Neri Da Fonseca v Brazil**
> 1. On December 7, 1995, during the visit of the Inter-American Commission on Human Rights (hereinafter "the Commission" or "IACHR") to Brazil, it received a complaint from the D. Luciano Mendes Defense Center (*Associação Beneficente São Martinho* [St.

[1] There is no suggestion here whatsoever that the judicial execution of ***any*** person; let alone someone under age 18, is not also a form at a minimum of psychological torture but that discussion is beyond the scope of this present inquiry.

'Murder' here refers to: (i) murder as a war crime under the Rome Statute (2002) (Article 8(2)(c)(1)) occurring in a non-international conflict situation where civilians among other protected persons are knowingly being killed and (ii) murder as a crime against humanity under the Rome Statute (2002) (Article 7(1(a)) where the killing of civilians occurred as part of an intentional systematic and widespread attack on civilians.
"Wilfull Killing" refers to the war crime of 'wilful killing' under the Rome Statute (2002) (Article 8(2)(a)(i)) where the killing of civilians among other protected persons under the 1949 Geneva Conventions occurred in the context of an international conflict (Note that the Rome Statute (2002) also addresses genocide through killing (Article 6(a)).
The term 'extra-judicial execution or killing' is here used to refer to a killing that occurs without legal due process and is carried out by an agent of the State while the term 'murder' or 'wilful killing' is used here to refer to a killing that is not necessarily carried out by an agent of the State (i.e. it could be committed by a rebel perpetrator).

S. C. Grover, *The Torture of Children During Armed Conflicts*,

DOI: 10.1007/978-3-642-40689-8_7,

Martin Charitable Association]), against the Federal Republic of Brazil (hereinafter "Brazil," or "the State," or "the State of Brazil), for the alleged extrajudicial ***execution of Jailton Neri da Fonseca, a child***, by members of the military police of the State of Rio de Janeiro.

...

7. The petitioners reported that on December 22, 1992, Jailton Neri da Fonseca, a child residing in the *favela* [shantytown or slum neighborhood] of Roquete Pinto, at Praia de Ramos [Ramos Beach], in the city of Rio de Janeiro, was summarily executed by members of the military police from the Ramos Community Police Station, a police unit located in that place.

8. **The petitioners indicated that Jailton Neri da Fonseca was 14 years old when he was killed,** and that he was the only surviving son of Mrs. Maria dos Santos Silva, a 40-year old widow who had a son, Marco Neri da Fonseca, 18 years old, who had been allegedly murdered by the military police, and another son, Alexandre, who died at 14 years of age of pulmonary edema.

11. According to the petitioners, the official report of the autopsy performed on the body of the child, attached to the court records, stated that Jailton Neri had been killed by five shots from a firearm– two shots to his neck, one in the back, one in the back of his left arm, and one just below the right eye–all fired at short range. Later, the ballistics report concluded that the bullets withdrawn from the body of Jailton were expelled by a weapon examined by the experts, who reported that it belonged to the Ramos Military Police and was carried by Military Police Soldier Eduardo Bezerra Matos

12. **The petitioners reported that local residents had seen the police dragging the child through the streets of the *favela* to a place close to the beach, where they shot him five times and killed him**....

Proven Facts
62. In a case in which several children were detained for several hours by police agents before executing them, the Inter-American Court of Human Rights determined as follows:

... it is worth recalling, as this Court has already stated, that a person who is unlawfully detained [forcibly disappeared in this case]... is in an exacerbated situation of vulnerability creating a real risk that his other rights, such as the right to humane treatment and to be treated with dignity, will be violated.

63. From the established facts in the present case [Jailton Neri Da Fonseca v. Brazil], it is evident that Jailton Neri da Fonseca was in the custody of the military police when he was forced to proceed through the Ramos *favela*. **It is reasonable to infer that Jailton was perfectly aware that his life was in serious and imminent danger and that such circumstance caused extreme fear and psychological and moral suffering in him. The Commission considers that *these acts constitute torture*, defined in Article 2 of the Inter-American Convention to Prevent and Punish Torture, for the purposes of this Convention, as:**

any act intentionally performed whereby physical or mental pain or suffering is inflicted on a person, for purposes of criminal investigation, as a means of intimidation, as personal punishment, as a preventive measure, as a penalty, for any other purpose. Torture shall also be understood to be the use of methods upon a person intended to obliterate the personality of the victim or to diminish his physical or mental capacities, even if they do not cause physical pain or mental anguish.

64. ***On this point, although this article leaves some room for interpretation in defining whether a specific act constitutes torture, in the case of children the highest standard***

must be applied in determining the degree of suffering, taking into account factors such as age, sex, the effect of the tension and fear experienced, the status of the victim's health, and his maturity, for instance.

65. **The Commission is of the opinion that Jailton Neri da Fonseca must have experienced extreme fear and terror in finding himself in the hands of the military police, not knowing where they were taking him. The IACHR considers that such circumstance brought on Jailson Neri da Fonseca a situation of extreme psychological and moral suffering.**

66. Based on the preceding considerations, the Commission concludes that the State of Brazil violated the right to humane treatment of Jailton Neri da Fonseca. Hence Brazil violated Article 5 of the American Convention [which includes the right to be protected from torture in all its forms]

...

86. **In this case, the State of Brazil, instead of providing special protection for the human rights of the 14-year old Jailton Neri da Fonseca, since his status as a child made him subject to special rights and guarantees, murdered him, through its State agents** (emphasis added).[2]

The Jailton Neri Da Fonseca case hence advances the proposition, endorsed here, that extra-judicial execution constitutes *psychological torture*. It is further contended by the current author that such extra-judicial killings or executions used as a strategy of war constitute the Rome Statute crime not only of 'murder' but also of 'torture'. Further, this author maintains that the Inter-American Commission was quite correct legally and factually in holding that where the victims of extra-judicial abduction and killings are children; *psychological torture* can be inferred to have occurred given the child's vulnerability and, for younger children especially, but not exclusively, absolute terror in being separated from family.

7.2 'Murder' and 'Wilful Killing' as Psychological Torture: The ICC Case of Prosecutor v Germain Katanga and Mathieu Ngudjolo Chui (Democratic Republic of Congo)

In the *Katanga and Chui* ICC case, not only were children the victims of murder as an international crime but children as child soldiers were also used to carry out this atrocity. It is here held that both the child murder victims; and (on order of the FNI and FRPI commanders); the child soldier perpetrators; were as a result the

[2] Inter-American Commission of Human Rights Report No. 33/04 in Jailton Neri Da Fonseca v Brazil 11 March 2004.

victims also of *psychological torture* as a war crime[3] and as a crime against humanity as defined under the Rome Statute:

> 12. In the Prosecution's Amended Charging Document, the Prosecution submitted that at the time of the attack on Bogoro village, Germain Katanga was the FRPI's top commander of all Ngiti armed forces [Force de Résistance Patriotique en Ituri]and Mathieu Ngudjolo Chui the FNI military leader [Front des Nationalistes et Intégrationnistes] of all the Lendu fighters based in military camps south of Bunia.
>
> …
>
> 282. **The evidence presented by the Prosecution is also sufficient to establish substantial grounds to believe that the attack was directed against civilians not taking direct part in the hostilities, including women and *small children*, who were killed inside their houses with gunshots or machetes**. The evidence also shows that the attacks on the civilian population lasted throughout the day.
>
> 458. **Based on the evidence tendered by the Prosecution, the majority of the Chamber, Judge Anita Usacka dissenting, finds, however, that the combatants, in attacking civilians during and in the aftermath of the 24 February 2003 attack on Bogoro, and by indiscriminately using machetes, firearms and heavy weapons against civilians in such attacks, had the specific intent to kill such civilians, rather than the intent to cause severe injuries. They commenced the execution of the conduct of killing civilians by means of a substantial step toward the killing of one or more persons, but did not achieve the act because of circumstances independent of the perpetrator's intent.**
>
> …
>
> 462. As already found by the Chamber in a previous section of the present Decision, including those related to the war crime of wilful killing, and the crime against humanity of murder, the evidence tendered by the Prosecution establishes substantial grounds to believe that FNI/FRPI members had the specific intent to murder the civilian population of Bogoro, and that the attack on Bogoro village on 24 February 2003 included that: (i) it was directed against the predominantly Hema civilian population; (ii) the civilian population was the first to be targeted; (iii) ***civilians, including elderly, women and children, were killed by gunfire and machete wounds, and some were killed by being burned alive;*** and (iv) civilians were killed inside their houses or while trying to flee, during and in the aftermath of the attack.
>
> 463. Therefore, in the view of the majority of the Chamber, the clear intent to kill persons cannot be transformed into intent to severely injure persons by means of inhumane acts solely on the basis that the result of the conduct was different from that which was intended and pursued by the perpetrators.
>
> 464. The majority of the Chamber therefore finds that, for the purposes of the decision whether or not to confirm the charge, the Prosecution has not tendered sufficient evidence to establish substantial grounds to believe that the combatants, in attacking civilians with deadly weapons by either indiscriminately shooting civilians with firearms or in striking civilians with lances or machetes, had the intent to only cause serious injury to body or to mental or physical health of the civilian population of Bogoro.

[3] The Pre-Trial Chamber in Katanga Chui characterized the conflict as an international conflict in Ituri District between, at least, August 2002 and May 2003 (Situation in the Democratic Republic of Congo: The Prosecutor v Germain Katanga and Mathieu Ngudjolo Chui Pre-Trial Chamber I Decision on the Confirmation of Charges 30 September, 2008 ICC-01/04-01/07, para 240).

547… **there is sufficient evidence to establish substantial grounds to believe that in the FNI and FRPI camps:**

i. child soldiers were trained using violent methods, they learned how to handle weapons, and at the end of their training received "armes blanches" (e.g. machetes and spears) and guns;

ii. soldiers were militarily trained under the orders of Germain Katanga and Mathieu Ngudjolo Chui and were often paraded in their presence;

iii. **Germain Katanga was the key decision-maker regarding the transfer of children to, from, and within FRPI camps**;

iv. **Germain Katanga also used child soldiers in his personal escort because:**

"[il] préférait être escortée [sic] par les enfants soldats âgés de moins de 15 ans parce qu'ils exécutaient sans oppositions."

v. **Mathieu Ngudjolo Chui also used child soldiers in his personal escort**.

According Witness 280, in the FNI camps, a significant number of children were in the Military Police; the Military Police was in charge of arresting soldiers who caused trouble in the camp or in the village (every camp had a Military Police whose size depended on the size of the camp).

548. There is sufficient evidence to establish substantial grounds to believe that Germain Katanga and Mathieu Ngudjolo Chui agreed on a common plan to "wipe out" Bogoro:

i. since their creation in late 2002, because of the traditional links between Lendu and Ngiti ethnic groups, the FNI and FRPI, fought together;

ii. in early 2003, there was an agreement or common plan between Germain Katanga, leader of the FRPI, and Mathieu Ngudjolo Chui, leader of the FNI, to attack the village of Bogoro by "wiping out" the village of its UPC military elements and of the Hema civilians;

iii. **Germain Katanga, and Mathieu Ngudjolo Chui, through Commander Boba Boba and others under his command, met in Aveba in early 2003 and planned the attack against the village of Bogoro**;

iv. after the meeting in Aveba, a written plan was handed over to Mathieu Ngudjolo Chui. The plan was distributed to commanders by both Germain Katanga and Mathieu Ngudjolo Chui;

v. a few days before the attack against the village of Bogoro, Germain Katanga and other commanders visited Mathieu Ngudjolo Chui at the Zumbe Camp. The day after Germain Katanga's visit to the Zumbe camp, Mathieu Ngudjolo Chui informed the soldiers that they were going to attack Bogoro; and

vi. the day before the attack, Germain Katanga, Mathieu Ngudjolo Chui and other commanders met at Cobra Matata's camp in Bavi and from there, on the eve of the attack against the Bogoro village, moved to implement the **common plan** as they took their respective positions in Medhu and Kagaba.

549. **The Chamber finds that there is sufficient evidence to establish substantial grounds to believe that there was a plan to "wipe out" Bogoro village by directing the attack against the civilian population, killing and murdering the predominantly Hema population and destroying their properties.**

553. There is sufficient evidence to establish substantial grounds to believe that ***Germain Katanga and Mathieu Ngudjolo Chui agreed upon the use of children under the age of fifteen years to actively participate in the attack on Bogoro village. This conclusion is not only substantiated by the fact that they themselves used child soldiers as their bodyguards but also by the fact that their militias were largely made up of child soldiers. Moreover, there is sufficient evidence to establish substantial grounds to believe that the suspects sent their own bodyguards, many of them being children under the age of fifteen, to participate in the attack on Bogoro village***

567. The majority of the Chamber, Judge Anita Usacka dissenting, finds that there is sufficient evidence to establish substantial grounds to believe that from the Aveba meeting in early 2003 to the day of the attack on 24 February 2003, ***Germain Katanga and Mathieu Ngudjolo Chui knew that, as a consequence of the common plan, rape and sexual slavery of women and girls would occur in the ordinary course of the events.***

568. Accordingly, in the view of the majority of the Chamber, this conclusion, in relation to the crimes against humanity of rape and sexual slavery of **women and girls**, is also substantiated by the fact that:

(i) rape and sexual slavery against of women and girls constituted a common practice in the region of Ituri throughout the protracted armed conflict;

(ii) such common practice was widely acknowledged amongst the soldiers and the commanders;

(iii) in previous and subsequent attacks against the civilian population, the militias led and used by the suspects to perpetrate attacks ***repeatedly committed rape and sexual slavery against women and girls living in Ituri;***

(iv) ***the soldiers and child soldiers were trained (and grew up) in camps in which women and girls were constantly raped and kept in conditions to ease sexual slavery***;

(v) Germain Katanga, Mathieu Ngudjolo Chui and their commanders visited the camps under their control, frequently received reports of the activities of the camps by the camps commanders under their command, and were in permanent contact with the combatants during the attacks, including the attack on Bogoro;

(vi) **the fate reserved to captured women and girls was widely known amongst combatants**; and

(vii) the suspects and the combatants were aware, for example, which camps and which commanders more frequently engaged in this practice.

569. Therefore, the majority of the Chamber, Judge Anita Usacka dissenting, finds that there is sufficient evidence to establish substantial grounds to believe that when they planned, ordered and monitored the attack on Bogoro and on other villages inhabited mainly by Hema population, **the suspects knew that rape and sexual slavery would be committed in the ordinary course of the events**

The Chamber unanimously
CONFIRMS, on the basis of the evidence admitted for the purposes of the confirmation hearing, that there is sufficient evidence to establish substantial grounds to believe that Germain Katanga and Mathieu Ngudjolo Chui are responsible, under Article 25(3)(a) of the Statute, for the charge of **murder constituting a crime against humanity within the meaning of Article 7(1)(a) of the Statute;**

CONFIRMS, on the basis of the evidence admitted for the purposes of the confirmation hearing, that there is sufficient evidence to establish substantial grounds to believe that Germain Katanga and Mathieu Ngudjolo Chui are responsible, under Article 25(3)(a) of the Statute, for the **charge of wilful killing as a war crime within the meaning of Article 8(2)(a)(i) of the Statute**

…

CONFIRMS, on the basis of the evidence admitted for the purposes of the confirmation hearing, that there is sufficient evidence to establish substantial grounds to believe that Germain Katanga and Mathieu Ngudjolo Chui are responsible, under Article 25(3)(a) of the Statute, for the charge of **using children to participate actively in hostilities, as a war crime within the meaning of Article 8(2)(b)(xxvi) of the Statute;**

CONFIRMS, on the basis of the evidence admitted for the purposes of the confirmation hearing, that there is sufficient evidence to establish substantial grounds to believe that Germain Katanga and Mathieu Ngudjolo Chui are responsible, under Article 25(3)(a) of the Statute, for the charge of **intentionally directing attacks against the civilian**

> **population of Bogoro village, constituting a war crime within the meaning of Article 8(2)(b)(i) of the Statute**
>
> ...
>
> DECLINES to confirm the charge of inhuman treatment as a war crime within the meaning of Article 8(2)(a)(ii), on the basis of Article 61(7)(b) of the Statute;
> DECLINES to confirm the charge of outrages upon personal dignity as a war crime within the meaning of Article 8(2)(b)(xxxi) of the Statute, on the basis of Article 61(7)(b) of the Statute;
>
> ...
>
> CONFIRMS, on the basis of the evidence admitted for the purposes of the confirmation hearing, that there is sufficient evidence to establish substantial grounds to believe that Germain Katanga and Mathieu Ngudjolo Chui are responsible, under Article 25(3)(a) of the Statute, for **the charge of sexual slavery as a crime against humanity within the meaning of Article 7(1)(g) of the Statute;**
>
> CONFIRMS, on the basis of the evidence admitted for the purposes of the confirmation hearing, that there is sufficient evidence to establish substantial grounds to believe that Germain Katanga and Mathieu Ngudjolo Chui are responsible, under Article 25(3) (a) of the Statute, for **the charge of sexual slavery as a war crime within the meaning of Article 8(2)(b)(xxii) of the Statute**
>
> CONFIRMS, on the basis of the evidence admitted for the purposes of the confirmation hearing, that there is sufficient evidence to establish substantial grounds to believe that Germain Katanga and Mathieu Ngudjolo Chui are responsible, under Article 25(3)(a) of the Statute, for the charge of **rape as a crime against humanity within the meaning of Article 7(l)(g) of the Statute;**
>
> CONFIRMS, on the basis of the evidence admitted for the purposes of the confirmation hearing, that there is sufficient evidence to establish substantial grounds to believe that Germain Katanga and Mathieu Ngudjolo Chui are responsible, under Article 25(3)(a) of the Statute, for the charge of **rape as a war crime within the meaning of Article 8(2)(b) (xxii) of the Statute** (emphasis added).[4]

In sum then the ICC Pre-Trial Chamber confirmed, amongst other charges, the charges of: (a) murder of civilians as a crime against humanity in the Katanga Chui case and (b) acknowledged the role of child soldiers in the commission of that grave international crime amongst others (confirming then that there was also a violation of Rome Statute Article 8(2)(b)(xxvi)). The Pre-Trial Chamber, however, declined to confirm the charges of 'inhuman conduct' as a war crime or 'outrages on personal dignity' as a war crime[5] or 'other inhumane acts' as a crime against humanity. It is here contended, however, that using children to perpetrate

---

[4] The Situation in the Democratic Republic of Congo: The Prosecutor v Germain Katanga and Mathieu Ngudjolo Chui Pre-Trial Chamber I Decision on the Confirmation of Charges 30 September 2008 ICC-01/04-01/07.

[5] This based on the Pre-Trial Chamber's contention that these two crimes were not part of the plan to "wipe out" Bogoro village but occurred incidentally after the attack without being part of the mental element of the two co-accused Katanga and Cui (see The Situation in the Democratic Republic of Congo: The Prosecutor v Germain Katanga and Mathieu Ngudjolo Chui Pre-Trial Chamber I Decision on the Confirmation of Charges 30 September 2008: The Prosecutor v Germain Katanga and Mathieu Ngudjolo Chui Pre-Trial Chamber I Decision on the Confirmation of Charges 30 September, 2008 ICC-01/04-01/07, para 570-571).

atrocities and inflicting atrocity on children in this and other ways (as occurred in the attack on Bogoro village and on other villages): (i) constitutes 'inhuman treatment' as a war crime and as a crime against humanity and (ii) *in addition*, produces severe physical and psychological suffering constituting inhuman treatment that rises to the level of *torture* for the children in particular (both the so-called child soldiers and their child victims).[6] In regard to the latter point note the position of the Katanga Chui Pre-Trial Chamber on the matter of making a finding of 'other inhumane acts:

> 449. The Chamber notes that, according to the jurisprudence of the ICTY Trial Chamber in The Prosecutor v. Blaskic, the conduct of intentionally causing serious physical or mental injury constitutes a serious violation of international customary law and of human rights of a similar nature and gravity to the crimes referred to in Article 7(1) of the Statute. **However, in determining whether such acts meet the requirements of Article 7(1)(k) of the Statute [the Rome Statute], the Chamber also considers that in each case:**
>
> consideration must be given to all of the factual circumstances. These circumstances may include the nature of the act or omission, the context in which it occurred, **the personal circumstances of the victim including *age*, sex and health, as well as the physical, mental and moral effects of the act upon the victim** (emphasis added).[7]

The ICC Pre-Trial Chamber in *Katanga Chui* thus held that[8] it is necessary to consider such factors as "*age* as well as the physical, mental and moral effects of the act upon the victim" in considering how the Rome Statute applies to the facts in the case. No such consideration, however, on the current author's estimation, was given in *Katanga Chui* to factors such as the *young age* of many of the victims and/or (child soldier) perpetrators.

The rapes and sexual enslavement of children by the FRPI and FNI and the use of so-called child soldiers by these armed forces to carry out atrocities constitute an attack on the personal dignity of the child victim perpetrators *and* the latter's child victims. (This author has elsewhere argued that children recruited and used as

---

[6] This is not to suggest that physical and torture was not also inflicted on the adults targeted in Bogoro village but rather to suggest that, as has been discussed, children are entitled to special protections that go beyond a basis just in their status as civilians. Further, as discussed here also previously, children as victims are held by experts on torture and those in the medical community who study this issue generally to have a lower threshold for pain and suffering including psychological suffering (see for example Quiroga (2009)). Hence, based on that empirical context; it was reasonable on the facts to infer that the children in Bogoro village in particular suffered torture due to the murderous attack planned and implemented by Katanga and Chui.

[7] The Situation in the Democratic Republic of Congo: The Prosecutor v Germain Katanga and Mathieu Ngudjolo Chui Pre-Trial Chamber I Decision on the Confirmation of Charges 30 September 2008: The Prosecutor v Germain Katanga and Mathieu Ngudjolo Chui Pre-Trial Chamber I Decision on the Confirmation of Charges 30 September, 2008 ICC-01/04-01/07, para 449.

[8] On 18 December 2012, Trial Chamber II acquitted Mathieu Ngudjolo Chui of the charges of war crimes and crimes against humanity and ordered his immediate release. On 21 December 2012, Mathieu Ngudjolo Chui was released from custody. The Office of the Prosecutor has appealed the verdict.

so-called child soldiers by State or non-State forces perpetrating mass atrocities retain their civilian status and are the victims of 'genocidal forcible transfer 'of a protected group to an unlawful criminal organization.[9] The facts in *Katanga Chui* reveal that both the child soldiers (persons under age 18) and their child victims were denied the special protections and care and respect owed to children during armed conflict as per, for instance, international customary and humanitarian law).[10]

Note that in *Katanga Chui* certain sexual violence charges were confirmed both as war crimes and as crimes against humanity (rape and sexual slavery) and these charges related also to the rape and other sexual violence against children in particular. The facts regarding sexual violence against children also support the necessity for there having been torture charges brought in the case. The rapes and sexual enslavement of the girls in particular constituted psychological and physical torture. Those girls not yet subjected to rape and sexual enslavement (if there were any such as yet non-sexually violated girls) also suffered psychologically with the knowledge that the same sexual violence and sexual enslavement was in all probability ultimately also to befall them in the FNI/FRPI military camps.

Hence, on the analysis here, at a minimum, *torture* as: (i) a crime against humanity (Rome Statute Article 7(1)(f)) and as (ii) a war crime (depending on the proper characterization of the nature of the armed conflict under Article 8 (2)(a)(ii) and/or Article 8 (2)(c)(i)) should have been included in the charges and confirmed by the ICC Pre-Trial Chamber in *Katanga Chui* (or alternatively, but less ideally, some of the facts already introduced by the Prosecutor legally re-characterised to allow for the bringing of torture charges in addition to the other charges). In the Katanga Chui case, as in all ICC cases to date, however, no torture charges were brought. Thus there was no consideration given to: (i) the issue of the severe pain and suffering inflicted on children in particular through (child) soldiering with; and sexual enslavement and other sexual victimization by; an armed group committing widespread atrocities; (ii) the lower thresholds of pain and suffering and particular and varied set of circumstances during armed conflict that may qualify as torture under the Rome Statute where children are the targeted victims or amongst the high priority selected victims nor to (iii) the fact that the torture of children in particular serves as a highly effective tool for intimidation of the targeted civilian population.

---

[9] See, for example, Grover (2013a), pp. 3–80.

[10] See for instance Protocol I Additional to the Geneva Conventions of 12 August (1949), (Article 77(1)): "Children shall be the object of special respect and shall be protected against any form of indecent assault. The Parties to the conflict shall provide them with the care and aid they require, whether because of their age or for any other reason." and Protocol II Additional to the Geneva Conventions of 12 August (1949), (Article 4(3)): "Children shall be provided with the care and aid they require…" Both these introductions to the respective articles in the Additional Protocols reflect international customary law codified on the special protection owed 'children' during armed conflict. These lines do *not* specify an age in referring to "children' but the term "children' here is interpreted by the ICRC as covering persons under 18.

References

Literature

Grover SC (2013a) Humanity's children: ICC jurisprudence and the failure to address the genocidal forcible transfer of children. Springer, Berlin

Quiroga J (2009) Torture in children. Torture (Journal on Rehabilitation of Torture Victims and Prevention of Torture) 19(2): 65–87

Materials

Protocol I Additional to the Geneva Conventions of 12 August (1949), and relating to the Protection of Victims of International Armed Conflicts (Protocol I), 8 June 1977. http://www.icrc.org/ihl.nsf/WebART/470-750099 Accessed 18 April 2013

Protocol II Additional to the Geneva Conventions of 12 August (1949), and relating to the Protection of Victims of Non-International Armed Conflicts (Protocol II), 8 June 1977 http://www.icrc.org/ihl.nsf/WebART/470-750099 Accessed 18 April 2013

Cases

Inter-American Commission of Human Rights Report No. 33/04 in Jailton Neri Da Fonseca v Brazil 11 March, 2004 http://cidh.org/annualrep/2004eng/Brazil.11634eng.htm Accessed 18 May 2013

The Situation in the Democratic Republic of Congo: The Prosecutor v Germain Katanga and Mathieu Ngudjolo Chui Pre-Trial Chamber I Decision on the Confirmation of Charges 30 September, 2008 ICC-01/04-01/07

Chapter 8
The International Legal Responsibility to Child Victims of Systematic Torture During Armed Conflict

8.1 Preliminary Comments

> Children have been detained and tortured in the pursuit of military objectives. Torture of children may be used as part of a collective punishment of a community, as a means of extracting information from the child, the child's peers or parents, or as entertainment. Allegations of cruelty to children ...involving solitary confinement while naked and blindfolded, beatings, electric shocks, and hosing with cold water—have all been documented by Amnesty International and corroborated by medical evidence.[1]

It is here argued that in not considering children as particularized high priority targets of various crimes under the Rome Statute that produce severe psychological and physical pain and suffering[2]; the occurrence of child *torture* (and in addition often also 'cruel or inhuman treatment' and 'outrages on personal dignity' perpetrated intentionally on children specifically[3]) has been to date unjustifiably disregarded by the ICC.[4] Respectfully then, on the view here, this inevitably results in the ICC not meeting its obligation to uphold in all respects, and in regards to victims of every age (including children), the *jus cogens* ICL prohibition against

[1] Plunkett and Southall (1998), p. 73.

[2] Here referred to are Rome Statute crimes during armed conflict such as 'enforced disappearance', rape and murder *where children in particular are targeted* (though not necessarily children exclusively) and where these crimes also constitute psychological and physical torture.

[3] See for example the Prosecutor v Thomas Lubanga Dyilo warrant for arrest (10 February, 2006).

[4] This being the case both in respect of the charges brought by the ICC OTP (i.e. absence of torture charges where children are prime victims) and in terms of the analysis of the case by the ICC Chambers (where the Chambers decline to legally characterize also as torture various crimes that amount to torture where children are the targeted victims. Recall in this regard the children's generally lower threshold for pain and suffering compared to that of healthy adults.)

S. C. Grover, *The Torture of Children During Armed Conflicts*,
DOI: 10.1007/978-3-642-40689-8_8, © Springer-Verlag Berlin Heidelberg 2014

torture. In this regard recall that the International Committee of the Red Cross has found as a rule of ICL that:

> Torture, cruel or inhuman treatment and outrages on personal dignity, in particular humiliation and degrading treatment, are prohibited[5]

On the view here; with respect; the failure *in practice* to acknowledge: (i) the systematic widespread ***torture*** of children during a specific armed conflict situation (i.e. torture through 'enforced disappearance', child soldiering, sexual enslavement, rape and through other vehicles) and (ii*)* the particularized targeting of children for ***torture***; amounts to the ICC exercising discretion as to when to acknowledge and when to deny the actual occurrence of torture (discretion in this respect that arguably has no foundation in international law). Further, the denial of children as particularized targets for *torture* is tantamount to inadvertently denying the personhood and dignity of the child victims. This is reminiscent of the contemporary debate about torture in some academic circles where the reality of torture having occurred in a particular situation is ostensibly defined away:

> the discussion of torture often generates an almost Orwellian use of language. Thus, President Bush's assertion that "we do not torture" needs the equivalent of a "decoder-ring" before one can have any idea what he might mean by such a statement.[6] Recall Humpty Dumpty's famous assertion, in Chapter Six of Lewis Carroll's *Through the Looking Glass*, that "when I use a word, it means just what I choose it to mean…." Upon Alice's protest that "the question is whether you can make words mean so many different things," Mr. Dumpty replies, "The question is which is to be master—that's all." **In many ways, the best way of understanding the contemporary debate about torture is as a fundamental struggle over who will get to be the "master" of the language we use when giving concrete definition to "torture"**(emphasis added).[7]

The torture of children refocuses our attention on the fact that deciding what constitutes torture in any particular set of circumstances should properly take into account factors such as, but not limited to; the age, maturity, health, disability status, and gender of the victims. This in that children; particularly younger children; due to their age, maturational status and vulnerability may experience severe physical and psychological pain and suffering at a lower threshold than would be the case for healthy adults not of elderly age. The issue of the torture of children then forces us to look at the realities on the ground and steer away from semantic gymnastics and a strictly abstract consideration of what constitutes torture on any particular set of facts. This is a very salutary process given that in recent years there have been notorious attempts, even by some democratic governments, to define away the reality of the torture they have imposed. An example of one such outrageous and misguided attempt to define away torture (i.e. as "harsh interrogation" techniques) came as is widely known during the Bush administration's implementation of torture in the

[5] Henckaerts and Doswald-Beck (2005), p. 315.

[6] This given the evidence of torture used at the Guantanamo Detention Centre; a U.S. facility.

[7] Levinson (2010), p. 236.

form of water boarding and selected other torturous techniques at Guantanamo.[8] Further, consideration of children as particularized targets for torture reminds us of the failure to fulfil the international obligation under international law owed to children regarding their 'special protection' during armed conflict over and above that protection afforded civilians in general (including protection against child soldiering). Adding grave insult to injury is the fact, as was here discussed, that where children have been particularized targets for torture during armed conflict in cases considered by the ICC: (i) torture has either not been charged or (ii) where charged; the fact that children were also specifically targeted in particular as part of the common plan was not addressed in any substantive manner (i.e. as an aggravating factor taken into account during sentencing[9]). Children as particularized victims of systematic and widespread torture (in whatever form) during armed conflict are entitled both to international criminal justice through the ICC (where the Court has jurisdiction and all other criminal justice avenues are blocked) and to reparations.

8.2 Lessons Yet to be Learned Given the Failure of the ICC to Acknowledge the Systematic Widespread Torture of Children During Armed Conflict[10]

8.2.1 Child Soldiering for Perpetrator Armed Forces as Torture

It has here been argued that recruitment and use of child soldiers by State or non-State forces perpetrating mass atrocities and/or genocide during hostilities and/or the use of children as sex slaves during armed conflict constitutes *'enforced disappearance' and 'torture'* under the Rome Statute.[11] Both of these types of perpetrator conduct during armed conflict (i) inflict severe psychological pain and suffering on the direct and indirect victims and (ii) adversely impact the integrity of the family unit (negating the child's right to family as well as the parents' or legal guardians' right to the children to whom they have lawful custody). For all intents and purposes these child soldiers are 'forcibly disappeared.' Due to being disappeared; and as a consequence of the stigma and alienation from family and community that arises as a consequence of the child's connection to the perpetrator group; family ties are dramatically disrupted or even in some cases broken.

[8] Lokaneeta (2010).

[9] In contrast, for example, to the situation with the handling of torture of children cases addressed by the Inter-American Court of Human Rights.

[10] This is not an exhaustive list of lessons yet to be learned *in practice* on acknowledging the occurrence of the international crime of torture of children as particularized victims during armed conflict and on prosecuting those most responsible.

[11] The issue of child soldiering for forces that respect ICL and international humanitarian treaty law is beyond the scope of this book (in the latter context child refers to children 15 or over).

This results in a continuing psychological torture for the children involved and for their families which frequently persists even if the children are recovered alive.

On the aforementioned analysis, hence, it is here contended that children under 18 and not just those under 15 are protected under the Rome Statute against the international crime of recruitment and use of children for active participation in hostilities (the term 'child soldier' used here to encompass children used as sex slaves in military camps and/or used for fighting or for combat support functions such as spying). That is, for instance, under the Rome Statute provisions concerned with 'enforced disappearance' and 'torture' (i.e. torture as a war crime or a crime against humanity or both depending on the fact pattern); children (persons under age 18) are protected against child soldiering with a State or non-State force perpetrating mass atrocities when *child soldiering is properly considered as a vehicle for torture and/or enforced disappearance.* It is here contended thus that the issue of child soldiering in ICC cases must not, if the matter is to be given a fair hearing, be approached *only* in terms of Rome Statute Articles 8(2)(b)(xxvi) or 8(2)(e)(vii).

So-called child soldiers (persons under age 18) appropriated by State or non-State forces perpetrating atrocities are, on the current author's analysis, *child civilians* entitled to protection from the State and international community under ICL and international treaty law whether in the context of an international or a non-international armed conflict.[12] Notwithstanding this fact, however, children have been routinely subjected to forced disappearance and torture as child soldiers for perpetrator State or non-State forces. On the view here; these children are to be considered in a broad sense *child civilian* detainees of the perpetrator force (held in the perpetrator force military encampments and, through threat and coercion, moving with the perpetrator force as the perpetrator group moves to the fluid frontlines in various locations). These children then are entitled during armed conflict to special protection under ICL, international human rights and humanitarian law notwithstanding the fact that they are ostensibly erroneously categorized by the perpetrator group as 'members' of that armed group and wrongly most often perceived as such by the adversary or segments of the larger civilian community (particularly if the children are 15 or over).[13]

These child victim detainees, whether over or under age 15, cannot then under international law properly be considered to have lawfully consented to their own *torture* (through child soldiering for a perpetrator group committing mass atrocities and/

[12] Recall in any case that Article 5 of the Universal of Declaration of Human Rights (1948) states that "no one shall be subjected to torture or to cruel, inhuman or degrading treatment or punishment" and that various international human rights treaties have stipulated that there is no derogation from this absolute prohibition (see Rodley NS Cited in Kaleck W; Ratner, M; Singelnstein T and Weiss P (2007), pp. 192–193.

[13] Children appropriated by a perpetrator group committing mass atrocities and/or genocide cannot be considered to have genuinely consented to having 'joined' such an armed force or group. This is the case given the extremely coercive circumstances surrounding their recruitment and induction into the perpetrator group. This author has argued elsewhere, furthermore, that these appropriated children are the victims of the grave international crime of 'genocidal forcible transfer of children' (see for instance Grover (2013a), Grover (2013b) and Grover (2012)).

or genocide)[14] regardless the alleged mechanism of their so-called 'recruitment' into the perpetrator group as child soldiers (i.e. alleged 'enlistment' or alternatively 'conscription'). Time and again this point has *not* been acknowledged by either international or domestic courts. Consider, for instance, the case of Omar Khadr in which the Canadian courts found that Omar Khadr, a minor, had been subjected to 'cruel treatment' at Guantanamo while in U.S. detention and certain justices found that this cruel treatment rose to the level of *torture*. However, the Canadian courts failed to consider or acknowledge Omar Khadr's child soldiering with Afghani extremist Taliban linked to Al Qaeda *as itself constituting torture of a child* under international criminal law to which treatment the child *cannot* be considered to have consented given: (i) the vulnerability of children who are entitled under ICL and international human rights and humanitarian treaty law to *special protection* during armed conflict; (ii) the coercive circumstances that led to his child soldiering (his father, after bringing the boy to Afghanistan on a trip from Canada, (it appears knowingly) left the Canadian boy in Afghanistan (when Omar Khadr was 14) in the house of extremist Taliban involved with Al Qaeda); and (iii) the international community's duty under ICL and human rights and humanitarian treaty law to protect children (persons under age 18) from various harms during armed conflict including from child soldiering[15]:

The Canadian federal courts, as mentioned, have recognized Omar Khadr's treatment at Guantanamo as 'cruel' and arguably rising to the level of 'torture' (in which treatment Canada to some extent was complicit). However, these same courts have not acknowledged that child soldiering for a perpetrator force committing grave international crimes against civilians is *in itself* a form of torture of children in particular:

Excerpts from Canada (Prime Minister) v. Khadr, 2010 **SCC 3:**

> [3] Mr. Khadr was 15 years old when he was taken prisoner on July 27, 2002, by U.S. forces in Afghanistan. He was alleged to have thrown a grenade that killed an American soldier in the battle in which he was captured.[16] About 3 months later, he was transferred to the U.S. military installation at Guantanamo Bay. He was placed in adult detention facilities
> ...
> [5] In February and September 2003, agents from the Canadian Security Intelligence Service ("CSIS") and the Foreign Intelligence Division of the Department of Foreign Affairs and International Trade ("DFAIT") questioned Mr. Khadr on matters connected to the charges pending against him and shared the product of these interviews with U.S. authorities. **In March 2004, a DFAIT official interviewed Mr. Khadr again, with the knowledge that he had been subjected by U.S. authorities to a sleep deprivation**

[14] That torture being inflicted, for instance, by having the appropriated children participate in and witness atrocities, and experience brutalization and sexual victimization during 'training' and 'orientation to the perpetrator group etc.

[15] In Omar Khadr's case, the boy was not forcibly disappeared from the family's perspective in that his family apparently willingly arranged for his involvement in the Taliban extremist group. However, under the Rome Statute "forcibly" can involve also "psychological oppression" and "abuse of power" (see footnote 5 to Article 6(e)) and arguably the boy had no choice under the circumstances but to acquiesce to the Taliban demands.

[16] Omar Khadr was severely injured in that battle in which he was ultimately captured and, were it not for the Americans providing medical aid, likely would have succumbed to his injuries.

technique, known as the "frequent flyer program", in an effort to make him less resistant to interrogation. During this interview, Mr. Khadr refused to answer questions. In 2005, von Finckenstein J. of the Federal Court issued an interim injunction preventing CSIS and DFAIT agents from further interviewing Mr. Khadr in order "to prevent a potential grave injustice" from occurring: *Khadr v. Canada*, 2005 FC 1076, [2006] 2 F.C.R. 505, at para. 46. In 2008, this Court ordered the Canadian government to disclose to Mr. Khadr the transcripts of the interviews he had given to CSIS and DFAIT in Guantanamo Bay, under s. 7 of the *Charter*: *Khadr v. Canada*, 2008 SCC 28, [2008] 2 S.C.R. 125 ("*Khadr 2008*").

...

[9] **After reviewing the history of Mr. Khadr's detention and applicable principles of Canadian and international law, O'Reilly J. concluded that in these special circumstances, Canada has a "duty to protect" Mr. Khadr** (2009 FC 405, 341 F.T.R. 300). He found that "[t]he ongoing refusal of Canada to request Mr. Khadr's repatriation to Canada offends a principle of fundamental justice and violates Mr. Khadr's rights under s. 7 of the *Charter*" (para. 92). Also, he held that "[t]o mitigate the effect of that violation, Canada must present a request to the United States for Mr. Khadr's repatriation to Canada as soon as practicable" (para. 92).

[10] The majority judgment of the Federal Court of Appeal (*per* Evans and Sharlow JJ.A.) upheld O'Reilly J.'s order, but defined the s. 7 breach more narrowly. The majority of the Court of Appeal found that it arose from the March 2004 interrogation conducted with the knowledge that ***Mr. Khadr had been subject to the "frequent flyer program", characterized by the majority as involving cruel and abusive treatment contrary to the principles of fundamental justice***: 2009 FCA 246, 310 D.L.R. (4th) 462...(emphasis added)[17]

Excerpt from Khadr v. Canada (Prime Minister), 2010 **FC 715,** [2010] **4 F.C.R. 36:**

[7] In February and September 2003, agents from the Canadian Security Intelligence Service (CSIS) and the Foreign Intelligence Division of Foreign Affairs and International Trade (DFAIT) travelled to Guantanamo Bay and questioned Mr. Khadr. The information obtained by these Canadian officials was provided to the U.S. Mr. Khadr was interviewed again in March 2004 by a DFAIT official who knew, prior to the interview, that Mr. Khadr had been subjected by U.S. authorities to a program of sleep deprivation. A report described this technique and its purpose:

In an effort to make him more amenable and willing to talk, [blank] has placed Umar [sic: should read Omar] on the "frequent flyer program." [F]or the three weeks before [the] visit, Umar [sic:should read Omar has not been permitted more than three hours in any one location. At 3 h intervals he is moved to another cell block, thus denying him uninterrupted sleep and a continuous change of neighbours. He will soon be placed in isolation for up to three weeks and then will be interviewed again (emphasis added).[18]

Note that Khadr was also isolated from any contact with persons outside of Guantanamo and did not even have contact with legal counsel until 2004.[19] This also constituted, on the analysis here, cruel treatment rising to the level of psychological torture.

Consider the following excerpts from Khadr v. Canada (Prime Minister) 2009 F.C.J. No. 462 [2009] FC 405 on the issue of whether Omar Khadr, a minor,

[17] Canada (Prime Minister) v. Khadr, 2010 SCC 3 Judgment 29 January, 2010.

[18] Khadr v. Canada (Prime Minister), 2010 FC 715, [2010] 4 F.C.R. 36.

[19] Khadr v. Canada (Prime Minister) [2009] F.C.J. No. 462 at para 10.

caught up with the Taliban in Afghanistan, was *tortured* at Guantanamo. These selected excerpts highlight the need to consider this question in the context of relevant international instruments as opposed to within a more limited legal context:

Excerpts from Khadr v. Canada (Prime Minister) 2009 **F.C.J. No. 462** [2009] **FC 405**
Relevant International Instruments

(i) The Convention against Torture and Other Cruel, Inhuman or Degrading Treatment of Punishment (CAT)

56 Torture is defined under the CAT as "any act by which severe pain or suffering, whether physical or mental, is intentionally inflicted on a person for such purposes as obtaining from him or a third person information or a confession" (Article 1). The Supreme Court of Israel has concluded that sleep deprivation "for the purpose of tiring [the suspect] out or 'breaking' him,... is not part of the scope of a fair and reasonable investigation" and harms "the rights and dignity of the suspect" (*Public Committee Against Torture in Israel* v. *Israel*, 38 I.L.M. 1471 at para. 31). ***Based on that decision, Justice Mosley concluded that the subjection of Mr. Khadr to sleep deprivation techniques offended the CAT.***

57 In addition to its obligation to prevent torture within Canada and to prosecute offenders, Canada also has a duty to "ensure that any statement which is established to have been made as a result of torture shall not be invoked as evidence in any proceedings" (Article 15). Canada turned over the fruits of its interrogation of Mr. Khadr to U.S. authorities for use against him, knowing that sleep deprivation techniques had been imposed on him.

(ii) Convention on the Rights of the Child (CRC)

58 Canada has a duty under the CRC to "take all appropriate legislative, administrative, social and educational measures to protect the child from all forms of physical and mental violence, injury or abuse, neglect or negligent treatment, maltreatment or exploitation, including sexual abuse, while in the care of parent(s), legal guardian(s) or any other person who has the care of the child" (Article 19.1). A child is a person under the age of 18 (Article 1).

59 In addition, Canada must ensure that "[n]o child shall be subjected to torture or other cruel, inhuman or degrading treatment or punishment", that "[n]o child shall be deprived of his or her liberty unlawfully or arbitrarily" and that the "arrest, detention or imprisonment of a child shall be in conformity with the law and shall be used only as a measure of last resort and for the shortest appropriate period of time" (Article 37*a*, *b*).

60 Canada must also ensure that "every child deprived of liberty shall be separated from adults" and "**have the right to maintain contact with his or her family through correspondence and visits", except in exceptional circumstances (Article 37c).** Further, every child in custody "shall have the right to prompt access to legal and other appropriate assistance, as well as the right to challenge the legality of the deprivation of his or her liberty before a court or other competent, independent and impartial authority, and to a prompt decision on any such action" (Article 37*d*).

61 Canada also has a duty to "take all appropriate measures to promote physical and psychological recovery and social reintegration of a child victim of: any form of neglect, exploitation, or abuse; **torture** or any other form of cruel, inhuman or degrading treatment or punishment; or armed conflicts" (Article 39).

62 **Finally, Canada has recognized "the right of every child alleged as, accused of, or recognized as having infringed the penal law to be treated in a manner consistent with the promotion of the child's sense of dignity and worth" (Article 40.1).**

63 The CRC imposes on Canada some specific duties in respect of Mr. Khadr. Canada was required to take steps to protect Mr. Khadr from all forms of physical and mental violence, injury, abuse or maltreatment. **We know that Canada raised concerns about Mr. Khadr's treatment, but it also implicitly condoned the imposition of sleep deprivation techniques on him, having carried out interviews knowing that he had been subjected to them.**

64 Canada had a duty to protect Mr. Khadr from being subjected to any ***torture*** **or other cruel, inhuman or degrading treatment or punishment, from being unlawfully detained, and from being locked up for a duration exceeding the shortest appropriate period of time. In Mr. Khadr's case, while Canada did make representations regarding his possible mistreatment, it also participated directly in conduct that failed to respect Mr. Khadr's rights, and failed to take steps to remove him from an extended period of unlawful detention among adult prisoners, without contact with his family**[20] (emphasis added).[21]

The Canadian court judgments in the Omar Khadr case[22] hence show a startling lack of consideration of **child soldiering as a form of torture *in itself*** such that the so called child soldier is properly viewed under ICL and international human rights and humanitarian treaty law as a non-culpable victim. That is; a victim recruited into child soldiering by direct force or indirect force due to coercive circumstances and propaganda and the knowledge that being a member of the perpetrator group committing mass atrocities might be the only realistic option for survival for any period. One form of coercion that is placed on the children to become child soldiers or to return if escaped or rescued is the fear that the perpetrator group will abduct one of the child's siblings or an adult in the family for instance as retaliation. Human Rights Watch documented such realistic concerns among returned LTTE child soldiers in Shri Lanka:

> Because the LTTE commonly demands the service of one child per household, many returnees expressed concern that their brothers and sisters might be taken in their stead if the former child soldier refused to return. Although most returnees clearly did not want

[20] Note that being deprived of contact with family for a significant period without justifiable legal basis, and contrary to the child's best interests, can constitute *psychological torture* of a child.

[21] Khadr v. Canada (Prime Minister) 2009 F.C.J. No. 462 [2009] FC 405.

[22] For additional discussion on the Omar Khadr case and related Canadian court judgements see for example Grover (2011) and Grover (2009).

> to rejoin the LTTE, many indicated that they would return to avoid the recruitment of a brother or sister.
>
> Seventeen-year-old Selvamani said,
> "If they try to take my brothers or sisters, I will have to rejoin again. I am worried." (Human Rights Watch interview with "Selvamani," Batticaloa district, August 2004)
>
> Manchula, now sixteen, said:
> "I don't want to go [back] under any condition. The problem is they can go all over and take children in public places, like when they go to temples. I am nervous that they will take my brother, so if that happens, I may have to go back. I have one brother and one sister." (Human Rights Watch interview with "Manchula," Batticaloa district, August 2004).[23]

Clearly, the LTTE child soldier returnees': (i) continuing fear of violence to family members (as retaliation for the returnees' escape or rescue) and (ii) the returnees' experience of pressure to go back to the LLTE lest the perpetrator group take one of their siblings; amounts to severe psychological torture for these ex-child soldiers.

8.2.2 The Rape of Children by Perpetrator Armed Forces as Torture

Amnesty International in a 2011 report on rape and sexual violence and human rights law and standards at the ICC stated that:

> Sexual violence, including rape, is one of the most significant aspects of discriminatory violence against women.[24]

The current author would amend the above statement to say that: "Sexual violence, including rape, is one of the most significant aspects of *gender based* discriminatory violence against women" *and girls*.[25] Note in regards to the gravity of sexual violence related, gender-based international crimes perpetrated during armed conflict that there is established precedent for considering *rape as a form of torture:*

---

[23] Human Rights Watch (2004), p. 42.

[24] Amnesty International (2011), p. 7.

[25] Boy 'child soldiers' are also often subjected to sexual violence as are girls thus reflecting a discriminatory selection of high priority targets based on young age (that is; children are frequently amongst the preferred targets for sexual victimization by members of perpetrator armed forces for a variety of reasons, including amongst others, demoralization of the larger targeted civilian populace and appropriation of the children to the perpetrator group through stigmatization).

> **The Committee on the Elimination of All Forms of Discrimination (CEDAW) has identified gender-based violence, which includes *rape, as a violation of the right not to be tortured*** (emphasis added).[26]
>
> **The Committee against Torture has also recognized *rape as a form of torture*** (emphasis added).[27]

Recall that in the Lubanga case, the former ICC Prosecutor; Mr. Moreno-Ocampo, was reluctant to advance any sexual enslavement, rape and other sexual violence charges pertaining to the child soldier female victims and ultimately did not do so.[28] No doubt part of his concern was that such charges might have become mired in debates about alleged consent of the girl child soldiers designated by the perpetrator group as so-called 'bush wives.' In this regard; consider: (i) the following statement of the former ICC Prosecutor in *Lubanga* on the issue of his failure to advance separate charges relating to gender-based sexual violence perpetrated against children in particular (including rape and sexual enslavement) and (ii) his tacit reference to the risk of a falsely perceived alleged consent of the so-called child 'bush wives' to their own sexual violation:

> We believe the facts are that girls were abused, used as sexual slaves and raped. We believe this suffering is part of the suffering of conscription. We did not allege and will not present evidence linking Thomas Lubanga with rapes. We allege that he linked it with the conscription [of children as child soldiers] and he knows the harsh conditions. So we believe in this case it is a different way to present the gender crimes. It presents the gender crimes not specific as rapes. Gender crimes were committed as part of the conscription of girls in -in the militias. **And it is important to have the charge as confined to the conscription, because if not …the girls are considered wife and ignored as people to be protected and demobilized and cared [for]**…(emphasis added)[29]

This author has elsewhere argued that, in her respectful view, it was unwise and unjust not to advance separate rape charges as these child victims of rape and other sexual violence referred to in *Lubanga* were entitled to a remedy, at a minimum, in terms of the ICC prosecution of their victimizers also for these international crimes.[30] It is essential that the various forms of coercion and force in regards to rape and other forms of mass sexual violence during armed conflict are recognized by the ICC and understood to be a form of *torture.*

It is here argued that endorsing the view that mass rape and other forms of systematic and widespread sexual violence during armed conflict as part of a common plan is torture presupposes the acknowledgement also of the mass rape and other sexual violence underlying the torture *additionally* as separate autonomous crimes. Consider also that international criminal law does not contemplate a victim of torture providing voluntary consent to be on the receiving end of torturous conduct. Hence acknowledging *mass*

---

[26] Amnesty International (2011), p. 42.

[27] Amnesty International (2011), p. 42.

[28] On the analysis here; child soldiers so-called are in fact child *civilians* forcibly disappeared through exploitation of their coercive circumstances or the use of more direct psychological or physical force or threats.

[29] Prosecutor v Thomas Lubanga Dyilo prosecutor Closing Statement (2011), p. 54.

[30] Grover (2013a), pp. 106–137.

rape as torture is an acknowledgement also of the forced nature of the sexual contact between perpetrators and victims. Put differently, consent is not a defence contemplated in regards to a charge of torture advanced under the Rome Statute unlike the situation for alleged rape. Therefore for that reason also legally characterizing mass rape as torture is legally supportable. Recall in this regard that Prosecutor Moreno-Ocampo's decision not to charge Lubanga with failing to prevent mass rape of child soldiers and other children was in large part premised on his fear that the defence would argue that the so-called girl child soldier 'bush wives' were in some sort of situation where a rape charge would be difficult to prove given their alleged quasi wife status. The issue of how to define rape and the matter of whether non-consent should be a central element was an issue also for the ad hoc international criminal tribunals for Rwanda and Yugoslavia:

> The scope of definitions of rape and sexual violence in the ad hoc International Criminal Tribunals for Rwanda and Yugoslavia have been the subject of intense scholarly attention. and significant jurisprudence, mainly on the central question of **how rape should be defined, whether by reference to the victim's lack of consent, or whether the perpetrator used coercion, force, or threat of force, or took advantage of coercive circumstances.**[31]

Framing mass rape which is part of the common plan of a particular perpetrator group during armed conflict as *torture*, on the view here, puts the focus where it belongs; namely on the perpetrator's use of coercion, force, threat of force, and/or exploitation of coercive circumstances. Note also that the Rome Statute Elements of the Crimes takes account of young age (i.e. age associated with childhood) as a factor negating the possibility of genuine informed and voluntary consent to various sex related acts underlying certain Rome Statute offences. Hence, a footnote to Article 7(1)(g)(i) *crime against humanity of rape* states:

> **It is understood that a person may be incapable of giving genuine consent if affected by** natural, induced or ***age related incapacity***. This footnote also applies to the corresponding elements of article 7(1)(g)-3, 5 and 6.[32]

Similarly a footnote in regards to rape as a war crime in either an international or a non-international armed conflict situation[33] recognizes that age may be a factor precluding genuine consent:

> **It is understood that a person may be incapable of giving genuine consent if affected by** natural, induced or **age related incapacity**. This footnote also applies to the corresponding elements of article 8(2)(b)(xxii)-3, 5 and 6.[34]

[31] Amnesty International (2011), p. 8.

[32] Rome Statute Elements of the Crimes (2002) specifies then that the crime against humanity of rape, the crime against humanity of enforced prostitution, the crime against humanity of enforced sterilization and the crime against humanity of sexual violence are crimes where young age can be considered a factor precluding consent.

[33] See footnote 64 to Article 8(2)(e)(vi)-1 war crime of rape (non-international context).

[34] Rome Statute Elements of the Crimes (2002) specifies that the war crime of rape, war crime of enforced prostitution, war crime of enforced sterilization and war crime of sexual violence are crimes where young age can be considered a factor precluding consent.

It should be understood that coercion is inherent in the power differential between adult perpetrator and child sex victim. Consider in regard to this point the following statement of the South African Law Commission on the new emphasis on considering the role of coercion in rape and other sexual violence as opposed to interrogating the subjective state of mind of the victim and then making inferences regarding the consent or lack of consent of the victim:

> **A shift from 'absence of consent' to 'coercion' represents a shift in the focus of the utmost importance from the subjective state of mind of the victim to the imbalance of power between the parties** .... This perspective also allows one to understand that coercion constitutes more than physical force or threat thereof, but may also include various other forms of exercise of power over another person: emotional,psychological, economical, social or organizational power (emphasis added).[35]

Note also the role of coercion in rape of the older child and the inadequacy of consent based approaches to the legal analysis of facts pertaining to alleged rape:

> **Consent-based approaches to the crime of rape do not capture the reality of how children under 18 are targeted for sexual violence.** The kinds of fearful submission to sexual acts that may be manifested by children ... are frequently portrayed as 'consent' by alleged perpetrators. This portrayal is particularly common when the alleged victim is an older child, especially an adolescent girl. **The importance of the coercion-based approach to the definition of rape and sexual violence is that it focuses on the perpetrator's actions, and how this affected the behaviour of the victim** (emphasis added).[36]

Framing as *torture* that part of the common plan during armed conflict involving systematic and widespread sexual violence perpetrated against children (including older adolescents) is a tacit affirmation of the coercion involved (for instance in the sexual victimization of girl child soldiers which typically involves repeated rapes and even gang rapes). Unfortunately, as in *Lubanga*, mass rape of children in particular (including girl child soldiers) during armed conflict has not to date been legally characterized as *torture* by the ICC. Furthermore, the *unique experience* of suffering of child victims of rape and of other sexual violence (given their special vulnerabilities) has not been considered by the ICC and this has contributed to the failure to regard the rape of children as torture.[37]

Child soldiers and other children associated with perpetrator armed groups or forces and who are the victims of gender-based crimes such as rape[38] *in that context*; strangely to date (as in *Lubanga*), have not for the most part, if at all, benefited from the Rome Statute Elements of the Crimes' somewhat progressive formulation of 'rape' (one which does *not* entirely focus on so-called consent of the victim issues).

---

[35] Amnesty International (2011), p. 19.

[36] Amnesty International (2011), p. 32.

[37] This is not at all to diminish the extent of suffering of adult victims of rape and of other sexual violence during armed conflict or to suggest that the rape of women is not also torture (physical and psychological).

[38] 'Gender-based crimes' here refers to the disproportionately higher victimization of women and girls through rape and other sexual violence. This is not to say that men and boys are not also victims of such crimes of sexual violence including rape especially during armed conflict but rather to suggest they are so in most instances to a lesser extent than are women and girls.

Rather rape charges have been brought in regard to the mass rapes of women and girls in the context of attacks on civilians rather than *also* as perpetrated against the perpetrator group's own child soldiers; see in this regard for instance the Harun case:

> CONSIDERING that there are reasonable grounds to believe that **during these attacks, the Sudanese Armed Forces and the Milita/Janjaweed committed several criminal acts against civilians primarily from the Fur, Zaghawa and Masalit** populations, between August 2003 and March 2004, namely murders of civilians, **rapes and outrages upon the personal dignity of women and girls**, attacks intentionally directed against the above-mentioned civilian populations and destruction of property belonging to the above-mentioned populations and pillaging of towns…
>
> **Count 10**
> Persecution in Bindisi town and surrounding areas constituting a crime against Humanity
> On or about 15 August 2003, Ahmad Harun, as part of a group of persons acting with a common purpose, contributed to the **persecution of the primarily Fur population of Bindisi town and surrounding areas, by acts** of murder, **rape, attack of the civilian population,** inhumane acts, pillaging, destruction of property and forcible transfer of the population (articles 7(l)(h) and 25(3)(d) of the Statute) (emphasis added)[39]

The Rome Statute elements of the crime of rape focus heavily on: (i) the perpetrator use of coercion, force, threat of force and/or (ii) the perpetrator exploitation of coercive circumstances; and/or (iii) the power differential that may exist between perpetrator and victim in various domains (psychological, physical, economic etc.) and/or (iv) the incapacity of the victim to consent based on age or other natural or induced states of incapacity.[40] All of the latter four factors are highly relevant also to child soldier victims[41] who have been appropriated by a perpetrator armed force. It is abundantly clear that child soldiers and other children associated with perpetrator armed groups cannot consent to being tortured through sexual victimization by members of the perpetrator force which has appropriated them (so too is consent *not* operative for child civilians subjected to sexual violence such as rape who are not 'recruited' as so-called child soldiers by the perpetrator group). Yet generally child soldier victims of the Rome Statute offence of *rape* are not considered as such in the ICC cases where rape has been charged only in relation to general attacks on the populace (though, as in *Kony*, 'sexual enslavement' as a crime against humanity charges may have been brought in regards to certain of the children abducted by the armed perpetrator group).[42] This is perhaps the ICC OTP

---

[39] Ahmad Muhammad Harun ("Ahmad Harun") and Ali Muhammad Ali Abd-Al-Rahman ("Ali Kushayb") Pre-Trial Chamber I Warrant of Arrest for Ahmad Harun (27 April, 2007) ICC-02/05-01/07.

[40] See for example Rome Statute Elements of the Crime: Article 7(1)(g)-1 and accompanying footnote 16: **Crime against humanity of rape at element 2**: "The invasion was committed by force, or by threat of force or coercion, such as that caused by fear of violence, duress, detention, psychological oppression or abuse of power, against such person or another person, or by taking advantage of a coercive environment, or the invasion was committed against a person incapable of giving genuine consent"… "…due to natural induced or age -related incapacity." Rome Statute Elements of the Crimes (2002).

[41] Child soldier here also includes girls sexually enslaved by perpetrator armed groups.

[42] Rome Statute 7(2)(c) "'Enslavement' means the exercise of any or all of the powers attaching to the right of ownership over a person and includes the exercise of such power in the course of trafficking in persons, in particular women and children" (Rome Statute 2002).

approach since: (i) the notion of non-consent is a priori built into the definition of the concept of 'sexual *enslavement*' whereas (ii) a defence of consent can defeat a rape charge and the ICC Prosecutor may be reluctant to open the perceived Pandora's box re 'consent' since child soldiers have been erroneously characterized as something other than forcibly disappeared children; particularly if it is alleged some 'enlisted.'[43]

The systemic mass rape of children as high priority targets and as part of a common plan during armed conflict is the quintessential illustration of torture (physical and psychological) through sexual violence. Consider further, child soldier/sex slaves and other children captured by the State military or ancillary forces or non-State militia and denied the freedom to leave and who, while detained, are repeatedly gang raped. This author concurs in respect of the latter situation with the Appeal Chamber in *Kumara* that certain "detentions amount to circumstances that [are] so coercive as to negate any possibility of consent."[44] The latter applies then, on the analysis here, also to child soldier members of perpetrator armed groups committing mass atrocities and/or genocide and negates the possibility of a consent defence to the charge of systematic rape of these child soldiers and girl child soldiers in particular..

In sum then the common occurrence of mass rape and other sexual violence committed against children during armed conflict by perpetrator armed groups is just one striking example illustrating that consideration of:

> **[t]he human rights of children [is] essential to an effective integration of relevant human rights principles into the jurisprudence of the Court [the ICC]** (emphasis added).[45]

Put somewhat differently; it is long overdue that the ICC acknowledged and prosecuted those most responsible for the *particularized targeting of children* as victims of any grave international crime set out in the Rome Statute *where the evidence warrants* and not only in respect of the Rome Statute child specific crimes of, for instance, child soldiering and the 'genocidal forcible transfer of children'.[46] Further, the current author holds that rape and all forms of sexual violence during armed conflict as part of a common plan should be properly charged by the ICC OTP cumulatively *also* as *torture*[47]; especially, but not exclusively, where the victims are children (including in regard to the sexual victimization of child soldiers and children enslaved primarily for sexual purposes by perpetrator armed groups). This in that the threshold for physical and psychological pain and suffering is generally

43 As noted here previously, the current author maintains that children 'recruited' to become members of an armed force perpetrating mass atrocities and/or genocide are the victims of the 'genocidal forcible transfer of children' and may also be regarded as 'forcibly disappeared'. Hence the notion of 'enlistment' of children as child soldiers into the perpetrator group under the coercive circumstances created for the general civilian population by the perpetrator armed group, is legally insupportable.

44 Prosecutor v Kunarac, Kovac and Vukovic Appeal Judgment (12 June, 2002) at para 132.

45 Amnesty International (2011), p. 32.

46 Note that 'genocidal forcible transfer of children' has never been prosecuted in fact by the ICC OTP.

47 Also the view here is that that the ICC Chambers should accept such cumulative charges as an appropriate and legally supportable in the circumstances here described.

lower for children for a variety of developmental and medical reasons, and children, in many instances, are more vulnerable to coercion and exploitation of their coercive circumstances. Further, the dishonour that is falsely attributed to the child victim of rape or other sexual violation during armed conflict is devastating. This in that it often ruins the prospects: (i) for marriage later on (especially for girl victims) and for (ii) a normal developmental course generally as frequently sexual victimization of children by the perpetrator group leads to a tragic breakdown in the child's family and community ties. The cumulative charging of rape and other sexual violence during armed conflict (as *also* constituting torture) allows the ICC to consider more substantively the adverse stereotypes that these sexual violence victims endure[48] and that cause them severe psychological suffering amounting to *ongoing psychological torture*.[49] The latter too supports the view that rape and other sexual violence against children as part of a common plan during armed conflict should be properly cumulatively charged *also* as psychological as well as physical *torture* and not only in terms of the rape and other sexual violence Rome Statute offences.

The evidence appears to indicate in the ICC and international criminal tribunal cases here discussed that rape and other forms of mass sexual violence during armed conflict as part of a common plan is perpetrated: (i) in a discriminatory fashion to a much greater extent against females victims and that (ii) children too are particularized high priority targets for perpetrator armed groups; especially girls. Thus rape and other sexual violence during armed conflict as part of a common plan often reflects: (i) a discriminatory purpose relating to *gender and young age* and (ii) the objective in large part of demoralizing and intimidating civilians; a purpose that is characteristic especially, but not exclusively, of torture as a weapon of war.

8.2.3 *Torture Under the Rome Statute and the Young Age of the Victims*

It is here argued that child victims have the right to have their situations as *particularized targets of grave international crimes* taken into account (i.e. in the charges brought by the ICC OTP and in the ICC Chambers' application of the law

[48] The adverse false stereotypes of sexual violence victims during armed conflict include but are not limited to the notion that female victims of mass rape and other sexual violence during armed conflict are immoral, that they consented to the sexual violation of their person, and that the rape victims are sympathetic to the perpetrator group.

[49] In addition, cumulative charging at the ICC of *rape also as torture* would allow for a challenge to other false stereotypes regarding gender-based sexual violence crimes occurring during armed conflict as part of a common plan; namely the *erroneous* presumptions that: "(a) rape is a less important crime; (b) that rape is inevitable and inescapable, [as an incidental aspect of war] rather than an intentional act of violence [as part of a common plan]; and that (c) rape is a natural result of perpetrators' sexual urges, rather than an intentional act of humiliation, discrimination and intimidation [as part of a common plan]." (Amnesty International 2011, p. 39).

to the facts). This right is based *in part* on: (i) international customary law (i.e. the Additional Protocols I and II to the 1949 Geneva Conventions[50] which are generally regarded as a codification of ICL) and (ii) various international human rights law instruments such as the Convention on the Rights of the Child[51] that set out the special protections to which children are entitled. In this regard, there is a pressing need for a better account to be made in *ICC practice* of the fact that the Rome Statute too is "part of a very comprehensive international *corpus juris*" which reflects fundamental principles that include, in part, "the protection of the child."[52] Recall that the Rome Statute does have certain provisions that deal *explicitly* with international crimes grounded on violation of the most fundamental rights of the child; in particular i.e. genocidal forcible transfer of children of the group to another group and the provisions on child soldiering. However, 'young age' of the victims (where 'young age' refers to under 18) is to be considered, it is here argued, in respect of all the provisions of the Rome Statute in interpreting the very nature of the crime and what would be appropriate sentencing. For instance, what qualifies as physical and psychological *torture of a child* may differ compared to what is the case for adults (given differences that may exist in many cases between healthy adults and children in terms of their comparative threshold levels for pain and suffering that crosses the line into the domain of torture). This then might properly result in a different ICC OTP charging approach taking into consideration the specific characteristics of the particular victims in a certain case and also other contextual factors.

8.2.4 Children's Juridical Personality, Their Right to the Full Measure of International Criminal Justice and to Reparations for Torture Suffered During Armed Conflict

It is here contended that the failure of the ICC to legally characterize as *torture* the particularized targeting, as part of a common plan during armed conflict, of children for (child) soldiering, mass rape, sexual enslavement and other forms of sexual violence is ultimately a denial of the children's juridical personality. This is the case in that the child victims' right to justice as persons before and under the law (here the Rome Statute) is being denied in regards to the Rome Statute grave

---

50 Protocol I and II Additional to the 1949 Geneva Conventions (1977).

51 Convention on the Rights of the Child (1990).

52 Inter-American Commission on Human Rights Report No. 33/04 in Jailton Neri Da Fonseca v Brazil 11 March, 2004 at para 81. The point made here by the Inter-American Commission of Human Rights concerning considering the Court's enabling statute in the broader context of international human rights and other international law, it is here contended, is equally applicable to the proper interpretation and application of the Rome Statute.

offence of torture as a crime against humanity and/or a war crime (depending on the particular fact pattern in the case).

It is arguably the case that: (i) the child victims (persons under age 18) experience the aforementioned perpetrator conduct as torture,[53] and (ii) the perpetrators commit these grave human rights violations as part of a common plan during armed conflict with the intent *also* to inflict torture (including psychological torture) not only on the direct child victims; but also on the general populace for the purpose of coercion and intimidation (and depending on the situation; even to facilitate ethnic cleansing/genocide as in Bosnia and Darfur). When the ICC fails to prosecute for torture (where the evidence would support such a prosecution); the children victimized in this way as part of a perpetrator common plan during armed conflict are then, *in practice*, unable to benefit from the *jus cogens* prohibition against torture also incorporated into the Rome Statute. In this way; children as particularized targets of the aforementioned international crimes do not have equal benefit of the international criminal law as embodied in the Rome Statute as it pertains to the offence of torture. The latter is contrary to what is required under Article 21(3) of the Rome Statute which prohibits indirect and direct discrimination based on age (among other grounds of discrimination) in the interpretation and application of the Rome Statute which discrimination based on young age undermines respect for the basic human rights of children (i.e. the right to justice for children who have been victimized as particularized targets for torture inflicted as part of a common plan during armed conflict).[54]

Rome Statute Article 21(3) also requires regard for international human rights law and other relevant treaties and that the interpretation and application of the Rome Statute be consistent with internationally recognized human rights and humanitarian norms and standards. Consider then the following statement from the 'Inter-American Institute of Children' on the rights of the child as codified in the Convention on the Rights of the Child[55]:

> The existence of a universal principle of protection of children has been recognized internationally, in view of the fact that they are in a position of "disadvantage and greater vulnerability" vis-à-vis other sectors of the population, and because they have specific needs. The Declaration on the Rights of the Child, adopted by the UN General Assembly in 1959, made a statement along these lines. **However, it was not until 1989, with the Convention on the Rights of the Child, that there was "a true qualitative transformation of interpretation, understanding of and attention to minors, and therefore of their social and *juridical condition*." Said Convention includes a number of principles**

[53] This is in fact clear from interviews with some of the child victims of child soldiering and sexual enslavement perpetrated by armed groups committing mass atrocities which interviews have been here previously excerpted and cited.

[54] "The application and interpretation of law ...must be consistent with internationally recognized human rights, and be without any adverse distinction founded on grounds such as ... age" (Article 21(3) Rome Statute (2002). Article 21(3) regarding the non-discriminatory interpretation of the Rome Statute is a foundational principle and speaks in part to the fact that the age of the victims is *not* a basis to deny them the full measure of justice under the Statute.

[55] Convention on the Rights of the Child (1990).

> **and provisions pertaining to the protection of children, and it is a paradigm that should provide guidance**...(emphasis added)[56]

The ICC has, however, it is here contended, not properly and fully considered: (i) what constitutes torture in children's subjective experience and also based on objective factors relating to, for instance, children's developmentally vulnerable status nor (ii) taken proper account of children's fundamental right to justice as human beings in their own right with *inherent* juridical personality.[57] This then results in discrimination based on young age in the interpretation and application of the law (such as in the interpretation and application of the Rome Statute articles concerning torture (or acts that can amount to torture in certain circumstances) as applies to *child victims* of torture as a war crime or crime against humanity). On the issue of the mechanisms of discrimination (i.e. in the interpretation and application of the law); it should be noted that discrimination can also result when the unique characteristics and situation of the victims as children are not taken into account:

> **'[t]he right not to be discriminated against in the enjoyment of ...rights**...is also violated when..without an objective and reasonable justification [the ICC] fail[s] to treat differently persons [children] whose situations are ... different' (emphasis added).[58]

It is here argued further that; (i) the ICC's pattern of not considering the fact that children are high priority perpetrator targets for *torture* as part of the common plan in the context of mass atrocities during armed conflict and (ii) the ICC's subsuming of the child victims with others under umbrella crimes such as attacks on the civilian population, reflects an implicit failure to acknowledge a new norm and standard of human rights which affirms that "children are subjects of their own rights."[59]

8.2.5 The Widespread and Systematic Targeting of Children for Torture as Intimidation of the Populace: A Cautionary Tale on the 'International Responsibility to Protect' the Vulnerable

> North Korea's first dictator, Kim Il Sung, instituted this practice of "three generations of punishment" to eliminate any opposition to the regime. "It's unique in the 20th or 21st

[56] The Inter-American Institute of Children August 7, 2001 brief. Cited in the Inter-American Court of Human Rights Advisory Opinion OC-17/2002 of August 28, 2002 on the Juridical Condition and Human Rights of the Child, p. 12–13.

[57] 'Juridical personality' it should be noted is distinguishable from 'legal capacity' (see Juridical status and human rights of the child, Advisory Opinion OC-17/02, August 28, 2002, Inter-Am. Ct. H.R. (Ser. A) No. 17 (2002) Concurring Opinion of Judge A.A. Cancado Trindade at point 8).

[58] Modified quote from Thlimmenos v. Greece, Judgment of 6 April 2000, no. 34369/97, para. 44 Cited in Xenos (2009), p. 598.

[59] The Inter-American Institute of Children August 7, 2001 brief. Cited in the Inter-American Court of Human Rights Advisory Opinion OC-17/2002 of August 28, 2002 on the Juridical Condition and Human Rights of the Child, p. 10.

> century," Hawk says. "Mao didn't do it. Stalin didn't do it. Hitler, of course, tried to exterminate entire families. *But in the post-World War II world, it's only [North] Korea that had this practice* (emphasis added)."[60]

The current author would argue, in contrast to what is suggested in the above quote, that the torture of children in particular (and of other relatives) of persons perceived to be part of an opposition or potential opposition is a commonplace feature of the global picture post WWII during armed conflict (internal or international). It appears that the international community, however, generally professes a kind of naivety and disingenuous shock about the fact that children are often targeted for torture in various forms during armed conflict *in part* due to their association to adults such as parents with perceived alleged affiliations to adversarial groups (i.e. as in Syria under Al Assad). Human Rights Watch reports on the torture of children in Syria:

> As with the total number of detainees, it is virtually impossible to establish how many children, women, and elderly persons the security forces have detained, but local activists have recorded the detention of 635 children and 319 women as of June 22, 2012. **Through interviews with children and other detainees who witnessed the torture of children during their detention Human Rights Watch has documented the detention and torture of children in 12 cases**. For example, Hossam, age 13, told Human Rights Watch that security forces detained him and a relative, also 13, in May 2011 and tortured him for three days at a military security branch about 45 min by car from Tal Kalakh:
>
> Every so often they would open our cell door and yell at us and beat us. They said, "You pigs, you want freedom?" They interrogated me by myself. They asked, "Who is your god?" And I said, "Allah." Then they electrocuted me on my stomach, with a prod. I fell unconscious. When they interrogated me the second time, they beat me and electrocuted me again. The third time they had some pliers, and they pulled out my toenail. **They said, "Remember this saying, always keep it in mind: We take both kids and adults, and we kill them both." I started to cry, and they returned me to the cell**
>
> **It was the detention and torture of children from the southern town of Daraa in March 2011 that triggered the first anti-government protests in Syria**, and in the following months several other cases, including the torture and death of 13-year-old Hamza Ali al-Khateeb, caused an outcry in Syria and internationally. **In cases documented by Human Rights Watch, the detained children were usually between 13 and 17 years old, although some witnesses and defectors reported seeing boys as young as eight in detention**. They were mostly held in the same cells and in the same conditions as adults, sometimes in solitary confinement, and subjected to many of the torture methods described above (emphasis added).[61]

In fact as certain of the cases here discussed illustrate (i.e. the Lubanga and Kony cases among others); the targeting for torture of children of the perceived opposition using various mechanisms is commonplace. The targeting of children in

---

[60] Statement of Human rights investigator David Hawk in an interview with CNN's Anderson Cooper (2012).

[61] Human Rights Watch (2012), pp. 31–32.

particular for torture (regardless whether the children were themselves engaged in any political activism of note and irrespective of the children's age) then is directed often toward suppressing that segment of the civilian population that is perceived as potentially offering or actually engaged in resistance to one or more perpetrator armed groups.[62] Despite the horrific reality of the systematic torture of children in particular in Syria, for instance, there has been no referral (at the time of writing) by the UN Security Council of the situation in Syria to the ICC. Clearly this is a stark example of a flagrant disregard of the 'responsibility to protect" through also the vehicle of holding perpetrators to account.[63] That disregard, it is here contended, contributes significantly to an erosion of respect for international human rights norms and even of the perceived legitimacy and relevance of international criminal law however codified. In a sense the ICC is itself a concrete embodiment of dedication to the notion of the international 'responsibility to protect' which notion is intimately related, in part, to effecting the criminal accountability of the perpetrators most responsible for grave international crimes.[64]

8.3 Speaking of Torture and the Complicity of the International Community

> In *This Side of Silence* **Tobias Kelly describes the key challenge torture poses as "not one of the failure of language but of the failure of recognition**. It is not the survivor's inability to speak; rather it is our inability to listen (emphasis added)."[65]

That 'failure to recognize' torture is reflected, in the context considered here, in a reluctance to: (i) legally characterize perpetrator conduct as torture under the Rome Statute *where children are the particularized high priority targets of torture* as certain of the ICC cases here discussed illustrate and in (ii) the grant of *de facto* immunity from ICC prosecution to certain of those who perpetrate the torture of children (as part of a common plan during armed conflict)

---

[62] We have considered in this inquiry also the torture of children of the same nationality and ethnicity as the perpetrator group; that torture coming in the form of 'recruitment' and use as a child soldier/sex slave for the perpetrator group.

[63] The contentious notion of a 'responsibility to protect' (R2P) as an international norm was accepted by the United Nations in 2005.

[64] Here then the concept of an international 'responsibility to protect' is more broadly construed to not only include State intervention in another State to prevent or stop mass atrocities and/or genocide but also States ensuring that the perpetrators most responsible for the aforementioned mass atrocities and/or genocide are held criminally to account by a competent criminal court or tribunal (for instance the ICC where the jurisdictional and admissibility criteria are met in a case).

[65] Kelly (2012).

notwithstanding that the perpetrator conduct fulfills the elements of the crime of torture per the Rome Statute (even where that torture is systematic and widespread and the perpetrators are those most responsible). In light of the foregoing (the failure of the ICC to prosecute the torture of child victims as a separable crime under the Rome Statute); we turn next to a consideration of the issue of gravity of the crime and the gravity threshold considered by the ICC OTP in relation to the number of victims as well as other criteria. We will examine the Nourain and Jamus ICC case[66] which was prosecuted by the ICC despite the small number of victims involved where UN peacekeepers were the ***victims.*** Next we will consider the grant of *de facto* immunity from ICC prosecution to perpetrators of the international crime of torture involving direct and indirect child victims where the ***perpetrators*** were UN peacekeepers. That is to say that the UN peacekeeper perpetrators of child torture in various forms were: (i) either not prosecuted by their home country or the host country or any international criminal tribunal or court or (ii) their prosecutions in their home country were closed military affairs (i.e. the Shidane Abukar Arone case discussed below)[67] such that the international community; the general populace in the home country and the host country in which the UN peacekeepers were stationed and perpetrated torture on children received neither the benefit of: (i) having the crimes widely publicized, and denounced nor (ii) there being easy access to :a) information regarding the details of this grave international crime perpetrated on the children; b) information regarding the micro and macro context in which the torture of the children by the UN peacekeepers occurred, or c) details of the trial and appeal procedural history and the various judgments and final disposition of the cases.

8.4 UN Peacekeepers and the Torture of Children as an International Crime

8.4.1 On the Issue of the Number of Victims and Gravity of the International Crime: UN Peacekeepers as Victims

While it is quite correct to say that only very few UN peacekeepers have engaged in the commission of the international crime of torture of children; that fact alone, on the view here, is not a justifiable or legal rationale for the failure to prosecute these persons at the ICC. Before we consider the issue of the immunity of UN

66 Situation in Darfur, Sudan in the Case of The Prosecutor v Abdallah Banda Abaeker Nourain and Saleh Mohammed Jerboa Jamus Corrigendum of the "Decision on the Confirmation of Charges 7 March, 2011.

67 Razack (2004), p. 87–101.

personnel as UN representatives; let us examine the matter of there being few UN peacekeepers who have been perpetrators of the torture of children while stationed in a jurisdiction on an official peacekeeping mission. The best evidence in support of the argument that the numbers of UN personnel involved as *perpetrators* should not matter regarding the issue of prosecution is the fact that when UN personnel are on the receiving end of atrocity; numbers have not mattered with respect to ICC prosecution of the perpetrators. UN peacekeepers are protected under ICL, treaty law (i.e. international humanitarian law) and the Safety Convention which states at Article 7:

Convention on the Safety of United Nations and Associated Personnel
Article 7
Duty to ensure the safety and security of United Nations and associated personnel

1. United Nations and associated personnel, their equipment and premises shall not be made the object of attack or of any action that prevents them from discharging their mandate.
2. States Parties shall take all appropriate measures to ensure the safety and security of United Nations and associated personnel. In particular, States Parties shall take all appropriate steps to protect United Nations and associated personnel who are deployed in their territory from the crimes set out in article 9.
3. States Parties shall cooperate with the United Nations and other States Parties, as appropriate, in the implementation of this Convention, particularly in any case where the host State is unable itself to take the required measures.[68]

Note that the Rome Statute provision protecting UN and associated personnel appears under "other serious violations of international humanitarian law" as:

> the first time [there has been] a specific provision envisioning for both international and non-international armed conflicts: the war crime of "intentionally directing attacks against personnel, installations, material, units or vehicles involved in a humanitarian assistance or peacekeeping mission in accordance with the Charter of the United Nations, **as long as they are entitled to the protection given to civilians**[69] **or civilian objects under the international law of armed conflict** (emphasis added)."[70]

There is *no* argument here in opposition to the view that UN peacekeepers should receive protections equivalent to that of civilians when they are *hors de combat*[71] An ICC case holding accountable those who attacked and killed UN peacekeepers is The Prosecutor v Abdallah Banda Abaeker Nourain and Saleh Mohammed Jerboa Jamus in relation to the situation in Darfur. That case involves an ICC prosecution against perpetrators of an attack on UN peacekeeping personnel, installations and vehicles that resulted in the death of 12 UN peacekeepers. The small number of victims in the Nourain and Jamus case (excerpts below) was hence not at all an impediment to ICC prosecution.

---

[68] Convention on the Safety of United Nations and Associated Personnel 15 January, 1999.

[69] That is, the UN peacekeepers have not taken a direct part in hostilities.

[70] Gadler (2010), p.593.

[71] Further, note these UN peacekeepers are not a party to the conflict.

8.4.2 *The Prosecutor v Abdallah Banda Abaeker Nourain and Saleh Mohammed Jerboa Jamus*

Excerpts from the Corrigendum of the "Decision on the Confirmation of Charges 7 March, 2011:

> On 29 September 2007, at the MGS Haskanita in Haskanita Village, Um Kadada Locality in North Darfur, the Sudan, in the context of and associated with an internal armed conflict, BANDA and JERBO together with JEM Splinter Group, SLA Unity and SLA Abdul Shafie forces under their command and control, acting pursuant to a common plan and orders issued by them, jointly with their forces,
>
> I. **attacked the MGS Haskanita and killed twelve (12) AMIS peacekeeping personnel and attempted to kill eight (8) AMIS peacekeeping personnel, with the knowledge that they were (1) personnel involved in a peacekeeping mission established in accordance with the UN Charter; and (2) taking no active part in hostilities and thus entitled to the protection given to civilians under the international law of armed conflict,** thereby committing a crime in violation of Articles 8(2)(c)(i) and 25(3)(a) and 25(3)(f) of the Rome Statute (Count 1: Violence to Life and Attempted Violence to Life (article 8(2)(c)(i) and Article 25(3)(a) and Article 25(3)(f) of theRome Statute);
> II. intentionally directed attacks against AMIS peacekeeping personnel, installations, materials, units and vehicles involved in a peacekeeping mission established in accordance with the Charter of the United Nations, which were entitled to the protection given to civilians and civilian objects under the international law of armed conflict, with the knowledge of the factual circumstances that established that protection, thereby committing a crime in violation of Articles 8(2)(e)(iii) and 25(3)(a) of the Rome Statute (Count 2: Intentionally directing attacks against personnel, installations, materials, units and vehicles involved in a peace keeping mission (Articles 8(2)(e)(iii) and 25(3)(a) of the Rome Statute);
> III. attacked the MGS Haskanita and appropriated property belonging to AMIS and its personnel including vehicles, refrigerators, computers, cellular phones, military boots and uniforms, fuel, ammunition and money, without the consent of the owners and for their private or personal use, thereby committing a crime in violation of Articles 8(2)(e)(v) and 25(3)(a) of the Rome Statute (Count 3: Pillaging (Article 8(2)(e)(v) and Article 25(3)(a) of the Rome Statute)."[72]
>
> ...
> FOR THESE REASONS, THE CHAMBER
> DECIDES
> that the charges brought against Abdallah Banda and Saleh Jerbo are confirmed and to commit them to a Trial Chamber for the trial on the charges as confirmed, pursuant to article 61(7)(a) of the Statute (emphasis added).[73]

As the ICC Nourain and Jamus case clearly illustrates; the need to uphold international humanitarian law and the ability of the UN to fulfil its mandate

---

[72] Situation in Darfur, Sudan in the Case of The Prosecutor v Abdallah Banda Abaeker Nourain and Saleh Mohammed Jerboa Jamus Corrigendum of the "Decision on the Confirmation of Charges 7 March, 2011, p. 4–5.

[73] Situation in Darfur, Sudan in the Case of The Prosecutor v Abdallah Banda Abaeker Nourain and Saleh Mohammed Jerboa Jamus Corrigendum of the "Decision on the Confirmation of Charges 7 March, 2011, p. 74.

require that the security of UN peacekeepers (who are acting *hors de combat*) be respected without qualification. The aforementioned principles or objectives are so significant that it appears that when UN peacekeepers are targeted for atrocity the gravity threshold is automatically reached for ICC prosecution. This regardless of the fact that the number of UN peacekeeper victims may in fact be small. This (automatic ICC persecution) is not the case when the victims are children who have been intentionally and knowingly tortured by a small number of UN peacekeepers despite the fact that: (i) this international crime also does tremendous damage to the perceived possibility in the international community for the rule of law and in fact (ii) grossly undermines the perceived legitimacy of international criminal law as per the Rome Statute. Consider in this regard that the small number of UN peacekeepers involved in committing atrocities against civilians they were charged with protecting should not *in itself* be a bar to ICC prosecution given: (i) the adverse impact on the international community and the local populace of such crimes committed in particular by UN peacekeepers and (ii) in that:

> One of the reasons behind the need for the Prosecutor to exercise discretion in choice of cases is that the ICC does not work with unlimited resources, and this is a valid motivation. That being said, a case involving crimes by peacekeeping personnel would be of a much smaller scale than the massive situations currently before the court, and as a result would require far less resources and time to investigate and prosecute. Therefore it would make sense for the Court to take on some smaller scale cases in order to advance its own jurisprudence and to demonstrate the ability of the Court to bring cases to completion, without having to rely only on cases that take years to investigate and prosecute.[74]

8.4.3 UN Peacekeepers as Perpetrators: The Torture and Murder of Shidane Abukar Arone by Canadian UN Peacekeepers as a Case Example

> At the very least, allegations of serious atrocities committed by peacekeepers date back to the time of the UN peacekeeping mission to Somalia in 1997. Canadian, Belgian and Italian peacekeeping troops were alleged to have been involved in atrocities [in Somalia] (emphasis added).[75]

Shidane Abukar Arone was a 16-year-old Somali tortured and murdered by Canadian peacekeepers Master Corporal Clayton Matchee,[76] and Private Kyle Brown. These two Canadian military persons took photos of themselves with

---

[74] O'Brien (2010), p. 325.

[75] Du Plessis and Pete (2004), p. 7.

[76] Matchee later tried to commit suicide and suffered permanent severe brain injury as a consequence of his suicide attempt rendering him incompetent to stand trial and as a result the charges against him were withdrawn.

Shidane Arone's battered head and body as if the young boy, having been tortured, was some sort of emblem of pride. Private Kyle Brown actually provided photos to his superiors implicating himself and Matchee in this atrocity which occurred on the night of 16 March, 1993.[77] Brown claimed he only hit Shidone Arone at one point. He was sentenced to 5 years imprisonment and dishonourable dismissal from the Canadian military and served only one third of his sentence.[78] Some may argue that this sentence is far too lenient given the severity of the crime of torture in which to some extent Brown was implicated in that he did not attempt to stop it from happening at the time and admitted that he had punched[79] Arone in the jaw. Two other soldiers were charged with aiding and abetting in the torture; David Brockelbank and Sergeant Mark Boland.[80] In addition; Boland as section commander; Sergeant Perry Douglas Gretsy, and persons higher up the chain of command; Captain Sox, Major Anthony Seward and Lieutenant Colonel Carol Mathieu were all charged with negligent performance of duty.[81] All of those charged had their cases heard by the military. Boland pleaded guilty to the charge of negligent discharge of duty and not guilty to torture and ultimately received a sentence of 1 year in prison and a demotion from sergeant to private.[82] Brockelbank was charged with failure to protect a civilian from violence he knew was occurring but was acquitted of all charges even though he had personally witnessed the torture for 40 min.[83] His defence lawyer in fact argued that there had been an order from superiors to 'abuse' the prisoners, that Brockelbank could not disregard that order and had noone to complain to and that his behaviour was not out of the norm.[84] It is very possible that such a defence would not have succeeded had the case been tried before the ICC given Article 33 of the Rome Statute:

Article 33
Superior orders and prescription of law

1. The fact that a crime within the jurisdiction of the Court has been committed by a person pursuant to an order of a Government or of a superior, whether military or civilian, shall not relieve that person of criminal responsibility unless:

(a) The person was under a legal obligation to obey orders of the Government or the superior in question;
(b) The person did not know that the order was unlawful; and
(c) **The order was not manifestly unlawful.**

---

[77] Razack (2004), p. 88.

[78] Gerster (16 March, 2013).

[79] Razack (2004), p. 97.

[80] Razack (2004), p. 88.

[81] Razack (2004), p. 88.

[82] Razack (2004), p. 96.

[83] Razack (2004), p. 100.

[84] Razack (2004), pp. 100–101.

2. For the purposes of this article, orders to commit genocide or crimes against humanity are manifestly unlawful (emphasis added).

The prohibition against torture is a *jus cogens* norm and torture as an international crime is 'manifestly unlawful' according to ICL. Torture as carried out by particular UN peacekeepers in isolated cases was yet arguably a crime against humanity in the context of Somalia in 1993. That is, for instance, the torture and murder of the child Shidane Abukar Arone occurred in a context where the civilian population was suffering widespread attacks and experiencing severe suffering due to atrocities committed by various Somali perpetrator groups. The UN peacekeepers were well aware of that fact given why they were in Somalia on a UN peacekeeping mission in the first place and equally aware that their torture and degradation of civilians, no matter how few, added to the suffering of the populace and in fact, in the result, aided and abetted the goal of the Somali perpetrators they had been sent to restrain. Indeed the fact that these were UN peacekeepers of various national origins carrying out the torture and murder of several children in Somalia (including Shidane Abukar Arone) contributed significantly to the demoralization of the populace despite the fact that there were few direct victims of the UN peacekeeper perpetrators. Hence the impact on the local populace of the crime of torture of children perpetrated by UN peacekeepers is great in significant part due to who are the perpetrators (UN peacekeepers) as well as who are the victims (children).

The current author is agreed with O'Brien that the fact that: (i) technically the UN peacekeeper perpetrators were not a party to the ongoing violence in the Somalia (they were neither on the side of the rebels nor that of remnant forces loyal to the previous fallen government) and that (ii) their direct victims were few; should not be a bar to considering the crimes perpetrated by UN peacekeepers against these children as crimes against humanity ripe for ICC prosecution. This given: (i) the impact of the UN peacekeeper international crimes of torture and murder on the local populace and the international community (a qualitative dimension of gravity of the crime) and (ii) the possibility of considering the UN peacekeeper commission of grave international crimes such as torture and murder as perpetrated intentionally with full knowledge that these crimes would: a) contribute to a widespread attack on the Somali civilian population and b) reinforce the objectives of the Somali perpetrators responsible for these widespread attacks on the general civilian populace (in the Somalia case; warlords, amongst others, who attacked civilians and prevented their access to humanitarian aid in various forms):

The ICC Prosecutor has in fact already set a precedent for lower numbers of victims by requesting arrest warrants for Sudanese rebel commanders for an attack on peacekeeping personnel that resulted in the death of 12 peacekeeping personnel and injured another eight. **Such an attack could be placed in the broader context of the ongoing armed conflict and alleged commission of crimes such as genocide in Darfur, rendering this one attack part of a large-scale commission of crimes.** ***This reasoning could be followed in the case of a peacekeeper committing a crime. It would not be relevant that a peacekeeper was not a member of a party involved in***

> ***the armed conflict (e.g. government forces or rebel forces), as the crime would still be part of the overall large-scale commission of international crimes.*** It is clear, however, that the Prosecutor has instead chosen to apply qualitative reasoning, and selected the incident [Nourain and Jamus case :the Sudanese attack on UN peacekeepers] due to such factors as the nature, manner and impact of the crimes. This is a promising application of *non-quantitative factors in gravity decisions* (emphasis added).[85]

On the view here then the actions of the UN peacekeeper perpetrators in the Shidane Abukar Arone case in 1993 properly should be considered in the context of the widespread attacks on civilians carried out by parties to the ongoing unrest following the collapse of the Siad Barre government. The torture of the child Shidane Abukar Arone[86] was carried out by the Canadian UN peacekeepers intentionally and with full knowledge of the fact that their actions would benefit in a major symbolic way the Somali perpetrators who were direct parties to the violence in the country. That is; the Shidane Abukar Arone torture and murder would further add to the demoralization and insecurity of the civilian population and the sense of civilians that access to humanitarian intervention was but a fantasy (i.e. the message communicated by the Shidane Abukar Arone torture and murder being that the rebels would continue to attack and interfere with humanitarian food deliveries etc. and UN peacekeepers could not be relied upon as saviours in the situation). Ultimately then the atrocity perpetrated by the UN peacekeepers reinforced the notion that any hope of support in resistance to the rebels and quashing their oppression of the populace was futile. From the aforementioned perspective then the Arone torture fulfills the elements of torture as a crime against humanity as per the Rome Statute. The defence of superior orders then does not apply to torture as a crime against humanity; that crime being 'manifestly unlawful.'[87] Note further in regard to the defence of superior orders that:

> ...international criminal law has created a norm with customary international law status in which an international crime committed by a subordinate is not to be exonerated as such by a plea that the accused acted upon superior orders issued either by military or civilian authorities. Such a plea may, at the most, mitigate the penalty...**The rationale for the principal exemption of the defense of obedience to superior orders is clearly the acceptance within contemporary criminal law that the defense of obedience of orders is not an absolute defense anymore.** ***This approach clearly applies equally to members of international peacekeeping operations*** **...irrespective of the rank held by the superior authority**...(emphasis added).[88]

What adds even more gravity to this appalling atrocity is the fact that many other military men had heard Shidane Abukar Arone's screams and/or personally

[85] O'Brien (2010), p. 316.

[86] It should be noted that the torture of the young Somali boy Shidane Abukar Arone by Canadian UN peacekeepers involved also sodomizing him with an instrument lest we forget that males also are not infrequently the victims of international crimes that include the severest forms of sexual violence as a vehicle for torture.

[87] Arguably torture as a war crime is also manifestly unlawful given the longstanding ICL prohibition against torture during armed conflict.

[88] Knoops Geert-Jan (2004), pp. 187–188.

observed in situ what was going on the night of March 16, 1993 in regards to the torture of Shidane Abukar Arone and did nothing to stop it.[89]

Shidane Abukar Arone had allegedly been trying to infiltrate the military camp of the Canadian UN peacekeepers; not for any terrorist-motivated reason but to access basic supplies such as food stuffs. It is important to understand that prior to the Shidane Arone torture and murder, Somalis who had tried to infiltrate the UN camp and commit petty thievery had been severely dealt with including of note *children t*hreatened with machetes etc.,[90] and "six-to-eight year old children being tied up, humiliated and left to sit in the scorching sun for two hours?"[91]

These were simply children trying to survive as best they could (as was their basic human right) in a dire situation where noone was effectively protecting and providing for them. Worse still; those tasked with protecting these children as civilians under international law (UN peacekeepers) at times and to varying degrees could rightfully be considered also as these children's adversary bent on doing them considerable harm. It is questionable whether domestic prosecutions in the home country via a rather closed military system as with the perpetrators in the Shidane Abukar Arone case or even national non-military national criminal court trials are adequate to address the need to publicly acknowledge and denounce for the international community such atrocities committed by UN peacekeepers.

8.4.4 Gender-Based International Crimes Perpetrated by UN Peacekeepers

Let us begin by considering some case examples of gender -based international crimes perpetrated by UN peacekeepers and consider whether the perpetrators were properly held accountable; if at all.

Based on many reports that Italian UN peacekeepers were perpetrating abuses and international crimes against Somali civilians; women and children in particular; the Gallo Commission set up by the Italian government provided a second report in 1998[92]:

> This report [the second Gallo Commission report] deemed it "credible" that in June 1993 a soldier near one entry to Mogadishu had beaten a 20 year old Somali woman semi-conscious, following which four soldiers had gang raped her. It was also considered "credible" that in November 1993 another Somali woman was raped with a pistol flare at a check-point in North Mogadishu. The Commission found it to be "probably true" that members of a tank division had attempted to rape a Somali woman with a pistol flare at the same check-point in August 1993. By July 1998, various investigations were being carried out into acts of violence committed by Italian soldiers in Somalia, including the

89 Razack (2004), pp. 88–100.

90 Razack (2004), p. 6.

91 Razack (2004), p. 6.

92 O'Brien (2004), p. 14.

> alleged rape of a Somali woman by soldiers at a check-point in Mogadishu. It is unclear as to the number, nature and status of the criminal investigations or disciplinary proceedings relating to violations, including whether these relate to the rapes mentioned. By January 1999, the Italian authorities stated that they were still investigating,with no criminal charges yet brought for rape.[93] Several *Belgian* soldiers have been tried in military courts for the ill-treatment or killing of Somalis. Most of these were acquitted or received suspended sentences. It is not evident precisely what crimes they were prosecuted for.[94]

> **In 2004, stories of the alleged involvement in rape and "survival sex" with women and children began to emerge**. The U.N. is investigating one case in which a French logistics employee videotaped himself torturing and abusing naked girls. Other peacekeepers allegedly lured girls as young as ten years old to have sex in exchange for a cup of milk, a few eggs, peanut butter or a dollar.[95]

On the view here, so-called 'sexual exploitation' of children or sex with women and children traded for the means necessary for these victims' survival is legally equivalent under international criminal law (i.e. the Rome Statute) to *rape as torture* since there can be no possibility of informed and voluntary consent in those circumstances.

It is apparent from these cases in Somalia, including the Shidane Abukar Arone case involving Canadian UN peacekeepers, that the pattern generally is that either the case is not prosecuted by the troop-contributing State or, if prosecuted, the defendants are acquitted or receive comparatively light sentences despite the credible evidence against them and the gravity of their international crimes. In the DRC in the context of UN peacekeeping operations; it was common knowledge that girls as young as 13 would sneak into the UN compound and exchange sex for food and that this practice was widespread with no UN command interfering in the practice.[96] It should be noted also that the sexual violation of these female DRC civilians including children (as in instances of sexual exploitation and violation by UN peacekeepers of civilians in other jurisdictions) also involves instances of babies being fathered and abandoned.[97] Thus more than one generation is often destined to suffer stigmatization and marginalization by the local community as rape victims or the offspring of rape victims.

Obviously, the code of conduct for the U.N. Mission in the Democratic Republic of Congo ("MONUC") intended to ensure honourable behaviour of these UN peacekeeper troops is having no impact on those who sexually exploit and abuse these children and women. Worse still; there appear to be rare or light legal ramifications, if any, in most instances for the direct perpetrators and those in command under whom these UN peacekeeper direct perpetrators 'serve':

> In May 2004 the UN announced that it would undertake an investigation into the allegations of 30 cases within the UN camp relating to sexual abuse perpetrated by Uruguayan,

---

[93] O'Brien (2004), p. 14.

[94] O'Brien (2004), p. 14.

[95] Notar (2006), p. 417.

[96] O'Brien (2004), p. 15.

[97] Notar (2006), p. 414.

Nepalese and Moroccan peacekeepers. In May, only one case was completed, although UN spokesman Fred Eckhard refused to reveal the identity or nationality of the offender, who has been repatriated and will *supposedly* be prosecuted by his national authorities (emphasis added)[98]

Certainly, without accountable command structures in their sending states, peacekeeping personnel think they can get away with it. This situation can be exacerbated when the contributing personnel come from sending states where the rule of law is not particularly strong (emphasis added).[99]

8.4.5 Prosecuting UN Peacekeepers at the ICC for Torture and Other Grave International Crimes Perpetrated Against Children

There are several barriers to holding UN peacekeepers accountable for grave international crimes committed while they served as peacekeepers:

Usually, in UN peacekeeping operations, status-of-forces agreements (SOFAs) are concluded between the UN and the host state, and contribution agreements (CAs) are concluded between the UN and the troop-contributing states ... **These agreements normally provide that the troop-contributing states will exercise criminal jurisdiction over the troops that they contribute.**[100] **This means that peacekeepers who commit crimes while on duty in another country are liable to prosecution for those crimes in terms of the (military) criminal law of their own state.** ***The problem, of course, is that different states may have different views on which, if any, crimes committed by their troops they wish to prosecute. Individual states may not be either willing or able to prosecute serious crimes committed by their troops while performing peacekeeping duties*** (emphasis added).[101]

Further the UN has no legal authority itself as an institution to hold UN peacekeepers criminally accountable nor to assure that the troop contributing State in fact does prosecute those of that State's troops deployed as UN peacekeepers who have committed grave international crimes.[102] Yet, at the same time:

While the U.N. is not a state party to international human rights conventions, at least one commentator has argued that it remains subject to customary international law of human rights in carrying out its work. The U.N. has explicitly stated that sexual

---

98 O'Brien (2004), p. 15.

99 O'Brien (2004), p. 14.

100 Note that civilian support personnel are an integral part of the military these days for many national forces and that they too are covered by SOFA (Ladley A (2005), pp. 84–85). Many home states have jurisdiction to prosecute only civilians serving on international missions *with the military* if these civilians commit international crimes abroad (if they have that jurisdiction at all). Even fewer home Sates have the jurisdiction to prosecute their civilian nationals who served on an international missions as staff but who did not serve as civilians with the military (see Ladley (2005), p. 86).

101 Du Plessis and Pete (2004), p. 6.

102 Du Plessis and Pete (2004), p. 6.

> exploitation and abuse [for example] violate such universally recognized legal norms (emphasis added).[103]

UN attempts at preventing UN peacekeepers and officials from perpetrating grave international crimes through, for instance, codes of conduct and UN training appear to date not to be fully adequate. The view endorsed here is that the international criminal law should apply equally to UN peacekeepers[104] as it does to others where the State contributing these troops is unable or unwilling to investigate or prosecute their own. It has been suggested that notwithstanding communiqués from the UN Secretary -General regarding the need for UN personnel and peacekeepers to respect international human rights and humanitarian law; in the final analysis: "The UN depends on sending states for funding, equipment and troops, and therefore is unwilling to antagonise these sending states."[105] At the same time disciplinary control over UN peacekeepers stays with the troop contributing State[106] and "Even if someone is repatriated by the UN, they are rarely disciplined by their national authorities as they should be."[107]

Individual States also not infrequently continue to appear to be obstructionist when it comes to facilitating the investigation and prosecution of their own nationals who, as UN peacekeepers, have committed grave international crimes. For instance, the Canadian Federal government appears (at the time of writing) to be attempting to pass a bill that would hamper domestic military prosecutions of Canadian peacekeepers who, while on a UN peacekeeping mission, committed atrocities:

> Last month, Glenn Stannard, chairman of the Military Police Complaints Commission, told a Commons committee the bill [bill C-15] would curtail guidelines that have been in place "since the period following the troubled Somalia deployment, which specifically sought to safeguard MP investigations from interference by the chain of command."[108], [109]

The ICC complementarity principle, it should be understood, translates into a lower probability of ICC prosecution should the State appear to be making efforts to investigate and, where legally supportable, prosecute their nationals for international crimes perpetrated abroad while serving as UN peacekeepers. However, in some instances, the State investigation and/or prosecution exercise may be a sham rather than a transparent effective search for justice for the victims and then, in theory at least, the ICC could (if it had jurisdiction also in all other respects) seize itself of the case.

[103] Notar (2006), p. 423.

[104] Any international crime committed by UN peacekeepers (considered UN personnel) cannot be considered 'official' conduct under the UN Charter and hence no immunity based on the perpetrators being part of a UN peacekeeping force attaches which would protect them from criminal prosecution by the troop sending State.

[105] O'Brien (2004), p. 21.

[106] O'Brien (2004), p. 33.

[107] O'Brien (2004), p. 34.

[108] Gerster (16 March 2013).

[109] O'Brien (2004), p. 21.

On the view here; considering that the State may in some; if not many instances, not be acting in complete good faith to deliver justice to the victims of international crimes committed by their nationals as UN peacekeepers; the possibility for prosecutions by the ICC should not be discounted. This author is furthermore agreed with Ladley that:

> it is contradictory for the UN to try to rebuild peace and security if the on the-ground 'rebuilders of the rule of law' enjoy effective impunity for their own criminal actions.[110]

It has been noted that ICC prosecution of UN peacekeepers for atrocities though highly improbable for various reasons (including the difficulty of obtaining the necessary sound evidence regarding the international crimes committed abroad),[111] if it does occur, is more likely to be for war crimes:

> There may be exceptions, but it is to be expected that in most cases, serious crimes committed by UN peacekeepers ...will be isolated in nature and the perpetrators of these crimes will not possess the necessary intent to enable such crimes to be classified as genocide or crimes against humanity. It is somewhat more likely that certain serious crimes committed by peacekeepers may amount to war crimes, although it is clear that the ICC is more concerned with war crimes committed on a wide scale than with isolated incidents....[112]

Note that while it is correct to say that Article 8 of the Rome Statute refers to a mandate that specifies that the Court "shall have jurisdiction in respect of war crimes *in particular* when committed as part of a plan or policy or as part of a large-scale commission of such crimes"[113]; it would be incorrect to suggest that the ICC could not per the Rome Statute prosecute isolated instances of war crimes such as torture. This in that Article 8 of the Rome Statute simply refers to the fact that the ICC, under normal circumstances, would prioritize those war crimes that are part of a plan or policy or were part of a large-scale commission of such crimes. **Where UN peacekeepers are the perpetrators, however, even isolated war crimes take on a special significance for the civilian population affected and for the international community as a whole.**[114] For instance, it is here argued that the war crime of torture as carried out by UN peacekeepers, even in cases where there are few direct victims, involves innumerable indirect victims. That is, the segment of the general populace aware of such perpetrator conduct by UN peacekeepers are significantly traumatized by such grave international crimes as it may be perceived as a signal that noone can be trusted and that there is noone to rely on for protection or for justice. Further, such UN peacekeeper conduct undermines the perceived effectiveness and legitimacy of international law and the rule of law generally. Thus the fact that UN peacekeepers were the *perpetrators* of atrocity in a particular case is as relevant to the issue of gravity of the crime and the need for

110 Ladley (2005), p. 82.

111 Ladley (2005), p. 84.

112 Du Plessis and Pete (2004), p. 14.

113 Rome Statute (2002) Article 8.

114 This then should, on the view here, properly result in a prioritizing of such cases for prosecution by the ICC where the State of origin is unable or unwilling to prosecute.

ICC prosecution (where a State has failed to deal with the matter or has done so in such a way as to deny the victims justice) as is the case when the UN peacekeepers are the *victims* of grave international crimes. In addition, it should be understood that while the *tendency* will be for the ICC to prosecute those who held command responsibility as per ICC OTP policy placing a high priority on such cases, there is no bar to prosecuting the rank and file members of a UN mission who have committed international crimes such as torture as set out under the Rome Statute:

> The ICC has addressed the issue of the Court prosecuting only the most senior leaders suspected of being most responsible, in the context of gravity. Pre-Trial Chamber I held in the *Lubanga/Ntaganda* Arrest Warrant ruling that the senior position of a perpetrator as a mandatory element of the gravity threshold…**On appeal, however, the Appeals Chamber deemed it more logical "to assume that the deterrent effect of the Court is highest if no category of perpetrators is *per se* excluded from potentially being brought before the Court…Further, the Appeals Chamber considered the Rome Statute itself, and that the prosecution of only senior leaders would conflict with a contextual interpretation of the Statute: the inclusion of command/superior responsibility as a separate mode of responsibility; Article 27(1) which provides that the Statute applies equally to all persons; and that the Preamble does not make reference to those 'most responsible', only "those responsible** (emphasis added)."[115]

This point is especially relevant in regards to the rank and file UN peacekeepers guilty of international crimes committed while serving on a UN mission. The commander who is in charge of thousands of UN peacekeeping troops may be entirely unaware of this criminal conduct of particular military personnel or civilians associated with the military all technically under his or her command (though this does not exclude the possibility of senior leadership themselves being perpetrators or complicit in some way in certain instances). In any case, the current author wholeheartedly endorsees O'Brien's view that:

> Clearly, peacekeeping personnel of senior ranking will be classified as big fish- particularly the Force Commander or the SRSG. **However…*all peacekeeping personnel, regardless of rank, should be considered 'big fish'. It is the position of peacekeeping personnel as protectors of civilians, as those who are tasked with advancing human rights and creating a secure and stable environment, that should render them 'big fish' [when it comes to being high priority for ICC prosecution] regardless of their actual rank or position… If peacekeeping personnel are afforded special status as victims, then a special status as perpetrators should also be bestowed upon them*** (emphasis added).[116]

It appears, however, that UN peacekeepers (of whatever rank) as *perpetrators* of atrocities against children and women in particular do *not* to date, at least judging from ICC case law, have a high priority status re the potential for their ICC prosecution. One is left to reasonably infer from this that the low status *in practice* accorded the child and female adult victims by the international community is at least one important factor in creating this status quo unjust situation in that a disproportionate number of the victims of these rogue UN peacekeeper pepetrators are women and children.

---

[115] O'Brien (2010), pp. 308–309.

[116] O'Brien (2010), pp. 311–312.

Consider also in regards to the issue of UN peacekeepers committing isolated atrocities while on a UN mission and the need to prosecute (where the sending and/or host State and/or a third State is unable or unwilling to prosecute):

> Even without the context of mass crimes, a single war crime should be enough for a prosecution [i.e. where UN peacekeepers are the perpetrators], and in fact such a case [prosecution of an isolated instance of atrocity by a low ranking military person] may have an unforeseen impact on the formulation of international criminal law precedent. The ICTY OTP came under fire, given the limited resources of the Tribunal, for the choice to prosecute a case that centred on a low-ranking perpetrator for his role in the rape of a single victim. **Yet that case became one of the most significant judgements in international criminal law. In *Furundzija*,** the **Tribunal found the accused guilty of *rape as torture and as outrages upon personal dignity*** (emphasis added).[117]

Recall in relation to the issue of the gravity threshold and ICC prosecution; the comments of the Pre-Trial Chamber in the Abu Garda case (a case involving in part attacks on UN peacekeepers).[118] Those comments make clear that the existence of a large number of direct victims is not the determinative criterion to be considered in deciding whether prosecution is merited when assessing gravity:

> 31. In the view of the Chamber, several factors may be taken into account in the assessment of the gravity of a case. **In this respect, the Chamber agrees with the Prosecution's view that, in assessing the gravity of a case, "the issues of the nature, manner and impact of the [alleged] attack are critical"**. ***Further, the gravity of a given case should not be assessed only from a quantitative perspective, i.e. by considering the number of victims; rather, the qualitative dimension of the crime should also be taken into consideration when assessing the gravity of a given case***.
>
> 32. The Chamber finds that certain factors that may be of relevance to the assessment of gravity are listed in rule 145(1)(c) of the Rules, relating to the determination of sentence. **The rule makes reference to "the extent of damage caused, in particular, the harm caused to victims and their families, the nature of the unlawful behaviour and the means employed to execute the crime", which, in the view of the Chamber, can serve' as useful guidelines for the evaluation of the gravity threshold required** by article 17(l)(d) of the Statute.
>
> 33. The Chamber notes the Prosecution contention that, as a result" of the alleged attack, killings and pillaging in the MGS Haskanita, "AMIS operations were severely disrupted, thus affecting its mandated protective roles with respect to millions of Darfurian civilians in need of humanitarian aid and security". The Prosecution further states that AMIS initially suspended and then reduced its activities in the area, and that this left a large number of civilians without AMIS protection, on which they had

117 O'Brien (2010), p. 316 This ICTY case *Furundzija* had nothing to do with UN peacekeepers as perpetrators of Rome Statute crimes. Rather the case is mentioned here to illustrate that **prosecution of low ranking perpetrators** can be valuable and instructive in terms of a fostering by example just application and development of international criminal law and is reasonable in certain instances (see The Prosecutor v Anto Furundzija 2 June, 1998).

118 Note that the Pre-Trial Chamber on 8 February, 2010 declined to confirm the charges against Abu Garda and 23 April, 2010 refused the ICC Prosecutor leave to appeal the refusal to confirm the charges. However, should the ICC Prosecutor obtain new additional enculpatory information, she will be able to file an appeal of the Pre-Trial Chamber refusal to confirm the charges.

> allegedly relied before the attack. **The Chamber thus finds that the consequences of the attack were grave for the direct victims of the attack, that is, the AMIS personnel, and for their families.**
>
> **In addition; the alleged initial suspension and ultimate reduction of' AMIS activities in the area as a result of the attack had a grave impact on the local population.**
>
> 34. In light of the foregoing, the Chamber is satisfied that the case brought before it is of sufficient gravity within the meaning of article 17(l)(d) of the Statute, and finds that the Case is admissible (emphasis added).[119]

It is here argued similarly that the gravity threshold for ICC prosecution is reached when UN peacekeepers are *perpetrators* of atrocity given "the harm caused to victims and their families, [and to respect for the rule of law] the nature of the unlawful behaviour and the means employed to execute the crime." That is, the harm caused by the torture of children and women by UN peacekeepers (physical and psychological torture) sometimes resulting in death of the victims is without question of extreme gravity and the damage irreparable to the direct victims and their families. Often these crimes are gender- based involving sexual violence causing enormous stigmatization to the direct child victims and to the families involved and undermining further the viability of a particular already highly vulnerable group such as internally displaced peoples living in IDP camps.[120] Often the victims targeted by UN peacekeeper perpetrators are disproportionately of a particular ethnic group adding an element contributing to the genocidal intent of non-UN perpetrators in the region as in Darfur. It can be said, at a minimum, that these UN peacekeeper perpetrators had knowledge that their international crimes against children (i.e. torture through rape and other modes) would contribute to the genocidal common plan of someone like Al Bashir even if they themselves as individuals were not personally motivated by genocidal intent.[121] The honour and good intentions of UN peacekeeping missions generally; and the ability of UN peacekeepers to keep the peace and provide security are all brought into serious disrepute when UN peacekeepers commit atrocities no matter the number of direct victims. Hence, when viewed from the aforementioned perspective; international crimes perpetrated by UN peacekeepers affect large numbers of peoples as indirect victims even if these incidents are isolated and targeted directly against only one or a very small number of victims by any individual UN peacekeeper perpetrator.

Let us consider then how feasible is ICC prosecution of UN peacekeepers who have committed Rome Statute international crimes while serving as peacekeepers (i.e. in cases where the troop-sending State with official criminal law

---

[119] The Situation in Darfur in the Case of the Prosecutor v Bahar Idriss Abu Garda Pre-Trial Chamber I Decision on Confirmation of Charges ICC-02/05-02/09 8 February, 2010 at paras 31–34.

[120] Children from IDP camps are often particularly vulnerable to sexual violence and exploitation as they often live in desperate circumstances.

[121] At the same time; some of the UN peacekeeper perpetrators may have harboured racist attitudes towards particular identifiable groups.

jurisdiction over these perpetrators is unwilling or unable to mount a proper genuine investigation and/or prosecution (though prosecution is legally warranted under international law principles) and where neither the host State nor any third State is willing to exercise universal jurisdiction (i.e. over UN perpetrators of torture of children and women in particular). We have discussed the fact that SOFA provide UN military peacekeepers immunity from prosecution in the *host State* while leaving them potentially criminally liable in their home country for atrocities committed abroad as peacekeepers. At the same time; recall that the Rome Statute at Article 27 stipulates that immunity arising from official status shall *not* be a bar to ICC prosecutions:

> **This is in part because the crimes are viewed as acts not committed as part of official capacity** "because they are neither normal State functions[122] nor functions that a State alone (in contrast to an individual) can perform" and in part because such crimes are so heinous that no immunity should bar prosecution…(emphasis added)[123]

This author is agreed with O'Brien that:

> All the UN documentation, from the Directives to the Convention on Privileges and Immunities explicitly state that immunity is granted in relation to all acts performed in an official capacity. **It should thus be the case that violations of international human rights and humanitarian law are considered to fall outside of the performance of official functions, and therefore immunity should not apply… Considering these crimes as part of official duties is to defeat the purpose of peacekeeping- that is, restoring peace and stopping these crimes.** (emphasis added).[124]
>
> **The bottom line is that immunity should not have to be waived in relation to these crimes [grave international crimes], if they are considered to be outside official duties. The immunities [for UN peacekeeper perpetrators] simply should not exist.** However, the reality shows that there is an unwillingness to apply this concept, and that the immunities still need to be lifted by the Secretary-General or the sending state. A major change needs to be made in this area (emphasis added).[125]

Yet Article 98 of the Rome Statute has been interpreted (erroneously on the respectful view here) to mean that *before* the ICC can proceed; the troop-sending State must *in effect* be willing to relinquish criminal jurisdiction over those of its nationals who perpetrated international crimes abroad as members of the UN peacekeeping force. For instance, Fleck interprets Rome Statute Article 98 to mean that the troop-sending State must be willing to agree to a waiver of the immunity granted by the host State before the perpetrator national(s) of the sending State can be turned over by the *host State* to the ICC for prosecution (that is, by the State in which the international crimes were perpetrated).[126] It could be argued, as does O'Brien, however, that where the troop-sending State is unable to prosecute (i.e.

[122] Note that these UN peacekeepers are first and foremost agents of their own sending State though they act also on behalf of and under the auspices of the UN.

[123] O'Brien (2010), p. 301.

[124] O'Brien (2004), p. 38.

[125] O'Brien (2004), p. 39.

[126] Fleck (2003) cited in O'Brien (2010), p. 301–302.

due to the breakdown of the judicial system); or is deemed likely to prosecute the UN peacekeeper perpetrators (the sending State's nationals) with but a 'sham' prosecution, if at all, that there is *not* then a bar to the host State transferring the perpetrators to the ICC for prosecution.[127] That is to say that under the aforementioned circumstances there is no precondition that the troop-sending State waive immunity before the possibility of ICC prosecution arises. It can further be argued justifiably that the international obligation (on the view here a mandatory obligation) to exercise universal jurisdiction to combat jus cogens violations such as torture[128] (in whatever form) *supersedes* any obligation to uphold an immunity agreement. Immunity cannot, in any case, apply to perpetrators of international crimes such as torture which are 'manifestly unlawful' under ICL and hence *ultra vires* of any State official function *or UN Charter mandate.*[129] On this view, a host State or a third State where (i) the troop-sending State is unable or unwilling to investigate and/or prosecute the UN peacekeeper perpetrators (its nationals) and where (ii) such investigation and prosecution is nevertheless warranted on the facts, may choose to exercise universal jurisdiction and prosecute the UN peacekeeper perpetrators domestically or may choose to transfer the perpetrators to the ICC.

As to the issue of a third State transferring UN peacekeeper perpetrators captured on its territory to the ICC, that State is *not* under any obligation to offer immunity to the perpetrators per a Status of Forces Agreement (SOFA):

> …the chance for the Court [the ICC] to interpret the application of a SOFA under [Rome Statute] Article 98 would only arise in the specific circumstances where the host state is seeking to surrender a national of a sending state to the ICC, *as only the host state is a party to the SOFA*. **Should a perpetrator be apprehended by a third state (i.e. not the sending state or the host state), that third state is under no obligation from the UN SOFA as it is not a party to the agreement**. (emphasis added)[130]

It is here argued that the obligation to exercise universal jurisdiction over violation of a *jus cogens* norm such as the prohibition against torture (in whatever form) would be operative for the third State as well. Hence, if that third State could not or was unwilling to hold the UN peacekeepers accountable domestically for torture; it would (i) under the CAT[131] for instance (if a State party to the latter)[132]

---

[127] O'Brien (2004), p. 39: O'Brien suggests that if the troop sending State cannot ensure an investigation and prosecution in good faith if warranted on the facts then the *host State* should have jurisdiction regarding accountability for the UN perpetrators that were operating within its territory where the crimes were committed. (This then would mean also that the host State may choose to surrender the UN peacekeeper perpetrators to the ICC at the latter's request).

[128] Torture being a violation of a *jus cogens* international norm.

[129] This mandatory obligation to exercise universal jurisdiction over violations of *jus cogens* norms (such violations constituting grave international crimes such as torture) would apply also to States that are *not* parties to the Rome Statute.

[130] O'Brien (2010), p. 302.

[131] Convention Against Torture (CAT) (26 June, 1987).

[132] The State's domestic laws may in certain instances also require the State to exercise universal jurisdiction over certain *jus cogens* crimes.

and (ii) under international customary law (ICL) mandating the exercise of universal jurisdiction in regard to torture; be required to transfer the perpetrators to the ICC for prosecution should an ICC arrest warrant have been issued.[133]

In sum then there is universal jurisdiction regarding holding to account perpetrators of the violation of *jus cogens* norms such as the prohibition against torture (i.e. whether torture as a crime against humanity and/or a war crime).The host State or a third State thus could conceivably hand over the ICC peacekeeper perpetrators under these States' right *and obligation* under ICL to exercise universal jurisdiction regarding the international crime of torture in its various forms.[134] The current author is thus disagreed with Casesse[135] that there is no mandatory obligation to exercise universal jurisdiction where grave international crimes such as torture have been perpetrated on the territory of the State in question (i.e. the host State for a UN peacekeeping mission) and the sending State is unwilling and/or unable to genuinely hold the perpetrators to account. Respectfully, the current author would maintain that successfully arguing that there is no *mandatory* obligation with regard to universal jurisdiction in holding to account perpetrators of the international crime of torture, for instance, would require a legally insupportable negation of the indisputable reality of the *jus cogens* nature of the *ICL norm* against torture.

The current author endorses the view of O'Brien that:

> These crimes are … deemed not just bad, but *malum in se*. The perpetrators are *hostis humani generi*. These crimes arè crimes of *jus cogens* for the reason that they "affect the interests of the world community as a whole because they threaten the peace and security of human kind and because they can shock the conscience of humanity". This was the view at the time of the Nuremberg Tribunal, and since then it can certainly be demonstrated to have **crystallised obligatory universal jurisdiction into customary law.** This is inherently captured in the preamble of the Rome Statute itself…(emphasis added).[136]

---

[133] O'Brien (2004), p. 43 maintains that (i) the court in the jurisdiction where the UN peacekeepers committed their international crimes will only need to obtain the consent for transfer of these perpetrators to the ICC from *non-State* parties to the Rome Statute whose nationals are implicated in these international crimes and that (ii) in contrast, ratification of the Rome Statute by States Parties *already* means acceptance of ICC jurisdiction where for whatever reason the State in question (host or troop sending State) cannot and/or will not properly investigate or prosecute the perpetrators (hence consent to waive immunity is **not** required in O'Brien's view, endorsed here, from States Parties to the Rome Statute). The current author also contends that transferring perpetrators to the ICC at ICC request where both the host or sending State cannot and/or will not investigate and prosecute (the prosecution being legally justified) is not then a violation of those State's parties' obligations under international criminal law, ICL or international human rights and humanitarian law. One could argue that SOFA are operative in terms of the sending State retaining criminal jurisdiction over its nationals serving as UN peacekeepers only where the troop sending State is able and willing to administer justice consistent with both national law and international criminal law and human rights substantive legal principles.

[134] See O'Brien (2004), p. 40 for a discussion on the issue of universal jurisdiction and the host State facilitating the transfer of UN peacekeeper perpetrators of gender-based crimes to the ICC.

[135] Cassese (2001), p. 264.

[136] O'Brien (2004), p. 264.

What is here suggested is that an authentic culture of accountability for grave international crimes such as torture, including those committed by UN peacekeepers (military or associated civilian members), requires the realistic possibility of prosecution of such perpetrators by the ICC.[137] The victims of these atrocities deserve nothing less and, furthermore, anything less undermines the international criminal justice system and respect for the rule of international law generally. Shamefully the UN Security Council has officially exempted in its referral of the situation in Sudan, for instance, certain UN peacekeeping personnel from ICC jurisdiction except in a particular limited circumstance:

> **…[T]he Security Council referral of the situation in Sudan to the ICC exempts nationals, current or former officials or personnel from a contributing state outside Sudan which is not a party to the ICC from ICC jurisdiction**. Such persons are declared "subject to the exclusive jurisdiction of that contributing State for all alleged acts or omissions arising out of or related to operations in Sudan established or authorized by the Council or the African Union, unless such exclusive jurisdiction has been expressly waived by that contributing State."[138]

This Security Council aforementioned exemption (in its referral of the situation in Sudan) of UN peacekeeper perpetrators from States not a party to the Rome Statute from ICC jurisdiction unless the troop-sending State waives jurisdiction is all the more uncalled for given: (i) the extreme and continuing vulnerability of the people of Northern Sudan under Al Bashir and (ii) the extreme atrocities which in particular (though not exclusively) women and children have suffered at the hands of certain UN mission personnel in Sudan.[139] This author would suggest in fact that the UN Security Council is violating its mandate under the UN Charter in providing this exemption. That mandate and purpose is in part stipulated in the following except from the preamble to the UN Charter:

> **PREAMBLE**
> **WE THE PEOPLES OF THE UNITED NATIONS DETERMINED**
>
> to save succeeding generations from the scourge of war, which twice in our lifetime has brought untold sorrow to mankind, and
>
> **to reaffirm faith in fundamental human rights, in the dignity and worth of the human person, in the equal rights of men and women and of nations large and small**, and
>
> **to establish conditions under which justice and respect for the obligations arising from treaties and other sources of international law can be maintained**…(emphasis added)[140]

Clearly the exemption of any UN peacekeeper perpetrator from possible ICC prosecution for jus cogens international crimes is contrary to the mandate set out in the UN Charter in that it: (i) undermines respect for the fundamental human rights of women and children who are predominately, but not exclusively, the

[137] Yet States may attempt to subvert the possibility of ICC prosecution. For instance, the U.S made several agreements with States parties to the Rome Statute not to hand over any U.S. perpetrators of grave international crimes to the ICC (see O'Brien (2010), pp. 302–303).

[138] O'Brien (2010), pp. 303–304

[139] Du Plessis and Pete (2004), pp. 7–8.

[140] UN Charter, Preamble (entry into force 24 October, 1945) Note that on this author's view the equal rights of children should also be mentioned in the Preamble but is not.

particularized victims of these UN perpetrators and (ii) fails to foster conditions under which justice and respect for the obligations arising from treaties and other sources of international law (i.e. ICL) can be maintained. Further this automatic exemption allowing for *potential* impunity for certain UN peacekeeper perpetrators is contrary to: (i) international customary law regarding the requirement to prevent torture and to hold the perpetrators of this *jus cogens* crime accountable and (ii) the CAT[141] which requires that the perpetrators of torture as an international crime and violation of a peremptory *jus cogens* norm be brought to justice regardless of their nationality or other status (i.e. UN peacekeeper or any other official status):

> … 'neither the text nor the spirit of the Charter conceives of the Security Council as *legibus solutus*.'[free of the constraints of law]. Thus projected compliance with international law is an intrinsic part of the Council's obligations and instrumental to its primary responsibility: or more specifically, *international law provides a framework for decision-making about the maintenance of international peace and security* (emphasis added).[142]

Note that before the Rome Statute entered into force, the U.S. tried to ensure immunity for U.S. military and civilian personnel engaged in UN peacekeeping operations. The U.S. advanced the argument, among others, that such immunity would facilitate the willingness of the U.S to participate in future UN peacekeeping operations and that such immunity if extended to UN personnel from other contributing States not parties to the Rome Statute would serve the same function also in regards to those States.[143] Ultimately the UN Security Council adopted resolutions 1422 and 1487 which extend immunity to UN peacekeepers from ICC prosecution where the contributing State is a non-party to the Rome Statute; with the resolution renewable every 12 months depending on the Security Council vote.[144] It has been noted that to the extent that UN member States refuse to surrender ICC requested UN peacekeeper perpetrators due to Security Council resolution 1422/1487 (given the international obligations these impose on States) this would subvert the rule of law.[145] Recall in this regard that the Parliamentarians for Global Action in fact attempted to *prevent the renewal* of resolution 1422 as it was not consistent with the intentions of Article 16 and arguably violates the UN Charter as "Chapter VII requires the existence of a threat to peace, breach of the

141 Convention Against Torture (CAT) (26 June, 1987).

142 Field SM (2013), p. 137.

143 Knoops Geert-Jan (2004), pp. 257–258.

144 UN Security Council Resolutions 1422 and 1487. Note that these resolutions are not legally binding on the ICC (Knoops Geert-Jan (2004), p. 270).

145 Knoops Geert-Jan (2004), pp. 270–271.

peace or an act of aggression before the Council can take such action."[146] Consider then Article 16 of the Rome Statute:

> **Article 16**
> **Deferral of investigation or prosecution**
> No investigation or prosecution may be commenced or proceeded with under this Statute for a period of 12 months after the Security Council, in a resolution adopted under Chapter VII of the Charter of the United Nations, has requested the Court to that effect; *that request may be renewed by the Council under the same conditions* (emphasis added).[147]

Any attempt to use Article 16 to *indefinitely* halt the investigation and prosecution of those most responsible for grave international crimes such as torture, whether UN peacekeeper perpetrators or others, on this author's view, is not at all consistent with securing peace and security. In fact; the ICC could "reject such a request [from the UN Security Council to halt an investigation or prosecution at any point] because it would not relate sufficiently to restoration of peace or security, on the basis of which Chapter VII of the Charter authorizes the Security Council to take extraordinary measures."[148]

References

Literature

Cassese A (2001) International law. Oxford University Press, Oxford

Field SM (2013). UN Security Council resolutions concerning children affected by armed conflict: In whose best interest?. Int J Children's Rights 21(1):127–161

Grover SC (2009) Canada's refusal to repatriate a Canadian citizen from Guantanamo Bay as a violation of the Humanitarian Values Underlying the Principle of Non- refoulement: a reanalysis of the reasoning in Omar Ahmed Khadr v the prime Minister of Canada et al. High Court Quart Rev 5(2):42–48

Grover SC (2013a) Humanity's children: ICC jurisprudence and the failure to address the genocidal forcible transfer of children. Springer, Berlin

Grover SC (2013b) Child soldiers as victims of 'genocidal forcible transfer': Darfur and Syria as case examples. Int J Hum Rights 17(3):411–427

Grover SC (2012) Child soldier victims of genocidal forcible transfer: exonerating child soldiers charged with grave conflict-related international crimes. Springer, Berlin

Gadler A (2010) The protection of peacekeepers and international criminal law

Knoops Geert -Jan A (2004) The prosecution and defense of peacekeepers under international criminal law. Transnational Publishers, Ardsley

Du Plessis M, Pete S (2004) Who guards the guards? the ICC and serious crimes committed by United Nations peacekeepers in Africa. African Secur Rev 13(4):5–17

Fleck D (2003) Are foreign military personnel exempt from international criminal jurisdiction under status of forces agreements? J Int Crim Justice 1(3):651–670

[146] Knoops Geert-Jan (2004), p. 281.

[147] Rome Statute (2002).

[148] Knoops Geert-Jan (2004), p. 271.

Henckaerts JM and Doswald-Beck L (2005) Customary international humanitarian law, vol 1. http://www.icrc.org/eng/assets/files/other/customary-international-humanitarian-law-i-icrc-eng.pdf. Accessed 20 May 2013
Kelly T (2012) This side of silence: human rights, torture, and the recognition of cruelty. University of Pennsylvania Press, Philadelphia
Ladley A (2005) Peacekeeper abuse, immunity and impunity: the need for effective criminal and civil accountability on international peace operations. Polit Ethics Rev 1(1):81–90
Levinson S (2010) In quest of a "common conscience: reflections on the current debate about torture. J Natl Secur Law Policy, 1:231–252 p. 252
Lokaneeta J (2010) A rose by another name: legal definitions, sanitized terms, and imagery of torture in 24. Law Cult Humanit 6(2):245–273
Notar SA (2006) Peacekeepers as perpetrators: sexual exploitation and abuse of women and children in the democratic republic of the Congo. J Gend Soc Policy Law 14(2):413–429
O'Brien M (2010) National and international criminal jurisdiction over United Nations peacekeeping personnel for gender-based crimes against women Doctoral Dissertation, University of Nottingham Available for download at http://etheses.nottingham.ac.uk/1492/. Accessed 31 May 2013
O'Brien M (2004) Overcoming boys-will-be-boys syndrome: is prosecution of peacekeepers in the international criminal court for trafficking, sexual slavery and related crimes against women a possibility? Masters thesis, International Human Rights Law, University of Lund, Faculty of Law http://lup.lub.lu.se/luur/download?func=downloadFile&recordOId=1554856&fileOId=1563466. Accessed 7 June 2013
Plunkett MCB, Southall DBP (1998) War and children. Arch Dis Child 1998(78):72–77
Razack SH (2004) Dark threats and white knights: the Somalia affair, peacekeeping, and the new imperialism. University of Toronto Press, Toronto
Rodley NS (2007) The prohibition of torture: absolute means absolute. In: Kaleck W, Ratner M, Singelnstein T, Weiss P (eds) International prosecution of human rights crimes. Springer, Berlin, pp 185–200
Xenos D (2009) The human rights of the vulnerable. Int J Hum Rights 13(4):591–614
Grover SC (2011) The supreme court of Canada's declining of Its jurisdiction in not ordering the repatriation of a Canadian guantanamo detainee: implications of the case for our understanding of international humanitarian law. Int J Hum Rights 15(3):481–508

Materials

UN Charter 26 June, 1945 (entry into force 24 October, 1945). http://www.un.org/en/documents/charter/intro.shtml. Accessed 16 June 2013
Amnesty International (2011) Rape and sexual violence": human rights law and standards in the international criminal court. http://www.amnesty.org/en/library/asset/IOR53/001/2011/en/7f5eae8f-c008-4caf-ab59-0f84605b61e0/ior530012011en.pdf. Accessed 26 May 2013
Convention on the Rights of the Child (1990) (entry into force 2 September 1990). http://www.ohchr.org/EN/ProfessionalInterest/Pages/CRC.aspx. Accessed 19 April 2013
Convention on the Safety of United Nations and Associated Personnel (1999) (entry into force 15 January 1999). http://www.un.org/law/cod/safety.htm. Accessed 30 May 2013
Gerster J (2013) Twenty years after Somalia affair of tortured teen, The Canadian Press. http://metronews.ca/news/canada/597698/saturday-marks-anniversary-of-somalia-affair/. Accessed 5 June 2013
Human Rights Watch (2012) Torture archipelago: arbitrary arrests, torture and enforced disappearances in Syria's underground prisons since March 2011. http://www.hrw.org/node/108415/section/5. Accessed 23 May 2013
Human Rights Watch (2004) Living in fear: Child soldiers and the Tamil Tigers in Sri Lanka November 2004 vol 16, No 13 (C). http://www.hrw.org/sites/default/files/reports/srilanka1104.pdf. Accessed 27 May 2013

Inter-American Court of Human Rights, Advisory opinion OC-17/2002 of August 28, 2002 on the Juridical Condition and Human Rights of the Child (2002). http://www.corteidh.or.cr/docs/opiniones/seriea_18_ing.pdf. Accessed 27 May 2013
Juridical status and human rights of the child, Advisory Opinion OC-17/02, August 28, 2002, Inter-Am. Ct. H.R. (Ser. A) No. 17 (2002). http://www1.umn.edu/humanrts/iachr/series_A_OC-17.html. Accessed 1 July 2013
Rome Statute Elements of the Crimes (2002) http://www.icc-cpi.int/NR/rdonlyres/9CAEE830-38CF-41D6-AB0B-68E5F9082543/0/Element_of_Crimes_English.pdf
Statement of Human rights investigator David Hawk in an interview with CNN's Anderson Cooper (2012) Horrors revealed at North Korean prison camp CBS News 30 November 2012. http://www.cbsnews.com/8301-18560_162-57556456/horrors-revealed-at-north-korean-prison-camp/. Accessed 23 May 2013
Universal Declaration of Human Rights (1948) G.A. Res. 217A(III) , UN Doc A/810. https://www.un.org/en/documents/udhr/. Accessed 20 May, 2013

Cases

Canada (Prime Minister) v. Khadr (2010) SCC 3 Judgment 29 January 2010
Inter-American Commission of Human Rights Report No. 33/04 in Jailton Neri Da Fonseca v Brazil 11 March 2004. http://cidh.org/annualrep/2004eng/Brazil.11634eng.htm. Accessed 18 May 2013
Khadr v. Canada (Prime Minister) (2010) FC 715, [2010] 4 F.C.R. 36
Khadr v. Canada (Prime Minister) (2009) F.C.J. No. 462 [2009] FC 405
The Prosecutor v Anto Furundzija (ICTY CASE NO.: IT-95-17/1-PT) Amended Indictment (2 June, 1998). http://www.icty.org/x/cases/furundzija/ind/en/fur-1ai980602e.pdf. Accessed 25 June 2013
The Prosecutor v Thomas Lubanga Dyilo warrant for arrest (10 February 2006). http://www.icc-cpi.int/iccdocs/doc/doc191959.PDF. Accessed 11 July 2013
The Situation in Darfur in the Case of the Prosecutor v Bahar Idriss Abu Garda Pre-Trial Chamber I Decision on Confirmation of Charges ICC-02/05-02/09 8 February 2010
The Prosecutor v Thomas Lubanga Dyilo Prosecutor Closing Statement (25 August 2011). http://212.159.242.181/iccdocs/doc/doc1210316.pdf. Accessed 26 May 2013
The Prosecutor v. Ahmad Muhammad Harun ("Ahmad Harun") and Ali Muhammad Ali Abd-Al-Rahman ("Ali Kushayb") Pre-Trial Chamber I Warrant of Arrest for Ahmad Harun 27 April 2007 ICC-02/05-01/07
The Situation in Darfur, Sudan in the Case of The Prosecutor v Abdallah Banda Abaeker Nourain and Saleh Mohammed Jerboa Jamus Corrigendum of the "Decision on the Confirmation of Charges 7 March 2011 ICC-02/05-03/09

Chapter 9
Conclusion

9.1 A Final Comment

In a 2010 report by the Innocenti Centre it was noted that:

> **In addition to being targeted alongside adults, children are sometimes specifically targeted because of their vulnerability, notably as a means to intimidate, harass or destroy their communities or groups**. Children are indeed more vulnerable than adults to being victimized and therefore likely to be affected in greater proportion. International law, including humanitarian law, recognizes that children's vulnerability entitles them to protection above and beyond the general protection afforded to them as part of the civilian population. ***Given the specific legal obligation to protect children, their particular vulnerability and the disproportionate impact of crimes on them, crimes committed against children should receive greater consideration. Yet, these crimes have not received systematic or even sustained attention from international courts*** (emphasis added).[1]

The frequency globally of the systemic and widespread use during armed conflict of the torture of children in particular as the unfettered implementation of a common plan by a perpetrator armed force is a striking indicator that the international legal regime responsible is failing in enforcing the *jus cogens* prohibition against torture. The systematic widespread use of torture during armed conflict as a separable form of criminal conduct and as military and political strategy is, it is here contended, a grave international crime on par with genocide (referring here to torture as a widespread war crime and/or torture as a crime against humanity). Torture as a common plan during armed conflict is often a precursor to or correlated with 'enforced disappearance' and other grave international crimes such as the intentional killings of civilians and creating conditions of life that cause great suffering and may not be survivable. The systemic and widespread use of torture in particular of children during armed conflict is in fact not infrequently an 'early warning bell' of a likely impending broader human rights disaster in terms of all manner of crimes against humanity, war crimes and/or genocide yet to

---

[1] Aptel (2010), pp. 87–88.

S. C. Grover, *The Torture of Children During Armed Conflicts*,
DOI: 10.1007/978-3-642-40689-8_9, © Springer-Verlag Berlin Heidelberg 2014

befall the targeted civilian populace. The need to be alert to 'early warning bells' (their nature unspecified) was in fact referred to in a UN document on the 'duty to protect':

> (d) The Summit recognized that early warning and assessment was a necessary, though hardly sufficient, ingredient for successful preventive and protective action by Member States, through the United Nations. As asserted…the international community should "support the United Nations in establishing an early warning capability". This would require: (i) the timely flow to United Nations decision makers of accurate, authoritative, reliable and relevant information about the incitement, preparation or perpetration of the four specified crimes and violations; (ii) the capacity for the United Nations Secretariat to assess that information and to understand the patterns of events properly within the context of local conditions; and (iii) ready access to the office of the Secretary-General. ***Too often, the alarm bells were not sounded at all or they failed to command attention or spur effective action at senior political ranks, whether in the Secretariat or in intergovernmental bodies*** …(emphasis added).[2]

Clearly, the alarm bells as an 'early warning' system for the implementation of the international community's 'duty to protect' continue to toll silently for the UN in respect of the systematic torture in particular of children as a strategy of war. This is certainly the case for the child victims in Syria as has been the case in relation to so many child torture victims in other armed conflict situations before. In fact at the time of writing; reports are emerging that chemical weapons have been used in Syria with there being civilian victims.[3] It is known that the government of Bashar al-Assad has chemical weapons at its disposal but the UN is being cautious in making any finding to date regarding who the perpetrators were.[4] Yet there is still no coordinated and effective action from the apoplectic international community to end the Al Assad regime's ever more severe torture of the Syrian people in various forms including of children.

The systemic and/or widespread use of torture as part of a common plan during armed conflict and/or the targeted torture of children in particular, it is here argued, should be sufficient to trigger vigorous international efforts toward prosecution of those most responsible for violation of the *jus cogens* prohibition against torture (i.e. ICC warrants of arrest and a willingness of States to surrender the perpetrators should they somehow gain custody and control over these offenders during a UN sanctioned

---

2 Report of the UN Secretary-General on the implementation of duty to protect (2009).

3 Report of the Independent International Commission of Inquiry on the Syrian Arab Republic to the UN Human Rights Council (4 June, 2013), p. 21.

4 Report of the Independent International Commission of Inquiry on the Syrian Arab Republic to the UN Human Rights Council (4 June, 2013), p. 21. Note that as of at least June, 2013 the U.S. has decided based on its intelligence that the Bashar al-Assad regime has used chemical weapons against its own people and on that basis has decided to provide certain selected categories of arms to the rebels. The use of chemical weapons by Bashar Al Assad's regime, the Obama administration had warned, would be crossing a red line but **apparently the torture of Syrian children which had occurred much earlier and continues in various forms was not such a 'game changer'**. Then again; recall that the U.S. has yet to ratify the Convention with the most ratifications of any international human rights instrument; namely the Convention on the Rights of the Child (1990).

intervention or through some other circumstance and the home State or any other State is unwilling or unable to prosecute). As things stand at present, however, that torture during armed conflict in a certain jurisdiction as a common plan, even of children as particularized targets, should trigger international condemnation and intervention is a notion not even agreed upon in principle let alone acted on in practice. Clearly the international community of States parties to the Rome Statute, and to various international human rights and humanitarian law treaties has some considerable distance to go to actually attaining the civilized standard that it so often professes to endorse. The current author expresses grave concern that children exposed to systematic torture in various forms during armed conflict (as part of a common plan of a perpetrator State or non-State force) are at continuing risk in contemporary times of having their suffering gone unaddressed as torture by the ICC as the cases here discussed reveal. One contributor to this failure to afford the aforementioned child torture victims the full measure of international criminal justice[5] is the misleading oversimplified prototypical image of the torture victim too often held in the international public consciousness:

> When the modern human rights movement began, its normative victim was an eastern European male prisoner of conscience...**But the "war on terror" has returned us, in many ways, to status quo ante: today, the normative human rights victim is once more a male prisoner, this time in Guantánamo; human rights offences by states are back at centre stage; and *crimes against women and children are again being marginalized*** (emphasis added).[6]

Hopefully this book has contributed to challenging those oversimplified stereotypes regarding who are the victims of torture as an international crime during armed conflict and allowed for a step closer, no matter how small, to gaining the international justice child victims of torture as an international crime are owed by the international community. At the time of writing the fact of the matter is that the horrific systematic *torture* of civilians during armed conflict, *including children as particularized targets*, continues unabated in places such as Syria as reported, for instance, in the following:

Item: **Human Rights Watch Report (4 June , 2013):** Between January and March 2013 at least 147 bodies have been found floating down the Aleppo river in government- controlled areas. There are 350 photos of these victims; *many if not all of them the victims of enforced disappearance and torture* (at the least severe

[5] Affording the mass child torture victims true international justice under the Rome Statute will require that the systemic and widespread rape and other grave sexual violence, enforced disappearance, extra-judicial killing and certain other Rome Statute crimes against children during armed conflict be recognized by the ICC OTP and ICC Pre-Trial, Trial and Appeal Chambers as torture. This recognition that the children have been the victims of torture as a common plan during armed conflict would be reflected in the cumulative charges advanced, the confirmation of the torture charges in addition to the separate other charges such as rape, the survival of the torture charges on defence appeal and the severe sentence imposed for the systemic targeted torture of children during armed conflict.

[6] Tax (13 December, 2010). It should be noted of course that it is the case that females have also carried out terrorist acts for domestic terrorist groups and for international terrorist organizations such as Al Qaeda (no doubt, at least at times, under great duress and, in other instances, due to the womens' adoption of a so-called 'political' extremist ideology) but that this is an infrequent occurrence compared to the incidence rate for males carrying out terrorist activities.

psychological torture) found with their hands tied behind their backs and tape over their mouth; shot in the head. *The ages range from childhood (age 11) to age 64.*[7] These cases were investigated by Human Rights Watch personnel who visited the site and interviewed local residents and activists including a forensic expert who examined the bodies and reviewed the photographs (emphasis added).[8]

Item: UN Report (4 June, 2013):

> **Massacres**
>
> …
>
> **Baniyas**
>
> 41. Government forces and affiliated militia attacked the village of Al-Bayda on 2 May and a neighbourhood in Baniyas, Tartous, on 3 May. **Video materials show dozens of *bodies of women and children* apparently killed at close quarters.**[9] Evidence gathered indicates the perpetrators are Government-affiliated militia. The investigation continues (emphasis added).[10]
>
> **Other unlawful killing**
>
> **Summary execution and the war crime of murder**
>
> **Anti-Government armed groups**
>
> **55. Video footage emerged showing a child participating in the beheading of two kidnapped men.**[11] Following investigation, it is believed that the video is authentic and the men were soldiers, killed as depicted. It was not possible to identify the perpetrators. Evidence indicates the Usud Al-Tawhid Brigade committed the initial kidnapping (emphasis added)[12]
>
> **Abductions, arbitrary arrests, detention and torture**
>
> **Government forces and affiliated militia**
>
> 99. Government forces and militia detained *children* at checkpoints and during house raids. Several arrests in Dara'a appeared to *target children of suspected FSA members.* Others *held children as hostage* in exchange for detainees held by the FSA. During the 10 April attack on Sanamayn, **children were forced to watch the torture or killing of parents**. In April, checkpoint personnel in Rastan, Homs, threatened to shoot two girls aged nine and seven who started crying during their father's interrogation (emphasis added).[13]
>
> **Recruitment and use of children**
>
> **Anti-Government armed groups**
>
> 101. Some armed groups recruit and use children for active participation in hostilities. A 14-year-old boy from Homs underwent training in use of weapons with the Abu

---

[7] Human Rights Watch (4 June, 2013b) Syria: A stream of bodies in Aleppo's River.

[8] Human Rights Watch (4 June, 2013b) Syria: A stream of bodies in Aleppo's River.

[9] The child victims obviously in particular would have suffered intense terror amounting to psychological torture as victims targeted during these massacres.

[10] Report of the Independent International Commission of Inquiry on the Syrian Arab Republic to the UN Human Rights Council 4 June, 2013, p. 9.

[11] Note that the UN did not in its report cite this as an instance of *psychological torture of the child* involved in the beheading.

[12] Report of the Independent International Commission of Inquiry on the Syrian Arab Republic to the UN Human Rights Council 4 June, 2013, p. 11.

[13] Report of the Independent International Commission of Inquiry on the Syrian Arab Republic to the UN Human Rights Council 4 June, 2013, p. 16.

> Yusef Battalion, which then used him to keep track of soldiers' movements in Al-Waar. Other groups reject underage volunteers. Commanders in Dayr Al-Zawr refused to accept a 15- year-old boy, calling his parents to collect him.
> 102. Casualty statistics indicate 86 children were killed in hostilities as combatants. Of those, nearly half died in 2013. **These figures suggest the use of children in combat is increasing** (emphasis added).[14]
>
> **Illegal Weapons**
> 139. ...In four attacks—on Khan Al-Asal, Aleppo, 19 March; Uteibah, Damascus, 19 March; Sheikh Maqsood neighbourhood, Aleppo, 13 April; and Saraqib, Idlib, 29 April—**there are reasonable grounds to believe that limited quantities of toxic chemicals were used**. It has not been possible, on the evidence available, to determine the precise chemical agents used, their delivery systems or the perpetrator. Other incidents also remain under investigation (emphasis added).[15]

Currently, children in Syria are under the psychological torture caused by the knowledge that at any moment they may be gravely injured or killed in mass attacks on civilians by the Syrian regime. Further, their schools are under attack making it clear to children of all ages attending school that they are expendable and, on the contrary, prized targets of the Syrian regime.

Adding to this psychological torture is the air of mistrust and the total lack of a sense of security, physical or psychological, for these child victims:

> There started to be a phobia of school. Teachers were informants. Families would say, "Don't talk to your teachers," or would just keep students home. A big portion of families would not send their kids to school.
> —Mostafa, guidance counselor at a boys' high school in Nimr, Daraa governorate, who fled to Jordan, November 2012.[16]

> In Syria's brutal and protracted armed conflict, children have suffered alongside the rest of the population. Many have been killed and wounded as their hometowns have been transformed into war zones. **They have endured torture and inhumane conditions in government detention**. And they have been tested by severe shortages of humanitarian aid and inadequate medical care.[17]

It should be recognized that under international human rights law; children too have political and civil rights[18] and the inherent right to exercise them in certain ways[19] such as through peaceful demonstration without suppression through attack, illegal arrest, *torture*, inhuman and degrading treatment or any other means:

> **Convention on the Rights of the Child**
>
> **Article 12**
> **1. States Parties shall assure to the child who is capable of forming his or her own views the right to express those views freely in all matters affecting the child** , the

[14] Report of the Independent International Commission of Inquiry on the Syrian Arab Republic to the UN Human Rights Council 4 June, 2013, p. 17.

[15] Report of the Independent International Commission of Inquiry on the Syrian Arab Republic to the UN Human Rights Council 4 June, 2013, p. 21.

[16] Human Rights Watch (2013c). Safe no more: Students and Schools under Attack in Syria, p. 1.

[17] Human Rights Watch (2013c). Safe no more: Students and Schools under Attack in Syria, p. 1.

[18] Convention on the Rights of the Child (1990).

[19] Grover (2012).

views of the child being given due weight in accordance with the age and maturity of the child....

Article 13
1. The child shall have the right to freedom of expression; this right shall include freedom to seek, receive and impart information and ideas of all kinds, regardless of frontiers, either orally, in writing or in print, in the form of art, or through any other media of the child's choice.
2. The exercise of this right may be subject to certain restrictions, but these shall only be such as are provided by law and are necessary:
(a) For respect of the rights or reputations of others; or
(b) For the protection of national security or of public order[20](ordre public), or of public health or morals.

Article 14
1. States Parties shall respect the right of the child to freedom of thought, conscience ...

Article 15
1. States Parties recognize the rights of the child to freedom of association and to freedom of peaceful assembly.
2. No restrictions may be placed on the exercise of these rights other than those imposed in conformity with the law and which are necessary in a *democratic society*...

Article 16
1. No child shall be subjected to arbitrary or unlawful interference with his or her privacy, family, or correspondence, nor to unlawful attacks on his or her honour and reputation.
2. The child has the right to the protection of the law against such interference or attacks.

Article 37
States Parties shall ensure that:
(a) No child shall be subjected to ***torture*** **or other cruel, inhuman or degrading treatment or punishment**. Neither capital punishment nor life imprisonment without possibility of release shall be imposed for offences committed by persons below eighteen years of age;
(b) No child shall be deprived of his or her liberty unlawfully or arbitrarily. The arrest, detention or imprisonment of a child shall be in conformity with the law and shall be used only as a measure of last resort and for the shortest appropriate period of time;
(c) Every child deprived of liberty shall be treated with humanity and respect for the inherent dignity of the human person, and in a manner which takes into account the needs of persons of his or her age. In particular, every child deprived of liberty shall be separated from adults unless it is considered in the child's best interest not to do so and shall have the right to maintain contact with his or her family through correspondence and visits, save in exceptional circumstances;
(d) Every child deprived of his or her liberty shall have the right to prompt access to legal and other appropriate assistance, as well as the right to challenge the legality of the deprivation of his or her liberty before a court or other competent, independent and impartial authority, and to a prompt decision on any such action.[21]

[20] That public order being founded on respect for human rights.

[21] Convention on the Rights of the Child (1990).

However, in attempting to exercise their civil and political rights, the children of Syria so engaged (among the other children not at all engaged in activism) have come under brutal attack by the Bashar al-Assad regime:

> The government of President Bashar al-Assad …has also carried out unlawful policies and practices targeting students and their schools. Witnesses from six schools in the Daraa, Homs, and the Damascus suburbs told Human Rights Watch that **authorities sent security officers and *used school officials to interrogate students* about their *political views and alleged anti-government activities by students and their parents*. Witnesses and students from the Damascus suburbs and Daraa described how security forces and pro-government militias used excessive force, even gunfire, against three peaceful student demonstrations** (emphasis added).[22]
>
> Government forces and shabiha, pro-government armed groups, assaulted and sometimes fired on anti-government, student-organized protest marches that students staged at the end of their school day. They also entered schools to arrest students, sometimes assaulting students and teachers, and firing guns in the air, terrifying the students.
>
> Government forces and shabiha also fired upon schools, including schools still in use as educational institutions. Salma, a high school student from Daraa, described hiding underneath her desk while machine gun fire hit her school walls. Marwan, a 12-year-old student, also from Daraa, said that he ran for safety as tank shells struck his school building.
>
> Syrian government air force fighter jets and helicopters dropped bombs—including what appeared to be improvised "barrel bombs" and incendiary weapons—on school buildings, causing extensive damage. Human Rights Watch documented two air strikes on school buildings. Witnesses interviewed said there were no opposition forces in or near the schools, suggesting that the attacks were unlawful….[23]

In Syria there is no public order with the regime violating ICL, international criminal, human rights and humanitarian treaty law to suppress the population. Those Syrian children in demonstrating for an end to these human rights abuses are standing up for their right as Syrians and the right of all Syrians to peace, security and public order founded on the respect for fundamental human rights and democracy. Neither the children's exercise of their inherent fundamental human right to free expression nor any other rationale can justify in international law the use of various forms of oppression and suppression by the regime including the torture of children. How pitiful and unforgivable that to date the international community has left these child human rights activists to fend for themselves even in the face of the Bashar al-Assad regime using torture as a common plan also against Syria's children in particular; activist or not.

It is long past due that the international community considers the use of torture (in whatever form), including of children as particularized high priority targets, (especially when a systematic practice as part of a common plan during armed conflict) as sufficient grounds for UN intervention. A case in point- Syria. The time is now to put an end to the abominable and inexcusable attacks by the Bashar al-Assad regime on civilians and to its infliction of suffering through

[22] Human Rights Watch (2013c). Safe no more: Students and Schools under Attack in Syria, p. 1.

[23] Human Rights Watch (2013c). Safe no more: Students and Schools under Attack in Syria, p. 2.

torture (psychological and physical) as part of a common plan. Likewise any member of the Syrian opposition engaged in, for instance, the psychological torture of a child through the children's participation in executions or as a rebel member, regardless the specific role of the children, or torture in any other manner whether psychological and/or physical must be held accountable by the ICC if no other mechanism is available. It is essential that the UN Security Council refer the situation in Syria to the ICC without further delay and authorize appropriate intervention to stop the violence.[24] The former step for the sake not only of the Syrian people but to help preserve the perceived viability of the ICC as an instrument of international criminal justice and to salvage the general perception, what of it remains, of equality of justice under international law for all peoples.

On the issue of a moral and legal imperative for a UN Security Council referral of the situation in Syria to the ICC (given the atrocities being committed by the Al Assad regime), recall that the UN itself as an institution has an obligation to uphold respect for fundamental universal human rights[25]; an objective and mandate expressed in the UN Charter. In addition note that the preamble to the UN Charter also specifically mentions *the obligation to protect children in particular* listing as a prime objective of the UN "to save succeeding generations from the scourge of war, which twice in our lifetime has brought untold sorrow to mankind"[26]

This author is agreed with Field that the UN Security Council is bound by international law including international human rights law regarding, in particular, preemptory norms:

> At a minimum ....the [Security] Council is bound by provisions of the CRC [Convention on the Rights of the Child] that reflect peremptory norms of international human rights law and also customary international human rights law.[27]

This means then that insofar as children are concerned; the UN Security Council is bound in particular by Article 37 of the Convention on the Rights of the Child[28] prohibiting the torture of children and reflecting a peremptory norm in this regard. To meet its legal obligation to uphold human rights then the UN Security Council must, among other vital steps, refer the situation in Syria to the ICC given the fact

---

[24] Such a referral is necessary if the ICC is to assume jurisdiction over the matter as Syria is not a party to the Rome Statute. Of course to make this possible members of the UN Security Council currently blocking the referral would have to relent and stop the transparent deadly 'game of smoke and mirrors' they have been playing with the lives of Syrian civilians (i.e. Russia now denying that there is credible evidence that the Al Assad regime has used chemical weapons against the people and, at the time of writing, Russia still blocking intervention or any UN Security Council referral to the ICC).

[25] Field (2013), p. 140.

[26] UN Charter 26 June, 1945

[27] Field (2013), p. 141.

[28] Convention on the Rights of the Child (1990): Article 37 States Parties shall ensure that: (a) No child shall be subjected to torture or other cruel, inhuman or degrading treatment or punishment. ...

that in Syria children's right to be protected against torture used as military and political strategy is being grossly violated by the Bashar Al Assad regime. Note that the protection of children during armed conflict is viewed by the UN Security Council (as reflected in its resolutions concerning children) as a factor intimately connected to the maintenance of peace and security:

> **As posited by the Council, serious violations of international law relating to children 'may constitute a threat to peace'. Thus positioned central to maintaining peace and security is preventing serious violations of international law relating to children** (emphasis added).[29]

Notwithstanding the foregoing UN resolutions, there has been according to some scholars, minimal engagement of the UN Security Council with the Convention on the Rights of the Child.[30] Further, as here discussed; the targeting during armed conflict of children in particular for torture has had virtually no impact on any UN Security Council decision-making to date regarding referral of situations to the ICC where the State is a non-party to the Rome Statute (as evidenced, for instance, by agents of the Syrian regime to date perpetrating mass atrocities including the torture of children in particular with impunity and absent any referral of the situation to the ICC).

Not only are the child and other victims of torture as a common plan in these contemporary conflicts, such as in Syria,[31] entitled to justice under international criminal law (i.e. the ICC where there is no workable alternative); but they are also entitled to reparations through whatever judicial means available (i.e. under domestic legislation, via transnational law suits, as a remedy in part through an international human rights commission or court or through the ICC victims fund if their case is heard and decided in their favor by the ICC).[32] The child victims of systematic and widespread torture used as central to a common plan in the armed conflict in Syria and elsewhere are *still* waiting for justice and for a show of a even a modicum of humanity from the international community.

References

Aceves WJ (2007) The anatomy of torture :a documentary history of Filartiga v Pena Irala Martinus Nijhoff Publishers, Leiden

Aptel C (2010) International criminal justice and child protection. In: Parmar S, Roseman MJ, Siegrist S, Sowa T (eds.) Children and transitional justice: Truth -telling, accountability and reconciliation, 67–113

---

[29] Field, p. 157.

[30] Field (2013), p. 159.

[31] According to Human Rights Watch; the UN inspectors' report on recent chemical attacks in Syria confirm the use of Sarin poisonous gas. Furthermore, the UN report provides data that allows for determination of the trajectory of the Sarin rocket delivery paths. The flight paths converge in origin on a military base of the Republican Guard serving at the pleasure of the Assad regime (Lyons, J 17 September, 2013).

[32] The topic of reparations for torture victims is beyond the scope of this book, however for discussions on this topic see for instance Echeverria (2012) and Aceves (2007).

Convention on the Rights of the Child (1990) (entry into force 2 Sept 1990). http://www.ohchr.org/EN/ProfessionalInterest/Pages/CRC.aspx. Accessed 19 April 2013
Echeverria G (2012) Do victims of torture and other serious human rights violations have an independent and enforceable right to reparation? Int J Hum Rights 16(5):698–716
Field SM (2013) UN Security Council resolutions concerning children affected by armed conflict: in whose best interest?. Int J Children's Rights 127–161
Grover SC (2012) Child soldier victims of genocidal forcible transfer: exonerating child soldiers charged with grave conflict-related international crimes. Springer, Berlin
Human Rights Watch (4 June 2013b) Syria: A stream of bodies in Aleppo's River. http://www.hrw.org/news/2013/06/04/syria-stream-bodies-aleppo-s-river. Accessed 9 June 2013
Human Rights Watch (2013c) Safe no more: Students and Schools under Attack in Syria. http://www.hrw.org/sites/default/files/reports/syria0613webwcover.pdf. Accessed 9 June 2013
Lyons J (2013) Dispatches:Mapping the Sarin Flight Path. https://www.hrw.org/news/2013/09/17/dispatches-mapping-sarin-flight-path Accessed 20 September, 2013
Report of the UN Secretary-General on the implementation of duty to protect (12 Jan 2009) A/63/677. http://www.un.org/ga/search/view_doc.asp?symbol=A/63/677. Accessed 23 May 2013
Report of the Independent International Commission of Inquiry on the Syrian Arab Republic to the UN Human Rights Council (4 June 2013) A/HRC/23/58 (Advance Unedited Version). http://www.ohchr.org/Documents/HRBodies/HRCouncil/CoISyria/A-HRC-23-58_en.pdf. Accessed 9 June 2013
Tax M (13 Dec 2010) Women have human rights too: The ICC's failure to prosecute gender violence is symptomatic of the way human rights advocacy has come to overlook women. http://www.guardian.co.uk/commentisfree/cifamerica/2010/dec/13/international-criminal-court-moreno-ocampo. Accessed 26 May 2013
UN Charter 26 June 1945 (entry into force 24 Oct 1945). http://www.un.org/en/documents/charter/intro.shtml. Accessed 16 June 2013

Index

S. C. Grover, *The Torture of Children During Armed Conflicts*,
DOI: 10.1007/978-3-642-40689-8, © Springer-Verlag Berlin Heidelberg 2014

MIX
Papier aus verantwortungsvollen Quellen
Paper from responsible sources
FSC® C105338

If you have any concerns about our products,
you can contact us on
ProductSafety@springernature.com

In case Publisher is established outside the EU,
the EU authorized representative is:
Springer Nature Customer Service Center GmbH
Europaplatz 3, 69115 Heidelberg, Germany

Printed by Libri Plureos GmbH
in Hamburg, Germany